AFRICAN CHILDHOOD

Are children's rights compatible with African Conceptions of Childhood?

REMEMBER MIAMINGI

To my darling wife Mrs. Alina Ramona Miamingi for loving without reserving some for herself, my son Crystal Sokifasi Miamingi and my daughter Emerald Natalia Dinee Miamingi who daily remind me of millions of weak and powerless people whose only guarantee for a future is their faith in the values and virtues of others; and to the memory of my mother Mrs. Margreat Abugu Baradio for her resilience in spite of all odds.

Table of Contents

Acknowledgement

In 1986, I inscribed on the wall of class 6, Source Yubu Primary School the following: 'HE. Dr. Remember Abishai Sokifasi, the President of the Republic of Sudan' little did I know that it would take 28 years, two refugee statuses, 1925 kilometres of trekking from Mboki, in the Central African Republic towards Bangui, the Capital city, days of sleeping under the Obalende Bridge in Lagos, Nigeria, working as a domestic servant and taxi driver; to realise the first part of this dream.

In the course of this journey, several individuals and institutions played different enabling roles. There are simply too many people to mention all by name. I am eternally grateful to my mother, late Mrs Abugu Baradio, who passed away on 3 January 2013 – the night I arrived in South Africa to start work on my LLD studies. She spent her life working to send 19 of us to school; to my mentor and step father, late Abishai Sokifasi, who stood by my decision and encouraged me to trek from Mboki to Bangui. Without him, I would not have had the courage to leap into the unknown in search of knowledge; to Mr John Yatta, who left Mboki with me, and we went through it all together. He still remains my constant source of inspiration and support. To Venerable Levi Opara, who picked us up from under the bridge and on the streets of Lagos and provided shelter for us at All Saints Church Yaba, Lagos, Nigeria. He remains a father to me. To my wife, Alina Ramona Miamingi, who left everything for nothing just to be with me, she endured loneliness and managed two hyperactive kids; for her many nights of editing work on my clumsy writing style and for her unconditional love. To my two kids whose love, confidence (and my desire to ensure that their own dreams never take as long to realise as mine did), kept me working. To Dr Mariana Obisanya and Dr Akin Obisanya, they made their home our home. To my brother and friend Seun Solomon Bakare who was and still is with me during the ups and downs of life.

To Prof. M Hansungule for provoking my thoughts on African philosophy and cultural heritage, Dr Martin Nsibirwa for providing guidance throughout my LLD studies that formed the basis for this book, to Prof Jegede Ademola, Dr Romola Adeola, Dr Azubike Onuoraoguno, Dr Ally Possi, Mr Bright Nkrumah and to all colleagues around the big table who contributed to refocusing my original LLD proposal during the Centre's monthly research meeting. To Mrs CM Viljoen for her exceptional organising skills that make the Centre for Human Rights an ideal place for my LLD sresearch, to Mrs I De Meyer, Mr H Meintjies, Mrs E Laubscher, Mrs Pienaar-Erasmus, Mrs Yolanda Booyzen, Mrs Lizette Hermann, Mr Eric Lwanga, Mrs Karen Stefiszyn, Ms Thuto Hlalele and Mr NA Taku for making the Centre for Human Rights a friendly family environment and for inspiring me to greater heights, thank you all. To the LLM Class 2008, thank you all!

Prof Frans Viljoen is my teacher, role model and my supervisor. His dedication, commitment, efficiency and foresight are outstanding. Thank you very much for your inspiration and support along this journey. I have learned what it takes to be a better student and a supervisor for the lack of a better word. Prof Ann Skelton, thank you very much for your attention to details, thoroughness, and inexhaustible energy for excellence enviable. Prof Julia Sloth-Nielsen, Prof Benyam Mezmur, Prof Magnus Killander and Prof Thoko Kaime: thank you very much for your insightful comments and support.

I am indebted to the following institutions for contributing to my studies: UNHCR, DAFI, Open Society Foundation, the European Union, Obafemi Awolowo University, University of Pretoria, Centre for Human Rights and the University of the Western Cape.

To all individuals and institutions I could not mention by name, Thank you!

TO GOD BE THE GLORY, HONOUR AND MAJESTY!

The Author

Dr Remember Miamingi advises the Political Affairs, Peace and Security Department of the African Union, Africa's premier intergovernmental body, on protecting civilians and child protection in conflict situations.

Earlier in his career, he was the Head of Research at the South Africa Human Rights Commission. He served as the Pan-African Advocacy and Institutional Relations Manager for Save the Children UK's Liaison Office to the African Union and the Coordinator for the Africa-wide Movement for Children. Dr Miamingi has lectured postgraduate students on international law, international human rights and democratization and humanitarian law at Addis Ababa University, Ethiopia and the University of Pretoria, South Africa. He has consulted for governments, intergovernmental bodies, UN agencies and international nongovernmental organizations.

Dr Miamingi holds an LLB law degree from Obafemi Awolowo University, Ile-Ife, Osun State, Nigeria, and LLM and LLD law degrees from the University of Pretoria, Pretoria, South Africa. Dr Miamingi's publications include books, book chapters and academic articles, including the Book "State Party Reporting and the Realization of Children's Rights in Africa" and the Book "African Union's Commitment to Child Protection in Conflict Situations."

CHAPTER 1

INTRODUCTION

1. Introduction

Legislation dealing with children and their rights,[1] academic writings,[2] state practices,[3] cultural beliefs and practices[4] relating to the child in different parts of the world indicate different understandings of childhood.[5] Three reasons underline these differences. First, childhood has become a political issue;[6] second, inherent in the conception of childhood is the contestable concept of

---

1 See, generally, African Child Policy Report: In the best interests of the child: Harmonisation of Laws on Children in Eastern and Southern Africa (2007) as well as 'Realising rights for children: Harmonisation of laws on children Eastern and Southern Africa 2007 available at: http://www.africanchildforum.org/site/index.php?option=com_content&view=article&id=86.

2 B Rwezaura 'Competing 'images' of childhood in social and legal systems of contemporary sub-Saharan Africa' (1998) 12 *International Journal of law, Policy and the Family* 255; P Veerman *The rights of the child and the changing image of childhood* (1992) 3; B Rwezaura 'The best interests of the child in changing social and economic contexts of sub-Saharan Africa' in P Alston *The best interests of the child: Reconciling culture and human rights* (1994) 82.

3 See generally, African Child Policy Report: In the best interests of the child: Harmonisation of Laws on Children in Eastern and Southern Africa (2007) as well as 'Realising rights for children: Harmonisation of laws on children Eastern and Southern Africa 2007 available at: http://www.africanchildforum.org/site/index.php?option=com_content&view=article&id=86.

4 B Rwenzaura 'Law, culture and children's rights in Eastern and Southern Africa: Contemporary challenges and present day dilemmas' in W Ncube (ed) *Law, culture, tradition and children's rights* (1998) 289; W Ncube 'The African cultural fingerprints: The changing concept of childhood' in W Ncube (ed) *Law, culture, tradition and children's rights* (1998) 11; L Sacramento & A Pessoa 'Implementation of the rights of the child in the Mozambican context' in M Freeman (ed) *Children's rights: Comparative perspective* (1996) 145.

5 F Kelly 'Conceptualising the child through an 'ethic of care': Lessons for family law' (2004) 4 *International Journal of Law in Context* 375; E Durkheim 'Childhood' in W Pickering (ed) *Durkheim: Essays on morals and education* (1911) 149; C Jenks (ed) *The sociology of childhood: Essential readings* (1982) 15.

6 N Scheper-Hughes *et al Small wars: The cultural politics of childhood* (1998) 163; A Richardson 'The politics of childhood: Wordsworth, Blake, and catechistic methods' (1989) 56 *English Literary History* 853; J Goddard *The politics of childhood: International perspectives, contemporary development* (2005) 44.

identity[7] and cultural sensitivity;[8] third, the role childhood plays in different socio- cultural as well as socio-political settings around the world is not only changing rapidly, but equally is contestable.[9]

In the light of these differences some scholars argue that universalising a particular conception of childhood is paternalistic.[10] Mead and Wolfenstein suggest that as much as there are differences in the experience of children, their needs and rights can fairly be addressed within a common framework.[11]

This debate is producing more heat than light:

> After centuries of debate and practice, we have still not achieved any consensus over the issue of childhood. Despite a long cultural commitment to the good of the child, and more recent intellectual engagement with the topic of childhood, what remains perpetually diffuse and ambiguous is the basic conceptualization of childhood as a social practice.[12]

An obstacle to finding a universal conception of childhood is that childhood is a social construct and, thus, is context specific.[13] Every community, every culture and every society possess as valid conceptions of childhood.[14]

---

7 R Ya'ir 'Redefining the child's right to identity' (2004) 18 *International Journal of Law, Policy and Family* 147; J Eekelaar 'Children between cultures' (2004) 18 I*nternational Journal of Law, Policy and the Family* 178; D Hodgson 'The international legal protection of the child's right to a legal identity and the problem of statelessness' (1993) 7 *International Journal of Law, Policy and the Family* 255; M Slaughter 'Contested identities: The adoption of American Indian children and the liberal state' (2000) 9 *Social and Legal Studies* 227.

8 N Mairead *et al Cultural diversity, heritage and human rights intersection in theory and practice* (2010) 450-300 *Kindle version;* A Boakye-Boaten 'Changes in the concept of childhood: Implications for children in Ghana' (2010) 3 *Journal of International Social Studies* 10.

9 M Slaughter 'Contested identities: The adoption of American Indian children and the liberal state' (2000) 9 *Social and Legal Studies* 227.

10 B Rwezaura 'Competing images of childhood in the social and legal systems of contemporary sub-Saharan Africa' (1998) 12 *International Journal of Law, Policy and the Family* 253; W Ncube 'The African cultural fingerprints: The changing concept of childhood' in W Ncube (ed) *Law, culture, tradition and children's rights* (1998) 11.

11 M Mead & M Wolfenstein *Childhood in contemporary cultures* (1954) 8.

12 C Jenks *Childhood* (1996) 2.

13 n 12, 4, see also P Veerman *The rights of the child and the changing image of childhood* (1992) 3.

14 M Freeman 'Culture, childhood and rights' (2011) 5 *The Family in Law* 15.

If childhood is a cultural and context-specific construct, are there conceptions of childhood in Africa? Do these conceptions of childhood in Africa share common features across cultures and communities? Are these African conceptions of childhood similar to the conception of childhood in the Convention on the Rights of the Child (CRC)? These are some of the questions that need to be booked.[15] It is important to know the extent to which makers and implementers of policy on child wellbeing in Africa have identified, acknowledged and documented the different conceptions of childhood. The extent to which an African human rights system negotiates these differences in the understanding of children in Africa has implications for the legitimacy of the system as well as an impact on the implementation and compliance with the standard setting instruments and decisions of monitoring bodies within the system.[16]

The norms and values that underpin the African human rights system should not be determined through neglecting the cultural values of Africans. The resulting human rights norms and standards will create tension within the African human rights system. As a result, the implementation and compliance with human rights norms are likely to encounter challenges and raise questions of legitimacy.[17]

An argument for the regionalisation of international human rights and international human rights laws is that the impact of human rights law depends, as do all laws, on changing the local consciousness of rights and relationships.[18] In order for human rights ideas to be effective they need to be translated into local terms and resonate, favourably, within local contexts of power and meaning. Regionalisation of human rights was supposed to narrow the gap between people and international human rights norms and mechanisms. It is believed that with a shared history, geography, and, in some

15 W Ncube 'The African cultural fingerprints: The changing concept of childhood' in W Ncube (ed) *Law, culture, tradition and children's rights* (1998) 11; B Rwenzaura 'Law, culture and children's rights in Eastern and Southern Africa: Contemporary challenges and present day dilemmas' in W Ncube (ed) *Law, culture, tradition and children's rights* (1998) 289.

16 T Kaime *The African Charter on the Rights and Welfare of the Child: A socio-legal perspective* (2009) 177.

17 H Steiner & P Alston *International human rights in context: Law, politics and morals* (2005) 366.

18 As above.

cases, language and religion, as well as a commonality of values, regions will most likely meet the human rights yearnings of their peoples as opposed to implementing human rights at the level of the United Nations.[19]

It was this desire to bring the benefits of international human rights closer to Africans, as well as to temper these benefits with the context-specific realities of the continent that resulted in the adoption of a regional human rights system.[20] Another reason that motivated the Organisation of African Unity (OAU) and its legal successor, the African Union (AU), to put in place human rights treaties is, in contrast to international human rights norms, that African countries wanted a system of human rights norms with an African cultural flavour.[21]

Regional human rights systems are conceived to perform at least two functions. First, it should provide the first port of call when something goes fundamental wrong at the country level and the country has failed adequately to address it. Second, it ought to provide a common minimum human right standard specific to the region.[22] As mentioned, regional specificity and the context-specific nature of human rights systems are among the virtues of regional human rights systems.

Context and cultural specificities of regional human rights norms and institutions are critical in the areas of children's rights and welfare.[23] Though African cultures tend to share core common values and understanding of childhood, there are significant differences within and among cultures in Africa.[24] For example, in many African cultures childhood is regarded as a rehearsal for adulthood and thus is a time to learn, to build character,

---

19 M Cerna 'Universality of human rights and cultural diversity: Implementation of human rights in different socio-cultural contexts' (1994) 16 *Human Rights Quarterly* 740.

20 V Nmehielle *The African human rights system: Its laws, practice and institutions* (2001) 75 see also F Viljoen *International human rights law in Africa* (2012) 219.

21 As above.

22 Cerna, n 19.

23 B Rwezaura 'Competing 'images' of childhood in social and legal systems of contemporary sub-Saharan Africa' (1998) 12 *International Journal of Law, Policy and the Family* 255; P Veerman *The rights of the child and the changing image of childhood* (1992) 231.

24 Rwezaura, n 23.

and acquire lifesaving skills that are needed in adulthood.[25] In addition, children provide a source of economic survival and continuity for families and communities in Africa. Children are seen as 'Africa's most valuable resources [to whom] we entrust ... our values and knowledge, our hope and our aspirations'.[26] Nevertheless, there is evidence to the effect that the understanding of childhood differs, in some respects, from culture to culture and even within cultures and from one time period to another.[27]

Culture is not static, nor is it a homogenous, integrated and consensual system that is to be accepted or criticized as a whole. Even though 'the universality of human rights requires respect for the diversity of ... cultures,'[28] culture cannot, legitimately, be cited as justification for a violation of human rights. Thus, human rights norms are expected to inform and influence cultural values, in the same way cultures are expected to inform and influence international and regional human rights norms and standards.

The drafters of the African Charter on the Rights and Welfare of the Child (African Children's Charter) sought to attain this compromise. As a result, even though the African Children's Charter is rooted in African cultural values and philosophy, it reflects and responds to the values and philosophy of the CRC.[29] Such balance could enhance the implementation of the rights provided for in the African Children's Charter without negative impacts on cultural norms and expectations relating to children in Africa. The potential for a negative impact has not been investigated adequately. Nevertheless, the African Children's Charter, in comparison with others, has been described as

25 B Rwenzaura 'Law, culture and children's rights in Eastern and Southern Africa: Contemporary challenges and present day dilemmas' in W Ncube (ed) *Law, culture, tradition and c children's rights* (1998) 289; W Ncube 'The African cultural fingerprints: The changing concept of childhood' in W Ncube (ed) *Law, culture, tradition and children's rights* (1998) 11; L Sacramento & A Pessoa 'Implementation of the rights of the child in the Mozambican context' in M Freeman (ed) *Children's rights: Comparative perspective*(1996) 145.

26 Ncube, n 15.

27 As above ; B Rwenzaura 'Law, culture and children's rights in Eastern and Southern Africa: Contemporary challenges and present day dilemmas ' in W Ncube (ed) *Law, culture, tradition and children's rights* (1998) 290.

28 S Merry 'Human rights and demonization of culture' (2003) 26 *Political and Legal Anthropology Review* 55.

29 T Kaime *The African Charter on the Rights and Welfare of the Child: A socio-legal perspective* (2009) 36; J Sloth-Nielsen & B Mezmur 'The dutiful child: The implications of article 31 of the African's Children's Charter' (2008) 52 *Journal of African Law* 159; D Chirwa 'The merits and demerits of the African Charter on the Rights and Welfare of the Child' (2002) 10 *International Journal of Children's Rights* 157.

'a pioneering treaty and the most progressive of the treaties on the rights of the child.'[30]

Though academic writings about the African Children's Charter are on the increase, fewer scholars have engaged with issues around the cultural legitimacy of the African Children's Charter. The earlier writers on the African Children's Charter were concerned with creating awareness around the treaty and highlighting its distinctiveness.

With a few exceptions,[31] the cultural legitimacy of the African Children's Charter is taken for granted even though there is no adequate textual evidence in the document itself to support this presumption.[32] The substantive difference between the African Children's Charter and the CRC, in the opinion of this writer, lies in the fact that the former emphasises African-specific challenges facing children, imposes higher standard in this regards and burdens children with duties. In its core philosophy as well as underlying values and principles, the African Children's Charter to a large extent, is substantively the same as the CRC.

---

30 G Van Bueren *The international law on the rights of the child* (1995) *402*.

31 T Kaime *The African Charter on the Rights and Welfare of the Child: A socio-legal perspective* (2009). So far, most writings on the African Children's Charter are restricted to comparative and textual analysis with the CRC and the provisions of the African Children's Charter itself. Few writings such as those by T Kaime (*The African Charter on the Rights and Welfare of the Child: A socio-legal perspective* (2009)) and J Sloth-Nielsen & B Mezmur ('The dutiful child: the implications of article 31 of the African's Children's Charter' (2008) 52 *Journal of African Law*) have attempted some philosophical analysis of the African Children's Charter. The earlier writings on the African Children's Charter attempted to critique the value adding role of the African Children's Charter such as the one by F Viljoen 'The African Charter on the Rights and Welfare of the Child' in C Davel (ed) *Introduction to child law in South Africa* (2000) 214 that attempts to challenge the value added nature of the African Children's Charter. There is a deficit of critical engagement with the rationale, the provisions of the African Children's Charter as well as with other writers. A good example of critical academic comment on the work of another writer with respect to the African Children's Charter is the one made by T Kaime (T Kaime *The African Charter on the Rights and Welfare of the Child: A socio-legal perspective* (2009) 27) on the work of B Thompson (in 'Africa's Charter on Children's Rights: A normative break with cultural traditionalism' (1992) 41 *The International and Comparative Law Quarterly* 432;) with respect to her opinion that the African Children's Charter was a revolutionary and transformative treaty that effectively challenges African cultural beliefs and practices relating to child rearing in Africa. However, there is an increase tendency now to re-examined human rights claims and norms, within the African context, from a multi-disciplinary perspective. For an example of this development see generally F Viljoen (ed) *Beyond the law: Multi-disciplinary perspectives on human rights* (2012).

32 With the exception of a vague reference in paragraph 6 of the Preamble, the inclusion of the duties and responsibilities and reference to parental respect, there are very few examples to justify this assertion. If anything, the document, apart from excluding group and community rights provided for in the African Charter on Human and Peoples' Rights (ACHPR), the African Children's Charter provided for rights that even adults in Africa were denied under the ACHPR). An example of such a right is the right to privacy provided for under the African Children's Charter and not under the ACHPR.

This book engages with the following questions: Why is it that a treaty specifically negotiated and adopted by African countries and with African children in mind should look so strikingly similar to the CRC? Could a lack of a different conception of childhood or an inability to identify, concretise and communicate such a conception of childhood be blamed for substantial deference to the conception of childhood presented in the CRC? If the CRC is considered biased toward a non-African conception of childhood,[33] does transplanting the norms in the CRC into an African children's rights treaty transform these norms into African cultural norms?

According to UNICEF, 88% of children in Africa live in rural areas.[34] Customs and traditions mainly govern the lives of people living in the rural parts of Africa. Even in the urban areas, the effect of traditional values and custom is evident.[35] As the influence of the state becomes weaker from urban to rural, the influence of traditional norms increases in many African communities. Protecting and promoting the wellbeing of children in Africa mainly on the basis of children's rights treaties that depend on states to implement is likely to exclude a majority of children from benefiting from such a regime. In addition, as the influence of the children's rights treaties in Africa increases, many children in the rural areas are likely to experience a hybrid conditions of childhood created by the multiplicity of the governing norms – children's rights treaties and traditional norms in Africa. Since 'children's rights is … still not … a primary societal value informing social policy in countries in Africa,'[36] a framework that excludes traditional African value systems from the protection and promotion of children's rights in Africa offers incomplete protection.

33 T Bennett *Human rights and African customary law under the South African Constitution* (1999) 98 noting that children's rights in international law have a decidedly Western slant.

34 http://www.unicef.org/sowc2012/pdfs/SOWC-2012-Chapter-1-Children-in-an-increasingly-urban-world.pdf; see also UNECA, The relevance of African traditional institutions of governance' (2007) 10 available at http://www.uneca.org/sites/default/files/publications/relevance_africantradinstgov.pdf.

35 C Kessides The urban transition in sub-Saharan Africa: Implications for economic growth and poverty reduction' (2005) Africa Region Working Paper Series No. 97 http://www.worldbank.org/afr/wps/wp97.pdf.

36 J Sloth-Nielsen & B Mezmur 'Surveying the book landscape to promote children's legal rights in an African context' (2007) 7 *African Human Rights Law Journal* 330.

1.1. Conceptual clarification

There are two concepts discussed in this book that needs delineation. These terms are: 'Traditional' and 'conception.' The 'image' and 'understanding' of childhood are used in this book interchangeably with the 'conception' of childhood.

1.1.1. 'Traditional values' or 'traditional community'

The expressions 'traditional values' or 'traditional community' as used by the scholars referenced in this work are seldom defined. The senses in which these expressions are used in the literature surveyed for the purpose of this work emphasis the contrast to modernity. 'Modern' is understood to mean a 'set of attitudes and values, and ways of feeling and acting, presumably of the sort either generated by or required for participation in a modern society.'[37] The sense in which the expressions 'traditional value' or 'traditional community' are used in this work is captured by Lassiter when he describes traditional values as:

> widespread sub-Saharan African core values, beliefs, cultural themes and behaviors as they existed prior to European contact; and as they still exist, especially in the rural areas and to a lesser extent in the urban areas of Africa; and upon which many, if not most, fundamental thought processes and behaviors of contemporary sub-Saharan Africans are based and continue to be derived from.[38]

The book analyses general features and trends in how traditional value systems in Africa have contributed to the conception(s) of childhood in Africa. The purpose of this analysis is to demonstrate that there are differences between the conception of childhood in the African Children's Charter and the understanding of childhood by traditional communities in Africa. These differences in the understanding of childhood between the African Children's

---

37 D Smith & A Inkeles *The om scale: A comparative socio-psychological measure of individual modernity* (1996) 353.

38 J Lassiter 'African culture and personality: Bad social science, effective social activism, or a call to reinvent ethnology?' (2000) 3 *African Studies Quarterly* 1.

Charter and communities in Africa is a major challenge to the effective and efficient implementation of the African Children's Charter in Africa.

The book examines how the African Committee of Experts on the Rights and Welfare of the Child (African Children's Committee) could discharge its mandate in a manner that will enhance context-specific implementation of the African Children's Charter. Negotiating the equilibrium between human rights and cultural norms and standards is the delicate task human rights treaty bodies, regionally and internationally, are called upon to discharge. Human rights treaty bodies supervise state parties' compliance with their obligations under a treaty, monitor progress and provide public scrutiny of the efforts aimed at realising human rights obligations. They assist states in assessing achievements and in identifying implementation gaps. They try to induce changes to laws, policies, and practices in member states and provide guidance in this regard to state parties.

1.1.2. 'Concept', 'conception', 'image', and 'understanding' of childhood

There is no conclusive definition of the expression 'conception of childhood' or 'concept of childhood.'[39] According to Archard, a concept of childhood requires that 'children be distinguishable from adults in respect of some unspecified set of attributes. A conception of childhood is a specification of those attributes.'[40] So, 'to have a concept of childhood is to recognise that children differ interestingly from adults; to have a conception of childhood is to have a view of what those interesting differences are.'[41] Therefore, a concept is more descriptive, while a conception could be said to be ideological. 'Images' or 'understanding' of childhood is commonly used without specific definition.[42] However, Hwang attempts a definition of 'images of

39 See generally C Hwang *et al Images of childhood* (1996) 27.

40 D Archard *Children: Rights and childhood* (2004) 27.

41 As above.

42 See, generally, B Rweraura 'Competing 'images' of childhood in the social and legal systems of contemporary sub-Saharan Africa' (1998) 12 *International Journal of Law, Polity and the Family* 253. A Dawes *Images of childhood in cultural perspective: Challenges to theory and practice* (1999); J Holt *What is a child? Popular images of childhood* (1992).

childhood'. According to Hwang, images of childhood are 'basic assumptions or conception about children and factors that influence their ontogeny.'[43] 'Understanding' of childhood also is usually not defined. For the purpose of this book, 'conception', 'image', and 'understanding' of childhood are used interchangeably to refer to a set of assumptions that adults and societies have about children and how those assumptions govern how children are seen, related with, and treated.

1.2. Problem statement

The drafters of the African Children's Charter justified the need for an African children's right treaty on the basis, amongst others, that the CRC was not in tune with an African worldview and cultural heritage.[44] The African Children's Charter was adopted to address this mischief. However, the conception of childhood in the African Children's Charter is strikingly similar to the one in the CRC. The majority of children in Africa live in rural areas and their lives are governed according to the norms and values of cultures in Africa.[45] On one hand, if the children's rights norms provided for in these two children's rights treaties are applied in disregard of the cultures of the families and communities' in which children live their lives, it could be disruptive and socially dislocative. On the other hand, there are cultural norms and practices that are harmful to the life, survival and development of children in Africa. How can the children's rights norms provided for in the two children's rights treaties be interpreted and applied in a way that is faithful to the texts of these treaties and culturally sensitive? Already the dual regime is problematic

43 C Hwang et al *Images of childhood* (1996) 27.

44 See generally ANPPCAN 'The rights of the child selected proceedings of a workshop on the draft Convention on the Rights of the Child: An African perspective' (1988); see also L Muthoga 'Analysis of international instruments for the protection of the rights of the child' in Community Law Centre (ed) International Conference on the Rights of the Child: Papers and reports of a conference convened by the Community Law Centre (1992) 123; S Wako 'Towards an African Charter on the Rights of the Child' paper delivered at the Workshop on the Draft Convention on the Rights of the Child, Nairobi, 9-11 May 1988 cited in T Kaime 'The foundations of rights in the African Charter on the Rights and Welfare of the Child: A Historical and philosophical account' (2009) 3 *African Journal of Legal Studies* 120; T Kaime 'The foundations of rights in the African Charter on the Rights and Welfare of the Child: A historical and philosophical account' (2009) 3 *African Journal of Legal Studies* 120.

45 http://www.unicef.org/sowc2012/pdfs/SOWC-2012-Chapter-1-Children-in-an-increasingly-urban-world.pdf; see also UNECA, The relevance of African traditional institutions of governance' (2007) 10 available at http://www.uneca.org/sites/default/files/publications/relevance_africantradinstgov.pdf.

to policy makers and to children. Policy makers contend with these multiple norms in an effort to protect children. Children struggle with the multiple conceptions of who they are or should be. What role can the African Children's Committee play to reduce the tension that arises between children's rights norms and the hybridity of children's lived experience in Africa as a result of the multiplicities of the conceptions of childhood? The central preoccupation, therefore, is how can the African Children's Committee discharge its mandate in a manner that reconciles these tensions?

1.3. Key questions explored in the book

This book answers the following questions:

1. What is the conception of childhood in the Convention on the Rights of the Child?
2. Is there a different and common understanding of childhood by communities in Africa?
3. Is the conception of childhood in the African Children's Charter compatible with the understanding of childhood by different communities in Africa?
4. Can the mandate of the African Children's Committee reconcile the differences between the image of childhood portrayed in the African Children's Charter and the understandings of childhood by traditional communities in Africa?

With respect to the first question the author contends that the CRC conceptualises the child as a human being and confers the child with almost all autonomy and liberty rights. The book further contends that by conceptualising childhood against the background of liberal philosophies, the CRC's conception of childhood excludes and renders unacceptable a conception of childhood in Africa that is not in line with its understanding of children.

In answering questions 2 and 3 the author contends that traditional communities in Africa have different and varying conceptions of childhood.

However, there are cross-cultural features and trends in the conceptions of childhood that are common to all cultures and traditions in Africa. Ethnography studies, academic writings and oral traditions in different parts of Africa are used to identify these common features in the understanding of childhood in Africa. These common characteristics of the understanding of childhood among different traditional communities in Africa can be distilled into a common African core conception of childhood. The book further argues that the common core conception of childhood in Africa, to an extent, is different in form and content from the image of childhood in the CRC and the African Children's Charter.

In answering question 4, the author notes unfortunately that the African Children's Charter does not sufficiently incorporate the understanding of childhood in traditional communities in Africa. Rather, it mainly is a transplant of the CRC. The book uses the definition of the child, autonomy and liberty rights, the best interests of the child, and child participation to demonstrate the fundamental similarities between the CRC and the African Children's Charter. The book concedes that the African Children's Charter has a number of unique features. However, it contends that these unique features do not amount to a different (African) conception of childhood, but rather are a provision of higher standards of protection for children in Africa. In addition, the author contends that due to the entry into force of the three Optional Protocols to the CRC and some of the expansive interpretations of the provisions of the CRC by the Committee on the Rights of the Child (the CRC Committee), the continued justification for the existence of the African Children's Charter subsequently have been eroded.

Since the African Children's Charter significantly defers to the CRC's conception of childhood, the African Children's Charter stands accused of unnecessary duplication and redundancy unless the African Children's Committee can demonstrate, irrespective of the similarities between the two children's rights treaties, that the African Children's Charter can be interpreted differently and context-specifically. However, not only are the mandate and the working methods of the African Children's Committee similar to those of the CRC Committee, but the African Children's Committee has also similarly interpreted the provisions of the African Children's Charter in the same way as the CRC Committee. Should this trend continue, the African Children's Charter would become increasingly superfluous. This book makes recommendations on how best the African Children's Committee could exercise its mandate in a way that reduces the chances of its voice being a mere echo of the CRC Committee.

1.4. The state of play

Primary and secondary source materials are used in the course of this book. The primary sources include official records of law making at regional and international levels, national, regional and international legislation and case law as well as non-binding human rights norms. State party reports are consulted and records of the practice of treaty bodies in considering state parties reports are used in the course of this work. Secondary sources that are used in the work include books, journal articles, reports, unpublished book, newspapers and Internet sources.

A number of authors have written on the African Children's Charter.[46] With few exceptions, these writings concentrate on the common and different features between the African Children's Charter and the CRC.[47] In addition, a significant number of these academic writings take for a fact that 'children's rights are a legitimate enterprise within African societies' thereby assuming 'the cultural legitimacy of children's rights in Africa.'[48] This work challenge

---

46 See, for example, F Viljoen 'The African Charter on the Rights and Welfare of the Child' in C Davel (ed) *Introduction to child law in South Africa* (2000) 214; B Thompson 'Africa's charter on children's rights: A normative break with cultural traditionalism, (1992) 41 *International and Comparative Law Quarterly* 432; A Lloyd 'A theoretical analysis of the reality of children's rights in Africa: An introduction to the African Charter on the Rights and Welfare of the Child' (2002) 1 *African Human Rights Law Journal* 11; D Chirwa 'The merits and demerits of the African Charter on the Rights and Welfare of the Child' (2002) 10 *International Journal of Children's Rights* 157; M Gose *The African Charter on the Rights and Welfare of the Child: An assessment of the legal value of its substantive provisions by means of a direct comparison to the Convention on the Rights of the Child* (2002), D Olowu, Protecting children's rights in Africa: A critique of the African Charter on the Rights and Welfare of the Child'(2002) 10 *International Journal of Children's Rights* 127.

47 W Ncube 'The changing concept of childhood: The African cultural fingerprints' in W Ncube (ed) *Law, culture, tradition and children's rights* (1998); B Rwenzaura 'Law, culture and children's rights in Eastern and Southern Africa: Contemporary challenges and present day dilemmas ' in W Ncube (ed) *Law, culture, tradition and children's rights* (1998); J Sloth-Nielsen & B Mezmur 'The dutiful child: the implications of article 31 of the African's Children's Charter' (2008) 52 *Journal of African Law* 159; T Kaime *The African Charter on the Rights and Welfare of the Child: A socio-legal perspective* (2009).

48 T Kaime 'The foundations of rights in the African Charter on the Rights and Welfare of the Child: A

this assumption of cultural legitimacy of children's rights in the African context. This book takes as its departure point the observation by Kaime that what is lacking in the academic discourse on children's rights in Africa is an 'affirmation of traditionalism in the whole enterprise of children's rights and the African Children's Charter.'[49] Therefore, to complete the work already done with respect of an upward review[50] of the African Children's Charter using the CRC as a benchmark, this book conducts a downward[51] cultural legitimacy and compatibility analysis of the provisions of the African Children's Charter with the understanding of childhood in traditional African communities. The book uses the definition of the child, children's autonomy and liberty rights, the best interests of the child and child participation, to identify African values and civilization that should characterise a meaningful implementation of children's rights in Africa.

The scope and the nature of this book are different from other scholarly work done in this area. First, this work identified general parameters for a common core conception of childhood in Africa. Second, this book used general features and trends in the conceptions of childhood in the CRC and the African Children's Charter in order to map out similarities and differences between the understanding of childhood in the CRC and the African Children's Charter, on one hand, and the conception of childhood by communities in Africa, on the other hand.[52] Third, the work used 'pluralistic universalism' as a theoretical framework that could diffuse the tension between a global conception of childhood and a communal understanding of childhood in Africa.

---

historical and philosophical account' (2009) 3 *African Journal of Legal Studies* 120.

49 AS above.

50 What is meant here is reviewing the African Children's Charter using the CRC standards.

51 By downward is referring to an assessment of the African Children's Charter using African cultural values as standards of measurement.

52 See n 40 above.

1.5. Significance of the book

The book identifies an alternative and equally valid conception of childhood in Africa. It elaborates on the challenges and implications in implementing the CRC and the African Children's Charter in Africa. It provides concrete suggestions as to how the African Children's Committee could minimise these challenges. The book seeks to recommend and influence an African approach and policy position on the child in Africa.

1.6. Scope and limitation of the book

The book is limited in a number of ways. First, its scope of engagement is limited to the general features and trends with respect to the conception of childhood in the CRC, the African Children's Charter and by communities in Africa. Inherent in this approach is a level of generalisation such as Western/non-western, individualistic/communitarian. The generalisation is necessary to identify and strengthen some points. The second limitation is the fact that this book could not examine the conception of childhood in every culture in Africa in order to arrive at the common features of the understanding of childhood in Africa. The book is designed to identify only general and comparable features of the different cultural conceptions of childhood in Africa using available sources. Time and resource constraints could not allow exploration of the understandings of childhood in every culture in Africa. The inability to conduct primary research is another limitation. Because the book examines common and comparable features of the understanding of childhood in Africa, empirical studies into one or two cultural norms could make the use of the findings of such book for the purpose of generalisation theoretically difficult.

1.7. Approaches to research

This book uses a combination of approaches. These include a socio-legal approach[53] and multi-disciplinary[54] as well as comparative[55] book methodologies. The book utilises qualitative tools in the conduct of the research.

A socio-legal approach was chosen because it provides an appropriate normative and empirical framework for robust analysis. It also provides an appropriate platform to approach book issues from the perspectives of more than one discipline simultaneously, thereby bridging different disciplines.

Comparatively, this book juxtaposes international, regional, country and some African communities' specific understandings of childhood as well as the images of childhood anticipated within the provisions of the CRC and the African Children's Charter. Given that childhood is a continuum with varying experiences along that continuum, the book examined, compared and contrasted the difference experiences of childhood within urban or rural settings.

In addition to the complexities involved in understanding the conception of childhood, examining the coneption (s) of childhood in Africa, a continent of over 900 million people with thousands of cultures, makes researching every community and culture impossible to attain within the framework of this work. Therefore, the book is limited to available information to establish general features and trends around the understanding and treatment of childhood in selected African communities. The general features and trends are compared with the provisions of the African Children's Charter to test the validity of the claims that the Treaty bears the fingerprint of African cultural heritage and traditions and, thus, is legitimate.

---

53 B Tamanaha 'Socio-legal positivism and a general jurisprudence' (2001) 21 *Oxford Journal of Legal Studies* 1; B Ehrlich *The fundamental principles of the sociology of law* (1975) 9; V Gessner & J Thomas 'Socio-legal book and policy studies: A review of the issues' (1988) 10 *Law and Policy* 85; C Menkel-Meadow 'Durkheimian epiphanies: The importance of engaged socio science in legal studies' (1990-1991) 18 *Florida State University Law Review* 91.

54 The book will transcend the boundaries of different disciplines.

55 Van de Vijver *Methods and data analysis of comparative book: Handbook of cross-cultural psychology: Theory and method* (1997) 257.

The work reviewed existing legal, sociological, anthropological and historical materials in the areas of childhood and child rights in Africa and constructed a conceptual framework that sustained this book. The definition of a child, the autonomy and agency of the child, the best interests of the child and child participation are used to construct a comparable image of childhood as presented in human rights law and African traditional understanding.[56] The emerging image or images of childhood from an African context are used to compare with the image in the African Children's Charter. Primary sources, such as the CRC and the African Children's Charter as well as general comments and concluding observations emanating from these documents, are examined textually.

The book is anchored in 'pluralistic universalism' as a theoretical basis. This theory is propounded by Corradetti in his book, 'Relativism and human rights: A theory of pluralistic universalism' (2009). He advances a theoretical framework that defends a relationship between universal validity and cultural pluralism. This theoretical framework anticipates cohabitation between universally valid human rights norms with culturally specific norms that are not necessarily repugnant to human dignity as a foundation of human rights. This author holds the view that such a flexible and robust theoretical framework could support a construction of childhood in Africa that incorporates context-specific features without unnecessarily jeopardising universally accepted safeguards. The reason for holding such a position is that even though childhood is a context and culturally specific construct that reflects the historical evolution of a particular community, it is rational to expect that aspects of specificity could be general to all childhood experiences. The generality of these possible specificities may not be captured comprehensively either by relativists or universalists.

The book makes an argument in favour of flexibility in the interpretation and application of children's rights norms in contexts that might have different

56 These concepts have been chosen to guide this book for two reasons: first, these concepts have been identified by different scholars as marking the main features of the children's rights movement and its conception of childhood. Second these concepts have dominated scholarly debate in the past decades and thus could easily facilitate comparative analysis. For this assertion see generally D Reynaert *et al* 'A review of children's rights literature since the adoption of the United Nations Convention on the Rights of the Child' (2009) 16 *Childhood* 518.

but equally valid norms governing childhood. Flexibility is used in the context of this argument as an exception to the rule of general application to children's rights norms and standards to all children. However, this exception must be context, child, and issue-specific and subject to the overriding best interests of the child.

1.8. Chapter outline

The book has six chapters. The first chapter introduces the book.

The second chapter identifies and examines the concept of childhood in the CRC and explores possible implications of the conception of childhood in the CRC on families and traditional communities in Africa.

Chapter 3 examines the conception of childhood in traditional African communities and compares and contrasts the traditional conception of childhood with the image of childhood in the CRC and the African Children's Charter. This chapter identifies the differences in the conception of childhood in the CRC and the African Children's Charter, on one hand, and the understanding of childhood in traditional African communities, on the other.

Chapter 4 identifies the understanding of childhood in the African Children's Charter and answers the question whether the image of childhood in the African Children's Charter is reflective of the conception of childhood in traditional communities in Africa or more in line with the way in which the CRC understands childhood. This chapter argues that the conception of childhood in the African Children's Charter is a mere transplant of the understanding of childhood in the CRC and therefore does not reflect the understanding of childhood in Africa.

Chapter 5 explores how the African Children's Committee can interpret the African Children's Charter in a manner that enhances the understanding of childhood in Africa without endangering the rights and welfare of children in Africa as agreed to at the international level. 'Pluralistic universalism' is recommended as a theoretical framework that could be used to ensure a context-specific interpretation of the African Children's Charter.

Chapter 6 offers a conclusion and recommendations.

CHAPTER 2

THE CONCEPTION OF CHILDHOOD IN THE CRC

This chapter is divided into three parts and a conclusion.

The first part presents an overview of the conception of childhood in the Convention on the Rights of the Child (CRC). It argues that the CRC's conception of childhood is overly legalistic and not universally shared. Law is rigid. Using law to define and universalise who a child is or what childhood entails is problematic. Laws operate optimally when they are context-specific. By attempting to envisage and enforce the laws on childhood from, mainly, universalist perspective, the CRC inevitably makes the implementation of its provisions challenging. Some communities around the world see and treat the norms and values of childhood in the CRC as alien and lack local counterparts. Laws, sometimes, are codifications of the culture of the lawmakers and forcing such laws on cultures and traditions in other parts of the world is not an easy task. Situating the conception of childhood in liberal thoughts and laws mainly rooted in the cultures and traditions of the West, makes the CRC at once a transformative treaty and dislocative of local and culturally based images of childhood in other parts of the world. The result of this dislocation is that the CRC's conception of childhood is divorced from the lived reality of children in non-Western societies.

The second part examines the understanding of the child as a human being with autonomy and liberty rights. This section argues that 'agency', as used in the CRC, as a basis to confer on children autonomy and liberty rights is used as an abstract attribute emptied of context and culture. The nature and scope of human agency is cultural and context-specific. Thus, how agency is understood and applied usually reflects the context and culture of the interpreters. Since the CRC is biased to favour liberal philosophy and understanding, agency, as seen in the CRC, also reflects the liberal feature of autonomous individuals whose interests are a primary consideration. Such a concept of agency may not be successfully implemented without a replacement or at least a reformulation of the concept of agency in other traditions of thought. The way children speak, decide and have their voice heard, an important component of agency, varies from context to context and from culture to culture.

The third part attempts to answer the question whether all peoples and cultures of the world share the image of childhood presented in the CRC. This section argues that the conception of childhood in the CRC is similar to how Western Europe and North America conceptualise childhood. However, there are features of the conception of childhood in the CRC that are in advance of the common understanding of childhood in Western Europe and North America. Evidence suggests that the CRC's child is rooted in a rationalistic, technical and philosophical concept not shared by all sectors of society, even in the West. In trying to sketch the conception of childhood in the CRC, the chapter argues that the child in the CRC is an autonomous, independent, competent child whose interest is a primary consideration and who is entitled to most of the autonomy rights adults are entitled to, in addition to other child-specific rights. Moreover, it is argued that this image of the child is rooted in the history of liberal thought.

Finally, the implications of the conception of childhood in the CRC on cultures and families that do not share such an understanding of the child are considered here. The conception of childhood in the CRC alters fundamentally how different traditional societies, such as those in Africa, have seen and relate to children and childhood. It is argued that the effective implementation of the CRC in contexts such as Africa, if not done in a context sensitive manner, might, in the long run, have negative implication for African cultural values, family forms and structure.

2. Introduction

Article 1 of the CRC defines a child as 'every human being below the age of eighteen years unless under the law applicable to the child, majority is attained earlier.'[1] This definition has at least three interrelated implications: First, a child is a 'human being'; second, 'childhood' is understood as the period below 18 years; and third, 'childhood', as envisaged in the CRC, is a purely legal question determined on the basis of a 'law applicable to the child'.

To consider children human beings was revolutionary, as children were mainly regarded as beings in the making.[2]. Using age (as opposed to a concept of childhood that is determined primarily by the operational demands and the underlying values of a social system) to delineate the structural space called childhood and qualify its inhabitants reduces the individual specificities of a child to a legal definition and an age group. The new age group created by law, is at once a rational proposition and a programme: A proposition that bases the understanding of child welfare and rearing practices, globally, on a common standard, and a programme which compels other peoples and cultures to accept this proposition. Hammel supports that argument when he asks the question: 'by what principle short of imperialism do we insist on the application of civil or human rights in societies that have not come to these ideas through their own histories?'[3]

The decision to adopt and universalise the image of childhood in the CRC seems not to have taken into account empirical knowledge to the effect that

1 Adopted by the General Assembly Resolution 44/25 of 20 November 1989 and entered into force 2 September 1990, in accordance with article 40 of the Convention.

2 First, because this puts to rest the dichotomy between 'being' and 'becoming' with respect to childhood. Second, this recognition confers children with the features of humanity upon birth and demands respect and protection. For the importance of, and clarity with respect to this distinction see A Ansell 'Children, youth and development' (2005) specially at page 22 where the author remarks that children 'are not "human becomings" but [are] "human beings" with a culture of their own'.

3 E Hammel 'Meeting the minotaur' (1994) 35 *Anthropology Newsletter* 48 quoted by P Werker 'Universal human rights and the problem of unbounded cultural meanings' (1997) 99 *American Anthropologist* 4.

the conceptions of a 'child' and 'childhood' are fluid,[4] evolutionary,[5] and time, place and context-specific.[6] Some scholars argue that the failure of those who drafted the CRC to recognise that childhood 'is not the same in all societies or cultures and may not even be the same at different places or different times within the same society or culture'[7] is at the root of difficulties encountered in implementing universal children's rights by different countries.[8] It has been argued that a successful realisation of human rights, in general, and children's rights, specifically, depends to a large extent on their approximation to varying contexts and on their voluntary acceptability by a global community.[9]

It is debatable whether for human rights, in general, and children's rights, specifically, to be realised that they must be rooted in and accepted by different cultures and community practices. Some scholars argue that the body of human rights laws as it stands, irrespective of its source in philosophy that inspired human rights development, is representative of values and practices universal to communities around the world. In the words of Asante:

> I reject the notion that human rights concepts are peculiarly or even essentially bourgeois or Western, and without relevance to Africa. Such a notion confuses the articulation of the theoretical foundations of the Western concept of human rights with the ultimate objective

---

4 See generally C Jenks (ed) *The sociology of childhood: Essential readings* (1982); specifically see A James & A Prout *Constructing and reconstructing childhood: Contemporary issues in the book of childhood* (1997) 8 summarising the fluidity of the concept of childhood; M Koller & O Ritchie *Sociology of childhood* (1964) 15; S Carey *Conceptual change in childhood* (1985) 257; M Mead 'An investigation of the thought of primitive children, with special reference to animism, personalities and cultures' in R Hunt (ed) *Personalities and cultures* (1967) 213.

5 See generally P Aries *Century of childhood: A history of family life* (1962); S Shahar *Childhood in the Middle Ages* (1992) 101; M Freeman 'The sociology of childhood and children's rights' (1998) 6 *International Journal of Children's Rights* 433.

6 See J Kociumbas 'Childhood history as ideology' (1984) 47 *Labour History* 1; A Skolnick 'The limits of childhood: Concept of child development and social context' (1975) 39 *Law and Contemporary Problems* 38; J Sommerville *The rise and fall of childhood* (1991) 183; A James & J Prout (eds) *Constructing and reconstructing childhood: Contemporary issues in the sociological studies* (1990) 6.

7 G Hegal *The philosophy of rights* (1942)100 Encyclopaedia Britannica.

8 T Kaime *The African Charter on the Rights and Welfare of the Child: A socio-legal perspective* (2009) 83; T Kaime *The Convention on the Rights of the Child: A cultural legitimacy critique* (2011) 77; T Kaime "Vernacularising' the Convention on the Rights of the Child: Rights and culture as analytic tools' (2010) 18 *International Journal of Children's Rights* 637; N Kaufman & I Rizzini 'Closing the gap between rights and realities of children's lives' in Qvortrup *et al* (eds) *The Palgrave handbook of child studies* (2009) 28.

9 A Imoh 'Realizing children's rights in Africa: An introduction' in A Imoh & N Ansell (eds) *Children's lives in an era of children's rights: The progress of the Convention on the Rights of the Child in Africa* (2014) 4.

> of any philosophy of human rights. Human rights quite simply, are concerned with asserting human dignity and they are ultimately based on a regard for the intrinsic worth of the individual. This is an eternal and universal phenomenon...[10]

Predicating the idea of human rights on the universal quest for human dignity strikes a familiar chord across time and space. Such an approach, however, cannot afford to 'assume *ab initio* that a particular cultural practice was offensive to human rights. It would respect cultural pluralism as a basis for finding common universality on some issues.'[11] A conscious consensus approach would minimise the perception that human rights are an 'epochal contest pitting savages, on one hand, against victims and saviours, on the other.'[12]

Herskovitz insists that the universality of human rights, under whatever pretext, must be rejected on empirical, epistemological and ethical grounds.[13] According to him, moral systems are different in form and content such that universal moral standard remain prescriptive and require making a moral judgement about the cultural values of others. Such judgements can hardly be objective since they are likely to be made against benchmarks established by universal values.[14] With no common agreed mechanisms for negotiating and aggregating this 'eternal and universal phenomenon' called human rights into universal moral standards, it is feared that the knowledge, value and culture that eventually become universal, in the form of universal human rights, might be those of the most powerful and influential countries, leading to 'moral imperialism' for others.[15] This debate is symptomatic of the tension between those who support a universalist approach and those who support a relative application of human rights.

10 Quoted in I Shivji *The concept of human rights in Africa* (1989) 12.

11 M Mutua *Human rights: A political and cultural critique* (2002) 8.

12 Mutua, n 11, 10.

13 M Herskovitz 'Statement on human rights' (1947) 49 American Anthropologist 539 cited in M Goodale 'Introduction to anthropology and human rights in a new key' (2006) 108 *American Anthropologist* 1.

14 Mutua, n 11, 11.

15 As above, 8.

Universalism and relativism are widely-known positions relating to the validity of the sources of human rights and the legitimacy of the outcomes as well as the implementation of human rights norms in all contexts; however, an in-between position is possible.

The middle ground includes multi-culturists,[16] pluralists,[17] universal pluralists[18] and relative pluralists.[19] The common denominator holding these theorists together, albeit loosely, is the belief that value and knowledge production are not disinterested processes, that human rights must be amiable to 'multiple perspectives,' and a rejection of the idea that 'there is only one possible answer (to the question of the validity and legitimacy of human rights) that everyone must accept.'[20] These different positions seem to have been born out of a common suspicion that human rights philosophy as it stands is 'favourable to political and cultural homogenization and hostile to difference and diversity.'[21]

These contestations around the nature, scope, extent, validity and legitimacy of international human rights laws have implications for the efficacy of human rights, in general, but specifically for children's rights, and ultimately for the life, survival and development of the child. Why specifically children's rights? First, like other special interest groups, a child is defined, and childhood delineated by international human rights law.[22] The challenges children

---

16 For a detailed discussion of multiculturalism see A Gutmann (ed) *Multiculturalism: Examining the politics of recognition* (1994); B Parekh *Rethinking multiculturalism: Cultural diversity and political theory* (2000); and for a critique see P Kelly *Multiculturalism reconsidered: Culture and equality and its critics* (2002); and B Barry *Culture and equality: An egalitarian critique of multiculturalism* (2001).

17 C Young *The politics of cultural pluralism* (1976) 23; C Young (ed) *The rising tide of cultural pluralism: The nation state at bay?* (1993) 3; and for critique of cultural pluralism see M Deveaux *Cultural pluralism and the dilemmas of justice* (2000) 180.

18 See, generally, C Corradetti *Relativism and human rights: A theory of pluralistic universalism* (2009).

19 D Wong 'Pluralistic universalism' (1996) 20 *Midwest Studies in Philosophy* 378; D Wong *Natural moralities: A defence of pluralistic universalism* (2006) 29.

20 P Singer *Ethics* (1994) 286.

21 M Mutua *Human rights: A political and cultural critique* (2002) 3.

22 Children are first defined before they are recognised and conferred with entitlements. Thus, their very legal existence as a category is a matter of international human rights law, in a sense. The Convention on the Elimination of all Forms of Discrimination against Women does not define womanhood, but rather discrimination against women, for example. It is debatable whether the Convention on the Rights of Persons with Disability defines disability or persons with disability.

face is not universally the same; they are not entirely relative either. What is universal is that the challenges children face has serious implications for their rights to life, survival and development. The exact nature of the challenges facing children, how they impact on a child and how society reacts to these challenges differ from child to child, from context to context and from culture to culture. Second, children were and, predominantly, still are subjects of these contestations that define them, confer them with entitlements and constrain them.[23] Third, the terms 'child' and 'childhood' are themselves subject to contestation.[24] The overarching debate on the validity of human rights has an implication and unintended consequences for children.

In addition to contestations around legitimacy and the validity of human rights, the content of the concepts of 'child' and 'childhood' are fiercely contested. Children's qualification as direct subjects and objects of rights is also hotly debated.[25] Primarily, there are two competing theoretical postulations, which bear on children's suitability for possessing rights. One group are the will or choice theorists,[26] and the opposing group are the interest or welfare theorists.[27]

---

23 F Ang *et al Participation rights of children* (2006) 18; J Boylan & P Ing ' 'Seen but not heard': Young people's experience of advocacy' (2005) 14 *International Journal of Social Welfare* 2; J Hemrica & F Heyting 'Tacit notions of childhood: An analysis of discourse about child participation in decision-making regarding arrangements in the case of parental divorce' (2004) 4 *Childhood* 449; M Lücker-Babel 'The right of the child to express views to be heard: An attempt to interpret article 12 of the UN Convention on the Rights of the Child' (1995) 3 *International Journal of Children's Rights* 391; N Thomas 'Towards a theory of children's participation' (2007) 15 *International Journal of Children's Rights* 199.

24 G Therborn 'Child politics: Dimensions and perspectives' (1996) 3 *Childhood* 29; N Lee 'The challenge of childhood: Distributions of childhood's ambiguity in adult institutions' (1999) 6 *Childhood* 455; A James *et al Theorizing childhood* (2002) 43; S Aitken 'Global crises of childhood: Rights, justice and the unchildlike Child' (2001) 33 *Area* 119; T Schapiro 'What is a child? (1999) 109 *Ethics* 715; J Holt *Escape from childhood: The needs and rights of Children* (1975) 25.

25 H Brighouse 'What rights (if any) do children have?' in D Archard & C Macleod (eds) *The moral and political status of children* (2002) 31; J Eekelaar 'The emergence of children's rights' (1986) 6 *Oxford Journal of Legal Studies* 161; J Griffin 'Do children have rights?' in D Archard & C Macleod (eds) *The moral and political status of children: New essays* (2002) 19; M Kramer 'Rights without trimmings' in M Kramer *et al A debate over rights, philosophical enquiries* (1998) 7; K Federle 'Rights flow downhill' (1994) 2 *International Journal of Children's Rights* 343; J Fernando 'Children's rights: Beyond the impasse'*(2001) 575 The Annals of the American Academy of Political and Social Science 8;* V Pupavac 'Misanthropy without borders: The international children's rights regime' (2001) 25 *Disasters 95;* R Roose & M Bouverne-De Bie 'Do children have rights or do their rights have to be realised? The United Nations Convention on the Rights of the Child as a frame of reference for pedagogical action' (2007) 41 *Journal of Philosophy of Education* 43; for more in depth discussion of why children should not be granted rights coterminous with that of adults see L Purdy '*In their best interests? The case against equal rights for children*' (1992) 55.

26 The choice group.

27 The interest group.

For the choice group, rights are 'the protected exercise of choice.'[28] In order to have rights, therefore, the right holder must have the capacity to enforce or waive any correlative duty arising from the right claim. The interest group conceives of a right as a protective cover for the paramount interest of a category of persons sufficiently important to warrant the imposition of duties the discharge of which allow the rights-holder to enjoy the interest in question.[29]

The implication for children of the position of the choice group is that since children, either as a biological category or a legal construct, lack the requisite cognitive and volitional capacities to exercise reasonable choice, they cannot reasonably be made possessors of rights. Children's vulnerability and lack of capacity mean that the child's wellbeing depends first and foremost on the voluntary exercise of love, care and affection by others.[30] The second reason why the choice group disputes that children possess rights is because of the corrosive impact of the language of rights on the fragile nature of the relationships that exists between children and their parents. The reason is that the nature of childhood and of the type of relationship that exists between a child and his or her caregivers disqualifies the concept of rights, at least in the legal sense, when talking about children. It is difficult to legislate love; yet love is an essential component of a good family environment for children.

So, the use of rights language is considered as eroding and eventually destroying the nature of the dispositions and attitudes that are essential to nurture and support the development and wellbeing of children.[31] The choice

28 H Hart 'Bentham on legal rights' in A Simpson (ed) *Oxford essays in jurisprudence* (1973) 171; see also generally, L Summer *The moral foundations of rights* (1987); H Steiner 'working rights'in M Kramer *et al A debate over rights, philosophical inquiries* (1998) and H Steiner *An essay on rights* (1994).

29 N MacCormick 'Children's rights: A test case' in N MacCormick *Legal rights and social democracy* (1982) 154; J Raz 'Legal rights' (1984) 4 *Oxford Journal of Legal Studies* 1; and M Kramer 'Rights without trimmings' in M Kramer *et al A debate over rights, philosophical enquiries* (1998) 17.

30 S Benporath 'Autonomy and vulnerability: On just relations between adults and children' (2003) 37 *Journal of Philosophy of Education* 127.

31 For a detailed discussion of the implication of the rights language on family environment and whether or not it is conducive for childcare see generally J Blustein *Parents and children: The ethics of the family* (1982); F Schrag 'Children: Their rights and needs' in W Aiken & H LaFollette (eds) *Whose child? Parental rights, parental authority and state power* (1980) 237; S Liao 'The right of children to be loved' (2006) 14 *Journal of Political Philosophy* 420; see generally also M Sandel *Liberalism and the limits of justice* (1982).

group argues that caregivers should have only moral rights and obligations to ensure conditions necessary for life, survival and development of a child.[32]

The interest group, on the other hand, maintains that it is precisely to enhance children's capacity and agency as well as to enhance preferences of children that they should be conferred with rights. In other words, if children are conferred with rights, that will facilitate the process of children acquiring the requisite capacity.[33] The interest group further maintains that using capacity to distinguish between childhood and adulthood is hard to reasonably justify. This is because 'to distinguish people with rights from people without rights [on the basis of capacity] can be shown to be arbitrary.'[34] Not all adults possess requisite capacity, just as not all children are without such capacity. The interest group further argues that because children are human, they ought to be treated in a way that is different from non-humans. Therefore, granting them rights accepts and recognises children's self-worth and dignity as members of the human family.

There are difficulties inherent in the positions of the two groups of theorists discussed above. On the one hand, lumping children together as one category and considering them as incapable of exercising rights glosses over a range of different categories of children within that age group called 'children'. The different categories include infants, young children and youths, and adolescents,[35] all of whom fall within this group and lay claim to varying degrees of capacity. On the other hand, the argument about best interests

---

32 W Aiken & H LaFollette (eds) *Whose child? Parental rights, parental authority and state power* (1980) 124; S Brennan & R Noggle 'The moral status of children: Children's rights, parents' rights, and family justice' (1997) 23 *Social Theory and Practice* 1; F Schoeman 'Rights of families: Rights of parents, and the moral basis of the family' (1980) 91 *Ethics* 6; for further discussion on the dynamics between different rights within family setting see O O'Neill & W Ruddick (eds) *Having children: Philosophical and legal reflections on parenthood* (1979); G Scarre (ed) *Children, parents, and politics* (1989).

33 N MacCormick 'Children's rights: A test case' in N MacCormick *Legal rights and social democracy* (1982) 154; J Raz 'Legal rights' (1984) 4 *Oxford Journal of Legal Studies* 1; and M Kramer 'Rights without trimmings' in M Kramer *et al A debate over rights, philosophical enquiries* (1998) 27.

34 H Cohen *Equal rights for children* (1980) 48.

35 In the African human rights system, for example, children, minors and youth or young people are defined and considered differently. The African Children's Charter defines a child as any human being below the age of eighteen years. The African Youth Charter on the other hand defines minors 'to mean young people age 15-17' subject to national laws; while youth or young people 'shall refer to every person between the ages of 15 and 35'. See definition section of the African Youth Charter available at: http://www.africa-union.org/root/ua/conferences/mai/hrst/charter%20english.pdf. This subject will be discussed in more detail in Chapter four of this book.

assumes that there is an identifiable and universally agreeable 'interest' capable of protection. Because 'child' and 'childhood' are cultural constructs, protectable interests will vary from culture to culture, from family to family, and even from one individual child to another.[36] So the task of identifying, consolidating and recognising which interests are capable of protection through the instrumentality of human rights is onerous.

International human rights law, especially the CRC, has attempted to minimise and streamline these arguments and counter arguments with respect to human rights and the child. It has done so by clearly defining the child, delineating childhood, and codifying the rights children have as human beings and as children. As a result, it is now possible to identify and define what a child is and what an ideal childhood should look like, at least within the context of international human rights law.[37]

2.1. The conception of childhood with reference to four aspects of the CRC

2.1.1. Who is a child in the CRC?

The question 'Who is a child?' can be approached from three perspectives. First, from a non-normative perspective, that is purely a biological statement of facts and, thus, an empirical question. Second, it could be regarded as a 'content of a status concept' and, as such, normative. Thirdly, as a social construct that depends upon and differs according to context. For instance, it is in a partly biological sense that Schapiro says:

> Treating someone like a child is prima facie wrong, unless, of course, the person in question really is a child. ... To treat someone like a child is, roughly, to treat her as if her life is not

36 L Kopelman 'Children and bioethics: Uses and abuses of the best-interests standard' (1997) 22 *The Journal of Medicine and Philosophy* 213.

37 Article 1 of the CRC and article 2 of the African Children's Charter defines a child as anyone below the age of 18 years. However, article 1 of the Covenant on the Rights of the Child in Islam, defines a child as 'every human being who, according to the law applicable to him/her has not attained maturity'. The implication of this for international human rights and the African human rights system will be the subject of discussion in chapter four of this book.

> quite her own to lead and as if her choices are not quite her own to make.[38]

The CRC regards childhood as a 'content of a status concept' and, as such, normative.

For a long time international law makers were comfortable using the category 'children' without attempting an overarching definition of the initial and terminal points of childhood.[39] Whenever an attempt was made to delineate an upper limit, it varied according to a particular and specific purpose.[40] The underlying reason for adapting a flexible position on the definition of childhood was that there were as many concepts of childhood as there were countries, cultures and legislative purposes.[41] Homogenising and universalising a particular brand of childhood was deemed detrimental to the harmonious development of children who fell outside specific contexts.[42]

---

38 T Schapiro 'What is a Child?' (1999) 109 *Ethics* 715.

39 It should be noted that this statement is only correct with respect to the CRC and, in some case, few purpose specific legal documents adopted after 1989 such as the ILO's Worse Forms of Child Labour Convention 182 of 2000 that equally peg the lower age limits for worse forms of labour at 18. The African Children's Charter also adopts the straight 18 position. However, the Optional Protocol to the Convention on the Rights of the Child on the Involvement of Children in Armed Conflict (2002); and the Rome Status of the International Criminal Court (2002) deviate from a straight 18 position of the CRC with respect to children's involvement directly and indirectly in armed conflicts under different circumstances. Older human rights and humanitarian law instruments also did not provide for clear lower or upper limits for all situations. For example, Article 77 of Additional Protocol I and Article 4(c) of the Additional Protocol II establish 15 years as the minimum age for recruitment and participation in hostilities. Both, the 1924 Declaration on the Rights of the Child, the 1959 Declaration on the Rights of the Child do not define childhood. Article 25(2) of the Universal Declaration of Human Rights provides for the protection of children without defining them, Article 24 of the International Covenant on Civil and Political Rights protects children without defining the category.

40 Some of these purposes were, for example, participation in hostilities, age of consent either for medical purpose or marriage; and age of criminal liability.

41 See the editorial by C Jenks '*Many childhoods*?' (2004) 11 *Childhood* 1; and see also the collections in this edition of childhood dealing with the varieties of childhoods around the world and its implication for policy making.

42 Aitken S 'Global crises of childhood: Rights, justice and the unchildlike child' (2001) 33 *Area* 119; Alston P 'The legal framework of the Convention on the Rights of the Child' (1992) 2 *Bulletin of Human Rights* 9; An-na'im A 'Cultural transformation and normative consensus on the best interests of the child' (1994) *8 International Journal of Law and the Family* 62; K Cheney 'Conflicting protectionist and participation models of children's rights: Their consequences for Uganda's orphans and vulnerable children' in A Imoh & N Ansell (eds) *Children's lives in an era of children's rights: The progress of the Convention on the Rights of the Child in Africa* (2014) 17; A Norman 'Children's Rights in the time of AIDS in KwaZulu-Natal, South Africa' in A Imoh & N Ansell (eds) *Children's lives in an era of children's rights: The progress of the Convention on the Rights of the Child in Africa* (2014) 34; S Okyere 'Children's participation in prohibited work in Ghana and its implications for the Convention on the Rights of the Child' in A Imoh & N Ansell (eds) *Children's lives in an era of children's rights: The progress of the Convention on the Rights of the Child in Africa* (2014) 92; K Bentley 'Can there be any universal children's rights? (2006) 9 *International Journal of Human Rights* 107.

The CRC deviate from this tradition. For the first time in international human rights law, it provides an overarching definition of childhood. The CRC defined a child as a human being who has not attained 18 years of age. The motivating factor was to ensure uniformity and widen the protective cover of its provisions. For policy convenience, the drafters of the CRC opted for an overarching definition of childhood and the setting of an upper age limit to distinguish between childhood and adulthood.[43] State parties, therefore, have the discretion to determine who qualifies as a 'child' for the purpose of the CRC. In theory, the position does not appear to be inflexible, deterministic and homogenising; in fact, it seems to be culturally and context sensitive. In practice, however, the CRC Committee, UNICEF, bilateral and multilateral donor agencies and armies of nongovernmental organizations have sustained pressure on governments, especially in developing countries, to harmonise their domestic legislation with the provisions of the CRC[44] prominent on the list is the demand that governments peg their upper age limit at 'straight 18.'[45]

There are a number of arguments in favour of a 'straight 18' definition of childhood. First, most national legislation classified children as human beings between the ages of 0 to 21 years old. So, 18 is a good compromise.[46] Second, the argument is that the higher the upper limit for childhood is, the better the chance for an enhanced protection for children.[47] The third argument is that even though 18 years may be arbitrary, so would any other number be arbitrary.

---

43 S Detrick *The United Nations Convention on the Rights of the Child: A guide to the travaux préparatoires* (1992) 115. The lower limit - when childhood should start was left to the 'margin of appreciation' of member states taking into consideration their economic, socio-political and socio-cultural peculiarities. See General Comment .17 (paragraph.4) on article 24 of the ICCPR on the Rights of the Child adopted by the Committee on Civil and Political Rights (1989). The CRC Committee has alluded to this reason. See the Implementation handbook for the Convention on the Rights of the Child (2007) 1.

44 See the summary of the recommendations of the CRC Committee concluding observations and recommendations to state parties in the Implementation Handbook for the Convention on the Rights of the Child (2007) 1-11.

45 Even though this straight 18 position is in line with article 2 of the African Children's Charter, it is argued that this very rigid definition of childhood is not in line with the understanding of childhood in traditional communities in Africa. Among traditional communities in Africa, a child could transit to adulthood before the age of 18 or remain a child after reaching the age of 18. See the discussion of chapter 3 of this book.

46 S Detrick *The United Nations Convention on the Rights of the Child: A guide to the travaux préparatoires* (1992) 115.

47 D Chirwa 'The merits and demerits of the African Charter on the Rights and Welfare of the Child' (2002) 10 *International Journal of Children's Rights* 157. See also B Memzur 'The African Children's Charter versus the UN Convention on the Rights of the Child: A zero-sum game?'(2008) 23 *SAPR/PL* 1.

In the absence of conclusive scientific explanation or justification for the insistence on this straight 18 position, it is reasonable to ask why the CRC Committee, UNICEF and NGOs insist on harmonising national constitutions and legislation to ensure that childhood ends only at 18. It raises doubt about the intention of the flexible provision of article 1 of the CRC as an attempt to secure a compromise during the negotiations of the CRC and, thereafter, to isolate state parties to ensure that the 'universal ideals' of the CRC are recognised and accepted. If the purpose of harmonisation is to ensure universality in the definition and conception of childhood, what is the implication of such an approach? Adhering to a sense of strict universality with respect to the conception of childhood poses a number of difficulties in the successful implementation of children's rights and, ultimately, with regard to the wellbeing of the child.[48] Among these challenges are the following:

a) *It divorces childhood from its lived reality*: As a structural space, 'childhood' is a normative as well as an operational concept. 'Childhood' is normative in the sense that it regulates interaction within society, and it is operational because it is meant to serve some agreed socio-economic and socio-cultural ends in a specific context. The interaction between a society and its children 'reflects not only its qualities of compassion and protective caring but also its sense of justice, its commitment to a future and its urge to enhance the human condition for coming generations.'49 Attempting to externally and arbitrarily regulate this relationship through the implementation of an alternative model of interaction is to pass a value judgement on a community's or society's sense of compassion and justice and, ultimately, their collective worthiness as a group. It creates a schism between the outside concept of childhood and the lived reality of children in their context.50

48 T Abebe & T Tefera 'Earning rights: Discourses on children's rights and proper childhood in Ethiopia' in A Imoh & N Ansell (eds) *Children's lives in an era of children's rights: The progress of the Convention on the Rights of the Child in Africa* (2014) 53, where the authors argue that the imposition of numerical age by NGOs instead of the social age known to traditional communities in Ethiopia is causing some social dislocations.

49 Javier Perez De Cuellar, UN Secretary-General, in his international message on the Convention on the Rights of the Child in September 1987 Statement made by the United Nations Secretary in 1978 as quoted in M Kruger 'The development of a protocol to ensure the recognition of the rights of children during a legal process' unpublished PhD book, University of Pretoria (2006) 1.

50 See C André & M Godin 'Children's Rights in the Democratic Republic of Congo and neoliberal reform:

b) *Using age as a distinguishing factor between childhood and adulthood is misleading*: Using age as the most important distinguishing factor between childhood and adulthood presupposes that majority is solely a function of numbers. It also presumes that all communities use a numerical indication for the purpose of delineating childhood from adulthood. Furthermore, how the CRC uses age is capable of creating two different worlds for children - children who are under 18 years but who have attained majority according to their national legislation, and children who are under 18 years of age but have not attained majority according to their national legislation.

c) *Placing the upper age limit higher to ensure wider protective coverage may inadvertently affect the quantity and quality of service available to children*: Fixing the terminal point of childhood at 18 means that more than half of the population of some developing countries is classified as 'children.'51 The economic burden created by this situation affects governments' ability to effectively and efficiently discharge their obligations to children.52 In addition, more than half of the population of these countries is automatically legally barred from participating in many productive economic activities simply because the law designates them as children. The argument is not to support harmful labour practices, but an argument rather that empowers children to acquire the skills needed to be self-reliant adults. The desire to protect children from abuse should be balanced against a determination to protect opportunities for children too.53

The case of mines in the province of Katanga' in A Imoh & N Ansell (eds) *Children's lives in an era of children's rights: The progress of the Convention on the Rights of the child in Africa* (2014) 72.

51 UNICEF estimates children and young people's population in Africa to be more than half of the total population of the continent see UNICEF's World Status of Children's Report 2010.

52 State reports to the Committee on the Rights of the Rights routinely ask for technical and financial assistance to help them meet their obligation under the CRC. See the Implementation Handbook on the United Nations Convention on the Rights of the Child (2007) 20-47. During the drafting session, delegates from developing countries already started complaining about the economic implications of 18 as the upper limit of childhood. For a detailed discussion on the drafting history of the Convention on the Rights of the Child see S Detrick *Commentary on the United Nations Convention on the Rights of the Child* (1999) 51.

53 See similar argument made by the following case studies: M Bourdillon & E Musvosvi 'What can children's rights mean when children are struggling to survive? The case of Chiweshe, Zimbabwe' in A Imoh & N Ansell (eds) *Children's lives in an era of children's rights: The progress of the Convention on the Rights of the Child in Africa* (2014) 105; E Omike 'In the best interests of the child: The case of child domestic workers in Ghana and Nigeria' in A Imoh & N Ansell (eds) *Children's lives in an era of children's rights: The progress of*

This is not to suggest that using age to define and limit childhood is not without merit. The legal value of regularity and universality, at least for policy makers in the area of childhood, is high. Allowing childhood to be delineated according to different cultural practices, the world over would make the task of protecting children internationally virtually impossible. It is submitted that when flexibilities have been agreed and made law, as is the case with respect to article 1 of the CRC, such flexibility should also be enforced in interpreting the provisions of that law. The argument made here with respect to defining childhood in a context-specific manner is alive to the fact that the 'diversities that distinguish one child from another are as important and as significant as the commonalities they might share.'[54] It is conceivable that the commonalities are universally perceived and predictable in expression.

The difficulty arises when the 'commonalities' prematurely are translated into immutable fact by the force of international human rights law seen through specific historical and philosophical lenses, thereby translating 'wide-ranging political questions into more narrowly framed legal questions.'[55] The danger is that 'universalisms . . . [may, in this case,] result from the elevation of a particularism to a universal status, so that the act of universal inclusion is always at the same time an act of exclusion.'[56] It may lead to a feeling that some cultures systematically are denied the right to rear their children based on their value system, culture and history. This perception is partially responsible for resentment against the wholesale implementation of the CRC. Some scholars hold the view that the CRC, in its

> drafting process, the resulting text, and in its implementation, takes as its starting point western, modern, childhood, which has been 'globalised' first through colonialism and then through imperialism of the international aid...[57]

---

the Convention on the Rights of the Child in Africa (2014) 123 and L Van Blerk 'Progressing street children's rights and participation in policy: Evidence from South Africa' in A Imoh & N Ansell (eds) *Children's lives in an era of children's rights: The progress of the Convention on the Rights of the Child in Africa* (2014) 191.

54 C James & A James *Constructing childhood: Theory, policy and social practice* (2004) 16.

55 W Brown & J Halley (eds) *Left legalism/left criticism* (2002) 19.

56 C Hall *Cultures of the empire: Colonizers in Britain and the empire in the twentieth centuries* (2000) 64.

57 J Ennew 'Outside childhood: Street children's rights' in B Franklin (ed) *The handbook of children's rights*

This perception begs the question: What is this Western and modern childhood that the CRC is accused of reflecting and how is that different, for example, from an African childhood? The next section will attempt to answer the question: First, by sketching the image of childhood in the CRC. Second, this image of childhood in the CRC will be juxtaposed with the understanding of childhood in the West. Third, a conclusion will then be reached by means of a comparative analysis. The question asked in respect of an African conception of childhood is the subject of another chapter and will not be discussed here.

2.1.2. Children's autonomy rights in the CRC

The CRC defines a child as a 'human being' who is under 18 years of age except when majority is attained earlier under a domestic legal system. The remaining substantive provisions of the CRC complete the image of preferred childhood and the entitlements of a child as a 'human being'. The consideration, conceptualisation and codification of the child as a 'full and complete' human being probably aimed to put to rest debates around the status of the child as 'not-yet-being', 'becoming' or an 'adult in the waiting.'[58] The conception of the child as a human being radically changes the way society sees and treats children, at least in policy terms.

By recognising the child as a 'human being,' the CRC protects the self-worth, dignity, personhood, agency, autonomy or self-determination and the best interests of children. Recognising a child as a human being endows that child with some of the irreducible attributes of humanness. The conception of the child as an independent, autonomous and responsible individual is theoretically sound but practically is fraught with challenges.[59] On the one hand, different subsets of the age category 'children' are biologically and physically immature, dependent, vulnerable and finite; on the other, children, as part of the human family, cannot logically be deprived of the essential

(1995) 202.

58 G Mathews 'Getting beyond the deficit conception of childhood: Thinking philosophically with children' in M Hand & C Stanley (eds) *Philosophy in Schools* (2008) 27.

59 L Purdy '*In their best interests? The case against equal rights for children* (1992) 87.

attributes of that family. An examination of the concepts of agency, autonomy and a primary interest of the child highlights this tension.

Rational, autonomous and moral agency is the essential attribute that distinguishes humans from other species.[60] Rational agency involves an appreciation of causality. Autonomous agency refers to the capacity to choose a course in life and the ability to pursue that course. Moral agency is the capacity to act in the light of moral reason.[61] This moral and rational personhood is something that Nussbaum addresses. Nussbaum asserts that by being human, all have equality of dignity and worth irrespective of where they are situated in society.[62] She further expressed the view that 'the primary source of this worth is a power of moral choice..., a power that consists in the ability to plan a life in accordance with one's own evaluation of ends.'[63] The implication of asserting the equal worth of all persons is that 'the moral equality of persons gives them a fair claim to certain types of treatment at the hands of society and politics.'[64] This approach 'addresses hierarchy across the board in the name of human dignity.'[65] This capacity to reflect on, to choose, and to pursue what we ourselves decide'[66] is at the core of human worth. Griffin says: 'to be an agent, in the fullest sense of which we are capable ... [is] not be dominated or controlled by someone or something else (autonomy). And ... others must also not stop one from pursuing what one sees as a good life (liberty).'[67] Agency is central to dignity, and dignity is pivotal to human rights. It is argued that dignity must be protected through human rights law.[68] Autonomy, liberty and welfare rights should flow naturally from the very fact

60 J Griffin 'First steps in an account of human rights' (2001) 9 *European Journal of Philosophy* 311.

61 M Hoffman 'The development of prosocial motivation: Empathy and guilt' in N Eisenberg (ed) *The development of prosocial behaviour* (1982) 281.

62 M Nussbaum *Cultivating humanity: A classical defence of reform in liberal education* (1997) 50.

63 Nussbaum, n 62, 57.

64 As above, 57.

65 As above, 71.

66 J Tasioulas 'Human rights, universality and the values of personhood: Retracing Griffin's steps' (2002) 10 *European Journal of Philosophy* 83.

67 J Griffin 'First steps in an account of human rights' (2001) 9 *European Journal of Philosophy* 311.

68 As above.

of seeing children as human beings. Therefore, the mere fact that a child is born of humans is a strong reason for according him or her, the same status and the same rights protection as other members of the human family.

Once the category 'child' was construed as a human being, the CRC logically conferred children with rights that in many respects are 'coextensive with those of adults,'[69] since children and adults are members of the same human family. This ideology led to the projection of the status and prospect of children that is 'rooted in [the] concept of the radically autonomous individual.'[70] Such an ideology can take the form of an extreme opinion, because 'kids are people too;'[71] they are masters of their own destiny and must be left alone. By allowing children to enjoy most of the entitlements of their personhood, the CRC bestows on children unprecedented personal and legal liberty and autonomous rights claims that are limited only by age, maturity and the evolving capacities of children. The purpose of liberty rights, usually, is to create an environment free from obstacles or coercion by the arbitrary will of others, for the enjoyment of conferred entitlements.

There are a number of difficulties with the above position. First, there is the presumption, by some, that all children possess similar levels of rational and autonomous agency. Second, the technicalisation of agency is used at the expense of its contextualisation. Third, there is the suggestion that whatever is significantly important for a dignified life must be converted into rights for safeguarding. Along a continuum from 0 to 18 years of age are infants, young children, children and youth or adolescents. Genuine agency in infancy and young children is difficult to ascertain.[72] In addition, agency is historically and geographically different. When contextually understood

69 J Stephen *et al* 'Children's rights' in *Encyclopaedia of education and human development* (2005) 363; but also see M Mason 'From father's property to children's rights' in L Kermit *et al The Oxford companion to American law* (1994) 95 where it is argued that children's rights are not coextensive with those of adults.

70 C Bruce & J Hafen 'Abandoning children to their rights' (1995) *First things First* 9 available at http://www.firstthings.com/article/2008/09/001-abandoning-children-to-their-rights-18.

71 A Lurie 'Representing the child-client: Kids are people too an analysis of the role of the legal counsel to minor' (1993) 11 *New York Law School Journal of Human Rights* 205.

72 J Griffin 'First steps in an account of human rights' (2001) 9 *European Journal of Philosophy* 311.

> agency ... is a matter not of fact but of interpretation attribution, value, and culture ... human agency, with its connotation of self-determination, is intrinsically constrained by forms of social external determination, which make up an irremovable background against which human agency is possible.[73]

Thus, selfhood and agency are 'not initially there at birth, but arise in the process of social experience and activity ... in the given individual as a result of his relations to that process as a whole and to other individuals within that process.'[74] The resultant agency attributable to a human being, therefore, is a result of a process in which the individual is 'becoming an object to himself by taking the attitudes [perspectives] of other individuals toward himself within an organized setting of social relationships'[75] that is a factor of culturalisation.

Placing agency within the broader meaning of context-specific value and power has implications for the structure, form and function of childhood and the family structure. In turn, it impacts on the local appreciation and application of international human rights, generally, and children's rights, in particular.[76] It is so because the conceptualisation of 'needs,' 'rights' and 'competencies' that accrue to childhood vary from context to context and from time to time.[77]

Articles 13 to 16 of the CRC best embody the spirit and purpose of liberty rights for children. Article 13 grants children 'the right to freedom of expression, including the right to seek, receive, and impart information and

---

73 C Jewei 'Evaluation of agency: A fundamental question for social and political philosophy' (2011) 42 *Metaphilosophy* 261.

74 J Mead quoted in J Martin & G Gillespie 'A neomeadian approach to human agency: Relating the social and the psychological in the ontogenesis of perspective coordinating persons' (2010) 44 *Integrative Psychological and Behavioral Science* 252; see also J Martin *et al* 'Taking and coordinating perspectives: From prereflective interactivity, through reflective intersubjectivity, to metareflective sociality' (2008) 58 *Human Development* 294.

75 J Mead 'The social self' in C Morris (ed) *Mind, self and society from the standpoint of social behaviourist* (1934) 225.

76 J Holt *Escape from childhood: The needs and rights of children* (1975) 39; J Ellis 'Different conceptions of a child's needs: Some implications of social work for Western African children and their parents (1977) 7 *British Journal of Social Work* 155.

77 J Ellis 'Different conceptions of a child's needs: Some implications of social work for Western African children and their parents (1977) 7 *British Journal of Social Work* 155.

ideas of all kinds, regardless of frontiers ... through any media of the child's choice'. This broad free speech guarantee is subject only to restrictions that are 'provided by law and are necessary to respect the rights or reputations of others' or to protect public security, order, health, or morals. Article 14 affirms 'the right of the child to freedom of thought, conscience and religion.' It respects parents' 'rights and duties' to 'provide direction' in this realm, but only 'to the child in the exercise of his or her right in a manner consistent with the evolving capacities of the child'. Article 16 establishes the child's privacy rights: 'No child shall be subjected to arbitrary or unlawful interference with his or her privacy, family, home or correspondence', the so called 'right to be left alone.'

According to the CRC Committee, these rights of children to speak, to decide, to have their voice heard and their opinion taken into consideration, as well as their rights to 'seek, receive and impart' information on all issues that affect them and, in all settings, constitute the basis of a social contract[78] between children, their families, and societies. To implement the terms of this social contract effectively, the CRC compels 'changes in political, social, institutional and cultural structures' the world over.[79] In other words, societies must fundamentally change the way they see and treat children. It is reasonable to think that the CRC could envisage such a radical transformative approach to child rearing because the image of childhood contemplated in the CRC is not rooted in all socio-political and cultural structures around the world, in which case existing socio-political and cultural infrastructure constitute stumbling blocks that must be dismantled.

Since the conception of the child as a liberal and autonomous individual with self-serving rights cannot be attained fully in different contexts without a reformulation of the nature and scope of socio-political, socio-economic and socio-cultural norms, values and institutions, it is arguable that the conception of childhood in the CRC constitutes a new culture, new norms and new values independent of existing ones. Such a new culture of child

---

78 See General Comment no. 12 (2009) *On the rights of the child to be heard*, of the CRC Committee. CRC/C/GC/12 20 July 2009.

79 CRC Committee, Report on the forty-third session, September 2006, Day of General Discussion, Recommendations, Preamble. For full text, see www.ohchr.org/english/bodies/crc/discussion.htm.

rearing has implications for childhood and the immediate environment in which childhood is spent. One such environment is the family. In this regard the CRC is not simply a child rights treaty; it is at the same time a family relationship guidebook. One of the first institutions that must 'bear the brunt' of this new culture is the family.[80] The nature, structure, roles and responsibilities of the family must change in order to facilitate a transformation in the fundamental nature of adult-child relationships that is needed to support the image of childhood advocated by the CRC.[81]

Therefore, in order to realise the ideas of the CRC, communities need to carve out new family arrangements, wherein parents are managers of upbringing, and children as 'autonomous, self-reliant, responsible'[82] individuals who take responsibility in a rational way.[83] It is not to say that the CRC does not provide for parental rights. It provides for respect of the 'responsibilities, rights and duties' of parents and other caregivers to provide 'direction and guidance', in line with the evolving capacities of children in the exercise of their rights.[84] However, parental rights are significantly curtailed by the CRC. Parental rights, as provided for in the CRC, are essentially functional: serving the best interests of the child.[85]

The family structure anticipated by, and the roles ascribed to families by the CRC are rights- based. Families have responsibilities, rights and duties to

80 S Brennan & R Noggle 'The moral status of children: Children's rights, parents' rights, and family justice' (1997) 23 *Social Theory and Practice* 1; for a view that says this assertion is over exaggerated see G Melton 'The child's right to a family environment: Why children's rights and family values are compatible' (1996) 51 *American Psychologist* 1234.

81 J Cornides 'Human rights pitted against man' (2008) 12 *International Journal of Human Rights* 107.

82 S Ruddick 'At horizons of the subject: Neoliberalism, neo-conservatism and the rights of the child part two: Parents, caregivers, the state' (2007) *14 Gender, Place & Culture: A Journal of Feminist Geography* 627.

83 C van Nijnatten 'Authority relations in families and child welfare in the Netherlands and England: New styles of governance' (2000) 14 *International Journal of Law, Policy and the Family* 107; J Muncie 'Governing young people: Coherence and contradictions in contemporary youth justice' (2006) 26 *Critical Social Policy* 770; U Beck 'Democratisation of the family' (1997) 4 *Childhood* 151; I Moqvist 'Constructing a parent' in M Bloch *et al* (eds) *Governing children, families and education: Reconstructing a welfare state* (2003) 117; M Vandenbroeck & M Bouverne-De Bie 'Children's agency and educational norms – a tensed negotiation' (2006) 13 *Childhood* 127.

84 Article 5 of the CRC.

85 S Detrick 'Family Rights' Under the United Nations Convention on the Rights of the Child' in N Lowe & G Douglas (eds) *Families across frontiers* (1996) 95; J Westman *Children's rights, parents prerogatives, and society's obligations* (1999) 29 *Child Psychiatry and Human Development* 315; S Tomanović 'Negotiating children's participation and autonomy within families' (2003) 11 International *Journal of Children's Rights* 51.

enable children to exercise their rights. The family anticipated in the CRC, in many respects, is expected to give to children love, care and material wellbeing and expect nothing in return. This form of family structure is not yet common to all societies.[86] Some societies have obligations-based family structures. These family arrangements emphasise 'adult obligations rather than children's rights [as] the appropriate social, political and educational basis for adult society's relations with children.'[87] Until the right-based family model advocated by the CRC replaces obligation-based family understanding, children's lived experience will straddle these models.

2.1.3. Best interests of the child in the CRC

The CRC's child is a human being with a primary interest that should be taken into consideration in all actions concerning the child. Though the inclusion of a 'best interests' of the child principle in the CRC was controversial,[88] it was not without precedent.[89] However, the application and implication of the concept in the CRC was, in breadth and depth, groundbreaking.[90] Its inclusion in the CRC serves a number of purposes. First, a 'best interests' principle supports, justifies and clarifies an approach or interpretation of issues covered by the CRC. Second, it serves as a conflict resolution mechanism either between competing rights or possibly between competing values and images of childhood. Third, it could serve a general evaluating function with respect to laws and practices of state parties on issues not covered by the CRC.[91] In all

86 U Beck 'Democratisation of the family' (1997) 4 *Childhood* 151.

87 S Benporath 'Autonomy and vulnerability: On just relations between adults and children' (2003) 37 *Journal of Philosophy of Education* 127.

88 S Detrick A *commentary on the United Nations Convention on the Rights of the Child* (1999) 89.

89 See generally P Alston (ed) *The best interests of the child: Reconciling culture and human rights* (1994) 4, 260; P Alston & B Gilmour-Walsh *The best interests of the child: Towards a synthesis of children's rights and cultural values* (1996) 3; L LaFave 'Origins of the evolution of 'the best interests of the child' standard' (1989) 34 *South Dakota Law Review* 459.

90 Detrick, n 88, 90.

91 S Parker 'The best interests of the child: Principles and problems' (1994) 8 *International Journal of Law and the Family* 26; P Alston & B Gilmour-Walsh *The best interests of the child: Towards a synthesis of children's rights and cultural values* (1996) 41.

matters not governed by positive rights in the Convention, article 3(1) will be the basis for 'evaluating the laws and practices of the state parties.'[92]

The meaning of the concept 'best interests of the child' is not as clear as its purpose may suggest. It is, in some cases, 'indetermined, vague and open-ended.'[93] The lack of clarity is both a virtue and a vice. It is a virtue because leaving it as a content-free-principle allows 'the meaning and implications of the best interests principle in any society [to be] open to challenge, reformulation and refinement through the processes of internal discourse and cross-cultural dialogue.'[94] Its weakness lies in the fact that, 'in the absence of legal rules or a hierarchy of values, the best interests approach depends upon the value system of the decision-maker. Absent any rule or guideline, that approach simply creates an unexaminable discretion in the repository of the power.'[95] A combination of human rights norms and local specificities should, wherever possible, provide guidance to decision makers while determining the best interests of the child. However, the tendency, so far at least, from the perspective of the CRC Committee is that 'it does not permit a degree of sensitivity to cultural factors.'[96] The unintended consequence of such inflexibility in relation to local context could fortify local resistance to the effective implementation of the CRC.

The CRC Committee is beginning to adopt a flexible stand on what constitutes the best interests of the child. In its General Comment 14 the CRC Committee gives guidance on how to interpret and apply best interests of the child principle. In this General Comment, the CRC Committee

---

92 S Parker 'The best interests of the child: Principles and problems' (1994) 8 *International Journal of Law and the Family* 26.

93 As above.

94 A An Na'im "Cultural transformation and normative consensus on the best interests of the child' (1994) 8 *International Journal of Law and the Family* 62.

95 Brennan, J in *Secretary, Dept of Health and Community Services* v *JWB and SMB FLC* 92-3 at 79,191 (1992).

96 P Alston & B Gilmour-Walsh *The best interests of the child: Towards a synthesis of children's rights and cultural norms* (1996)17. It must be noted, however, that the Committee on the Rights of the Child is an evolving treaty body. On some issues it has conceded some flexibility to context. A case in point is the approach that the Committee on the Rights of the Child recommends in the determination of the best interests of the child in its General Comment 14 discussed below. But this flexibility is still not a common feature of the approach of the Committee on the Rights of the Child.

acknowledges that 'the concept of the child's best interests is complex, and its content must be determined on a case-by-case basis,'[97] and that the

> concept of the child's best interests is flexible and adaptable. It should be adjusted and defined on an individual basis, according to the specific situation of the child or children concerned, taking into consideration their personal context, situation and needs.[98]

This flexibility must be assessed in the context of the CRC Committee's insistence that 'a right based approach'[99] that respects the universal, indivisible, interdependent and interrelated nature of children's rights, and recognises children as right holders[100] must be used as the parameter in determining what is in the best interests of a child.

What the CRC Committee says is that universal human rights values are the benchmark against which 'the social and cultural context in which the child or children find themselves'[101] are to be assessed in order to determine what is in the interests of the child. Since the values of individualisation, of individual autonomy and liberty rights espoused in the CRC rights are not universally held, it is possible that the norms of the cultures that have attained universality within the framework of international human rights treaties, such as the CRC, will be the yardstick used to judge what is and what is not in the best interests of children in other parts of the world.

Therefore, it is possible that in formulating, interpreting and implementing the 'best interests' of the child principle, the emerging 'best interests' interpretation merely reflects, responds to, and, in the process, universalises the norms and institutional features of the values of cultures fairly represented in the CRC. The result of such a process will be to create a child and the supporting social institutions in the image of the values of the cultures that inform the values in the CRC or that of members of the CRC Committee and

97 Para 32 of the General Comment 14 of the CRC Committee.

98 Para 32 of the General Comment 14 of the CRC Committee.

99 Para 5 of the General Comment 14 of the CRC Committee.

100 Para 16 (a) and (b) of the General Comment 14 of the CRC Committee.

101 Para 48 of the General Comment 14 of the CRC Committee.

those technocrats supporting the Committee whose determination of what is in the best interests of the child may be motivated by their own training, individual experience and professional orientation. However, the requirement in General Comment 14 to ensure children's participation in determining what is in their own interests is a useful balance.

2.1.4. Participation rights in the CRC

The CRC's child is a talking, thinking and deciding child. She is an active citizen participating in all decisions affecting her. Every child capable of forming his or her own views should have the right to express those views freely and such views are to be given due weight in accordance with the age and maturity of the child.[102] Generally, participation rights involve four levels: to be informed, to express an informed view, to have that view taken into account, and to be the main or joint decision-maker.[103] The CRC limits the right to participation to the first three levels, implying that decision-making power still rests with adults.[104] Participation is considered in the CRC as a fundamental right, as well as a means to realising all the other rights of the child.

Seen as a vertical right that mainly regulates child's participation in public decision-making, participation rights should be non-problematic. In societies where participation in public decision-making is a distant dream even for adults, talking of the child having participation rights may not be without problems and pitfalls. The challenge arises when child participation rights are viewed as applying within the family context.[105] First, in a significant number of families living in traditional settings Africa, family's decision-making is a hierarchical business mainly taken by those who have the capacity

102 See Article 12 of the Convention on the Rights of the Child.

103 B Percy-Smith *A handbook of children and young people's participation: Perspectives from theory and practice* (2010) 6.

104 See article 12 of the CRC.

105 E Ochaita & M Espinosa 'Children's participation in family and school life: A psychological and development Approach' (1997) 5 *International Journal of Children's Rights* 279; S Tomanović 'Negotiating children's participation and autonomy within families' (2003) 11 *International Journal of Children's Rights* 51; S Tomanović-Mihajlović 'Young people's participation within the family: Parent's accounts' (2000) 8 *International Journal of Children's Rights* 151.

to implement the decisions.[106] Second, there is the practical difficulty with how to ensure that the right to participation is implemented within a family setting. The concern here is predicated on the fact that 'the law does not have the capacity to supervise the fragile, complex interpersonal bonds between child and parent.'[107] In order to effectively regulate and monitor family environment, the machinery of the 'state is too crude a treaty.'[108]

The image of the child in the CRC is that of a universal, significantly autonomous, thinking, talking and deciding human being. His or her interest is central to family and public decision-making. She or he is endowed with rights[109] as a human being and, additionally, as a result of an inherent vulnerability of a child, as well as a child's incapacity. The CRC's child does not have any active corresponding obligation, duty or responsibility. The child, as conceptualised in the CRC, is under no obligation to give anything in return to family or society, certainly not as a matter of rights. This universal child is too rational and technical to be contextual. A view of a child who takes but gives nothing is a mismatch to the values in a number of communities around the world.

Conceptualising childhood mainly at such a rational and technical level has implications for the wellbeing of the child, the nature, structure, form and purpose of the family and the harmonious existence of societies.[110] Children are inherently dependent persons, a concept less of law than of nature.[111] John Stuart Mill in his doctrine of individual 'liberty' limits the concept 'to human

---

106 S Tomanović 'Negotiating children's participation and autonomy within families' (2003) 11 *International Journal of Children's Rights* 51; S Tomanović-Mihajlović 'Young people's participation within the family: Parent's accounts' (2000) 8 *International Journal of Children's Rights* 151.

107 M Freeman 'The best interests of the child? Is the best interests of the child in the best interests of children?' (1997) 11 *International Journal of Law, Policy and the Family* 360.

108 As above.

109 Except those rights that are temporally withheld by law so as to protect children and adults from the consequences of the immaturities of childhood these include rights to vote, or driving, age of sexual consent etc.

110 J Coons *et al* 'Puzzling over children's rights' (1991) *Brigham Young University Law Review* 307; see also A Alstott 'Is the family at odds with equality? The legal implications of equality for children' (2008) 82 *South California Law Review* 1.

111 A Appell 'The pre-political child of the child-cantered jurisprudence' (2009-2010) 46 *Houston Law Review* 703.

beings in the maturity of their faculties. We are not speaking of children [who] must be protected against their own actions as well as against external injury.'[112] The US Supreme Court noted:

> The peculiar vulnerability of children their inability to make critical decisions in an informed, mature manner and the importance of the parental role in child rearing leads to the conclusion that the constitutional rights of children cannot be equated with those of adults.[113]

To confer children with a full range of choice rights is to confer them with the burdens and responsibilities of adult status before '[their] understanding be fit to take the government of [their] will.'[114] This situation, therefore, could result into more vulnerability for children.

Placing children and their parents on the same footing as co-autonomous persons in their relation with the state and, at the same time, insisting that parents and people with responsibility to take care of children should leave children alone, let them speak for themselves and decide how their needs should be met, conflicts with the understanding of family functioning in a number of traditional societies.[115] Such an attempt by the CRC to reformulate family setting is an unnecessary intrusion of the law and state in the functioning of the family.[116] This concern, in the US, for instance, is based on the prominent doctrine of law that the 'parent-child relationship antedates the state just as natural individual rights antedate the state in the Constitution's political theory.'[117] The parent-child tie is 'a relationship having

---

112 J Mills 'On liberty' (1860) *Harvard Classics* 25.

113 In *Re Gault* 387 US 1 (1967).

114 J Locke *Two treaties of government and a letter concerning toleration* (2005) 89.

115 N Ansell 'The Convention on the Rights of the Child: Advancing social justice for African children? in A Imoh & N Ansell (eds) *Children's lives in an era of children's rights: The progress of the Convention on the Rights of the Child in Africa* (2014) 228.

116 A Skolnick 'The limits of childhood: Conceptions of child development and social context' (1975) 39 *Law and Contemporary Problems* 38; J Dolgin 'Transforming childhood: Apprenticeship in American law' (1996-97) 31 *New England Law Review* 1113; J Zainaldin 'The emergence of modern American family law: Child custody, adoption and the courts, 1796-1851' (1978-79) 73 *Northwest University Law Review* 1039.

117 B Hafen 'Children's liberation and the new egalitarianism: Some reservations about abandoning youth to their 'rights'' (1976) 605 *Brigham Young University Law Review* 644.

its origins entirely apart from the power of the state.'[118] Parents, therefore, are not 'trustees who receive authority to rear their children through delegations of state power over children.'[119]

If it is a fear of the negative effects of absolute parental authority that drives the policy positions of the CRC with respect to child-parent relationship, the CRC's conception of childhood must significantly take into account the full exercise of parental rights and responsibilities. Replacing parental paternalism with state paternalism does not, in and of itself, confer children with autonomy and liberty. Instead, atomising the social context of childrearing with roots in a child's setting and replacing that context with an internationally imposed child-rearing paradigm will weaken parent-society-child ties:

> To the extent that governmental policies foster noncommittal attitudes on the part of parents--either because parents believe they have no right to give direction to their children, or because they fear that in giving them direction they might meet . . . state-supported resistance . . . both the children of those families and the larger society will suffer.[120]

Conceptualising childhood in a manner incompatible with the norms and values of different family forms endangers the essential institution whose health and harmonious cohesion is imperative to the life, survival and development of the child. This is not to suggest that the prototype of a universal child espoused in the CRC is not compatible with family values and norms in some parts of the world. The question is: If the image of the child in the CRC is not the conception of childhood in all the parts of the world, whose conception of childhood is projected in the CRC? Answering this question will have implications as to how and why such an image of the child ought to be adopted by others.

---

118 *Smith v. Organisation of foster families for equality and reform* 431 US, 845 (1977).

119 B Hafen & J Hafen 'Abandoning children to their autonomy: The United Nations Convention on the Rights of the Child' (1996) 37 *Harvard International Law Journals* 449.

120 As above.

2.2. Sources of the concept of childhood in the CRC

The CRC conceptualises childhood 'within the context of liberal political philosophical presuppositions about autonomy and paternalism.'[121] Liberalism is fractured into different types and competing visions of a liberal society; therefore, it is difficult to define. An important contribution of liberalism was to expand the categories of legal subjects.[122] Blacks', women's and children's empowerment activists relied heavily on liberal norms and standards to advocate that these excluded groups should be considered as subjects and not objects of the law.[123] According to Hobbes, the liberal subject existed independently and in antagonism to other subjects, and the role of the state is to prevent the possibility of a 'war of all against all.'[124]

A common thread that runs through different variants of liberalism is liberty. According to Locke, human beings are in a 'state of perfect freedom to order their actions ... as they think fit ... without asking leave, or depending on the will of any other man'.[125] Central to the tenets of liberalism is an 'exemption from compulsion by others.'[126] A person is free only if he/she is self-directed or autonomous. So a liberal society is composed of individuals who are 'autonomous, self-reliant, responsible, and able to personally negotiate and take risk.'[127] The only compelling justification to limit individual liberty is the freedom of another individual. The moral primacy of the individual's claim against any social collectivity is paramount in liberal thoughts.

---

121 D Archard *Children: Rights and childhood* (2004) 77.

122 S Ruddick 'At the horizons of the subject: Neo-liberalism, neo-conservatism and the rights of the child part one: From 'knowing' fetus to 'confused' child' (2007) 14 *Gender, Place & Culture: A Journal of Feminist Geography* 513.

123 As above.

124 T Hobbes Leviathan (1948 [1651]) Michael Oakeshott (ed) ch1, 12.

125 P Laslett (ed) Locke, John (1960 [1689]) *The second treatise of government in two treatises of government* 287.

126 T Green (1986 [1895]) Lectures on the principles of political obligation and other essays, Paul Harris and John Morrow (eds) 229.

127 S Ruddick 'At the horizons of the subject: Neo-liberalism, neo-conservatism and the rights of the child part one: From 'knowing' fetus to 'confused' child' (2007) 14 *Gender, Place & Culture: A Journal of Feminist Geography* 513.

Liberalism has its roots in the West.[128] Liberalism was and still is a propelling force in the propagation of human rights norms and values. Liberalism inspired the human rights movement while human rights sustain liberal thought. Liberalism and human rights, in turn, have influenced the conception of childhood in law and policy making in the West.[129] The 'West' here refers to Western Europe and North America.[130]

2.2.1. Child and childhood in the West

The 'immaturity of children is a biological fact of life but the ways in which this immaturity is understood and made meaningful is a fact of culture'.[131] Historically, every culture, nation and people have their own conception of childhood. Some people and nations concretised, theorised and communicated more effectively their version of childhood than others. Western Europe and North America are examples of regions where childhood has been given significant academic, philosophical and professional attention. Historical, cultural, religious, political and economic factors, primarily in Western Europe and North America, triggered and influenced attention on children and their relationship with the adult world. This attention resulted in and reinforced the direction of the childhood philosophies of different professional disciplines including psychology, sociology, philosophy and the law. The childhood that was refined and processed through these disciplines, specifically, was a product of the cultures of the West.

The relationship between culture, religion and professional disciplines interested in understanding the child and childhood, on one hand, and the emerging image of a child or childhood, on the other, is interlocking

---

128 See, generally, A Arblaster *The rise and decline of Western liberalism* (1984).

129 S Benporath 'Autonomy and vulnerability: On just relations between adults and children' (2003) 37 *Journal of Philosophy of Education* 127.

130 The author is aware and concedes that there are different and unique cultural, philosophic and academic conceptions of childhood in Western Europe and North America. Even within and between European countries different people and communities would see and treat children differently. While acknowledging these differences, there are similarities between the conceptions of childhood in Europe and North America in some areas. Also, there are cross-cultural similarities with respect to how communities within countries in Europe see and treat children. The focus of this work is on these similarities at a more general level.

131 A James & A Prout *Constructing and reconstructing childhood: Contemporary issues in the sociological book of childhood* (1990) 7.

and mutually reinforcing. The child in Western thought[132] typifies this complementary relationship. The child and childhood in the West are a product of a Western specific interaction among different biological, social, economic, political and historical complexities over time and space.[133]

Western philosophy, Christianity, Enlightenment, industrialisation and the concomitant social dislocations play a significant role in the way societies in the West perceive children and act towards them.[134] For instance, Aristotle's conception of childhood as an incomplete and biologically immature phase has influenced the conception of childhood as a preparatory phase for responsible adulthood, predominated the understanding of children and childhood in the West for a long time.[135] Piaget's stage theory development of childhood supported a 'deficit conception of childhood.'[136] Descartes' and Locke's exchanges about cognitive development threw more light on the nature of children and childhood in their time. Descartes maintained that 'a clear and distinct knowledge of the world can be constructed from resources innate to the human mind;'[137] whereas Locke held the view that the 'materials of reason and knowledge'[138] come from experience. Rousseau's, Piaget's and

132 Given the scope of this work, it is not possible to engage in an elaborate discussion of childhood in Europe. This work will be limited only to a general discussion of features, trends and some social change triggers of childhood in Europe. For a more elaborate discussion on childhood in Europe see generally the following: C Heywood *A history of childhood: Children and childhood in the West from medieval to modern times* (2001); P Fass & M Grossberg (eds) *Reinventing childhood after World War II* (2012); C Heywood *A history of childhood from medieval to 20th century* (2001); L Pollock *forgotten children: Parent-child relations from 1500 to 1900* (1983); H Cunningham *Children and childhood in Western Society since 1500* (1995); L deMause (ed) *The history of childhood* (1976); H Henddrick 'The evolution of childhood in Western Europe c.1400-c.1750' in M Freeman (ed) *Law and Childhood Studies: Current legal issues volume 14* (2012) 99.

133 See generally P Fass & M Grossberg (eds) *Reinventing childhood after World War II* (2012); C Heywood *A history of childhood from medieval to 20th century* (2001); L Pollock *Forgotten children: parent-child relations from 1500 to 1900* (1983); H Cunningham *Children and childhood in western society since 1500* (1995).

134 J Kociumbas 'Childhood history as ideology' (1984) 47 *Labor history* 1; R Vasanthi 'The politics of childhood: Perspective from the south' (2000) *Economic and Political Weekly* 4055.

135 For a discussion of how philosophical thinking specific to Europe influenced the development of childhood in the European system see G Matthews 'Getting beyond the deficit conception of childhood: Thinking philosophically with children' in M Hand & C Hunt (ed) *Philosophy in schools* (2008) 27; and G Matthews 'Philosophy and developmental psychology: Outgrowing the deficit conception of childhood' in H Siegel (ed) *The Oxford handbook of philosophy of education* (2009) 162.

136 G Matthews 'Getting beyond the deficit conception of childhood: Thinking philosophically with children' in M Hand & C Hunt (ed) *Philosophy in schools* (2008) 27; and G Matthews 'Philosophy and developmental psychology: Outgrowing the deficit conception of childhood' in H Siegel (ed) *The Oxford handbook of philosophy of education* (2009) 162.

137 R Descartes in J Cottingham *et al* (trans.), [PW] *The philosophical writings of Descartes* (1985) *volume* 1.

138 J Locke [EHC] An *essay concerning human understanding* (1959) *volume* I.

Kohlberg's works in the areas of cognitive and moral development in children animated scholars and childhood practitioners in the West.[139]

Christianity's contradictory conception of childhood played itself out also in the image of childhood in the West. Some doctrines of the Christian religion conceive human nature as tainted with sin from the point of conception. The Bible declares 'behold, I was sharpened in iniquity; and in sin did my mother conceive me.'[140] According to Augustine, 'no man is free from sin, not even a child who has lived only one day on earth.'[141] Based on these authorities, evangelical Christians concluded that 'all children are by nature evil, and while they have none but the natural evil principle to guide them, pious and prudent parents must check their naughty passions in any way they have in their power.'[142] In the same religion, childhood is seen as a special period, because 'Christ loved childhood, mistress of humility, rule of innocence, model of sweetness' thus 'out of the mouth of babies come words of wisdom.'[143]

Everyone in the West did not accept Christianity's conception of childhood based on the ideas of depravity and original sin as plausible.[144] The West's continued search for a plausible conception of childhood led it to a rediscovery of 'the nature of the child and all of its richness.'[145] Rousseau championed a 'romantic' conception of the child and childhood, because 'everything is good as it leaves the hands of the author of things, everything degenerates in the hands of man.'[146] Though a child is born innocent, 'prejudices, authority, necessity, example, all the social institutions in which we find ourselves

---

139 L Kohlberg *Essays on moral development* (1981) *volume* I; and L Kohlberg Essays *on moral development* (1984) *volume* II.

140 Psalm 51: 5 English Standard Version (2001) of the Holy Bible, a book used by followers of the Christian religion.

141 Cited in I Feldman & M Ticktin *In the name of humanity: The government of threat and care* (2010) 76; M Sherwood *The history of the fairchild family* (2010) 186.

142 Cited in F Joseph *Children's books in England: Five centuries of social life* (2011) 175.

143 Pope Leo in his great preaching cited in C Heywood A *history of childhood: Children and childhood in the West from medieval to modern times* (2001) 15.

144 H Hendrick 'The evolution of childhood in Western Europe c.1400 – c.1750' in M Freeman (ed) *Law and childhood studies: Current legal issues volume 14* (2012) 99.

145 P Riche & D Alexandre-Bidon *L'Enfant au moyen age* (1994), 20 cited in C Heywood *A history of childhood: Children and childhood in the West from medieval to modern times* (2001) 16.

146 Cited by L Cooper *Rousseau nature: The problem of the good life* (1962) x.

submerged stifle him or her.'[147] The 'romantic' conception of childhood saw children as 'creatures of deeper wisdom, finer aesthetic sensitivity, and a more profound awareness of enduring moral truth.'[148]

The interaction between ideas and technologies in the West led to the Industrial Revolution and framed new social, political and economic realities for children and their families. The Industrial Revolution 'increased social and psychological investment in children with more thought given to child rearing and teaching methods and a new sympathy towards children.'[149] Society was faced with new ways and methods of generating income for families without child work; children became 'economically worthless, but emotionally priceless.'[150] The increased demand for labour meant families had little time properly to rear children.[151] Child rearing was gradually professionalised, institutionalised and segmented.[152]

The character, scope and consequence of the Industrial Revolution on the nature, structure and form of families in the West impacted on the conception of the child and childhood.[153] Traditionally, in the West the family father figure was, and still is in many communities, the basis upon which property, power and prestige rested.[154] With economic development and increasing

---

147 L Cooper Rousseau *Nature: The problem of the good life* (1962) x.

148 D Grylls *Guardians and angels: Parents and children in nineteen-century literature* (1978) 37.

149 V Zelizer *Pricing the priceless child: The changing social value of children* (1985) 3. Zelizer notes that in the West, before the Industrial Revolution, neither 'childhood' nor 'family,' as the terms are now understood existed. To the colonial American, 'child' in its present meaning, would have meant little. And 'family,' in its present meaning, would have meant little. Families existed; but as organic units which mirrored in small society as an organism defined by values grounded in its nature. For complex economic and political reasons, with the advent of the Industrial Revolution a striking shift in the conception of family, and therefore of childhood, occurred. As Industrialization rapidly produced a domain of commerce, its cultural antibook was also produced: the domain of family, a domain of love, of permanent, non-negotiable commitment, utterly different from the domain defined by contract, profit, and autonomous self-interest. For the first time in the history of the West, the family was conceived of as a sacred buffer against the self-interest of industrial commerce, and the best interests of children as a social imperative.

150 V Zelizer *Pricing the priceless child: The changing social value of children* (1985) 3.

151 H Zeiher 'Institutionalization as a secular trend' in J Qvortrup *et al the Palgrave handbook of childhood studies* (2009) 127.

152 As above, 128.

153 J An-Magritt 'Pluralization of family forms' in J Qvortrup *et al The Palgrave handbook of childhood studies* (2009) 140.

154 As above, 144.

access to economic resources by women, power and its dynamic nature within family was reconfigured.[155] In turn, it resulted in the

> 'evolution of the family as a single unit before the law, with a single legal identity to one based on an individual and right based, wherein husbands and wives have rights not only against the state but also against each other.'[156]

These changes had an impact on the child within the family.

Not long after the Enlightenment and industrialisation, women started vigorously to demand equal rights with their male counterparts. Increasingly, women agitated for political and economic participation. Women became more autonomous and increasingly participated in the political, economic and social sectors of society. It was in the interest of autonomous mothers to have autonomous children.[157] The disappearance of an exact and predictable family environment, fading extended family infrastructure in a number of communities in the West, and an increased economic burden of training 'economically worthless' children,[158] meant the traditional image of children as dependent, vulnerable and incapable of making competent decisions needed modification.[159] Children needed a new legal status that linked them directly to the state as citizens, to facilitate the sharing of the blessings and burdens of child bearing.[160]

The basis of support for a new status for children and childhood was readily available in the humanistic, rationalistic and individualistic thinking of the liberal philosophers of the Enlightenment period.[161] The core project of

155 As above, 152.

156 A Appell 'The pre-political child of child-centered jurisprudence' (2009-10) 46 *Houston Law Review* 703.

157 H Zeiher 'Institutionalization as a secular trend' in J Qvortrup *et al The Palgrave handbook of childhood studies* (2009) 136.

158 V Zelizer *Pricing the priceless child: The changing social value of children* (1985) 3; see also C Degler *At odds: Women and the family in America from the revolution to the present* (1980) 66 where she notes 'the precious children of middle-class nineteenth century homes were no longer 'object[s] of utility.' They had become 'object[s] of sentiment.'

159 Zeiher, n 157, 134.

160 J Gillis 'Transitions to modernity' in J Qvortrup *et al The Palgrave handbook of childhood studies* (2009) 114.

161 A Langlois 'The narrative metaphysics of human rights' (2005) 9 *The International Journal of Human*

the Enlightenment 'was the displacement of local, customary or traditional moralities and of all forms of transcendental faith, by a critical or rational morality, which was projected as the basis of a universal civilisation.'[162] Enlightenment philosophy gave the individual moral primacy over claims, which may be advanced by any social collectivity.[163] The society, anticipated by this liberal and individualistic thinking, was 'an association of individuals, as founded – logically or historically – on a contract between them, and it elevates the individual human person and his freedom and happiness to be the goal and end of all human association.'[164]

As autonomous human beings, children were conceptualised as part of this 'association of individuals' whose freedom, happiness and best interests were the 'goal and end' of society. To safeguard this acquired state, children and childhood in the West were 'legally, legislatively, socially, medically, psychologically, educationally and politically institutionalized.'[165] The state presented the family and the society with lists of things they should do for children and a list of things they could not be permitted to do to children.[166] Consequently, the culturally, religiously, philosophically and professionally construed child and childhood gave way to a more rational, technical and legalistic conception of childhood in the West, at least for the purpose of public policy.

The epistemological, moral and political philosophy grounded in the rationalistic and empirical traditions of the Enlightenment period interpreted,

Rights 369; see also J Dolgin 'Transforming childhood: Apprenticeship in American law (1996-97) 31 *New England Law Review* 1113; A Skolnick 'The limits of childhood: Conceptions of child development and social context' (1975) 39 *Law and Contemporary Problems* 38 ; E Scott 'The legal construction of childhood' (2000) *Public Law and Legal Theory Book Papers*, Working Paper No. 00-18 available at http://papers.ssrn.com/paper.taf?abstract_id=244666; J Gray *Enlightenment's wake: Politics and culture at the close of modern age* (1995); J Gray *Two faces of liberalism* (2000) 5.

162 J Gray *Enlightenment's wake: Politics and culture at the close of modern age* (1995) quoted in B Bowden *The empire of civilization: The evolution of an imperial idea* (2009) 134.

163 J Gray *Enlightenment's wake: Politics and culture at the close of modern age* (1995) 19.

164 E Kamenka 'Thinking and teaching about human rights' in E Kamenka & T Erh-soon (eds) *Human rights* (1978) 1, 6.

165 H Hendrick 'Constructions and reconstructions of British childhood: An interpretative survey, 1800 to the present' in A James & A Prout *Constructing and reconstructing childhood: Contemporary issues in the sociological book of childhood* (1997) 36.

166 C Degler *At odds: Women and the family in America from the revolution to the present* (1980) 78.

understood and socially institutionalised child and childhood as a dependant, inchoate and precapacitated category in the West. Industrialisation further strengthened and crystallised the binary between childhood and adulthood.[167] With economic change came office work, the decline of farming and increased separation between family and work.[168] The rise of industrialisation and urbanisation meant fewer roles for children, and childhood was made dependant on the working adult who had the experience and expertise demanded by this mode of production.[169] Snchez-Eppler explains that the

> same patterns of urbanization and industrialization that separate[d] workplace from home, labour from leisure, simultaneously function[ed] to commodify leisure time and to idealize middle - class domesticity, especially that of childhood.[170]

Children's immaturity, vulnerability, and consequent dependency conferred on parents, adults and caregivers the authority to guide, train and represent children and their needs.[171] By conceptualising childhood as a time of physical, cognitive and emotional development, children were safely tucked away from polity and market, effectively naturalising, domesticating and privatising childhood in the West, at least for a period.[172]

The struggles for humanisation and individualisation by the civil rights movement, as well as, to an extent, feminist scholars, began to challenge a naturalised and privatised childhood.[173] The rights movement and a supportive judiciary started to reconstruct children and childhood as autonomous individuals with purposeful competency. The individualistic and

---

167 A Appell 'The pre-political child of child-cantered jurisprudence' (2009-10) 46 *Houston Law Review* 703.

168 V Zelizer *Pricing the priceless child: The changing social value of children* (1985) 3; see also C Degler *At odds: Women and the family in America from the revolution to the present* (1980) 67.

169 As above.

170 K Sanchez-Eppler 'Playing at class' (2000) 67 *ELH* 819.

171 E Scott 'The legal construction of childhood' (2000) *Public Law and Legal Theory Book Papers*, Working Paper No. 00-18 available at http://papers.ssrn.com/paper.taf?abstract_id=244666.

172 A Appell 'The pre-political child of child-cantered jurisprudence' (2009-10) 46 *Houston Law Review* 703; V Zelizer *Pricing the priceless child: The changing social value of children* (1985) 3; see also C Degler *At odds: women and the family in America from the revolution to the present* (1980) 66.

173 See generally B Gross & R Gross *The children's rights movement: Overcoming the oppression of young people* (1977); T Cockburn 'Children and the feminist ethic of care' (2005) 12 *Childhood* 71.

individualising image of the child was purely legalistic and, as such, failed to delegitimise dependency but denaturalised and de-privatised childhood.[174] In other words, even though children were conferred with personhood, and thus had the right to be left alone, this was to be understood within the boundaries of dependency on parents and state.

The feminist contribution to understanding childhood was confined to or by a paradigm within its own struggle:

> Feminist theories of motherhood have been ... trapped in the dominant cultural assumptions about mothering. These, in turn, rest on unexamined notions of childhood ... as constraints on women, making children into women's 'appendices' while necessarily treating women and children as adversaries. Thus, the feminist theoretical project about the liberation of women could not simultaneously consider the liberation of children. Therefore, a separate 'child question' never arose.[175]

After the Great Depression, the West faced challenges to its institutions and economic model. Western countries responded to a labour crisis with an extended childhood exit period, creating a new class of children, 'teenagers,' and assiduously ensuring children spent a longer time in the school system:

> With schools cutting back for lack of funding, rising adult unemployment, and youth competing for those same jobs, 'there was a growing consensus that children had to be removed from the labour force and put in the classroom.' The effect of this was to keep children in school until at least sixteen and to raise the demarcation between childhood and adulthood, effectively increasing the capacity or length

174 A Appell 'The pre-political child of child-cantered jurisprudence' (2009-10) 46 *Houston Law Review* 703; E Scott 'The legal construction of childhood' (2000) *Public Law and Legal Theory Book Papers*, Working Paper No. 00-18 available at http://papers.ssrn.com/paper.taf?abstract_id=244666.

175 L Alanen 'Gender and generation: Feminisms and the 'child question' in J Qvortrup *et al* (eds) *Childhood matters* (1994) 27, 33; also cited in A Appell 'The pre-political child of child-cantered jurisprudence' (2009-10) 46 *Houston Law Review* 703.

> of childhood and creating a new group of children eventually known as 'teenagers.'[176]

The economic changes had implications for the family. Industrialisation had atomised family structure, creating a unit of co-autonomous individuals; the Great Depression further removed incentives for permanent, predictable and large family sizes.[177] Since the child was 'socioeconomically a family member, a student, a consumer' whose main job was to become an adult, child rearing was a burden calling for sharing.[178] A review of literature around this time reveals:

> The duties of parenthood have become increasingly onerous as the rewards, extrinsic and intrinsic, of rearing children one by one disappear ... Parents can no longer expect in their later year's reciprocation of the support, emotional and physical, which they provide to their children ... [179]

The above review of the general features and trends in the conception of child and childhood in the West, arguably, led to the following images of childhood:

a) Children are considered immature and vulnerable. This results in the status of dependency for children.
b) The beginning and the end of childhood are case and purpose specific.
c) Children are granted qualified autonomy, freedom, and independence to participate in activities that would transform them into self-sufficient, democratic, productive, and autonomous adults.
d) The interest of children is made an object of private and public policy.

What is obvious is that these conceptions of childhood came about as a result of Western cultural, religious, philosophic, political and socio-economic

---

176 S Mintz *Huck's part: A history of American childhood* (2004) 238.

177 See, generally, K Sanchez-Eppler *Dependant states: The child's part in the nineteenth century American culture* (2005); A Appell 'The pre-political child of child-cantered jurisprudence' (2009-10) 46 *Houston Law Review* 703; S Mintz *Huck's part: A history of American childhood* (2004) 155.

178 Appell 'The pre-political child of child-cantered jurisprudence' (2009-10) 46 *Houston Law Review* 703.

179 D Baumrind 'Children's rights – adult responsibilities' (1974) (unpublished book review) cited in A Skolnick 'The limits of childhood: Conceptions of child development and social context' (1975) 39 *Law and Contemporary Problems* 76.

factors that are specific to these regions. The conception and re-conception of childhood was consequential as well as instrumental in making meaningful their histories and lived realities. This conception was used to guide psychology, sociology, medicine, education, health, political processes, and the law in their dealing with the child and childhood.

2.2.2. The law and childhood in the West

There is a correlation between conceptions of childhood and policy decisions on children.[180] Whatever the policy, decisions taken in the best interests of children must be predicated on the perceived needs and capacities of children, on how these needs and capacities, or lack thereof, change with age, what circumstances or environment is good or bad for children, and how to ensure that the transition from childhood to adulthood is less abrupt.[181] It is the instrumentality of the law that

> operates as one of the main regulatory devices that shape the space of childhood. It does this through developing social policies... that seek to control the kinds of activities that children can do; the social and material environments they inhabit and the resources they have access to.[182]

The law has matured, over time, in its understanding of, and dealing with children. From its root in the Roman doctrine of *patria potestas* – paternal power – that conferred a parent with rights 'to all the service and all the acquisitions of his child, as much as those of his slave, but he had the same absolute control over his person,'[183] to the present when the law recognises children as

---

180 A Skolnick 'The limits of childhood: Conceptions of child development and social context' (1975) 39 *Law and Contemporary Problems* 38.

181 E Scott 'The legal construction of childhood' (2000) *Public Law and Legal Theory Book Papers*, Working Paper No. 00-18 available at http://papers.ssrn.com/paper.taf?abstract_id=244666 (accessed 20 March 2013).

182 A James *et al* 'Care and control in the construction of children's citizenship' in A Invernizzi & J Williams (eds) *Children and citizenship* (2008) 85.

183 J Hadley 'Introduction to Roman law in twelve academical lectures' (1873) 119, quoted in B Garner (ed) *Black's Law Dictionary* (2009) 1287.

> human beings in their own right with individual minds and wills, views and emotions, which should command serious attention. A child's wishes are not to be discounted or dismissed simply because he is a child. He should be free to express them and decision makers should listen.[184]

In the United States of America, the Supreme Court declared unequivocally that 'neither the Fourteenth Amendment nor the Bill of Rights is for adults alone;'[185] children also are entitled to constitutional rights.

Nevertheless, there are issues about which the position of the law has not changed for centuries. The law still sees children as immature, incompetent, dependent, malleable and thus vulnerable to both influence and harm by others.[186] The result is that the law restricts what children can do, shields them from the legal consequences of their action, and confers others with authority and responsibility to control children's actions and provide them with care, material assistance, and the tools and skills of life to ensure the life, survival and the development of children.[187]

The position of the law in the West is broadly characterised by this tension: on one hand, it recognises children as human beings with rights; on the other, children's 'lack of maturity and an underdeveloped sense of responsibility ... often result in impetuous and ill-considered actions and decisions.'[188] The law's response has been to combine a respect for the autonomy of children with the need to protect them from the consequences of certain decisions until they have reached an age of majority by which law makers are satisfied that these children can make reasonable decisions by and of themselves.[189]

---

184 Bingham MR in *Re S (A minor) (Independent representation)* (1993) 3 All ER 36 at 46-47.

185 *Re Gault* (1967) US 387 at 12.

186 A Appell 'The pre-political child of child-cantered jurisprudence' (2009-10) 46 *Houston Law Review* 703.

187 J Tobin 'Courts and the construction of childhood: A new way of thinking' in M Freeman (ed) *Law and childhood studies: Current legal issues 2011* (2012) 55; see also J Herring 'Vulnerability, children, and the law' in M Freeman (ed) *Law and childhood studies: Current legal issues 2011* (2012) 243.

188 *Roper v Simmons* (2005) 125 S. Ct 1183.

189 See generally L Ferguson 'The end of an age: Beyond age restrictions for minor's medical treatment decisions (2004) Law Commission of Canada. Available at: http://papers.ssrn.com/sol3/papers.cfm?abstract_id=998227.

This balancing act is borne out of the recognition that

> an infant does not possess full legal competence. Since he is regarded as of immature intellect and imperfect discretion, English Law, while treating all acts of an infant which are for his benefit on the same footing as those of an adult, will carefully protect his interests and not permit him to be prejudiced by anything to his disadvantage.[190]

Second, historically, the law gives authority to others over important decisions that affect the lives of children. For instance, under certain aspects of American family laws, primary responsibility for taking care of the welfare of children and authority over their lives was vested in their parents:[191]

> The law's concept of a family rests on a presumption that parents possess what children lack in maturity, experience and capacity for judgment required to make life's difficult decisions. More importantly, historically it has recognized that natural bonds of affection lead parents to act in the best interests of their children.[192]

In the English legal system in the past, the opinion was that any move by the court to override 'the natural jurisdiction' of a parent over his or her child 'would be really to set aside the whole course and order of nature and it seems to me it would disturb the very foundation of family life.'[193] The state interfered with parental rights only in the event of an effective failure by the parents of the child to discharge this legal obligation. The state or its institutions, as *parens patriae,* step in to act for the protection of those who cannot care for themselves.[194] There has been a significant change in position in English law. Increasingly, parental control is proportional to the evolving capacity of the child, because 'parental right yields to the child's right to make

190 C Sugiyama 'Inter vivos and transplantation and the human tissue gift act, S.O. 1971 C.83' (1976) 34 *University of Toronto Faculty of Law Review* 124.

191 A Appell 'The pre-political child of child-cantered jurisprudence' (2009-10) 46 *Houston Law Review* 703.

192 *Panham v J.R* (1979) 442 U.S 584, 602.

193 Bowen L.J. *in Re Agar-Ellis* (1883) cited in L Mackee & M O'brien *The father figure* (1982) 27.

194 A Appell 'The pre-political child of child-cantered jurisprudence' (2009-10) 46 *Houston Law Review* 703.

his own decisions when he reaches a sufficient understanding and intelligence to be capable of making up his own mind on the matter requiring decision.'[195]

The presumption of incompetence played in the interest of children in the judicial process, especially in criminal proceedings: the 'laws against crimes are as inapplicable to children as they would be to idiots.'[196] Children could not be 'responsible, on their view, because they lacked the capacity for reasoning, moral understanding and judgment on which attributions of blameworthiness must rest.'[197] Instead, the state ensures

> the child of the proper age to be under the jurisdiction of the juvenile court is encircled by the arm of the state, which, as a sheltering, wise parent, assumes guardianship and has power to shield the child from the rigors of the common law and from the neglect and depravity of adults.[198]

In light of the benefits and legal burdens that accrue to children and childhood, the law in the West tried as much as possible to delineate childhood from adulthood.[199] So the law concerned itself with establishing criteria and bench marks for determining maturity. In most cases, age became the proxy for maturity in relation to liberty rights.[200] Thus,

> although capacity is to be determined based on the facts and circumstances of each case, there are milestones in our society that legislatively recognize the maturation process and the transition from child to adult. Age is resorted to in some circumstances as a proxy for capacity.[201]

---

195 Lord Scarman in *Gillick v West Norfolk and Wisbech Area Health Authority* (1986) AC 112 at 186.

196 B Lindsey, an early judge of the Denver Juvenile Court cited in F. Scott 'Legal construction of childhood' in M Rosenheim et al (eds) *A century of juvenile justice* (2002) 117.

197 E Scott & L Steinberg *Rethinking juvenile justice* (2008) 67.

198 E Scott 'Legal construction of childhood' in M Rosenheim *et al* (eds) *A century of juvenile justice* (2002) 131.

199 E Scott & L Steinberg *Rethinking juvenile justice* (2008) 67; E Scott 'Legal construction of childhood' in M Rosenheim *et al* (eds) *A century of juvenile justice* (2002) 131.

200 L Schaffner 'An age of reason: Paradoxes in the US legal construction of adulthood' (2002) 10 *International Journal of Children's Rights* 201.

201 See generally L Ferguson 'The end of an age: Beyond age restrictions for minor's medical treatment decisions' (2004) Law Commission of Canada. Available at: http://papers.ssrn.com/sol3/papers.cfm?abstract_

Though the child, in the West, was legally conceptualised as an autonomous individual with enforceable rights, as a vulnerable person, parents, society and state must guide and direct the child and provide all that is necessary for his or her life, survival and development. Even though childhood ends at different times for different purposes, age is used to determine the end point of childhood.

2.3. Comparison between the conception of childhood in the West and the CRC

There is a degree of correlation between the norms, value systems, legal and academic traditions of 'civilised nations' and the norms and values espoused in international human rights law.[202] Either as international customs, general principles of law recognised by 'civilised nations' or judicial decisions and teachings of renowned scholars, the specific culture of these nations is imported into human rights instruments and then exported as universal norms.[203] To illustrate how this works in practice is to trace the trajectory along which President Franklin Roosevelt's Four Freedoms[204] found their way into the Universal Declaration of Human Rights and the International Bill of Rights. According to Roosevelt:

> In the future days, which we seek to make secure, we look forward to a world founded upon four essential freedoms . . . The first is freedom of speech and expression . . . The second is freedom of every person to worship God in his own way . . . The third is freedom from want . . . The fourth is freedom from fear. That is no vision of a distant

id-998227.

202 See generally B Hermandez-Truyol (ed) *Moral imperialism: A critical anthropology* (2002); B Hermandez-Truyol & S Rush *Culture, nationhood and human rights ideal* (2000); M Baderin & M Ssenyojo *International human rights law: Six decades after the UDHR and beyond* (2010).

203 Article 38 1(a-d) provides for the sources of law applicable in determining international disputes submitted by the International Court of Justice. These sources influence proceeding before other international judicial and quasi-judicial bodies globally. The interaction between jurisprudence of different courts makes the infusion of these jurisprudences into national, regional and international human rights instruments easier. For a full discussion of this possibility see N Croquet 'The International Criminal Court and the treatment of defence rights: A mirror of the European Court of Human Rights jurisprudence? (2011) 11 *Human Rights Review* 91; G Ress 'The effect of decisions and judgements of the European Court of Human Rights in domestic legal order' (2004-2005) 40 *Texas International Law Journal* 359.

204 F Roosevelt's Four Freedom Speech available at: http://www.u-s-history.com/pages/h1794.html.

millennium. It is a definite basis for a kind of world attainable in our own time and generation.[205]

Animated by the Four Freedoms, the American Law Institute (the Institute) in 1942 set itself the assignment of elaborating a global restatement of 'essential human rights.'[206] To do this, it had to answer the question whether certain human rights had already become part of the 'common law of mankind.'[207] The Institute congregated an international committee of experts 'representing the principal cultures of the world.'[208] The outcome document, the ALI Statement of Essential Human Rights, played a significant role in the drafting process of the Universal Declaration.[209]

One of the authors of the first draft of the Declaration stated that 'the best of the texts from which I worked was the one prepared by the American Law Institute, and I borrowed freely from it.'[210] Articles from the Statement of Essential Human Rights also found their way into the International Bill of Rights.[211] Essentially, what was a leader's value or vision transformed itself through the instrumentality of human rights law into universal values and vision.

This is not an isolated case but part of a trend. *Travaux préparatoires* of international human rights instruments reveal evidence of a relationship between the cultures, religions, values and legal traditions of participating nations and the nature of compromise and principles that emerges as

205 F Roosevelt's Four Freedom Speech available at: http://www.u-s-history.com/pages/h1794.html.

206 T Rensmann 'Munich alumni and the evolution of international human rights law' (2011) 22 *The European Journal of International Law* 973.

207 As above.

208 As above.

209 As above.

210 John Humphrey, who as the Director of the Human Rights Division in the UN Secretariat prepared the first draft of the Universal Declaration, revealed in his memoirs that this was no coincidence. Quoted in T Rensmann 'Munich alumni and the evolution of international human rights law' (2011) 22 *The European Journal of International Law* 973.

211 T Rensmann claims that Arts 14(1)(2), 21(2), 22(2)(1) ICCPR; Arts 4, 8(1)(a)(c) ICESCR could be directly traced to the ALI Statement of Essential Human Rights adopted earlier by the American Institute for Human Rights. See T Rensmann 'Munich alumni and the evolution of international human rights law' (2011) 22 *The European Journal of International Law* 973.

international human rights.[212] In fact, this relationship is good for the legitimacy of international human rights law, but participation deficit and unequal power dynamics between participating nations, in practice, tend to favour countries with greater means.[213]

International law-making is a political process.[214] Like any political process, the power to influence the process and the outcome of international law-making processes is determined by numbers, innovative strategies, political energy and skills. Powerful states, mostly in the West significantly influence the process of international treaty making. However, even though powerful states tend to exert significant influence over what and why an issue should be a subject of international law-making, how and where the process should proceed, in international law-making, power and influence are not synonymous. Factors such as the number of like-minded states taking a position on the issue that is to be a subject of international law making process,[215] the position and influence of non-state actors[216] and the nature of the issue impact on the extent of influence of powerful states. However, when power, numbers, and the nature of the issue that is to be the subject of law-making favour powerful states, then influence is synonymous with power.

This is what happened when the CRC was being drafted. During the drafting process of the CRC, power, numbers and the nature of the issues up for deliberation at international level favoured countries in the West. For instance, numerically, East and West European countries constituted the largest negotiating bloc that participated in the nine sessions of the Open-

212 For a detailed discussion of this interaction see F Martin *et al International human rights and humanitarian law: Treaties, cases & analysis* (2006) 307; J Bair *'The International Covenant on Civil and Political Rights and its (first) optional protocol: A short commentary* (2005); M Bossuyt *Guide to the 'Travaux Preparatoires' on the International Covenant on Civil and Political Rights* (1987); and M Nowak *UN Convention on Civil and Political Rights: CCPR Commentary* (1993).

213 G Fox 'Right to political participation in international law' (1992) 17 *Yale Journal of International Law* 539.

214 A Boyle & C Chinkin *The making of international law* (2007) 103.

215 A good example is the success of the group of 77 developing states in UNCLOS III processes or the success of the association of small high island state during the process leading to the Framework Convention on Climate Change. See J Evensen 'Working methods and procedures in the 3rd UNCLOS' (1986-iv) 199 *Recueil Des Cours* 425 cited in A Boyle & C Chinkin The making of international (2007) 103.

216 A Boyle & C Chinkin *The making of international law* (2007) 41.

ended Working Group that negotiated and drafted the CRC.[217] Only two Latin American countries (Argentina and Brazil) and two countries from Asia and the Pacific participated in all nine sessions of the Working Group. From North America, the United States and Canada attended all nine sessions; from Africa, out of the three countries that participated in the drafting process, Senegal managed to attend seven of the nine sessions, the other African countries that participated attended fewer sessions.[218] A lack of 'trained personnel and financial resources to commit the time and energy necessary to participate effectively'[219] were cited as the reasons responsible for the minimal participation by countries of the third world. According to Leblanc, 'in strictly quantitative terms …Western states and, to a somewhat lesser extent, the East European states were the principal drafters'[220] of the CRC. Interestingly, within the first few years of the CRC entering into force, countries in Latin America and Africa ratified it in high numbers.[221]

Substantively, the European bloc and the United States and Canada exerted significant influence on the norms and standards that eventually became universal standards for children. For instance, when Senegal, supported by the Holy See, proposed that article 1 of the CRC should define childhood as starting from the moment of conception, Australia, Canada, Denmark, Germany, the Netherlands, Norway and Sweden, amongst others, strongly opposed the proposal and it was dropped.[222]

In addition, article 5[223] of the CRC has its roots in a proposal by the United States and Australia in 1987.[224] Because of the strong position of the

---

217 L Leblanc *The Convention on the Rights of the Child: United Nations law making on human rights* (1995) 30.

218 L Leblanc as above, 33.

219 L Leblanc as above, 34.

220 L Leblanc as above, 33.

221 L Leblanc as above, 46.

222 L Leblanc as above 68.

223 'States Parties shall respect the responsibilities, rights and duties of parents or, where applicable, the members of the extended family or community as provided for by local custom, legal guardians or other persons legally responsible for the child, to provide, in a manner consistent with the evolving capacities of the child, appropriate direction and guidance in the exercise by the child of the rights recognized in the present Convention.'

224 L Leblanc *The Convention on the Rights of the Child: United Nations law making on human rights* (1995) 113.

United States on parental rights, this provision went beyond the traditional definition of family and fundamentally changed the 'traditional triangular responsibility'[225] of the child, parents and the state.

As a result of their numerical strength, political power and human and financial resources, countries in the West determined what should or should not be global norms on children's rights and welfare. In the process, as it is usually the case with international law-making processes, it was the national values, norms and interests of countries in the West that dominated the CRC drafting process and their norms eventually became the values and norms that the rest of the world was urged to incorporate and to harmonise their values and norms accordingly.

For example, the records of proceedings of the negotiations and drafting processes of the CRC bear witness to the fact that the definition of a child, what kind of rights accrue to children, the 'best interests' of the child standard, the type of family arrangement envisaged under the CRC, monitoring processes and mechanisms[226] were discussed and agreed within the frame of national laws, values and practices of mainly Western participating countries.

It is the striking similarity between the images of the child and childhood in the CRC and the contemporaneous images of childhood in the West that triggers the accusation that the CRC is a Western imperialist treaty designed to export and impose the prevailing images of the childhood in Western societies on non-Western societies.[227] Though it is reasonable to argue that the conception of childhood in the CRC predominantly reflects the conception in Western societies, the accusation is self-serving.

The image of childhood and of the child in the CRC contains elements that are additions to whatever understanding of the child and childhood existed before the CRC in societies in the West.[228] The following are examples: the

225 As above, 114.

226 See generally S Detrick *A commentary on the United Nations Convention on the Rights of the Child* (1999).

227 V Pupavac 'Misanthropy without Borders: The international children's rights Regime' (2001) 25 *Disasters* 95.

228 It has been argued that even though the best interests principle, child participation and autonomy rights existed in Western legal systems before the coming into effect of the CRC, their provisions in the CRC went beyond the limits that existed before then in societies in the West. For discussion of these see generally, S

straight 18 definition of what a child is for all purposes covered by the CRC except when national laws provide otherwise;[229] the elevation of the best interests of the child as a primary consideration in all matters concerning the child;[230] the significant granting of autonomy rights to all children below 18 years of age.[231] The age of criminal liability and the nature of child-parent relationship[232] envisaged in the CRC, arguably, contain elements that were not commonly acceptable in most Western societies.

The nature and extent of reservations by countries in the West, including Poland, might be symptomatic of the fact that not all the values incorporated in the CRC are rooted in a Western tradition. On ratifying the CRC, Poland (the author and proponent of the first draft of the CRC) made a reservation to the following effect:

> The Republic of Poland considers that a child's rights as defined in the Convention, in particular the rights defined in articles 12 to 16, shall be exercised with respect for parental authority, in accordance with Polish customs and traditions regarding the place of the child within and outside the family.[233]

The Netherlands entered a reservation to the following effect:

> The Kingdom of the Netherlands accepts the provisions of article 37(c) of the Convention with the reservation that these provisions shall not prevent the application of adult penal law to children of

---

Detrick *A commentary on the United Nations Convention on the Rights of the Child* (1999); E Ochaita & M Espinosa 'Children's participation in family and school life: A psychological and development approach' (1997) 5 *International Journal of Children's Rights* 279; S Tomanović 'Negotiating children's participation and autonomy within families' (2003) 11 *International Journal of Children's Rights* 51; S Tomanović-Mihajlović 'Young people's participation within the family: Parent's accounts' (2000) 8 *International Journal of Children's Rights* 151; P Alston (ed) *The best interests of the child: Reconciling culture and human rights* (1994); P Alston & B Gilmour-Walsh *The best interests of the child: Towards a synthesis of children's rights and cultural values* (1996).

229 S Detrick *A commentary on the United Nations Convention on the Rights of the Child* (1999) 51.

230 As above, 91.

231 See articles 12-16 of the CRC.

232 Detrick, n 229, 296.

233 (CRC/C/2/ Rev.8, p. 36).

sixteen years and older, provided that certain criteria laid down by law have been met.[234]

The United Kingdom of Great Britain and Northern Ireland following upon ratification declared:

a) The United Kingdom interprets the Convention as applicable only following a live birth.

b) The United Kingdom interprets the references in the Convention to 'parents' to mean only those persons who, as a matter of national law, are treated as parents. This includes cases where the law regards a child as having only one parent, for example where a child has been adopted by one person only and in certain cases where a child is conceived other than as a result of sexual intercourse by the woman who gives birth to it and she is treated as the only parent.[235]

Although the US played a significant role in drafting the CRC, it is yet to ratify it.[236] A tedious ratification process has been officially cited as a reason for non or delayed ratification by the government of the US, but there are indications that the problem might be more fundamental than bureaucracy.[237] One of the main reasons why the US is yet to ratify the CRC is perhaps that the US Congress perceives the CRC as advocating a conception of childhood, and, by extension, of the family as well as the relationship between the child

234 Available at http://treaties.un.org/Pages/ViewDetails.aspx?src=TREATY&mtdsg_no=IV-11&chapter=4&lang=en#EndDec.

235 Available at http://treaties.un.org/Pages/ViewDetails.aspx?src=TREATY&mtdsg_no=IV-11&chapter=4&lang=en#EndDec.

236 E Bartholet 'Ratification by the United States of the Convention on the Rights of the Child: Prons and cons from a child's rights perspective' (2011) 633 *The ANNALs of the American Academy of Political and Social Science* 80; L Blanchfield 'The United Nations Convention on the Rights of the Child: Background and policy issues' (2009) *Congressional Book Service Report for Congress*; J Todres *et al* (eds) *The U.N. Convention on the Rights of the Child: An analysis of treaty provisions and implications of U.S ratification* (2006).

237 E Bartholet 'Ratification by the United States of the Convention on the Rights of the Child: Prons and cons from a child's rights perspective' (2011) 633 *The ANNALs of the American Academy of Political and Social Science* 80; L Blanchfield 'The United Nations Convention on the Rights of the Child: Background and policy issues' (2009) *Congressional Book Service Report for Congress*; J Todres (eds) *et al The U.N. Convention on the Rights of the Child: An analysis of treaty provisions and implications of U.S. ratification* (2006).

and parent, fundamentally at variance with the US Constitution and its conception of the child and the family.[238]

One concludes that the 'child' and 'childhood' in the CRC, although inspired by childhood development over centuries in the West, are not entirely a reflection of western values; the child in the CRC is also a technical, rational and philosophical child.

One possible reason for the disparity between the position of some state parties to the CRC during the negotiation and drafting process and the final text of the CRC could be attributed to the role played by NGOs in the drafting process of the CRC. Law making process at the UN level involves basically two steps: agenda-setting and norm-setting.[239] During the drafting process of the CRC, the NGO Ad Hoc Group had a remarkable impact on agenda setting.[240] According to one account, at least 13 of the proposals made by the NGO Ad Hoc Group were incorporated into the Convention 'either [as] individual paragraphs or entire articles.'[241] The NGOs' influence with respect to the text is evident throughout the Convention.[242] Examples include the 'use of gender-free language' and the inclusion of 'standards for school discipline, encouragement of breast-feeding and discouragement of "traditional practices" (female circumcision).'[243] An area where the NGO Ad Hoc Group made a considerable difference in terms of norm-setting was juvenile justice. Article 37 and 40 of the CRC were significantly shaped by the NGOs.[244]

---

238 See generally J Todres *et al* (eds) *The U.N. Convention on the Rights of the Child: An analysis of treaty provisions and implications of U.S. ratification* (2006).

239 E Turkelli et al 'NGO impact on law-making: The case of a complaints procedure under the International Covenant on Economic, Social and Cultural Rights and the Convention on the Rights of the Child' (2013) 6 *Journal of Human Rights Practice* 1.

240 E Turkelli & W Vandenhole 'The Convention on the Rights of the Child: Repertoires of NGO participation' (2012) 12 *Human Rights Law Review* 33. The authors estimate that about 60% to 70% of all the inputs from the NGOs were incorporated into the draft CRC.

241 OHCHR *Legislative history of the Convention on the Rights of the Child*, Volume II (2007) 936.

242 E Turkelli et al 'NGO impact on law-making: The case of a complaints procedure under the International Covenant on Economic, Social and Cultural Rights and the Convention on the Rights of the Child' (2013) 6 *Journal of Human Rights Practice* 1.

243 P Cohen 'The role of Non-Governmental Organizations in the drafting of the Convention on the Rights of the Child' (1990) 12 *Human Rights Quarterly* 142.

244 E Turkelli & W Vandenhole 'The Convention on the Rights of the Child: Repertoires of NGO participation'

However, the NGOs did not succeed in getting all their proposals accepted. For instance, proposal for the inclusion of an article protecting children born out of wedlock did not gain the acceptance of states.[245] Also the proposal to prohibit the use of children for medical experimentation was not adopted.[246] In addition, NGOs' proposal with respect to the protection of children within the context of armed conflict failed to gain consensus.[247] Therefore, even though the influence of NGOs was instrumental in the drafting of the CRC, it largely occurred with the consent of states.

2.4. Conclusion

Using general features and trends in the conception of childhood in the CRC, the chapter argued that the child in the CRC is an autonomous, independent, competent child whose interest is a primary consideration and who is entitled to almost all autonomy and liberty rights adults are entitled to in addition to other child-specific rights. Further, it has been argued that even though this image of the child is rooted in the history of the West, the image of the child in the CRC is not entirely Western. The CRC child is rooted in a rationalistic, technical, philosophical and moral tradition that is not necessarily in agreement with all Western cultures and traditions.

The chapter also looked at the possible implications of this conception of the child on cultures and families, and, ultimately, on the child. The way in which childhood is conceived in the CRC fundamentally alters in type and in kind the way in which different societies in different parts of the world see and relate to children and childhood. Therefore, the core understanding of childhood in the CRC is not common to all cultures. If the gap between the

(2012) 12 *Human Rights Law Review* 33. Article 37 gives children protection against unlawful infringements by states such as the prevention of torture, of arbitrary detention and the prohibition of capital punishment and life imprisonment. Article 40 sets provides for the protections of the rights of children during criminal justice proceedings.

245 OHCHR *Legislative history of the Convention on the Rights of the Child*, Volume II (2007) 888.

246 P Cohen 'The Role of Non-Governmental Organizations in the Drafting of the Convention on the Rights of the Child' (1990) 12 *Human Rights Quarterly* 192.

247 E Turkelli et al 'NGO impact on law-making: The case of a complaints procedure under the International Covenant on Economic, Social and Cultural Rights and the Convention on the Rights of the Child' (2013) 6 *Journal of Human Rights Practice* 1.

image of childhood in the CRC and the understanding of childhood in other parts of the world is not narrowed, it is likely that the effective implementation of the CRC around the world will continue to be a tedious and costly exercise.

CHAPTER 3

THE CONCEPTION OF CHILDHOOD IN AFRICA

> The new born full of potentialities of human nature, is entirely geared towards the future. In the present he is nothing but expectation, power in search of actualisation. The culture he is entering without his choice, which will impose itself upon him as he progressively makes it his own, will make some of these potentials reality, but it will suffocate others, which will never emerge. This passage from nature to culture … from power to action represents a kind of limitation, a necessary narrowing.[1]

3. Introduction

This chapter is sub-divided into four parts. The first part sketches the common parameters that distinguish the conception of childhood in traditional communities from the understanding of childhood in the CRC and the African Children's Charter. It is argued in this part that unlike the conception of childhood in the CRC and the African Children's Charter, which is rooted in liberal traditions, the conception of childhood in traditional communities in Africa is inspired by communitarian philosophy and the understanding of personhood in African philosophy.

The second part compares and contrasts the common core features of the conception of childhood by different traditional communities in Africa with

1 P Erny *Childhood and cosmos: The social psychology of black African child* (1973) 23.

the CRC's core features of the understanding of childhood. These common features of the CRC are: 'Who a child?'; children's autonomy rights; the best interests of children; and child participation. It is argued that even though the two conceptions of childhood share some common features and have some similar outcomes, there are significant differences. It is further argued that the understanding of childhood in the CRC receives its validity from universal human rights framework, while the conception of childhood by traditional communities in Africa operates more on the basis of responsibilities, duties and obligations. African oral traditions are used to illustrate how the concepts of respect, reciprocity, reproduction and restrain govern the child-adult interaction in Africa within the framework of duties and obligations.

The third part concedes that the 'pure' traditional conception of childhood is fast giving way to a mixed conception of childhood. Some children and their families in Africa live in traditional settings, others transiting from traditional settings to modernity, while others straddle between these different settings. This experience is influencing the conception of childhood in Africa. A number of legal and non-legal factors are identified as contributing to changes in the conception of childhood in Africa. Colonialism, foreign religious beliefs and practices, the human rights movement, and social factors such as poverty and HIV are discussed as intervening factors in the transformation of traditional understanding of childhood in Africa.

The final part concludes, in the absence of a cultural adjustment program for Africa, that efforts to better promote and protect children's rights in Africa must take cognizance of these different conceptions of childhood. Implementing children's rights in Africa based on the claim to superiority of the conception of children's rights as espoused in the CRC or African Children's Charter is fraught with challenges. An approach that accommodates differences in the understanding of childhood within the African continent should be preferred to one which, in the process of harmonising differences, simply eliminates them.

3.1. Conception of childhood in traditional African communities

According to Therborn, 'if the African family has a single supreme value, it is probably fertility.'[2] Generally, in traditional African communities it is believed that without children, 'a person will leave no heirs to survive him or her and to die childless is to die completely.'[3] Children are the glue and the epicentre around which African families, communities, societies, cultures and traditions revolve.[4] The 'unique and privileged position' that children occupy in Africa imposes a collective responsibility on communities to determine and assign roles, responsibilities and privileges to children. In most cases, the roles and responsibilities are intertwined with and determined by the values of these families, communities, societies, cultures and traditions. In Africa, the understanding of the concept 'childhood' is a communal and cultural undertaking.

Any effort to understand what childhood is in Africa is first and foremost a cultural enterprise. Since culture varies between and within communities in Africa, the image of childhood, its roles and responsibilities differ accordingly. However, in the light of geographical proximity, mobility between and within communities, and a shared history and experiences have led to cultural similarities and trans-cultural commonalities. Some African philosophers and scholars hold the view that these transcultural commonalities between and within different African societies are strong enough to constitute an African 'identity;'[5] an African 'mind;'[6] and African 'psyche;'[7] and, ultimately,

2 G Therborn 'African families in a global context' in G Therborn (ed) *African families in a global* (2006) 29.

3 P Erny 'First steps in the life of a black African child: Birth and early childhood' in A Nsamenang *Human development in a cultural context* (1992) 149.

4 B Rweraura 'Competing 'images' of childhood in the social and legal systems of contemporary sub-Saharan Africa' (1998) 12 *International Journal of Law, Polity and the Family* 253.

5 J Nyasani *The African psyche* (1997) 197; A Appiah *In my father's house: Africa in the philosophy of culture* (1992) 173.

6 Nyasani, n 5, 57

7 As above, 58.

an African man or woman. Other scholars and philosophers hold opposite views.[8]

To talk about an African 'identity', 'mind' or 'psyche' might seem excessive; centuries of inter-communal and intra-communal interactions in Africa probably have given rise to a common core of cultural norms and practices. What needs further investigation is the extent to which different cultures and communities have influenced each other in Africa. But this work is not an attempt to determine the degree of cross-cultural influence in Africa; rather, it is an attempt to investigate whether within existing and established cross-cultural norms in Africa there is a common understanding of childhood. If there is a core commonality in the conception of childhood in traditional African communities, the question the book poses is how such an understanding facilitates a better promotion and protection of children's rights in Africa.

All children in all places do not universally experience childhood the same way at all times.[9] It is reasonable to expect that the conceptions of 'child' and 'childhood' in Africa are different, at least to some extent, from the image of childhood in other parts of the world.[10] The image of childhood in the CRC does not derive from that in traditional African cultures; as a result, the understanding of childhood in the CRC differs from the image of childhood in traditional communities in Africa.[11] What is not clear is the nature of, and the reason for that difference and the potential implication(s) of such a

8 For general discussion of the views of scholars for and against this position see J Lassiter 'African culture and personality: Bad social science, effective social activism, or a call to reinvent ethnology? (1999) 3 *African Studies Quarterly* 1 available at: http://www.africa.ufl.edu/asq/v3/v3i3a1.htm.

9 A James & A James *Constructing childhood: Theory, policy and social practice* (2004) 8.

10 The terms 'West' and 'Western' are used in this work to refer to concepts and philosophical orientation. It is used in the same way that Clarence Dias (quoted by A An-Na'im 'Cultural transformation and normative consensus on the best interests of the child' (1994) 8 *International Journal of Law and the Family* 62) uses the terms 'North' and 'South' to refer to concepts rather than regions. Therefore, just as there are pockets of these Western philosophical orientations within Africa, there is supporting evidence of African philosophical orientation within the West. However, as stated earlier, 'West' is used in this work to refer to geopolitical entities as well sometimes.

11 R Zimba 'Indigenous conceptions of childhood development and social realities in southern Africa' in R Zimba *Between culture and biology: Perspectives on ontogentic development* (2002) 89; A Armstrong *et al* 'Towards a cultural understanding of the interplay between children's and women's rights: An Eastern and Southern African perspective' (1995) 3 *International Journal of Children's Rights* 333; W Ncube *Law, culture, tradition and children's rights in East and Southern Africa* (1998) 8.

difference for the effective promotion and protection of children's rights and welfare in Africa.

Those who hold the view that there is a different image of childhood in Africa point to the following: First, in many African societies the difference between childhood and adulthood is primarily a functional, as opposed to a normative or numerical distinction.[12] In other words, whether a person is considered a child, or an adult may depend on what activity that person wants to undertake. Second, in traditional African societies, though childhood starts from conception,[13] it does not have any definite endpoint. Childhood ends as soon as a child practically demonstrates maturity or takes on mature roles and responsibilities.[14] Third, the term 'child' or 'childhood' have social connotations in Africa, which differ from the sense they have elsewhere; for example, they may refer to a perpetual relationship of mutual dependence between parents and their offspring, irrespective of age and maturity.[15] In addition, starting a family or undergoing certain rituals, for example, might qualify an individual who has not demonstrated enough maturity in a cultural sense, to be considered an adult, irrespective of age or status. On the other hand, a failure to start a family or to pass through a particular ritual might result in an individual being viewed as a child, irrespective of age.[16] Moreover, boys and girls in traditional communities in Africa attain maturity differently.

---

12 A Armstrong *et al* 'Towards a cultural understanding of the interplay between children's and women's rights: An Eastern and Southern African perspective' (1995) 3 *International Journal of Children's Rights* 333.

13 R Zimba 'Indigenous conceptions of childhood development and social realities in southern Africa' in R Zimba *Between culture and biology: Perspectives on ontogentic development* (2002) 89; A Armstrong *et al* 'Towards a cultural understanding of the interplay between children's and women's rights: An Eastern and Southern African perspective' (1995) 3 *International Journal of Children's Rights* 333; W Ncube *Law, culture, tradition and children's rights in East and Southern Africa* (1998) 8; J Marah 'The virtues and challenges in traditional African education' (2006) *1 The Journal of Pan African Studies* 15; C Golomski 'Rites of passage: 1900 to present: Africa' in A Stanton *Cultural sociology of the Middle East, Asia, & Africa: An Encyclopedia* (2014) 4; J Timyan cultural aspects of psychosocial development: an examination of West African childrearing practices A report prepared for the Regional UNICEF Workshop: Toward a strategy for enhancing early childhood development in the West and Central Africa region January 18-22, 1988 Abidjan, Cote d'Ivoire. Available at http://www.ecdgroup.com/download/aa1capda.pdf. Also see the discussion on abortion on page 161 to 166 of this book for more details.

14 S Seba & R Matango *The road to umumura in Kuria Community - A brief description of the upbringing of the youth among the Kuria community of Tanzania and Kenya Mimeo Tarime* (1976) 1.

15 R Zimba 'Indigenous conceptions of childhood development and social realities in southern Africa' in R Zimba *Between culture and biology: Perspectives on ontogentic development* (2002) 89.

16 A Armstrong *et al* 'Towards a cultural understanding of the interplay between children's and women's Rights: An Eastern and Southern African perspective' (1995) 3 *International Journal of Children's Rights* 333.

Finally, the equivalent of the concepts of 'child' or 'children' in many local languages are used mainly for young children between the ages of 1 to around 12 years.[17]

Therefore, unlike in the West or even in human rights law where childhood and contestations around it are primarily legal, any contestation about who is a child in Africa is primarily cultural though, gradually, it is taking a legal form. Largely, though, childhood in Africa is still a cultural undertaking, and it is culture that provides it with its goals and meanings.[18] Different cultural norms translate into different conceptions, beliefs and practices relating to childhood.[19] In the light of various cultures across and within African countries, it is contestable whether, in the absence of an African culture, there is an African childhood and, as such, an African understanding of it.

For some scholars there is no such thing as an African culture or tradition, but cultures and traditions in Africa.[20] For where there are similarities between cultures and traditions in Africa, these similarities constitute, at best, 'streams' of cultures and traditions and not an African culture or tradition.[21] These scholars further contend that if in the past there was anything such as an African culture, it no longer exists. This is because:

> [the] African today is a living confluence of cultural rivers, the major rivers being, on the one hand, the traditional culture with its tributaries of religion, social structure, language, values and world

---

17 L McNee 'The languages of childhood: The discursive construction of childhood and colonial policy in French West Africa' (2004) 7 *African Studies Quarterly*. Available at: http://www.africa.ufl.edu/asq/v7/v7i4a2.htm. Margaret Mead described lap children (infants, aged 0±1), knee children (toddlers, 2±3), yard children (preschool, 4±5), and community children (juveniles in middle childhood, 6±12) or the developmental stages of the human person in terms of the five stages of human growth and development that are common to Homo sapiens: infancy, childhood, juvenility, adolescence, and adulthood (Bogin 1999) closely resembles this traditional African thinking.

18 M Rosenthal 'Home to early childhood service: A ecological perspective' (2000) 4 *Childrenz Issues* 7; M Rosenthal 'Out-of-home child care book: A cultural perspective' (1999) *23 International Journal of Behavioural Development* 477; and see, generally, R Serpell 'Cultural models of childhood in indigenous socialization and formal schooling in Zambia' in L Hwang & I Sigel *Images of childhood* (1996) 129; J Kagan *The nature of the child* (1984) 166 and D Lee *Freedom and culture* (1959) 101.

19 M Rosenthal 'Out-of-home childcare book: A cultural perspective' (1999) 23 *International Journal of Behavioural Development* 477.

20 See generally J Lassiter 'African culture and personality: Bad social science, effective social activism, or a call to reinvent ethnology?' (1999) Available at http://web.africa.ufl.edu/asq/v3/v3i2a1.htm.

21 M Mugambi 'Forget your past, thank colonialism' (1998) *The People's Digest* 111.

> view, and, on the other hand, the Christian-Western culture (and other alien cultures including Islam) with its own tributaries.[22]

These scholars maintain that even if there were such a thing as an African culture in the past, romanticising such African tradition and culture is delusionary and a wish to elevate such a culture today is to do a disservice to Africa and to Africans. For example, Nyasani advocates that African cultures or traditions should be discarded, because such a culture or tradition produced in Africa an:

> endemic and congenital trait of what could be described as a natural benign docility generally brought about by years of blind social submission and unquestioning compliance to the mystique of higher authority that reigns surreptitiously yet effectively in all black African societies in varying degrees. This benign natural docility is generally regarded as positive, legitimate and virtuous strictly within the context of a traditional social regime.[23]

There are a number of difficulties relating to this position. The assertion that there is a culture of 'benign natural docility' evident in 'all black African societies' reflects the dangers inherent in overgeneralisation and it is unscientific. The position of these scholars conflates a distinction between something that does not exist and something that cannot be found. Theoretically, it is possible for that thing to exist. To state that there are no significant cross-cultural themes and patterns unique to Africa from which cultural generalities could be distilled would be valid only if a thorough search for these themes and patterns yielded no result.[24] Such a search is just starting to take place within the African context:

> [s]ince the 1960s, the predominant approach to social and cultural book among social scientists has been to examine a clearly defined society, population, sector, geographically defined area, or topic.

22 T Okere 'African culture: The past and the present as an indivisible whole' in T Okere *Identity and change: Nigerian Philosophical Studies* (1996) 10.

23 Nyasani, n 5, 113.

24 K Thairu *The African civilization* (1975) 168.

> Such book tends to steer away from cultural and psychological generalizations at higher levels of social organization such as the ethnic group, society, nation or geographical regions such as sub-Saharan Africa.[25]

Makgoba holds the view that Africans 'are linked by shared values that are fundamental features of African identify and culture.'[26] According to him, 'the existence of African identity is not in doubt.'[27] This identity stems from a peculiar African philosophy of life and view of man and society, which partly manifests itself in the African conception of kinship, the family and the place of an individual in society.[28]

According to Mbiti, African philosophy manifests strongly through the understanding of the place of kinship, the family and the individual in the society. He sees kinship as a network that ensures that 'each individual is a brother or a sister, father or a mother, grandmother or grandfather, or a cousin, or a brother-in-law, uncle or aunt, or something else, to everybody else.'[29] The result, at least for children in Africa, is that they are 'born into corporate envelopes of related and connected persons, ancestral spirits and the unborn.'[30] Thus, the traditional environment into which children in Africa were born had:

> the heavy accent on family – the blood relatives, the group kinsfolk held together by a common origin and a common obligation to its members, to those who are living and those who are dead. For the family is conceived as consisting of a large number of people, many of whom are dead, a few of whom are living and countless numbers of whom are yet to be born. The [child] is brought up to think of

25 J Lassiter 'African culture and personality: Bad social science, effective social activism, or a call to reinvent ethnology?' (1999) Available at: http://web.africa.ufl.edu/asq/v3/v3i2a1.htm.

26 M Makgoba *Mokoko, the makgoba affair: A reflection on transformation* (1997) 197.

27 As above,198.

28 J Mbiti *African religions and philosophy* (1990) 100.

29 As above,102.

30 R Zimba 'Indigenous conceptions of childhood development and social realities in southern Africa' in R Zimba *Between culture and biology: Perspectives on ontogentic development* (2002) 98.

> himself [and herself] always in relation to this group and to behave always in such a way as to bring honour and not disgrace to its members.[31]

To assert that there is an 'African culture' in the light of available evidence probably overstretches the argument. What is evident, in the opinion of the author, is that African cultures and traditions share some common features. These cultural similarities define certain aspects of life and the philosophy or worldview, in Africa. The book explores these cultural communalities in order to determine if they constitute a source for the conception of childhood in Africa.

3.1. Sources of the conception of childhood in Africa

3.1.1. Communalism

Communalism is a cultural feature that many scholars agree is common to many communities in Africa. Scholars of African philosophy tend to agree that the Zulu expression *umuntu umuntu ngabantu* (a person is only a person with other people),[32] encapsulates the essence of African communalism. Communality, used in this sense, is different from:

> [a] mere collection of self-interested persons, each with his private set of preferences, but all of whom get together nonetheless because they realize, each to each, that in association they can accomplish things which they are not able to accomplish otherwise.[33]

Communalism in African philosophy is used as a social platform that ensures that 'whatever happens to the individual happens to the whole group, and whatever happens to the whole group happens to the individual.'[34] The individual can only say: 'I am, because we are; and since we are, therefore

---

31 K Busia *The challenge of Africa* (1962) 33.

32 A Shutte *Philosophy for Africa* (1993) 46.

33 I Menkiti 'Person and community in African traditional thought' in R Wright (ed) *African philosophy* (1984) 171.

34 J Mbiti *African religions and philosophy* (1969) 109.

I am.'[35] Thus, the individual is the very essence of the community, and the community is the essence of the individual; without the individual there is no community and without the community there is no individual.

It has been said that African communalism is 'amphibious, for it manifests features of both communality and individuality.'[36] It is

> based both on the community and on the person ..., because it was founded on dialogue and reciprocity, the group had priority over the individual without crushing him, but allowing him to blossom as a person.[37]

The South African Constitutional Court supported this description of an African philosophy of communalism or 'Ubuntu' in *S v Makwanyane.* Langa J described it as

> [a] culture, which places some emphasis on communality and on the interdependence of the members of a community. It recognises a person's status as a human being, entitled to unconditional respect, dignity, value and acceptance from the members of the community such person happens to be part of. It also entails the converse, however. The person has the corresponding duty to give the same respect, dignity, value and acceptance to each member of that community. More importantly, it regulates the exercise of rights by the emphasis it lays on sharing and co-responsibility and mutual enjoyment of rights by all.[38]

In *DPP v Pete,* the Court of Appeal of Tanzania referred to communal ethics in the following terms:

> The co-existence of the individual and the society, and also the reality of the co-existence of rights and duties of the individual on one hand, and the collective of communitarian rights and duties of society

35 L Mbigi *New life for a new year* (1997) 37.

36 K Gyekye *The unexamined life: Philosophy and the African experience* (1988) 31.

37 L Senghor *Negritude* (1966) 5.

38 1995 (3) SA 391.

> on the other means that the rights and duties of the individual are limited by the rights and duties of the society, and vice versa.[39]

African philosophy emphasises a consensual system and style of life in African societies that ensures that individual and communal relationships 'avoid the excesses of the two exaggerated systems, while allowing for a meaningful, albeit uneasy, interaction between the individual and the society.'[40] Harmony is possible in this African philosophy because the 'self', the individual, is 'outside' and subsists in a relationship to what is other, the natural and social environment.'[41] It is in contradiction with the philosophical thought in the West that regards the 'self' as something that is 'inside a person, or at least as a kind of container of mental properties and powers.'[42] The difference in Western and African thought with regards to the conception of communalism stems from the difference in how Africa and the West understand the concept of personhood.

3.1.2. Personhood

Personhood has been described as 'attributes, capacities, and signs' of what it means to be, 'properly' a social person in a particular society.[43] Scholars hold the view that there is a fundamental difference in the conception of personhood between the West and Africa.[44] The claim is, in Africa, that it is the community that defines the person as a person, not an isolated, static quality of rationality, will, or the right to be left alone. Persons become persons only after a process of incorporation into and by a community.[45] In the West, a person is someone who has a soul, or rationality, or will, or memory. This

---

39 No. 28 of 1990, Court of Appeal of Tanzania.

40 K Gyekye *The unexamined life: Philosophy and the African experience* (1988) 32.

41 A Shutte *Philosophy for Africa* (1993) 46.

42 As above, 47.

43 G Herdt *Rituals of manhood: Male initiation in Papua New Guinea* (1982) 99.

44 D Kaphagawani 'African conceptions of personhood and intellectual identities' in P Coetzee & A Roux *Philosophy from Africa: A text with readings* (1998) 169; J Trimier 'The myth of authenticity: Personhood, traditional culture, and African philosophy' in R Solomon & K Higgins (eds) *From Africa to Zen: An invitation to world philosophy* (2003) 173.

45 D Kaphagawani 'African conceptions of personhood and intellectual identities' in P Coetzee & A Roux *Philosophy from Africa: A text with readings* (1998) 169.

conception of personhood in the West has been described as minimalistic, whereas the understanding of personhood in traditional African philosophy is seen as maximalistic.[46]

In his theory of justice, Rawls observed that

> [e]qual justice is owed to those who have the capacity to take part in and to act in accordance with the public understanding of the initial situation. One should observe that moral personality is here defined as a *potentiality that is ordinarily realized in due course.*[47] It is this potentiality which brings the claims of justice into play . . . The sufficient condition for equal justice [is] the capacity for moral personality.[48]

Though Rawls' preoccupation here was not personhood but moral personality, African philosophy tends mainly to consider the latter the precondition for the former. Maybe describing this 'potentiality' Sartre said that an individual is 'nothing [and] will not be anything until later, and then he will be what he makes of himself.'[49] Though Sartre made this statement within the framework of existentialism, it is relevant to communal view of personhood for the reason that while individualisation is pivotal to existentialism, community is central to communitarianism. Although Sartre's emphasis is on 'he will be what he makes of himself' and the emphasis of communalism is on what 'the community will make of him', Sartre's discussion about 'potentiality' is relevant to both.

These descriptions of personality correspond, to some extent, to the African image of personhood as something which is acquired, but there are also differences. In the former, 'reason' and 'freedom' are held to be the determining factors. An essentialist view holds that 'man does not exist in order to be free; subsequently, there is no difference between the being of

---

46 I Menkiti 'Person and community in African traditional thought' in R Wright (ed) *African philosophy* (1984) 171.

47 Emphasis provided.

48 J Rawls *A theory of justice* (1971) 505.

49 J Sartre *Being and nothingness: An essay on phenomenological ontology* (1956) 25 translated by Hazel E. Barnes.

man and his being free.'[50] Scholars of African philosophy argue that these are not the determining factors of personhood. They argue that 'if possession of reason is part of our nature, then we cannot be enslaved by reason …; for no entity can be enslaved by its own nature.'[51] In the West, a person is a person *a priori*, whereas in African philosophy personhood is achieved.

According to Menkiti, as 'far as African societies are concerned, personhood is something at which individuals could fail, at which they could be competent or ineffective, better or worse.'[52] In various traditional societies in Africa the ability to attain the status of full personhood was directly proportional to the ability to discharge various communal obligations accruing to one's station in life. Personhood, thus, was a function of responsibility, achievement(s) and recognition.

This view of personhood in Africa has been disputed on at least two grounds: First, those who maintain a gradual approach to the attainment of personhood confuse the attributes of personhood with the conception of personhood. According to some scholars, in contrast, in traditional African thought:

> [a] human person is a person whatever his age or social status. Personhood may reach its full realization in community, but it is not acquired or yet to be achieved as one goes along in society. What a person acquires are status, habits, and personality or character traits: he, qua person, thus becomes the subject of acquisition, and being thus prior to the acquisition, he cannot be defined by what he acquires.[53]

Gyekye is of the opinion that in African philosophy one is a person because of what he is, not because of what he acquires.[54]

---

50 As above.

51 W Abraham *The mind of Africa* (1962) 20.

52 I Menkiti 'Person and community in African traditional thought' in R Wright (ed) *African philosophy* (1984) 171.

53 K Wiredu & K Gyekye *Person and community: Ghanaian philosophical studies* (1992) 102.

54 K Gyekye *An essay on African philosophical thought* (1995) 85.

Second, these scholars hold the view that the proponents of incremental acquisition of personhood stratify people into 'lesser persons' and 'more persons.' Such a stratification of traditional communities introduces a class system into traditional African societies, a concept that was alien to that system. In addition, the philosophy of a progressive realisation of personhood, if taken to its logical conclusion, will disadvantage children and women, whose status and social position traditionally precluded them from acquiring those attributes necessary for the attainment of full personhood. It is maintained that although children and women were not considered equal to adults or elders or men, there is insufficient evidence to suggest that they were treated as non-humans or non-persons. They were persons in different ways.

The difference between the gradualist school of personhood in African philosophy and those who insist that personhood is vested upon birth into the human family is not the aim of this book. What is of interest to this work is to establish in what way African philosophy and African traditional or cultural beliefs and practices affect the understanding of childhood in Africa.

According to Dewey, philosophy is 'a social hope reduced to a working programme of action, a prophecy of the future.'[55] Rorty suggests that philosophy 'is best seen as a series of efforts to modify people's sense of who they are, what matters to them, what is most important.'[56] Even though these definitions tend to invoke a relationship between philosophy and culture, they are different spheres of academic interest. If there is a relationship between the two, there is much disagreement among scholars about the nature of such a link.[57] Practically, it seems that there is a measured relationship between cultural values and moral philosophy.

The idea that philosophical thought is culturally informed has been conceptually and empirically studied.[58] Some of the findings suggest that:

---

55 J Dewey 'Experience and nature' in J Boydston (ed) *The later works*, vol.1 (1925) (1988b) 72.

56 R Rorty *Philosophy as cultural politics* (2007) 71.

57 As above, 3.

58 E Machery *et al* 'Semantics, cross cultural style' (2004) 92 *Cognition* B1 and J Weinberg *et al* 'Normativity and epistemic intuitions' (2001) 29 *Philosophical Topics* 249.

> [some philosophical] concepts are culturally influenced, and that philosophical theories based on concepts may reflect the attitudes of a cultural group, rather than universally shared understanding of the target domain.[59]

A cultural concept that is influenced by philosophy is the concept of childhood. The influence of philosophers such as Aristotle, John Locke, and Jean-Jacques Rousseau on the understanding of childhood in the West is visible in the way children are seen and treated in law, policies and practice.[60] Not only does philosophy inform cultural norms and practices but culture influences and modifies the nature, status and direction of philosophy.[61] The mutual interaction between philosophy and culture and its impact on the understanding, roles, boundaries and dimensions of childhood are evident in the African *milieu*.

Culture, understood as the 'sum total of the integrated learned behaviour patterns characteristic of members of a society,'[62] plays a major role in the way society sees and treats children. There is considerable conceptual and empirical support for the relationship between culture and the image of childhood.[63] It is culture that establishes 'the proper status of the king and minister... rulers and the ruled ... elders and the juniors; or how to establish moral relationship between the sexes, parent, children and others.'[64]

---

59 J Prinz 'Culture and cognitive science' (2011) *The Stanford Encyclopaedia of Philosophy* URL = http://plato.stanford.edu/archives/win2011/entries/culture-cogsci/.

60 For a discussion of how philosophical thinking specific to Europe influenced the development of childhood in the European system see G Matthews 'Getting beyond the deficit conception of childhood: thinking philosophically with children' in M Hand & C Hunt (ed) *Philosophy in schools* (2008); and G Matthews 'Philosophy and developmental psychology: Outgrowing the deficit conception of childhood' in H Siegel (ed) *The Oxford handbook of philosophy of education* (2009) 162.

61 R Rorty *Philosophy as cultural politics* (2007) 71.

62 P Onwauchi *African identity and black liberation* (1972) 241.

63 J Berry 'Cultural relations in plural societies: Alternatives to separation and their socio-psychological implications' in N Miller & M Brewer, (eds) *Groups in contact: The psychology of desegregation* (1984) 228; see, generally, also J Gonzalez-Mena *Multicultural issues in child care* (1997).

64 Watch Tower, Mankind Search for God. Pennsylvania: Watch-tower Bible and Tract Society, 1990 quoted in K Oweh *Elements of complementary reflection as a philosophy of integration* (2006) available at http.//www.frasouzu.com/Issues%20and%20Papers/Kidzu%20T.%20Oweh%20on%20Elements%20of%20Complementary%20Reflection.pdf.

Culture, perceived as the customs, traditions, norms, values, beliefs, practices, provides a group with meaning, direction and coherence as it passes through the 'timeless rhythm of human life.'[65] The family, as 'the custodians of moral and traditional values'[66] of a community, is the platform that defines, constructs, reconstructs, legitimises and guards the basic cultural fingerprints of a society. The cultural beliefs and attitudes of the family regulate childrearing values and expectations.[67] For instance, in Western societies, 'individualistic' cultural values such as competence, independence and competition, as well as the emphasis on cognitive abilities, verbal skills and other signs of 'egocentric autonomy' are considered adaptive in that cultural setting.[68] The family inculcates cultural values in their children. A cultural script that is 'collectivist' motivates families in non-Western communities: 'inter-dependent cultural scripts that tend to emphasise harmony with one another, cooperation, altruism and social responsibility.'[69] African cultural values and experience set the meaning, purpose and goal for childrearing in Africa.

The discussion of the philosophical conception(s) of community and personhood in Africa demonstrates the positive, as well as negative influences of African philosophy and cultural heritage on the image of childhood in Africa. Children are seen and treated as a collective or a group; interests and needs of children are defined, determined and safeguarded on the basis of a collective identity. In addition, children are born into a community and it is the collective role and responsibility of the community to attend to the needs and interests of children. In Africa, children are literally born in a 'partnership with society and caregivers whose presence, attention and care focused on the needs of the child.'[70]

---

65 J Mbiti *African religions and philosophy* (1990)103.

66 Article 18 of the African Charter on Human and Peoples' Rights (1986) (Adopted 27 June 1981, OAU Doc. CAB/LEG/67/3 rev. 5, 21 I.L.M. 58 (1982), entered into force 21 October 1986).

67 See, generally, C Hwang *et al Images of childhood* (1996); M Rosenthal 'Out-of-home child care book: A cultural perspective' (1999) 23 *International Journal of Behavioural Development* 477; M Rosenthal 'Home to early childhood service: An ecological perspective' (2000) 4 *Childrenz Issues* 7.

68 H Trandis *et al* 'Individualism and collectivism: Cross cultural perspectives on self-in group relationships' (1988) 54 *Journal of Personality and Social Psychology* 323.

69 As above.

70 M Hecker 'Be born and you shall be attended' (1992) 13. An informal progress report on the education of Ju/'hoan children of Namibia presented to the Nyae Nyae Foundation.

This shared social responsibility for the upbringing of children is a community's investment in itself and in its children. Such an investment is usually expected to yield returns to the community.[71] That is probably why, in many communities in Africa, children constitute an insurance policy that facilitates material survival and a lineage continuity policy for the community. A complex system of reciprocal responsibilities and duties has been developed to safeguard what has been described as 'wealth-in-people': a socio-economic system that is developed around childbearing.[72] If not managed well, this concept impacts negatively on the understanding of childhood. Since children are expected to provide in return to the community, it has meant that for many children 'the task of growing up, work and learning are interwoven and not separated.'[73] Therefore, though communalism is a useful social security system in Africa; its complex nature makes it amenable to be abused: sometimes the law is a blunt instrument for dealing with such abuses.

The ineffectiveness of the law to deal with possible misuse of the communal system arises from the fact that communalism is more a 'socio-ethical'[74] concept than a legal or even a political doctrine. The closest the law has come to deal with it is captured in the concept of 'peoples' rights' incorporated under the African Charter on Human and Peoples' Rights.[75] The concept of 'peoples' rights' tries to capture the pre-eminence of the community in the life of individuals. However, the African Children's Charter does not recognise the group rights of children in the same sense as a 'peoples' rights.' This positive cultural heritage of African thought within the ambit of the African Children's Charter, its benefits and protection do not extend to children.[76]

---

71 W Ncube (ed) *Law, culture, tradition and children's rights in East and Southern Africa* (1998) 16.

72 C Bledsoe *Women and marriage in Kpelle society* (1980) 48.

73 M Woodhead 'In search for the rainbow: Pathways to quality in large scale programmes for young disadvantaged children' (1996) 10 *Early Childhood Development: Practice and Reflections* 10.

74 K Gyekye *The unexamined life: Philosophy and the African experience* (1988) 24.

75 The African Charter on Human and peoples' Rights (1986) (Adopted 27 June 1981, OAU Doc. CAB/LEG/67/3 rev. 5, 21 I.L.M. 58 (1982), entered into force 21 October 1986).

76 However, it could be argued that since the African Charter on Human and Peoples' Rights provides for the concept of a people and that children as human beings are covered within the scope of this treaty, the omission in the African Children's Charter is not fatal. The concern with this argument is that it could be argued that the explicit omission of this concept in the African Children's Charter which was drafted after the African Charter on Human and Peoples' Rights meant that the drafters of the African Children's Charter deliberately omitted this concept as not applying to children.

It is arguable that the conception of personhood in African philosophy has implications for the image of childhood in Africa. The progressive nature of personhood, how and why full personhood is attained, and the kind of relationship that exists between individuals at different stages on this continuum of personhood have implications for the understanding of childhood in traditional African communities. There seems to be a general understanding that African societies are hierarchical. This is because:

> [the] progression of the individual to the state of personhood is a common feature of hierarchically ordered societies, in which identity cannot be separated from the attributes attached to the position and the functions of the person within society, at successive stages in life.[77]

According to Smitherman, the African 'universe is hierarchical in nature, with God at the head of the hierarchy, followed by lesser deities, the "living dead" (ancestral spirits), people, animals, places.'[78] That is why it has been said in Africa that personhood is

> [acquired] along an evolution undertaken over an entire lifetime, of which ancestorhood represents the culmination. It is not attained at birth, but through the fulfilment of a number of requirements which include procreation in marriage, and reproduction through the procreation of one's own children.[79]

In other words, personhood is only 'conferred as a consequence of living out a life considered by society as 'proper."[80] This view has serious implications for the conception of childhood in traditional African societies.

First, children are considered as 'adults-in-the-making' or persons in the process of becoming 'full persons.'[81] According to Morris, in Malawi, for example, children are not considered full human beings until *kutenga Mwana,*

---

77 A Ottino *The universe within a Balinese village through its ritual practices* (2000) 275.

78 G Smitherman *Talking and testifying: The language of black American* (1977) 75.

79 A Ottino *The universe within a Balinese village through its ritual practices* (2000) 274.

80 U Neisser & D Jopling *The conceptual self in context: Culture, experience, and self-understanding* (1997) 43.

81 K Wiredu & K Gyekye *Person and community: Ghanaian philosophical studies* I (1992) 108.

a birth ritual, is performed.[82] This ritual prepares a child for full personhood, which is fully attainable only at adolescence. In Kenya, among the Babukusu, the child is given at birth only a temporary name; a permanent name is given when the child attains full personhood at adolescence.[83]

The community's role in the journey of helping a child attain full personhood, therefore, is to make culturally acceptable and socially responsible adults out of children. This role is a delicate one because the community fails when children fail to be socially responsible and culturally acceptable adults. Such a role has been described as being as 'delicate as holding an egg in one's palm. Holding the egg too tight crushes it; a careless handling of the egg may fall from the palm and be destroyed too.'[84]

Second, childhood is understood to be a period to learn, to form a character and to acquire the social and technical skills that are needed to live life as a socially responsible adult. Orchardson in his book *The Kipsigis* observes, with respect to the Kipsigis children of Tanzania, that those children

> learn how to observe. They show endless interest in the plant, animal and insect worlds ... can name almost every tree, bush, grass or weed, and describe where they grow and what their flowers and seeds are like; how insects behave, where birds nest, and what they say when they sing.[85]

Different rituals punctuate this learning period. In addition to serving as public notice of attainment of certain milestones along the continuum to adulthood, rituals are used to teach children to show respect to their equals and elders, to treat strangers courteously and generously, to be polite to those younger than they, to display moderation and control over their instincts and

---

82 B Morris *Animals and ancestors: An ethnography* (2000) 75.

83 A Nasiniyu-Wasike *Polygamy: A feminist critique* (1992) 47.

84 A Boakye-Boaten 'Changes in the concept of childhood: Implications on children in Ghana' (2010) 3 *The Journal of International Social Book* 105.

85 I Orchardson *The Kipsigis* (1961) 49.

emotions and, more generally, to be hard working, trustworthy, sincere and kind to others.[86]

Third, it would mean that when childhood starts, and ends is not the function of age but deeds. That is why some African communities hold the view that 'it is one's deeds that are counted, not one's years.'[87] In trying to emphasise the relative importance of achievements over age in the Igbos conception of childhood, Achebe said of Okonkwo: 'age was respected among his people, but achievement is revered.'[88]

The culture of respect and hierarchy in traditional Africa has come under attack from African philosophers. According to Nyasani

> [the]fundamental difference between the traditional African child and a child in the Western culture [is rooted in the culture of hierarchy and respect]. The child in Africa was muzzled right from the outset and was thereby drilled into submission to authority from above.[89]

However, such sweeping criticism of traditional African values should be approached cautiously.

It seems some African scholars are determined to take from African values, practices and literature only the attitudes that they bring to it.[90] A holistic view of culture in its full diversity of values, practices and literature and what these say about African traditions, might give a more balanced view. To approach cultures and societies purely from a point of view of what information about these societies can be used to attain in order to achieve a pre-determined outcome is problematic.[91] A balanced approach to research will reveal many

---

86 I Orchardson *The Kipsigis* (1961) 51.

87 P Ikuenobe 'The idea of personhood in Chinau Achebe's things fall apart' (2006) 9 *Philosopia Africana* 117.

88 C Achebe *Things fall apart* (1994) 12.

89 J Nyasani *The African psyche* (1997) 129.

90 This is an adaptation from J Ellis *Literature lost: Social agendas and the corruption of the humanities* (1996) 13 where he says: 'if we are determined to take from literature only the attitudes that we bring to it, it ceases to have any point'. A large group of contemporary scholars, Ellis notes, 'have no real interest in what literature might say (in its full diversity), and only an interest in what they can use it for'.

91 Adapted from J Ellis *Literature lost: Social agendas and the corruption of the humanities* (1996) 13 where he notes 'academic literary criticism has been transformed' from traditional inquiry into a overarching search for relevance and significance applicable to modern society. That literature and humanistic inquiry are subverted

positive potential contributions African traditional values could make to the promotion and protection of the rights of children in Africa, as well as their negative impact.

In the absence of a cultural adjustment programme for and in Africa, the understanding of childhood will continue, for the foreseeable future, to be dominated by culture. It would be helpful to concentrate efforts on balancing the tension between international human rights law and the communal understanding of childhood in Africa. Equilibrium cannot be attained simply by eliminating one side of the image of childhood, but only in a genuine search for accommodation and harmony. Any 'systematic attempt to ignore and dismiss the intrinsic value of African culture, customs and practices'[92] in the human rights discourse of children in Africa is not helpful. Such a move will 'leave [children in Africa] in a [cultural and philosophical] vacuum that can only be filled with confusion, loss of identity, and a total break in intergenerational communication.'[93]

The search for accommodation and harmony must be done with the understanding that a number of children in Africa no longer live in and experience 'pure' African cultural and traditional experience, but rather a 'hybrid'[94] of cultural realities with its own implications and configurations. Any discourse about childhood in Africa must be alive to the cultural mix and its hybrid nature. Such a discourse must ensure the centrality of the African cultural heritage without negating other non-African cultural experiences that enrich childhood experience. There are different sources from which an African cultural heritage can be ascertained: one such source is the oral traditions of many communities in Africa.

---

to quests for political power such that 'the universities should have an overtly political function, work directly for social and political change, and inculcate a particular political viewpoint in their students.'

92 N Matos 'The nature of learning, teaching and book in higher education' in P Higgs *et al* (eds) *African voices in education* (2000) 18.

93 F Boateng 'African traditional education: A method of dissemination cultural values' (1983) 3 *Journal of Black Studies* 335.

94 Y Kanu 'Tradition and educational reconstruction in Africa in post-colonial and global times: The case of Sierra Leone' (2007) 9 *African Studies Quarterly* 187; compare this with H Bhabha 'Signs taken for wonders: Questions of ambivalence and authority under a tree outside Delhi, May 1817 (1985) 12 *Critical Inquiry* 144.

African oral tradition is rich in indications of how Africans understand childhood. Inherent in a people's oral tradition is a sense of the value system of the people. For centuries, history, knowledge and value system were passed from generation to generation through oral traditions. These oral traditions show an understanding of childhood, as well as the goals and expectations of childhood in Africa.

The West African saying that 'a Fulani will lie but he will not make a lying proverb'[95] describes the integrity and credibility attached to oral traditions in Africa. African oral traditions constitute evidence of the commonalities that exist between and among cultures and traditions in Africa. Proverbs, folklore, linguistic expressions, religious beliefs, rituals, customs, traditions and myths, as components of Africa's oral traditions, are difficult to attribute, with exactitude, to a specific culture or tradition in Africa. What is a Shona proverb could be similar to an Akan saying and this similarity is reflected in other communities in Africa. Oral traditions in Africa conceal philosophical ideas, concepts and prepositions common to African communities, and provide evidence of how these communities ordered their social relationship and guided their institutions.

Mbiti is of the opinion that African ideas relating to science, metaphysics, logic and religion can be distilled from African proverbs.[96] Makinde concurs and suggests that traditional African sayings should be considered valuable source materials for serious academic endeavour, because

> [a]lthough ... it is not a philosophy, it has in it a great stock of ideas that generate various philosophical issues, including metaphysics, ethics, epistemology, and science, of which the most developed is traditional medical science.[97]

95 H Courlander *A treasury of African folklore: The oral literature, traditions, myths, legends, epics, tales, recollections, wisdom, sayings and humor of Africa* (1975) 38.

96 J Mbiti *African religions and philosophy* (1970) 69.

97 M Makinde *African philosophy, culture and traditional medicine* (1988) 5; see also A Makinde 'A philosophical analysis of the Yuruba concepts of ori and human destiny' (1985) 17 *International Studies in Philosophy* 53.

African oral tradition provides 'sources of insights into African orientations to life'.[98] Various African proverbs, folklore and myths espouse how African traditional communities see and treat children. A discussion of few of these components of African oral tradition is apt. The discussion of these oral traditions will be arranged around the following themes: What is a child? What are the rights of children in traditional African communities? What is considered to be in the best interests of the child from a cultural perspective? And what is meant by child participation. These themes are a means to assess the understanding of childhood in African cultural traditions.

3.2. The child in African tradition

3.2.1. Who is a child in African tradition?

The answer to the question 'who is a child?' in traditional African communities is more complex than the picture presented in the CRC and the African Children's Charter. In many communities, the prerogative to declare a person either a child or an adult is vested in the traditions and customs of the community. This determination of status is based not on the number of years one has lived on the planet but on how the person has demonstrated maturity. According to Ncube

> in the African cultural context childhood is not perceived and conceptualised in terms of age but in terms of inter-generational obligations of support and reciprocity. In this sense an African "child" is often always a "child" in relation to his or her parents who expect and are traditionally entitled to all forms of support in times of need and in old age.[99]

Whether a human being is a baby, a child, a youth, an adult or an elder is determined on the basis of biology, physical development, ability, purpose and status, in traditional African societies. With the exception, perhaps,

98 N Dzobo 'African Symbols and Proverbs as sources of knowledge' in G Arthur & R Rowe (eds) *Akan Cultural Symbols Projects* (2001) http:// www.mogaby.com/indidgenous.

99 W Ncube 'The African cultural fingerprints: The changing concept of childhood' in W Ncube (eds) *Law, culture, tradition and children's rights* (1998) 18.

of babyhood, each milestone has special protection, privileges as well as roles and obligations. Rituals are performed to mark the exit from one stage of development and to qualify an individual for entry into the next developmental phase. These rituals are 'social shifters that usher in changes in social roles, cultural perceptions and expectations, and a re-actualisation of personal rights and obligations.'[100]

The practical implication is that, on one hand, a human being is a 'child' as long as he or she lives, behaves, thinks and feels like a 'child' and, on the other, an individual has matured enough to be an adult once he or she has become physically strong, emotionally stable, and socially responsible. In traditional African society childhood starts at conception,[101] but its end is not so certain. It is possible that an individual can be 14 and already an adult, or he or she can be 21 and still be considered a child.[102] Adulthood is not automatic; it is to be achieved. In traditional Africa thought,

> the notion that someone by some magic wand, on the stroke of a pen turns into a fully competent, mature, wise and autonomous individual upon attaining a certain arbitrarily fixed age has ... no basis in fact and reality.[103]

---

100 M Aguilar *The politics of age and gerontocracy in Africa* (1998) 15.

101 R Zimba 'Indigenous conceptions of childhood development and social realities in southern Africa' in R Zimba *Between culture and biology: Perspectives on ontogentic development* (2002) 89; A Armstrong *et al* 'Towards a cultural understanding of the interplay between children's and women's rights: An Eastern and Southern African perspective' (1995) 3 *International Journal of Children's Rights* 333; W Ncube *Law, culture, tradition and children's rights in East and Southern Africa* (1998) 8; J Marah 'The virtues and challenges in traditional African education' (2006) *1The Journal of Pan African Studies* 15; C Golomski 'Rites of passage: 1900 to present: Africa' in A Stanton *Cultural sociology of the Middle East, Asia, & Africa: An Encyclopedia* (2014) 4; J Timyan 'Cultural aspects of psychosocial development: An examination of West African childrearing practices A report prepared for the Regional UNICEF Workshop: Toward a strategy for enhancing early childhood development in the West and Central Africa region January 18-22, 1988 Abidjan, Cote d'Ivoire. Available at http://www.ecdgroup.com/download/aa1capda.pdf. Also see the discussion on abortion on page 161 to 166 of this book for more details.

102 It should be noted, however, that leaving the upper age limit open could, in some instances, negatively affect children. This is so because a child in the African context is a child in traditional settings, a child in transition, living in, shuttling between traditional values and modern or Western cultures, and a child who is participating fully in the contemporary, industrial and post-industrial world. see K Peltzer 'Person and personality perception in Africa' (2002) 30 *Social Behaviour and Personality* 83. Therefore, an upper limit will make it easier to ascertain when this child should qualify to participate in some forms of formal processes such as legal contracts or elections, to mention but a few.

103 W Ncube *Law, culture, tradition and children's rights in east and Southern Africa* (1998) 20.

Evidence suggests that the position taken in traditional communities in Africa that age is not the only consideration when it comes to the beginning and the end points of childhood is closer to reality than the position adopted in the African Children's Charter, for example. The author argues that that an individual's level of maturity does not necessarily correspond to the chronological age.[104] In addition, maturity is attained at different ages by the sexes.[105] The brain of a male child reaches full maturity later than 21 whereas a female child is fully mature, in some cases, as early as 17.[106] The traditional African believes that maturity is not a function of age; the CRC alludes to this fact when it states:

> States Parties shall assure to the child who is capable of forming his or her own views the right to express those views freely in all matters affecting the child, the views of the child being given due weight in accordance *with the age and maturity* of the child.[107]

To distinguish 'age' from 'maturity' is to acknowledge and accept that one could be present without the other being a determining factor.

The terminology 'child' or 'children' connotes something different in various traditional African communities. For example, among the Tallensi in Ghana, the early period of life is divided into stages: babyhood and the childhood.[108] Babyhood is considered to be the period from 0 to 3 at an age when the baby is weaned from its mother's milk; childhood starts at 4 and ends at around 8 years old. Until the child reaches 12 to 14 its occupation most of the time is play.[109] The answer to the question 'Who is a child?' is not straightforward. A child is an individual who is yet to satisfy the requirements for adulthood.

---

104 See generally M Freeman *Law and neuroscience: Current legal issues volume 13* (2011).

105 M de Haan & M Gunnar *Handbook of developmental social neuroscience* (2009) 378.

106 R Dahl 'Adolescent brain development: A period of vulnerabilities and opportunities' (2004) 1021 *ANNALS , New York Academy of Science* 12; see also T Maroney 'Adolescent brain science and juvenile justice' in M Freeman (ed) *Law and neuroscience* (2011) 255; see generally, M Freeman (ed) *Law and neuroscience* (2011).

107 Article 12 of the Convention on the Rights of the Child (1989)

108 M Fortes *The web of kinship among the Tallensi: The second part of an analysis of the social structure of a transvolta tribe* (1957) 190.

109 M Fortes *The web of kinship among the Tallensi: The second part of an analysis of the social structure of a transvolta tribe* (1957) 191.

The understanding of who a child is and the means of establishing the boundaries of childhood in traditional African societies differ significantly from the image of the child presented by the CRC as well as the African Children's Charter. It is submitted that if this difference is not highlighted, negotiated and aligned, it will become increasingly problematic in the realisation of the rights and wellbeing of children in Africa. Policy makers understand that in the African context

> the normative universality achieved in the definition and formulation of children's rights has to contend with diverse and varied cultural and traditional conceptions of childhood, its role, its rights and obligations.[110]

Oral African tradition has no definitive answer to the question: 'Who is a child?' Rather, the words 'child' or 'children' are used mainly in their biological, social and functional senses. In its biological sense, references to children in proverbs, folklore, myths, songs and poems are mainly related to a generic, perpetual and mutually interdependent relationship that exists between parents and their offspring. In this sense, childhood is seen basically as a relational and an operational concept – 'I am your father, and you are my child' - irrespective of age and status. African sayings, such as 'As you do for your ancestors, your children will do for you;'[111] 'A child is one blood with its father and its mother;'[112] 'When you follow behind your father, you learn to walk like him;'[113] 'When your mother is poor you do not leave her and go and make someone else your mother,'[114] use the word 'child' in the generic sense.

In the oral tradition of communities in Africa, childhood is synonymous with a period of learning. So, the answer to the question 'Who is a child'? could simply be: 'a child is a learner'. The following proverbs common to

---

110 W Ncube 'Prospects and challenges in Eastern and Southern Africa: The interplay between international human rights norms and domestic law, tradition and culture' in W Ncube (ed) *law, culture, tradition and children's rights in Eastern and Southern Africa* (1998) 5.

111 R Rattry 'The African child in proverb, folklore and facts' (1933) 6 *Journal of the International African Institute* 456.

112 As above.

113 http://afritorial.com/the-best-72-african-wise-proverbs/.

114 http://www.bellaonline.com/articles/art64042.asp.

many communities in Africa outline the reason and purpose for childhood as a period of learning and becoming: 'Train a child the way he should go and make sure you also go the same way;'[115] 'A child who is carried on the back will not know how far the journey is;'[116] 'What you help a child to love can be more important than what you help him to learn;'[117] 'It is the habit that a child forms at home, that follows them to their marriage;'[118] 'If a mother steals with a child strapped in the back what do you expect of the child;'[119] 'A child is what you put into him;'[120] 'One should punish a child the first time he comes home with a stolen egg, otherwise the day he returns home with a stolen ox, it will be too late;'[121] 'We desire to bequest two things to our children - the first one is roots; the other one is wings;'[122] 'Parents give birth to the body of their children, but not always to their characters;'[123] 'He who fears the crying of a child, will cry himself;'[124] and 'The youth walks faster than the elderly but the elderly knows the road.'[125]

It seems that who a child is in oral tradition is so obvious that the answer to the question: 'Who is a child?' seems to be: 'when you see a child, you will know.'

115 R Rattry 'The African child in proverb, folklore and facts' (1933) 6 *Journal of the International African Institute* 456.

116 As above.

117 http://www.bellaonline.com/articles/art64042.asp.

118 http://www.motherlandnigeria.com/proverbs.html.

119 http://www.allgreatquotes.com/african_proverbs4.shtml.

120 http://www.worldofproverbs.com/2012/03/child-is-what-you-put-into-him-african.html.

121 http://www.special-dictionary.com/proverbs/source/e/ethiopian_proverb/185569.htm.

122 http://www.bellaonline.com/articles/art64042.asp.

123 http://www.special-dictionary.com/proverbs/source/g/ganda_proverb/178594.htm.

124 R Rattry 'The African child in proverb, folklore and facts' (1933) 6 *Journal of the International African Institute* 456.

125 http://www.special-dictionary.com/proverbs/source/n/nilotic_proverb/163394.htm.

3.2.2. Autonomy rights in traditional Africa

According to de Jouvenal, 'social contract theories are views of childless men who must have forgotten their own childhood.'[126] A human rights regime is partly based on the idea of social contract. The debate as to whether human rights, as articulated in the International Bill of Rights, are similar or the same as conception of roles, responsibilities, duties and obligations in traditional African societies is on-going. The applicability of this contestation to children in Africa will be attempted in this section.

The concept of rights that insists that a right-holder is entitled to an indisputable claim; that such a claim is not contingent upon the goodwill or the charitable nature of anyone; that such a claim cannot validly be denied without giving the rights-holder access to a higher authority to vindicate that right, is predicated on a particular conception of personhood and society that is different from the one envisaged in traditional African societies.[127]

This conception of right is appropriate in an individualistic society in which the ultimate survival, happiness and progress of an individual member of society depends on the construction of a clear shield of defence and attack against other members of the society, individually or collectively. In such a society, the role of human rights is not necessarily to make the individual and her or his interests supreme, but to curtail the excesses of the society and to secure equality of weaknesses as well as strengths. Since society is as strong or as weak as its constituent members, a community of weak and disconnected individuals is also weak and disconnected socially. Human rights conceived in this sense cannot meaningfully be held against the community *per se*. Rights could legitimately, until recently, be held only against the state. The rationale is that states, as an artificial representation of common will, interests and good, if not constrained, could abuse this commonwealth. The human rights tool is one for the weak individual against a strong common representation. Since the state conceptually was a representative of its constituent individuals,

---

126 B de Jouvenal *The pure theory of politics* (1963) 45.

127 R Panikkar 'Is the notion of human rights a Western concept?' (1982) 30 *Diogenes* 75; see also J Cobbah 'African values and human rights debate: An African perspective' (1987) 9 *Human Rights Quarterly* 309.

the concept of rights inherently was a right against a state's excesses, as well as those of other members of that state.

The condition *sine qua non* for the operation of human rights, in the sense outlined above, is the existence of a powerless individual and a powerful artificial representation of individuals with an inherent tendency to exploit and abuse its position of representation. In such a society 'each man has to use his own power as he will himself, for the preservation of his own nature that is to say, of his own life…'[128] Therefore, to balance competing interests, there was a need to create another entity that represents only virtue and not any person – the courts - with the function of maintaining societal equilibrium.

The balancing of competing interests is a feature of all societies, but how societies go about this differs from one society to another. No method of maintaining societal equilibrium, therefore, should be superior to the other. What matters is whether competing interests have been fairly balanced. Pannikkar is of the view that '[n]o culture, tradition, ideology, or religion can today speak for the whole of humankind, let alone solve its problem. Dialogues and intercourse leading to a mutual fecundation are necessary.'[129]

In traditional African societies, there are common core features of how different African society is organised to secure a fair balance of the competing goals of their members. They did so by linking individuals in a common web of relationships, so that what touches an individual invariably touches everyone. The individual was simply a part of the whole. This situation is expressed metaphorically in the Bible as follows:

> for even as the body is one and yet has many members, and all the members of the body, though they are many, are one body … if the foot says, 'Because I am not a hand, I am not a part of the body,' it is not for this reason any the less a part of the body. If the whole body were an eye, where would the hearing be? On the contrary, it is much truer that the members of the body which seem to be weaker

---

128 T Hobbes '*Of man, being the first part of Leviathan: Of the first and second natural laws, and of contract' (1588-1679) XIV The Harvard Classics* (1909-14) available at: http://www.bartleby.com/34/5/14.html.

129 R Panikkar 'Is the notion of human rights a Western concept?' (1982) 30 *Diogenes* 75.

> are necessary; and those members of the body which we deem less honourable, on these we bestow more abundant honour, and our less presentable members become much more presentable.[130]

In traditional African society equality was primarily a functional concept in the sense that 'the working of the human body or of the universe itself requires equality of its parts.'[131] The equality of the whole was the equality of each. The interests of an individual should not be at odds with that of the community but be adequately secured within the network of social relationships and social structure. The autonomy of an individual's action is protected within that network.

The difference in thought and style between a society organised around the notion of human rights and that organised around African traditional values is reasonably wide but is not irreconcilable on the basis of mutual respect, trust and understanding. The difference, according to Turner, between a society organised on the basis of Western philosophy and one predicated on African traditional values is that the former is:

> Liberal and individualist, the other "communitarian" and "holist." The one sees the individual, and his freedom, his interest and his projects at the centre of the field, society and social relationships as marginal to the hard irreducible core of his individuality, the other starts with the social relationships themselves and sees the individual as a function of them, regards the individual not as an independent being related only externally to others, but as a being whose whole nature is constituted by the character of the social relations in which he stands.[132]

Both styles of thought involve respect, restraint, responsibility and reciprocity, but the sources and goals of these values are different. One is rooted in the

---

130 1 Corinthians 12: 12. Scripture taken from the New American Standard Bible®, Copyright © 1960,1962,1963,1968,1971,1972,1973,1975,1977,1995 by The Lockman Foundation.

131 G Frug *City making: Building communities without building walls* (1999) 30.

132 J Cobbah 'African values and human rights debate: An African perspective' (1987) 9 *Human Rights Quarterly* 309.

individual and designed to protect the individual; the other is rooted in the community and designed to protect the individual in a community.

The conception of the place and role of the individual in traditional African societies has implications for the roles and duties of children in Africa. It is possible to argue that in traditional African communities, children's needs for protection and care are provided for within the framework of parental and communal duties and obligations rather than from a human or children's rights framework. There is evidence of happy and healthy children that are secure within this web of duties and obligations.

In his report to the Minister of Colonies in 1935, Governor General Brévié, described West Africans' attitudes toward children in the following terms:

> The very young black child has such an importance in the family that many observers remain surprised by it: one gives in to all of his caprices, arrested by the little personality that is awakening, this spirit of the child that so contains so much of the unfamiliar and which, for the black as for many others, but for all of our blacks, provokes an admiration that is a bit troubled.[133]

Parents and communities take care of children not because the law requires so, but because it is in the best interests of the children, the family and communities to do so. The culture, traditions or customs of the people require this. Traditional mechanisms for ensuring the welfare of children exist in many communities in Africa, but not as a matter of rights. These traditional mechanisms protect the best interests of children within the limits available to them. These communal constraints are generally accepted mechanisms of community control by an adult over children.

The traditional control mechanisms are running down due to different factors. Increasingly, it is becoming difficult to rely solely on these traditional values to secure the wellbeing of the young and vulnerable children in Africa. A mechanism that recognises whatever existing virtues are left in traditional African values and complements these with what is good in the human rights

133 L McNee 'The languages of childhood: The discursive construction of childhood and colonial policy in French West Africa' (2001) *African Studies Quarterly* http://www.africa.ufl.edu/asq/v7/v7i4a2.htm.

frameworks is needed in Africa to ensure that the best interests of children continue to be promoted and protected.

It should be noted that the frameworks for analysis, as outlined in the methodology for this book, are: 'Who is a child?', autonomy rights, the 'best interests' principle, and child participation. In this section, roles and responsibilities are used instead of rights because in the course of the book it became apparent that although there is sufficient conceptual support for the position that children have rights in traditional communities in Africa, the author could not find sufficient evidence indicating that such concepts of duties and obligations relied on by traditional communities in Africa are in consonance with human rights as espoused in international and regional instruments.

Children in traditional African communities have a claim to special care and protection arising from their vulnerability, special entitlements and privileges rather than on the basis of rights as understood in the in the CRC or the African Children's Charter. Although the outcomes of a rights regime or obligations and duties regime, if implemented, might be the same, the process and power inherent in the two regimes might not be the same. In discussing childhood in traditions in Africa, therefore, roles, responsibilities and privileges, rather than rights, best highlight the understanding of childhood. Oral traditions, as a subset of African cultures, demonstrate this responsibility and duty-based understanding of childhood.

The roles and responsibilities of children, as portrayed through oral traditions in Africa, are those of respecting elders, being socially and culturally responsible, reciprocating received care with services, obedience and loyalty, being emotionally restrained, and reproducing the cultural values and family lineage. Since 'a child is everyone's child' and 'it takes a whole village to raise a child,'[134] these roles and responsibilities accrue to the family as well as to the society. A brief look at what oral traditions say about respect,

134 http://www.afriprov.org/index.php/african-proverb-of-the-month/23-1998proverbs/137-november-1998-proverb.html.

responsibility, reciprocity and reproduction is necessary in order to appreciate the understanding of childhood in traditional African communities.

Respect: The cardinal value of a good childhood as depicted in oral tradition in Africa is respect for elders, peers and self. Respect is considered essential to learning and learning is viewed as the foundation of a successful childhood. What are to be respected are humanity, age, knowledge and wisdom, because 'what an old man sees sitting down, a young man cannot see standing up.'[135] Respect has results, such as 'When a child knows how to wash his hands thoroughly, he and his elders can partake of food together;'[136] but 'When a child does not listen to the words of its father or mother, it partakes of food in which there is no salt.'[137] Respect begs respect. Oral traditions show that respect is earned. Thus, the saying: 'Respect a little child, and let it respect you.'[138]

Responsibility: Oral traditions depict an ideal childhood as that which is responsible. Responsibility is seen and treated in oral traditions as a normative as well as a functional tool. In the former sense, children are expected to live responsibly. This could mean being neat, hardworking, disciplined, altruistic, and obedient. In the latter sense, children are expected to take care of their younger siblings, family members and of societal needs, depending on their social status. Even though it is the duty of parents and communities to instil these qualities in children, it is ultimately the responsibility of children to play these roles. Thus, the saying: 'Parents give birth to the body of their children, but not always to their characters.'[139]

Reciprocity: The sustaining principle for individual, family and communal survival, as seen through the lens of oral traditions in Africa, is reciprocity. The family and community are traditionally obliged to care for and protect

---

135 I Menkiti 'Person and community in African traditional thought' in R Wright (ed) *African philosophy* (1984) 171.

136 R Rattry 'The African child in proverb, folklore and facts' (1933) 6 *Journal of the International African Institute* 456.

137 As above.

138 As above.

139 http://www.bellaonline.com/articles/art69184.asp.

children in their time of vulnerability so that when members of the family or community become frail, children will, in turn, care for and protect them. That is one reason why it is said that 'A child's ring does not fit an elder's finger, but as for his (the child's) food it goes into the elder's mouth.'[140] This intergenerational transaction was not only a social security scheme that was mutually beneficial, but also a training field for a responsible life. Thus, 'when a woman has ten children, there is nothing that happens in the night that she does not know about.'[141]

Restraint: Seen through the wisdom of oral traditions, childhood is a period to acquire mastery over emotional instincts. The emphasis differs between the sexes. Control over emotions of fear, sex, selfishness, pride, laziness and so on marked the dividing line between childhood and adulthood. Different rituals were conceptualised to improve emotional control and enhance restraint. A number of sayings in traditional Africa are woven around these themes, a good example being: 'A child which is to turn out any good is not reared entirely on a beautiful mat.'[142] Another saying admonishes: 'When your child dances badly, tell him saying, "your dancing is not good;" don't say to him, "dance just as you want to;"[143] or 'If a child keeps saying "it is my father's, let me take it; it is my mother's, let me take it" that brings a child to stealing.'[144]

Reproduction: Families, communities and cultures that do not have children become extinct; having children is not seen as the responsibility and wish of an individual or a family in traditional societies. Traditional communities have in place mechanisms to ensure that every individual or family perpetuates itself. For example, the custom of 'putting a child in another womb' in a case where a woman is infertile or dies without having a child: a child may be 'put into the womb' of another woman or, if it is a man, a member of the family might impregnate his wife on his behalf to provide a child. Another example of these

140 R Rattry 'The African child in proverb, folklore and facts' (1933) 6 *Journal of the International African Institute* 456.

141 http://www.allgreatquotes.com/african_proverbs9.shtml.

142 Rattry, n 136.

143 As above.

144 AS above.

mechanisms is the so-called 'ghost marriages', in which a widow enters into a procreational relationship in the name of her deceased husband and grants paternity posthumously to the dead husband.

Sayings such as 'A loving wife is often blessed with the birth of a tenth child;'[145] 'One is born, one dies; the land grows;'[146] 'Birth is the only remedy against death;'[147] 'We will be grateful to flowers only if they have born fruits;'[148] 'The woman who gives birth to a child is like the banana tree that breaks under the weight of its fruit;'[149] are indicative of the role of reproduction in the conception of childhood by traditional communities in Africa. The emphasis on reproduction shapes the understanding of childhood in at least two ways. First, it emphasises that children are precious and should be cherished. Second, it underscores that childhood is more meaningful if it reproduces itself.

The above examples of oral traditions in Africa indicate that African communities see and treat the relationship between children and their societies as an exchange of responsibilities. Society must act in the interest of children, and children must conduct themselves in the best interests of their communities. This conception of childhood in traditional Africa informs and influences the conception of childhood in customary laws in Africa.

African customary law has occupied a central place in the regulation of children's lives for hundreds of years.[150] The recognition of cultural rights by international human rights and, increasingly, by constitutions in African countries [151] represents a perpetuation of the influence of custom on children's

145 http://www.bellaonline.com/articles/art69184.asp.

146 http://www.bellaonline.com/articles/art69184.asp.

147 http://www.bellaonline.com/articles/art69184.asp.

148 http://www.bellaonline.com/articles/art69184.asp.

149 http://www.bellaonline.com/articles/art69184.asp.

150 P Martin & M Buyi 'An exploratory book on the interplay between African customary law and practices and children's protection rights in South Africa' (2011) available at http://resourcecentre.savethechildren.se/sites/default/files/documents/5383.pdf.

151 See K Cuskelley Customs and constitutions: State recognition of customary law around the world (2011) 6. International Union for the Conservation of Nature and Natural Resources. Available at www. https://portals.iucn.org/library/efiles/documents/2011-101.pdf. According to Cuskelley 'The highest level of recognition of customary law is found in African constitutions, both in terms of the number of countries with relevant provisions and the breadth of aspects of customary law covered. Of 52 African constitutions analysed, 33 referred to customary law in some form. As discussed below, there is a high level of recognition

rights.[152] However, the relationship between custom and children rights, as seen from the human rights perspective, is that of a master and a servant in which custom services human rights and when there is conflict human rights prevail.[153]

Customary laws are normative transformation of practices socially acceptable and considered obligatory by members of a particular group, community or society. Such laws are generally unwritten and serve as an oral repertoire of a people's norms and values. Customary law is said to be either official or living. It is official when presented as a 'rigid and inflexible system of fossilised rules written down by white colonialists and enforced by white judges;'[154] and it is living if it represents presently accepted social practices of the people.

The difference between fossilized and living customary law is important when discussing children's rights within the customary regime, because the 'practices of contemporary customary law are often more accommodating to women's [and children's] needs than the official customary law.'[155] The emphasis and preference for living customary law is because 'one of the most striking features [of customary law] is its flexibility; it appears to have been always subject to motives of expediency, and it shows unquestionable adaptability to altered circumstances without entirely losing its character.'[156]

---

of traditional and customary institutions, as well as a broad recognition of customary law in the courts and relating to land. At the weakest level of recognition of customary law, a large number of African constitutions have provisions relating to the protection of culture or tradition'.

152 See for example The Universal Declaration of Human Rights Article 27, the International Covenant on Economic, Social and Cultural Rights Article 15, the African Charter on Human and People's Rights Article 17 recognise the African Children's Charter art 12, and the Convention on the Rights of the Child article 30.

153 See, for example, articles 1(3) and 21 of the African Children's Charter require that:
'Any custom, tradition, cultural or religious practise that is inconsistent with the rights, duties and obligations contained in the present Charter ...to the extent of such inconsistency be discouraged; and [that] 'State parties ... take all appropriate measures to eliminate harmful social and cultural practices affecting the welfare, dignity, normal growth and development of the child and in particular ...customs and practices (a) prejudicial to the health or life of the child, and (b) discriminatory to the child on the grounds of sex or other status.'

154 P De Vos 'Time for rethink on traditional leaders' (2010) available at: Constitutionally speaking: http://constitutionallyspeaking.co.za/time-for-rethink-on-traditionalleaders/.

155 E Curran & E Bonthuys 'Customary law and domestic violence in rural South African communities (2004) Centre for the Book of Violence and Reconciliation available at http://www.csvr.org.za/docs/gender/customarylawand.pdf.

156 Osborne CJ in *Lewis v. Bankole* (1908) 1 N.L.R.81. pp. 100-101.

The CRC and the African Children's Charter confer children with the right to 'participate freely [and fully] in cultural life' and put the obligation on the state to ensure that children are 'not to be deprived of the right to enjoy [their] own culture.'[157] These rights and obligations have both negative and positive implications. They entitle the rights holder to non-interference and constrain the state to desist from putting obstacles in the way of the right holder to practice cultural rights.[158] Positively, the state, individuals and communities actively promote the conservation, preservation, strengthening and development of positive African cultural practices, values and customs.[159] The state and its actors are obligated to protect and preserve positive past practices and also to develop them. This development 'implies some departure from past practice - a change/evolution or forward movement on a continuum.'[160]

Customary law is conditionally received into formal law and, by implication, human rights law. Customary law is only law if it is 'not . . . repugnant to natural justice, equity and good conscience.'[161] According to the African Children's Charter, 'any custom, tradition, cultural or religious practice that is inconsistent with the rights, duties and obligations contained in the present Charter. ...to the extent of such inconsistency be discouraged.'[162]

The unequal relationship that exists between human rights law and customary values of communities is problematic in that it entails a value judgment as to what is repugnant or inconsistent, and mainly according to the values and conscience of one side. Seen in this light, the consequences of human rights law are to create cultures in its own image and breathe its own life into customary practices. In communities in which some areas of human rights-

157 Article 12 of the African Children's Charter.

158 African Children's Charter, Articles 11(2); International Covenant on Economic, Social and Cultural Rights, Article 15(2); African Charter on Human and Peoples' Rights, Articles 17(3), 22(1) and 29(7).

159 L Mwambene & J Sloth-Nielsen 'Benign accommodation? Ukuthwala, "forced marriage" and the South African Children's Act' (2011) 11 *African Human Rights Law Journal* 1.

160 As above.

161 Osborne CJ in *Lewis v. Bankole* (1908) 1 N.L.R.81. pp. 100-101.

162 Article 21 of the African Children's Charter.

friendly values may not be discernible, the transformative mission of human rights could be identity altering and socially dislocative.[163]

Customary laws vary within and between communities in Africa. Such variation can be attributed to various factors, such as origin, history, language, proximity, social structure and economy. However, similarities in philosophical thought and cultural value systems within and between communities across Africa make for core commonalities in customary law in Africa.[164] Some scholars prefer to call these common features African customary law.[165] Some of the common features have bearing on the rights, the best interests and the participation of children in Africa.

How customary law sees and treats children, to a large extent, is determined by the living customary values and practices. The issues customary laws deal with in many African communities range across the extended family, damages for extra-marital pregnancy, decision making, communal ethics, dispute resolution and harmful cultural practices, inheritance and custody of children. A number of children's laws in Africa have recognized the intersection between culture and the law.[166]

Parental care, custody, inheritance, the best welfare of the child, and the family environment dominate the conversation between child law and customary law in Africa. For instance, the South African Children's Act and its Ghanaian counterpart define the family environment of the child to include extended

---

163 D Waldman 'A situational analysis of human rights effects on gender justice' (2011) unpublished book submitted to the University of Walden; see also A An-Na'im 'Human rights and Islamic identity in France and Uzbekistan: Mediation of the local and global' (2000) 22 *Human Rights Quarterly* 906.

164 H Courlander *A treasury of African folklore: The oral literature, traditions, myths, legends, epics, tales, recollections, wisdom, sayings and humor of Africa* (1975) 3 where he observes that 'Even though Africa is wide, it shares common ideas, themes, suppositions and truth in certain areas.' See also M Makgoba *Mokoko, the makgoba affair: A reflection on transformation* (1997)197; A Shutte *Philosophy for Africa* (1993) 46; A Ottino *The universe within a Balinese village through its ritual practices* (2000) 275; G Smitherman *Talking and testifying: The language of black American* (1977) 75; and J Anderson *Conjure in African American society* (2005) 144.

165 M Makgoba *Mokoko, the makgoba affair: A reflection on transformation* (1997) 197; A Shutte *Philosophy for Africa* (1993) 46; A Ottino *The universe within a Balinese village through its ritual practices* (2000) 275; G Smitherman *Talking and testifying: The language of black American* (1977) 75; and J Anderson *Conjure in African American society* (2005) 144.

166 C Chimonga 'African customary law and children's rights: Intersections and domains in a new era' in J Sloth-Nielsen (ed) *Children's rights in Africa: A legal perspective* (2008) 71.

family members and further state in a custody case that this family structure should be taken into consideration.[167]

3.2.3. The best interests of the child in traditional African society

The notion of the best interestss of the child, with very few exceptions, is influenced, nurtured and even created by the culture and traditions of a people. Since cultural goals for childbearing and childrearing differ from culture to culture, what is in the best interests of the children vary, in some sense, from one community to another. As a result, the best interests's consideration is more of a process than an outcome-oriented mechanism. In a strong communal culture like in Africa, the 'best interests' principle might ideally emphasize the cultural wellbeing of the child, social intelligence and responsibility, family harmony, communal acceptance and integration. In other settings, academic intelligence, competition and individual independence might be the goal.

The CRC Committee considers the best interests of the child as the 'guiding principle in the application of the Convention.'[168] In theory, the concept of the 'best interests' of the child principle should be an 'empty universal' concept that is flexible and sensitive enough to cultural variations; in practice:

> [The Committee] has not used the principle as a vehicle by which to permit a degree of sensitivity to cultural factors, in situations in which such leeway might be appropriate and consistent with the obligations contained in the Convention.[169]

The 'best interests' principle, as used by the CRC Committee, is an advocacy tool to push for more resource allocation to sectors that benefit children, a guiding principle for all government activities that concern children, as well as a transformative mechanism to change specific and targeted issues affecting

---

167 As above.

168 R Hodgkin & P Newell *Implementation handbook for the Convention on the Rights of the Child* (2007) 36.

169 P Alston & B Gilmour-Walsh *The best interests of the child: Towards a synthesis of children's rights and cultural norms* (1996) 17; see also S Harris-Short 'International human rights law: Imperialist, inept and ineffective? Cultural relativism and the UN Convention on the Rights of the Child' (2003) 25 *Human Rights Quarterly* 130;

children.[170] These specific issues include juvenile justice, child labour, inter-country adoption, corporal punishment and child marriage.[171] To appreciate the difference in the understanding of what is in the best interests of children between the CRC Committee and traditional African societies, it is apt to examine three specific issues that the CRC Committee has referred to with respect to Africa: corporal punishment, child marriage, and child labour.

3.2.3.1. Corporal punishment and the best interests of the child in traditional Africa

Corporal punishment is a specific issue that brings to the surface the content of the best interests of the child in the view of the CRC Committee and traditional value system in Africa. The Committee defines corporal punishment as follows:

> any punishment in which physical force is used and intended to cause some degree of pain or discomfort, however light. Most involves hitting ("smacking", "slapping", "spanking" or any punishment which belittles, humiliates, denigrates, scapegoats, threatens, scares or ridicules the child.) children, with the hand or with an implement - a whip, stick, belt, shoe, wooden spoon, etc.[172]

The CRC Committee differentiates disciplinary measures from physical punishment and allows the use of 'reasonable restraints' only in 'exceptional circumstance' wherein 'the principle of the minimum necessary use of force for the shortest necessary period of time must always apply.'[173] The rationale for the CRC Committee's opposition to corporal punishment is:

170 P Alston & B Gilmour-Walsh *The best interests of the child: Towards a synthesis of children's rights and cultural norms* (1996) 35.

171 As above, 42.

172 The CRC Committee General Comment 8 (2006) *The right of the child to protection from corporal punishment and other cruel or degrading forms of punishment* (arts. 19; 28, para 2; and 37, inter alia) CRC/C/GC/8 2 March 2007 available at http://www2.ohchr.org/english/bodies/crc/comments.htm.

173 The CRC Committee General Comment 8 (2006) *The right of the child to protection from corporal punishment and other cruel or degrading forms of punishment* (arts. 19; 28, para 2; and 37, inter alia) CRC/C/GC/8 2 March 2007 Available athttp://www2.ohchr.org/english/bodies/crc/comments.htm.

> [T]he practice directly conflicts with the equal and inalienable rights of children to respect for their human dignity and physical integrity. The distinct nature of children, their initial dependent and developmental state, their unique human potential as well as their vulnerability, all demand the need for more, rather than less, legal and other protection from all forms of violence.[174]

The view of the CRC Committee finds favour with major international and regional human rights treaties.[175] However, in some instances, it is incompatible with the childrearing practice in the traditional value system of many African communities.[176] No conclusive evidence links physical punishment with negative outcomes in child development.[177]

The Western model of childrearing, as represented in the CRC, regards corporal punishment as not in the best interests of the child. A number of traditional communities in many parts of Africa hold the view that 'sparing the rod spoils the child;'[178] a view corroborated by the biblical injunction that '[he] that spareth his rod hateth his son: but he that loveth him chasteneth him betimes.'[179] It is believed in traditional Africa that 'he, who fears the

---

174 The CRC Committee General Comment 8 (2006) *The right of the child to protection from corporal punishment and other cruel or degrading forms of punishment* (arts. 19; 28, para 2; and 37, inter alia) CRC/C/GC/8 2 March 2007 Available athttp://www2.ohchr.org/english/bodies/crc/comments.htm (accessed on 25 September 2013).

175 See article 19 of the CRC; Articles 11, 16, 19, 20, 21 and 31 of the African Children's Charter

176 M Damien 'Attitudes of stakeholders towards physical punishment on pupils of international and national schools in Kampala District, Uganda' (2012) 2 *World Journal of Education* 96; P Ebigbo 'Street children: The core of child abuse and neglect in Nigeria' (2003) 13 *Children, Youth and Environments*; J Korbin 'Culture and child maltreatment: Cultural competence and beyond' (2002) 8 *Child Abuse and Neglect: The International Journal* 637; J Korbin 'Social cultural factors in child maltreatment: A neighbourhood approach' in G Melton & F Barry (Eds) *Protecting children from abuse and neglect* (1994) 182.

177 There are contradictory scientific positions on the actual impact of corporal punishment on the wellbeing of children. Compare M Straus *et al* 'Spanking by parents and subsequent antisocial behavior of children' (1997) 151 *Archives of Paediatrics and Adolescent Medicine* 761 with R Larzelere *et al* 'Do nonphysical punishments reduce antisocial behavior more than spanking? A comparison using the strongest previous causal evidence against spanking' (2010) 10 *BMC Paediatrics* 10 for example, the former claims there is a strong link between corporal punishment and antisocial behaviour, the latter said the outcomes could be explained by reason of other factors than just corporal punishment.

178 This saying in Proverbs 13:24 encapsulate the reasoning in traditional African communities. See M Damien 'Attitudes of stakeholders towards physical punishment on pupils of international and national schools in Kampala District, Uganda' (2012) 2 *World Journal of Education* 96.

179 Proverbs 13:24. the King James Version of the Bible.

crying of a child, will cry himself;'[180] chastisement is seen not as a punishment for wrongdoing but as a tool for inculcating good character in the child and, therefore, it is in the child's best interests.[181]

The disciplining of children was not unregulated in traditional Africa. The society put in place mechanisms to guard against abuses and to promote reasonable chastisement.[182] The guiding principles of these mechanisms can be distilled from oral traditions such as the following: 'when a child cries, he is not punished by being fastened to a log;'[183] 'the child who goes for water is the one to break the pot;'[184] 'you cannot beat a child to take away its tears;'[185] 'a child is an axe; when it cuts you, you still pick it up and put it on your shoulder.'[186] There is considerable difference in the understanding of punishment between human rights and traditional or cultural value systems in Africa on the issue of corporal punishment.

The clash of human right norms with strongly held cultural norms calls for a mechanism to regulate the contestation. The provisions of human rights treaties, such as the CRC or the African Children's Charter, trump inconsistent cultural practice and value systems.[187] But on what authority do the human rights norms rest their claim to superiority? For instance, the legitimacy of the African Children's Charter is derived from international human rights treaties: there are communities in Africa that might not consider these sources as providing a legitimate basis for challenging or changing their traditional norms.

---

180 Proverbs 13: 24; the King James Version of the Bible.

181 P Ebigbo Street 'Children: The core of child abuse and neglect in Nigeria (2003) 13 *Children, Youth and Environments1*

182 M Last 'Children and the experience of violence: Contrasting cultures of punishment in Northern Nigeria (2000) 70 *Africa: Journal of the International African Institute* 359.

183 R Rattry 'The African child in proverb, folklore and facts' (1933) 6 *Journal of the International African Institute* 456.

184 R Rattry 'The African child in proverb, folklore and facts' (1933) 6 *Journal of the International African Institute* 456.

185 http://www.bellaonline.com/articles/art64042.asp.

186 Sayings usual & unusual: A classified list of sayings and a source of bon mots (2007) Wordsworth reference Series.

187 Articles 1(3) and 21 of the African Charter on the Rights and Welfare of the Child.

It is possible to justify corporal punishment as it is to ban the practice. Just as many scholars will agree that corporal punishment is not in the best interests of children, others would argue that a "'smack' is not violence, does not inflict injury, is not abuse or maltreatment.'[188] Human rights should not close off the debate, and human rights norms, as a basis for policy making, should accommodate other norms and value systems. In some cases, the challenge to human rights norms might not be inherent in those norms but rather how policy makers address conflicts within value systems. The concept of positive discipline is not alien to traditional values in Africa. It is easier to use these values to counter the abuse of children.

3.2.3.2. Child marriage and the best interests of the child in traditional Africa

In a number of communities in Africa puberty signifies readiness for marriage. If a girl who has reached puberty refuses to get married, she can be banished her from the community.[189] In such communities, girls are faced with the choice of being married and respected or refusing to get married and be disowned by the community.[190] The emotional and physical challenges associated with such arrangements are obvious. Families face a hard choice. In her ethnographic work among the Maasai, Archambault captured the dilemma of a father:

> We tried to educate all our children but it depended on our cows and goats and poverty. . . I have had children in six different schools, so I am a very good man for education. The problem is [too few] animals.[191]

Discussing and analysing the phenomenon of child marriage on the basis of a human rights violation may strip these practices of 'their social meanings and

188 M Freeman 'Culture, childhood and rights' (2011) 5 *Family in Law* 16. For example, in England the defense of reasonable chastisement is allowed if a child is only assaulted, without actual bodily harm as a result. See Children's Act 2004, para 58.

189 C Archambault 'Ethnographic empathy and the social context of rights: "Rescuing" Maasai girls from early marriage' (2011) 113 *American Anthropologist* 632.

190 As above.

191 As above.

subjectivities and conceal the ambiguities and contingencies that are at the heart of acts of injustice.'[192]

In a broader context, child marriage might be seen as a family's social security plan to secure their daughter's future and interests by placing her in trusted and well-connected families; the reason for marriage might be to provide girls with economic and social security.[193] Instead of seeing the family as trying to advance their selfish interests at the expense of the girl, the family could be seen as concerned and caring in a time of

> [c]ultural change and growing poverty and marginalization. Land and resource fragmentation and dispossession, increasing climactic instability, continued state neglect, and rising population pressure have weakened the viability of pastoralism as an exclusive livelihood practice for the majority of young people.[194]

The practice of child marriage could be seen as mutually beneficial and intrinsically fluid, permeable and unbounded in the context of economic, cultural and traditional issues, and not as a violation of human rights.

These arguments cannot justify the act of child marriage but are to illustrate the point that what is in a child's best interests are more meaningful if seen in the cultural context in which the child lives. Local economic and socio-political factors play roles in a community's perception of what is in their children's best interests. The CRC Committee does not see such an approach useful; child marriage is a harmful cultural practice, an age and health-oriented issue that must be eradicated through awareness raising, legislation and programmes.[195]

It could be argued that child marriage is not in all its manifestations simply a harmful cultural practice; for example, the arranged marriage of a child aged 9 to a child aged 16 is not the same as a 17-year-old girl who falls in love

---

192 As above.

193 Archambault, n 189, 632.

194 C Archambault 'Ethnographic empathy and the social context of rights: "Rescuing" Maasai girls from early marriage' (2011) 113 *American Anthropologist* 632.

195 See Committee on the Rights of the Child, General Comment No 4, 2003, and CRC/GC/2003/4.

with a 20 year old man and wants to marry. In communities where there are few options for earning a livelihood and no chance of education, the law vitiates the free and informed consent of such a girl without offering her an alternative. In countries where the age of sexual consent is below 18, is it reasonable to expect a girl to lawfully consent to sex but not to marriage? With respect to this age group a flexible, case by case and context-specific approach can be adopted to determine whether or not it will be in the girl's best interests to marry a man of her choice or of her own age.

3.2.3.3. Child labour and the best interests of the child in traditional Africa

In traditional African communities, the art of growing up, learning and working are intertwined.[196] Age and gender-appropriate working skills and ethics are considered in the best interests of the child.[197] In communities that survive on hard and sometimes hazardous work, the best way of training children in the art of survival is to train them in that work. For instance, some scholars have attributed the resilience demonstrated by children in Africa in the face of HIV/AIDS pandemic to the training children receive in communities.[198] Some of this training was not undertaken within the framework of human rights.

Child work or child labour[199] is a contentious issue that highlights the permeability of the principle of the 'best interests' of the child and the factors

196 B Rwezaura 'Law, culture and children's rights in Eastern and Southern Africa: Contemporary challenges and present day dilemmas' in Ncube W (eds) *Law, culture, tradition and children's rights*(1998) 289; B Rweraura 'Competing "images" of childhood in the social and legal systems of contemporary sub-Saharan Africa' (1998) *12 International Journal of Law, Polity and the Family* 253 and B Rwezaura 'The best interests of the child in changing social and economic contexts of sub-Saharan Africa' in Alston P The best interests of the child: Reconciling culture and human rights (1994) 82.

197 B Rwezaura 'The best interests of the child in changing social and economic contexts of sub-Saharan Africa' in Alston P The best interests of the child: Reconciling culture and human rights (1994) 82.

198 See for example T Rochat & Hough 'Enhancing resilience in children affected by HIV and AIDS: Children's views and experiences of resilience enhancing family and community practices' (2007) Child, Youth, Family and Social Development Human Sciences Book Council Available at http://www.childhope.org.uk/wcore/showdoc.asp?id=1098.

199 There is no conclusive definition and clear distinction between the concepts of child labour and child work. There are two main conventions that regulated child labour. These are: the Minimum Age Convention no.138 of 1973 and the Worst Forms of Child Labour Convention no.182 of 1999. The Minimum Age Convention no.138 of 1973 does not explicitly define child labour. The International Labour Organisation defines 'child labour as work that "is mentally, physically, socially or morally dangerous and harmful to

that determine its content from culture to culture. Most of the work children engage in, in traditional communities, could be deemed not to be in the best interests of children in a human rights framework.[200] Child-led organisations have asked for a right to work because children have responsibilities and need an income to meet those responsibilities.[201] In some rural communities, these income-generating activities are not child-friendly.[202] In situations where children are forced by their living experience to generate income, if decent working conditions are not within their grasp, it is problematic to ascertain whether stopping children from working is, in the short-term, in the best interests of these children. Sometimes, in the spirit of child participation, children[203] should be allowed to decide what they can do to meet their immediate needs. The understanding of different communities and the context in which childhood is lived in many communities in Africa might indicate a level of difference in the understanding of child work in traditional communities and child labour as described in human rights instruments.[204]

The concept of work is a cultural concept.[205] Work serves different cultural purposes. Beyond livelihood, work is an important component to becoming

---

children; and interferes with their schooling by: 1) depriving them of the opportunity to attend school; 2) obliging them to leave school prematurely; or 3) requiring them to attempt to combine school attendance with excessively long and heavy work'. Article 3 of this Convention prohibits work for anyone under 18, work which by its nature or circumstances are likely to harm, the health, compromise safety or morals of young persons

200 S Okyere 'Children's participation in prohibited work in Ghana and its implications for the Convention on the Rights of the Child' in A Imoh & N Ansell (eds) *Children's lives in an era of children's rights: The progress of the Convention on the Rights of the Child in Africa* (2014) 92.

201 The African Movement of Working Children and Youth was established among other things to advocate for the rights of children and young people to engage in income generating activities. See http://maejt.org/page%20anglais/English%20about%20us%20objectives.htm.

202 T Nhenga-Chakarisa 'Who does the law seek to protect and from what? The application of international law on child labour in an African context' (2010) 10 *African Human Rights Journal* 161.

203 For example children aged 15-17.

204 T Bennett 'Human rights and the African cultural tradition' (1993) 22 *Transformation* 40; J Cobbah 'African values and the human rights debate: An African perspective' (1987) 9 *Human Rights Quarterly* 309; and T Nhenga-Chakarisa 'Who does the law seek to protect and from what? The application of international law on child labour in an African context' (2010) 10 *African Human Rights Journal* 161.

205 S Schwartz 'A Theory of cultural values and some implications for work' (1999) 48 *Applied Psychology: An International Review* 23; R Fernández & A Fogli 'Culture: An empirical investigation of beliefs, work, and fertility' (2006a) *NBER Working Paper* No. 11268; A Greif 'Cultural beliefs, and the organization of society: A historical and theoretical reflection on collectivist and individualist societies' (1994) 102 *Journal of Political Economy* 912; see generally A Greif 'Institutions: Theory and history. Comparative and historical institutional analysis' (2005); L Guiso *et al* 'Does culture affect economic outcomes' (2006) 20 *Journal of Economic Perspectives* 23; G Mailath & A Postlewaite 'The social context of economic decisions' (2003)

a 'full person' and, therefore, an acceptable and responsible individual in traditional African communities. Work is also a pedagogical platform by which social intelligence and responsibility, as well as harmony and collaboration, are taught.[206] Work could show an individual as being mature. Traditional African communities believe that the ability and willingness to work is progressively acquired.[207] Denying children work in traditional communities would be seen to mean robbing them of a future and a means of respectable livelihood and, therefore, not in their best interests.[208] Whatever has a use can be abused. Work for children has been abused using traditional mechanisms. An appropriate solution to the abuses of work cannot effectively be provided without efficiently using traditional values and systems.

Oral traditions in Africa reflect cultures that, at least in theory, considered the interest of children as paramount. The following sayings could be considered as allowing for a consideration of what is good for children: 'no one sends a child up aloft and then knocks away the ladder from beneath him;'[209] 'an elder does not roast a hot stone and place it in the hand of a child;'[210] 'when an old woman is hungry she says, 'roast something for the children that they may eat.''[211] There is evidence that cultural norms and practices in Africa took into consideration the wellbeing of children. The danger with leaving the best interests of the child to be culturally determined in terms of a process as well as an outcome is to say that culture becomes the investigator, the prosecutor and the judge of what is good for children.

---

1 *Journal of the European Economic Association* 354 and C Reimers 'Cultural differences in labor force participation among married women' (1985) 75 *American Economic Review Papers and Proceedings* 251.

206 S Schwartz 'A Theory of cultural values and some implications for work' (1999) 48 *Applied Psychology: An International Review* 23.

207 T Nhenga-Chakarisa 'Who does the law seek to protect and from what? The application of international law on child labour in an African context' (2010) 10 *African Human Rights Journal* 161.

208 R Fernández & A Fogli 'Culture: An empirical investigation of beliefs, work, and fertility' (2006a) *NBER Working Paper* No. 11268.

209 R Rattry 'The African child in proverb, folklore and facts' (1933) 6 *Journal of the International African Institute* 456.

210 As above.

211 http://cogweb.ucla.edu/Discourse/Proverbs/Ashanti.html.

What is really in the best interests of children? Is it what the culture says or what the law says or what a judge says, or a combination of these? Whichever choice is made as to the regime that best protects the best interests of children, it must contend with the difficulties involved in determining what is in the immediate, medium and long-term best interests of the child as an individual or as a category. In collective and consensual societies, the distinction between the best interests of the child/ children or that of the family or community may not be as clear as it is in individualistic-oriented societies. Even though what is in the best interests of children were largely determined by their families and communities, there is evidence in the oral tradition that children participate in some decision making and, therefore, in determining what is in their best interests.

3.2.4. Child participation in traditional Africa

Traditional communities have mechanisms for fostering children's participation in decision-making. These mechanisms included songs, proverbs and joking relationships. Evidence suggests that these participation mechanisms facilitate children's inputs into family, as well as public, decision-making as it affects children.[212] Children's participation in traditional African communities is not mandatory and is entirely at the discretion of the adults.[213] Oral tradition provides evidence of the roles children played in saving families and communities, in leadership position and in wars across traditional communities in Africa.[214]

The CRC Committee considers these traditional mechanisms for child participation as 'the charity mentality and paternalistic approaches.'[215]

212 C Ngara 'African ways of knowing and pedagogy revisited' (2007) 2 *Journal of Contemporary Issues in Education* 7; I Goduka 'Indigenous epistemologies - Ways of knowing: Affirming our legacy' (1999) 13 *South African Journal of Higher Education* 26; M Runco 'Creativity as an extra cognitive phenomenon' in L Shavinina & M Ferrari (eds) *Beyond Knowledge: Extra cognitive aspects of developing high ability* (2004) 17.

213 C Himonga 'The rights of the child to participate in decision making: A perspective from Zambia' in W Ncube *Law, culture, tradition and children's rights in East and Southern Africa* (1998) 115.

214 See generally H Courlander *A treasury of African folklore: The oral literature, traditions, myths, legends, epics, tales, recollections, wisdom, sayings and humor of Africa* (1975).

215 The CRC Committee General Comment 12 (2009) *The right of the child to be heard* CRC/C/GC/12 20 July 2009.

According to the CRC Committee, meaningful child participation should provide the child with the right to

> express views and to participate in various activities, according to her/his evolving capacities… to speak, to participate, to have their views taken into account: these three phases describe the sequence of the enjoyment of the right to participate from a functional point of view. The new and deeper meaning of this right is that it should establish a new social contract. One by which children are fully recognized as rights-holders who are not only entitled to … This implies, in the long term, changes in political, social, institutional and cultural structures.[216]

Culture and traditions, in the view of the CRC Committee, are among the major obstacles to children freely expressing their views. A more helpful approach could be to explore possibilities for building upon and complementing existing traditional mechanisms to enhance the quality of participation of children. As mentioned above, traditional African culture and traditions provide for child participation mechanisms that, though insufficient, could be improved to enhance children's participation.

In traditional African value system, it is believed that 'the art of negotiating is acquired from childhood.'[217] Oral traditions in Africa do not seem to support the claim that in Africa 'children are seen but not heard.'[218] Proverbs, songs, folklore and myths point to a variety of ways and tools available to children to communicate and participate in decision-making in their societies. For example, the Bemba community in Zambia says *amano yafuma mwifwasa yaya muchulu:* knowledge is transferred from a small stone into an anthill.[219] This is a suggestion that knowledge could be transferred from a child to an adult. In a song among the Goba, children sing *singchimbere nga nzife tione megariro*

---

216 See the preamble to the general Comment of The CRC Committee General Comment 12 (2009) *The right of the child to be heard* CRC/C/GC/12 20 July 2009.

217 https://twitter.com/AfricanProverbs/status/316264478696173568.

218 I Mbikusita–Lewanika Pre–*school education in Zambia: A survey analysis and evaluation* (1979) 103.

219 C Himonga 'The rights of the child to participate in decision making: A perspective from Zambia' in W Ncube *Law, culture, tradition and children's rights in East and Southern* Africa (1998) 115.

taneta kutaura, all old people should die, we are tired of them.[220] These are a culturally acceptable way of getting adults to take children seriously.[221] There are many such examples across Africa that demonstrate the active participation of children in society and their own education.[222]

In a book of custody under customary law in some African communities, Himonga found that children participated in custody decisions.[223] In addition, traditional learning was an active and lifelong process that involves child-rearing practices, age-grade organizations, initiation ceremonies, apprenticeship systems and festivals – marriages, births, rituals and funeral ceremonies. All these mechanisms and platforms afforded children with an opportunity to participate in the cultural life of the community thus, enabling children to participate actively in these learning activities. Even though, traditionally, old men 'built up a store of claim which places them in the enviable position of owing nothing to any living being, their authority linked to the ancestors,'[224] there was space to learn from children. In the folklore of the Akans of Ghana, in an argument between a father and a son the son advises his father about possible danger. The father initially insists on his authority by virtue of age, but later realises how his wise son's advice saved his life and lamented

> by all the lesser gods,' said he, 'I might as well be dead; I thought I had all the wisdom in the whole world, yet some remained which even I did not possess, and lo, this still sucking infant has shown it me.[225]

---

220 As above.

221 As above.

222 A Ndofirepi & E Ndofirepi '(E)ducation or (e)ducation in traditional African societies?' (2012) 10 *Stud Tribes Trabals* 13.

223 C Himonga 'The rights of the child to participate in decision making: A perspective from Zambia' in W Ncube *Law, culture, tradition and children's rights in East and Southern Africa* (1998) 115.

224 L McNee 'The languages of childhood: The discursive construction of childhood and colonial policy in French West Africa' (2007) African Studies Quarterly 1 http://www.africa.ufl.edu/asq/v7/v7i4a2.htm.

225 R Rattry 'The African child in proverb, folklore and facts' (1933) 6 *Journal of the International African Institute* 456.

It suggests that children traditionally are not powerless, voiceless victims of adult oppression, but that children participated, and adults listened to their voice.[226] To what extent children's participation in traditional communities can be said to be meaningful is debatable. But improving and not transplanting participatory mechanisms is what children need to enable them to take part meaningfully in decision making. Whether human rights mechanisms are the most appropriate means of achieving this improvement is yet to be seen.

The three thematic issues of child marriage, child labour and child participation, and how these practices interact with the best interests of the child demonstrate the divergence between how traditional communities view what is in the best interests of children and how human rights experts interpret these cultural norms and practices. These differences in interpretation could translate into differences in expectation. Differences in expectations could easily lead to conflict of norms. Human rights norms have enormous expertise, resources and empirical evidence on their side, but the traditional communities have years of experience showing the benefit of custom and traditions, which human rights must contend if the goal is to replace traditional values and norms with human rights standards.

3.3. Factors affecting the conception of childhood in Africa

A 'pure' African conception of childhood is increasingly giving way to a mixed picture in the definition of childhood in Africa. This transition from a traditional conception of child to a version which combines tradition and modernity is facilitated by legal and non-legal factors in Africa.

3.3.1. Legal factors

The notion of 'childhood', as seen from a human rights perspective is the product of the law. The constructions of the concept, the content and contour of childhood have been made through the instrumentality of the law. Legitimate laws are inspired and instigated by the values and norms rooted in the culture and commonly accepted practices of a people. The complex

226 C Himonga 'The rights of the child to participate in decision making: A perspective from Zambia' in W Ncube *Law, culture, tradition and children's rights in East and Southern Africa* (1998) 115.

relationship that exists between law and culture has been described in the following terms: 'the law creates the conditions of culture… the law as cultural product… the law is to some extent a mandarin text, it is itself a subject of popular culture.'[227] Therefore, law is not 'a mere technical add-on to a morally (or immorally) finished society, it is, along of course with a whole range of other cultural realities … an active part of it.'[228]

Human rights law has recognized and deepened the relationship between law and culture. Articles 22 and 27 of the Universal Declaration of Human Rights acknowledge the right to take part in cultural life. Articles 13 and 14 of the International Covenant on Economic, Social and Cultural Rights reiterate these rights. The Preamble to the African Charter on Human and Peoples' Rights places the concept of human rights in Africa within the 'virtues of … historical tradition and values…which should inspire and characterize their reflection on the concept of human and peoples' rights.' The Preamble to the African Children's Charter reiterates the centrality of the 'virtues…cultural heritage, historical background and values of African civilization' in the understanding of the rights and welfare of children in African.

There are growing numbers of national laws on children that recognize the role culture and tradition play in the harmonious development of the child. However, this recognition does not seem to affect how different governments in Africa undertake new law reform on children. The provisions of the CRC and its general principles predominantly inspire these law reforms.[229] This assertion is obvious when considering the definition of the child, the autonomy rights of the child, best interests of the child, and child participation. The drive to 'harmonize' national laws on children with either the provisions of the CRC or the African Children's Charter is increasingly leading to the marginalization of African culture and traditions within the frameworks of national children's law in Africa.

---

227 C Weisbrod *Emblems of pluralism* (2002) 2.

228 C Geertz *Local knowledge: Further essays in interpretive anthropology* (1983) 218.

229 See generally ACPF's 'In the best interests of the Child: Harmonization of laws on children in East and Southern Africa' and in 'West and Central Africa' available here: http://www.africanchildforum.org/site/index.php/programmemess/the-african-child-law-programmeme/harmonisation-of-laws-on-children-in-africa.html.

The CRC Committee spearheads the wave of harmonization of laws relating to children in Africa. The Committee

> believes ... a comprehensive review of all domestic legislation and related administrative guidance to ensure full compliance with the Convention is an obligation. The review needs to consider the Convention not only article by article, but also holistically, recognizing the interdependence and indivisibility of human rights. The review needs to be continuous rather than one-off.[230]

Africa has a complex patchwork of legislation dealing with children's rights at the national level. This complexity poses a significant challenge to the effective promotion and protection of children's rights in Africa. Therefore, harmonization of laws is a necessary mechanism to reduce the barriers to effective implementation of laws and policies relating to children. The limitation of the current drive to harmonize national laws is its upward focus concentrating only on harmonization with international and regional standards at the expense of a downward accommodation that is balancing international and regional standards with cultural contexts.[231] If this trend continues, African countries may have perfectly harmonized laws that increasingly lack cultural legitimacy and, thus, provide new hurdles to effective implementation.

3.3.1.1. Who is a child?

There is no uniform definition of what a child is for all purposes or when childhood starts or ends in statutes relating to children in African countries.[232]

---

230 CRC Committee General Comment 5 (2003) General measures of implementation of the Convention on the Rights of the Child (arts. 4, 42 and 44, para. 6) CRC/GC/2003/5 27 November 2003.

231 There are few exceptions. See for example ACPF's Child friendly laws in Africa outline some examples of these few deviations: https://app.box.com/shared/t2k1hv9fn8.

232 See for example section 335 of Burundi's family law code it states that a person attains majority at 21 years; while article 88 of the same law dealing with marriage states that a boy child is mature for the purpose of marriage before 21 years a girl child at 18 but the governor can grant permission for marriage before 18 for a girl. The age of majority in Chad is still appreciated differently according to the texts. Under the French Civil Code of 1958 still in force in Chad, civil majority is 21 and the legal age for marriage is 15 years for girls and 18 for boys. Article 277 of the penal code seems to suggest that the age for marriage is 13 for girls. The code reads that: 'la consommation d'un mariage coutumier avant que la fille n'ait atteint l'âge de treize ans est assimilé au viol et punie comme telle.' (Sexual intercourse with a girl under 13 is considered as rape and punished as such). While 52 of the same Code say Children cannot be employed in any profession before the

There are different upper age limits for criminal responsibility, for sexual consent, for employment, and age when children are allowed to marry. In a survey of nineteen countries in East and Southern Africa, African Child Policy Forum (ACPF) reports that nine countries do not have an overarching definition of childhood in their constitutions or laws.[233] In a similar review, in 11 West and Central African countries, five countries did not have an overarching definition of the child.[234] These surveys are indicative of the fact that the move towards a uniform conception of the child across the continent for all-purposes is rapidly gaining momentum.

While the endpoint of childhood seems to be certain – eighteen years in many countries in Africa - when childhood starts, is not. In Rwanda, for example, the Rwanda Family Code[235] provides that childhood starts at conception. This is in line with the philosophical beliefs of most cultures in Africa.[236] The Islamic Charter on the Rights of the Child, which is reflective of the beliefs and practices in many Muslim communities in Africa, considers life to start at conception. Most countries with consolidated laws relating to children that have an overarching definition of childhood are mainly concerned with the upper limit. This focus is another reflection of the growing influence of the CRC Committee on law reform in Africa. The Committee will usually admonish state parties to

> review its legislation so that the definition of the child, the age of majority, and other minimum age requirements conform to the

---

age of fourteen except there is an exemption from the minister of labour or social security or public health. Parent consent is required. Article 276 of the family code of Senegal puts the age of majority for boys and girls at 18. However, for the purpose of marriage article 111 of the said Code provides that the minimum age required for girls is 16 and for boys 18 expect the president of the regional tribunal decides otherwise. Article 492 of the Civil Code of Gabon fixes the age of majority for both sexes at 21, but for marriage at 15 for girls and 18 for boys.

233 ACPF 'In the best interests of children: Harmonising laws in Eastern and Southern Africa' (2007) available at https://app.box.com/s/cb97350a04a4c0c732b0/1/47727956/474659866/1.

234 ACPF 'In the best interests of the Child: Harmonising laws on children in West and Central Africa' (2011) available at https://app.box.com/s/cb97350a04a4c0c732b0/1/47727956/4207935130/1.

235 Article 11 LAW N°54/2011 OF 14/12/2011 relating to the rights and the protection of the child Official Gazette n°26 of 25/06/2012 Available at: http://www.migeprof.gov.rw/IMG/pdf/Law_relating_to_the_rights_the_protection_of_the_Child_O-G-no_26_of_25-06-2012_-4.pdf.

236 R Zimba 'Indigenous conceptions of childhood development and social realities in Southern Africa' in R Zimba *Between culture and biology: Perspectives on ontogentic development* (2002) 91.

> principles and provisions of the Convention, and that they are gender neutral, and ensure that the laws are enforced.[237]

Technical partners, like UNICEF, and civil society organizations usually interpret this recommendation to mean a simple 18-year definition of the child and use available leverages to cajole the state into adopting this position.

As noted, African traditions and customs do not provide for a one-size-fits-all approach in defining who a child is. In tradition, childhood is a functional concept, which is purpose- specific. Also, the African worldview and life cycle consider that life starts at conception and, thus, a foetus is part of the community of the living and of the 'living dead'. The Rwandan Law Relating to the Rights and the Protection of the Child is more in tune with the traditional African view of the starting point of childhood. This law defines a child as someone below the age of 18 years and declares that 'the child shall enjoy his/her rights as of conception and he/she is reputed born whenever his/her interests are concerned.'[238] From the analysis, it seems that the current wave of children's law reform in Africa, driven mainly by international human rights law, is not cultural and context-specific when dealing with who a child is, and does not pay attention to some of these peculiarities. The law reform is primarily driven by civil society organizations through the CRC Committee. Through its reporting mechanism, the CRC Committee acknowledges its own influence in this process:

> the Committee notes with satisfaction that several of its concerns expressed and recommendations (CRC/C/15/Add 76) made upon the consideration of the State party's initial report (CRC/C/28/Add. 4) have been addressed through legislative measures and policies.[239]

---

237 This recommendation is routinely given to countries that are yet to harmonise laws. See, for example, Concluding Observations of the CRC Committee, Saudi Arabia, U.N. Doc. CRC/C/15/Add 148 (2001).

238 Article 11 LAW N°54/2011 OF 14/12/2011 relating to the rights and the protection of the child Official Gazette n°26 of 25/06/2012 Available at: http://www.migeprof.gov.rw/IMG/pdf/Law_relating_to_the_rights_the_protection_of_the_Child_O-G-no_26_of_25-06-2012_-4.pdf.

239 This is an example of similar observations the Committee gives out to State parties on regular basis. See for example CRC Committee Concluding observations CRC/C/15/Add 269 12 October 2005.

Areas of concern and a target for the CRC Committee and its civil society partners for reform are usually: definition of the child, age of sexual consent, birth registration, corporal punishment and ill-treatment, neglect and abuse of children, female genital mutilation and early and forced marriages, economic exploitation, discrimination against certain vulnerable groups of children, and the reform of the juvenile justice system. In all these areas, the reference point is the CRC.[240] Even though the CRC enjoins the CRC Committee to keep in mind the rights of the child 'to participate freely in [the] cultural life' of his community, culture is hardly a positive reference point in the recommendations of the CRC Committee.

Most constitutions in Africa do not define the beginning or the end of childhood. [241] Some of the constitutions that do define the upper limit of

240 As part of this work, the author examined the concluding observations for countries in Africa and identified these common areas of concern relevant to this work.

241 The following African Constitutions do not provide for the definition of who a child is. Even though many of them provide for the rights of children: The Constitution of the People's Democratic Republic of Algeria adopted on 19 November 1976, amended on 28 November 1996 and on 10 April 2002; Constitution of the Republic of Benin adopted at the referendum of 2 December 1990; The Constitution of Botswana adopted in September 1966. Last amended in 1999; The Constitution of Burkina Faso adopted on 2 June 1991, promulgated on 11 June 1991, amended on 27 January 1997 and on 11 April 2000; Constitution of the Republic of Cameroon adopted on 18 January 1996, amendment to the Constitution of 2 June 1972; Constitutional Law of the Republic of Cape Verde adopted on 25 September 1992, amended on 23 November 1995 and in 1999; Constitution of the Central African Republic adopted on 28 December 1994, promulgated on 14 January 1995; Fundamental Law of the Union Comoros adopted on 23 December 2001; Constitution of the Republic of Cote D'Ivoire adopted on 24 July 2000; Constitution of Djibouti Approved on 4 September 1992; The Constitution of the Arab Republic of Egypt after the amendments ratified on May 22, 1980 Referendum; Constitution of the Republic of Equatorial Guinea, 1996; The Constitution of Eritrea Ratified by the Constituent Assembly, On May 23, 1997; The Constitution of the Federal Republic Of Ethiopia, 1995; Constitution of The Gabonese Republic adopted on 26 March 1991, amended on 22 April 1997; Fundamental Law of The Second Republic Of Guinea Approved on 23 December 1990; Constitution of the Republic of Guinea-Bissau adopted in 1984, amended in 1991, 1993, 1996; The Constitution of Kenya 2010; Constitution of Lesotho adopted in 1993, Amended 1996, 1997, 1998, 2001; Constitution of the Republic of Liberia approved on 3 July 3 1984, entered into force on 6 January 1986; Constitution of the Republic of Madagascar adopted on 19 August 1992, amended in 1995 and 1998; Constitutional Proclamation of Libya adopted on 11 December 1969; The Constitution of Mali Adopted by referendum on 12 January 1992 and promulgated on the 25 February 1992; amended 1999; Constitution De La Republique Islamique De Mauritanie (avec les projets d'amendements soumis au référendum du 25 juin 2006); The Constitution of Mauritius 1968; The Constitution of Morocco adopted on 13 September 1996; The Constitution of Mozambique Approved and enacted on 2 November 1990; Constitution of the Fifth Republic of Niger adopted on 18 July 1999, promulgated on 9 August 1999; Constitution of the Federal Republic of Nigeria 1999; The Constitution of the Republic of Rwanda Adopted on 26 May 2003; Political Constitution of São Tomé and Príncipe adopted on 5 November 1975, Amended on 10 September 1990 through Law 7/90; Constitution of the Republic of Senegal adopted on 7 January 2001; Constitution of the Republic of Seychelles approved on 18 June 1993, Amended by Act No 14 of 1996; the Constitution of Sierra Leone adopted on 1 October 1991; Interim Constitution of Sudan 2005; The Constitution of the Kingdom of Swaziland Act, 2005 (Act No: of 2005); This Edition of the Constitution of the United Republic of Tanzania, 1997, and the first draft of the Tanzanian Constitution made public in June 2013; Constitution of Tunisia Adopted on 1 June 1959, Amended on 12 July 1988 and by Amendment Act No 93-105 of 8 November 1993 and the Constitution of Zambia 1996.

childhood do not do it for all,[242] thus opting for a functional approach to defining children according to specific purposes. Many of the constitutions provide for rights as well as duties consistent with the reciprocal obligation of children to take care of their parents and communities.[243]

Many constitutions in Africa hardly conceptualise childhood outside the family boundaries.[244] However, there are a few constitutions that provide for a definition of childhood consistent with the African Children's Charter,[245] which provide for the 'best interests' principle and provide an elaborate section on the rights of children.[246] The constitutions that provide for African Children's Charter or CRC also offer some African features, such as extended family, duties and responsibilities. Countries with more CRC or African Children's Charter features in their constitutions, coincidentally, are countries with high civil society activities index.[247]

---

242 Article 35 of the Togo Constitution sets 15 years as the end period for mandatory education; article 14 (c) of the Transitional Federal Charter of the Somali Republic 2004 provides 18 years as the period to vote; article 15(2) (3) of the Constitution of Namibia provides for 16 and 14 years respectively for periods of employment and when a child cannot be employed in factor or mine work respectively and article 15(5) outlawing preventive detention for persons under 16 years of age; article 23(5) of the Constitution of Malawi defines children for the purpose of work as persons under the years of 16; article 29(2) of the Constitution of the Second republic of Gambia outlaws economic exploitation of persons under 16 years of age; article 23 of the Constitution of the Republic of Congo makes mandatory education until the age of 16 and article 34 of the Constitution prohibits work by persons under the age of 16.

243 For example article 40 of the Constitution of the Democratic Republic of Congo provides 'children have the duty to assist their parents'; article 22(3) of the Constitution of Eretria provides 'parents have the right and duty to bring up their children with due care and affection; and, in turn, children have the right and the duty to respect their parents and to sustain them in their old age'; and article 25(4) of the Transitional Federal Charter of Somali Republic provides 'Children, who are of full age, are obliged to support their parents when the latter are unable to support themselves.'

244 The Transitional Federal Charter on the Somali Republic; the Constitution of the Republic of Senegal; the Constitute of the Republic of Niger; the Constitution of the Gabonese Republic; the Constitution of Eritrea; the Constitution of the Democratic Republic of Congo; the Constitution of the Republic of Congo; and the Constitution of the Central African Republic; are good examples.

245 Article 41 of the Constitution of the Democratic Republic of Congo states 'every person who has not yet completed 18 years of age is a minor, without distinction on grounds of sex'; article 28(5) of the Constitution of Ghana provides ' for the purposes of this article, "child" means a person below the age of eighteen years'; so article 81 of the Constitution of Zimbabwe and article 17(4) of the Transitional Constitution of the Republic of South Sudan and article 28(3) of the Constitution of South Africa are examples.

246 Article 41 of the Constitution of the Democratic Republic of Congo states 'every person who has not yet completed 18 years of age is a minor, without distinction on grounds of sex'; article 28(5) of the Constitution of Ghana provides ' for the purposes of this article, "child" means a person below the age of eighteen years'; so article 81 of the Constitution of Zimbabwe and article 17(4) of the Transitional Constitution of the Republic of South Sudan and article 28(3) of the Constitution of South Africa are examples.

247 See CIVICUS State of the world Civil Society Report 2013 available at: http://socs.civicus.org/wp-content/uploads/2013/04/2013StateofCivilSocietyReport_full.pdf.

The different inclinations of the constitutions-making processes and the child rights-law making processes in Africa are interesting. For example, the constitutions are friendlier to the unique features of African cultural heritage than many of the child rights laws. It would have been easier to analyse the problem if constitutions that were made before 1989 were more child rights unfriendly and those after this period were child rights friendly. The pattern of the constitutionalisation of children's rights in Africa is not linear. Probably the nature, implication and the scope of the processes that lead to constitution making might be a factor. Whatever the reason, what is clear is the fact that the process of the constitutionalisation of children's rights in Africa is more in tune with the traditional African conception of childhood than the process of statutory law making.

3.3.1.2. Autonomy rights

Statutory law as well as constitutional laws in Africa that provide for autonomy rights for children do so by incorporating the provisions of the CRC or the African Children's Charter. The analysis of autonomy rights already undertaken in discussing the relevant provisions of the CRC and African Children's Charter relating to autonomy rights for children applies here. Those discussions will not be repeated.

3.3.1.3. The best interests of the child

The 'best interests' principle has been provided for in most of the laws dealing with children's rights and welfare in Africa.[248] The CRC and the African Children's Charter influence the way the lawmakers have interpreted and applied the principle in Africa. The principle is mainly used to safeguard the welfare of children in formal proceedings against perceived negative cultural practices and beliefs, resource allocation, and to ensure child-friendly law reforms.[249] In interpreting for and influencing state parties to incorporate the

---

248 ACPF 'In the best interests of the Child: Harmonising laws on children in West and Central Africa' (2011) available at https://app.box.com/s/cb97350a04a4c0c732b0/1/47727956/4207935130/1 and ACPF 'In the best interests of children: Harmonising laws in Eastern and Southern Africa' (2007) available at https://app.box.com/s/cb97350a04a4c0c732b0/1/47727956/474659866/1.

249 P Alston & B Gilmour-Walsh *The best interests of the child: Towards a synthesis of children's rights and cultural norms* (1996) 17.

best interests principle in their domestic laws, the CRC Committee has not encouraged a context and cultural sensitive understanding of the principle.[250]

The 'best interests' principle should not be seen and used as a universalizing tool or transformative mechanism to spread a specific image of childhood across cultures and contexts. Its purpose should be to preserve a minimum core obligation society owes to children's welfare within its meaning and means. The 'best interests' principle should facilitate and accommodate conversation between cultures and civilizations around childbearing and childrearing norms and practices. State parties should encourage and be encouraged to engage in and deepen this conversation. The failure by African countries to forcefully provide an alternative and culturally sensitive understanding of the best interests of children has probably meant that the CRC Committee has not been afforded with a rich philosophical tradition from which to interpret this fundamental principle.[251]

3.3.1.4. Child participation

Increasingly, law reform efforts in Africa take on board children's rights to participate in decision-making at all levels. With respect to child participation, law reform is driven by UN agencies like UNICEF, civil society organizations, and the CRC Committee. Unfortunately, instead of taking advantage of traditional ways of promoting children's participation in decision making in African communities, the CRC Committee considers 'traditional practices and attitudes' as 'paternalistic and authoritarian' and, as such, a hindrance to children participation that must be dismantled through 'national awareness-raising campaigns to change traditional adult-centered attitudes which hinder children's right to express their views freely in all matters that affect them;' and through skills-training programmes in community settings.'[252]

In addition to the danger of overly characterizing children as victims in their own culture and traditions, this approach to law reform risks alienating law

250 As above, 41.

251 As above, 17.

252 CRC Committee General Comment 12 (2009) *The right of the child to be heard* CRC/C/GC/12 20 July 2009.

and children from their communities. Characterizing a people's worldview and way of life as 'paternalistic and authoritarian'[253] that needs to be replaced is unnecessarily antagonizing contextual value systems that could aid interventions on behalf of children. This helps to augment the view that the CRC principles are foreign, that can effectively and efficiently be implemented only with the support of a massive cultural adjustment programmes.

3.3.2. Non legal factors

Childhood is a fluid concept and there is continuum of experience in the structural place called 'childhood.' A number of factors contribute to the construction, interpretation, understanding and institutionalisation of a particular image of childhood in any society. Culture, law and children's reaction to, or experience of the interaction between culture and the law are contributing factors to the construction of childhood.[254] Specifically in Africa, the slave trade, colonialism and foreign religious imposition, poverty and HIV/AIDS add to the list of factors responsible for the changing image of childhood in Africa. The roles colonialism, religion, poverty and HIV/AIDS have possibly played in shaping childhood in Africa will be examined.

3.3.2.1. Colonialism

According to Diptee and Klein, 'during the colonial era... real efforts were made to control, remake, and/or manipulate African childhoods.'[255] The motivation, methods, means and mechanisms of colonialism in Africa impacted on childhood and children's experience in Africa. How exactly colonialism impacted on the conception of childhood in Africa is difficult to ascertain with exactitude.

First, scarcity and the nature of the source materials make it difficult to authoritatively draw conclusions based on them.[256] Second, the multiplicities

---

253 CRC Committee General Comment 12 (2009) *The right of the child to be heard* CRC/C/GC/12 20 July 2009.

254 A James & A James *Constructing childhood: Theory, policy, and social practice* (2004) 13.

255 A Diptee & A Klein 'African childhoods and the colonial project' (2009) 20 *Journal of Family History* 1.

256 A Diptee & A Klein 'African childhoods and the colonial project' (2009) 20 *Journal of Family History* 1;

of children's lives and experience under colonialism were extremely diverse and varied.[257] Third, there is the difficulty of ascertaining who children were and for what purpose because during the colonial period, in some cases, colonial and missionary officials depicted even adult Africans as children.[258] Therefore, to determine from official records who were actual children would be a tedious task. This lack of terminological clarity is compounded by the fact that during the colonial period 'most ... African societies did not use age, but social criteria for distinguishing children from adults. Rather than using age to define social status, then, social status defined age'.[259]

However, it is possible and reasonable to infer from the pervasive nature and impact of colonial policies and practices that childhood as a space and the experience of those inhabiting that space were affected. Children are the means through which societies reproduce themselves biologically and culturally; if the colonialists wanted a future for European ways of thinking and doing things in Africa, it is possible to expect that colonial policies were used to control the manner in which the next generation of Africans thought and behaved.

Colonialism is a system of rules predicated on the rights of a people to impose their ways of thinking and doing things on the cultural, social and political lives of others. According to the Concise Oxford Dictionary of Politics, colonialism is the policy and practice of a strong power extending its control territorially over a weaker nation or people.[260] Inevitably it leads to a culture

---

for some additional reading on some of the experience of children and colonialism see A Diptee, 'African children in the British Slave Trade during the late eighteenth century' (2006) 27 *Slavery & Abolition* 183; A Gottlieb *The afterlife is where we come from: The culture of infancy in West Africa* (2004); B *Grier Invisible hands: Child labor and the state in colonial Zimbabwe* (2006); L McNee 'The languages of childhood: The distinctive construction of childhood and colonial policy in French West Africa' (2004) 7 *African Studies Quarterly*1; W Cohen 'The colonized as child: British and French colonial rule' (1970) 3 *African Historical Studies* 107.

257 O Nwanosike & F Onyije 'Colonialism and education' (2011) Proceedings of the International Conference on Teaching, Learning and Change 624.

258 W Cohen 'The colonized as child: British and French colonial rule' (1970) 3 *African Historical Studies* 107.

259 L McNee, 'The languages of childhood: The distinctive construction of childhood and colonial policy in French West Africa' (2004) 7 *African Studies Quarterly*.

260 Oxford University Press, 2013.

of dominance and dependence in all spheres of interaction and, consequently, results in political, psychological and moral damage to the colonized.

Children occupied a central role in the colonial experience; 'children were often targeted by slavers in Africa;' because they constituted a 'highly valued labour source'.[261] In addition to cultural contestations, the colonial state, European settlers, and children themselves contested the idea of childhood in Africa not only within the framework of patriarchy, but also colonial laws, education, religion and culture.[262]

Laws, education, culture and religion were used by the colonial powers to redefine, reformulate and reconfigure childhood and its experience in Africa. The colonial officials used the instrumentality of law to define, constrain and control African childhood.[263] Laws were used to categorise and differentiate infants from children, and children from young people and adults. Colonial laws described juvenile crimes and established categories of offenders. Laws, in the hands of the colonial powers, attempted to relocate the conception of childhoods from the cultural to the legal domain. The partly successful attempt to relocate the understanding of childhood from the cultural domain to a public and legal concept means that the lived experience of children continues to straddle between legal prescriptions and cultural norms.

The norms and value system of the colonial powers were passed on to children and communities in Africa through education. The type and method of education practiced during the colonial period in Africa have been accused of being designed 'to extend foreign domination and economic exploitation of the colony.'[264] The process of education has been viewed as 'an attempt to strip the colonized people away from their indigenous learning structures and draw them towards the structures of the colonizers.'[265]

---

261 A Diptee & M Klein 'African childhoods and the colonial project' (2009) *Journal of Family History* 1.

262 As above.

263 S Heap 'Their days are spent in gambling and loafing, pimping for prostitutes, and picking pockets: Male juvenile delinquents on Lagos Island, 1920s-1960s' (2010) 35 *Journal of Family History* 48.

264 G Kelly & G Philip *Introduction 'the four faces of colonialism': Education and colonial experience* (1984) 1.

265 W Rodney *How Europe underdeveloped Africa* (1972) 141.

For example, education in the British colonies was primarily designed

> [to] form a class who may be interpreters between us and the millions whom we govern, –a class of persons [African] in blood and colour, but English in tastes, in opinions, in morals and in intellect.[266]

The effect of such an education was a 'lack of identity and a limited sense of [the] past'[267] which inculcates in the learners 'hybrids of two vastly different cultural systems'[268] and consequently 'annihilates a people of belief in their names, in their language, environment, heritage of struggle, unity, capacities and ultimately in themselves.'[269]

Colonialism, predicated on a belief in the cultural superiority of the colonizers, expressed in a desire to civilise other cultures. As a result, a combination of law, education and missionary activity was deployed by the colonial powers and their collaborators to define what was acceptable, what was barbaric and what was supportive of the colonial project in the cultural norms and practices of traditional African communities. The emerging cultural experience added a new dimension to the experience of children in Africa. The influence of this confluence of cultures on childhood was more visible on urban child dwellers. With the number of children in the urban centres increasing, the impact of this cultural clash on children in Africa is more obvious.

After the colonial experience in many African countries, African childhood presents a half full-half empty scenario. On one hand, it is influenced by African cultural norms and practices; on the other hand, a colonial heritage has left an indelible mark on the conception of childhood.

---

266 Sir T Macaulay to British parliament dated 2 February 1835 quoted in Y Lulat *A history of African higher education from antiquity to the present: A critical synbook* (2005) 32. Though this was probably a personal opinion of Sir Macaulay, it symbolises the perception of British education at the time.

267 G Kelly & G Philip *Introduction 'The four faces of colonialism' education and colonial experience* (1984) 1.

268 O Nwanosike & F Onyije 'Colonialism and education' (2011) Proceedings of the International Conference on Teaching, Learning and Change 624.

269 W Ngugi Decolonizing the mind: The politics of language in African literature (1986) cited in O Nwanosike & F Onyije 'Colonialism and education' (2011) Proceedings of the International Conference on Teaching, Learning and Change 624.

3.3.2.2. Religion

Africans are religious people.[270] Religion is a pervasive presence in a number of facets of the life of many Africans. As a way of life for many in Africa, religion affects the way Africans see and treats children. Africa's triple religious heritage - African traditional religion, Islam and Christianity - has impacted on the conception of the place, the position, and the prospect for childhood in Africa. Religion is a conduit for cultural transmission. African childhood, therefore, is a result of religious 'cultures pieced together in a shared heritage.'[271]

International human rights instruments, either at global or regional levels, recognise or protect the freedom of religion as well as the freedom to practice a religion of one's choice. Exercising this choice in the African context is fraught with challenges. For example, in many communities in Africa children cannot choose their religion. These communities expect children to be the recipients of the values, norms, roles and responsibilities that are expected by the religion into which they are born. The three major religions in Africa expect children to respect elders, peers and themselves, to exercise sufficient restraint over their natural instincts, to reciprocate parental and social goodwill, and to reproduce the religious norms of the community. These expectations are similar to the understanding of childhood under traditional African systems. However, there are divergences between the immigrant religions and African traditional image of childhood. The two main immigrant religions - Islam and Christianity - are discussed briefly below to elucidate how they impact on childhood in Africa.

3.3.2.2.1. Islam

Islam is a monotheistic religion revealed to the Prophet Muhammad in the 7th century CE. Islam arrived and spread in Africa around 647 AD.[272] It has

270 Sub-Saharan Africa now is home to about one-in-five of all the Christians in the world (21%) and more than one-in-seven of the world's Muslims (15%). See Pew Forum's 2009 report, 'Mapping the Global Muslim Population'; other estimates based on data from the World Religion Database.

271 This phrase is adapted from the preamble to the Rome Statute establishing the International Criminal Court. Paragraph one of the Preamble reads: 'Conscious that all peoples are united by common bonds, their cultures pieced together in a shared heritage, and concerned that this delicate mosaic may be shattered at any time'.

272 J Esposito *Islam the Straight Path* (2005) 32; J Esposito *Oxford history of Islam* (1999) 10 and J Esposito *What everyone needs to know about Islam* (2002) 139.

been said that 'the Koran, its sacred book, [was] read from the 'Atlantic to the Red Sea and from the Mediterranean to the Congo.'[273] Today it is estimated that there are around 234 million Muslims in Africa. More than half of this population is under 18 years old. Islamic culture, laws and practices govern every aspect of the lives of its followers.[274]

There are divergent views on the impact of Islam on African cultures and traditions. According to some historians, the arrival of Islam in Africa ensured that 'these backward regions commenced an upward progress,'[275] in the outdated view that 'the Negro who accepts Muhammudanism acquires at once a sense of the dignity of human nature.'[276] Some scholars believe that Islam had a negative impact, culturally speaking, in Africa, as it 'stifled everything by its arid and desolating simplicity.'[277] The influence of Islam on customs, ceremonies, death rituals, dances, and social functions in Africa is noticeable.

The relationship between Islam, Islamic culture and traditional African cultures was and still is symbiotic. Unlike Christianity, Islam is more tolerant and more accommodating of African traditions and culture,[278] in its process of 'transformative localisation.'[279] Islamic missionaries in Africa worked hard to ensure that 'Islamic civilization harmonized indigenous forms of cultural expression with the universal norms of its sacred law, Islamic jurisprudence.'[280] The ability of Islam to adapt to local exigencies has been described as

---

273 J Thompson quoted be G Ellis 'Islam as a factor in Western African culture' (1911) 2 *The Journal of Race Development* 105.

274 A Oba 'Islamic law as customary law: The changing perspective in Nigeria' (2002) 51 *International Comparative Law Quarterly* 817.

275 J Thompson quoted be G Ellis 'Islam as a factor in Western African culture' (1911) 2 *The Journal of Race Development* 105.

276 R Smith Muhammud and Muhammudanism, Lecture I, p. 32. Cited in J Thompson quoted be G Ellis 'Islam as a factor in Western African culture' (1911) 2 *The Journal of Race Development* 105.

277 J Thompson quoted be G Ellis 'Islam as a factor in Western African Culture' (1911) 2 *The Journal of Race Development* 105.

278 L Sanneh *West African Christianity* (1983) 227; L Sanneh *Piety and power between the world of Islam and that of the West* (1996) 3 and A Byaruhanga-Akiiki *Africa and Christianity: Domestication of Christian values in the African Church* (1993) 179.

279 W Binsbergen 'Islam as a constitutive factor in African 'traditional' religion the evidence from geomantic divination' forthcoming in A Breedveld *et al* (eds) *Islam and transformations in Africa* available at: http://www.shikanda.net/african_religion/islampaper_def_2003_RTF.pdf.

280 U An Nawawi 'Islam cultural and the imperative' (2003) 8 *Journal of Islamic Law and Culture* 89.

> a crystal clear river. Its waters (Islam) are pure, sweet, and life-giving but - having no color of their own - reflect the bedrock (indigenous culture) over which they flow. In China, Islam looked Chinese; in Mali, it looked African.[281]

There is a case to be made that Islam is more tolerant to local context than Christianity. According to the Prophet Muhammad, the flexibility of Islam was a deliberate move so that the 'the Jews and Christians know there is latitude in our religion.'[282] As a result, Islam and Islamic culture and practices prevalent in Africa today are Islam with an African flavour.

Islam has a special place for childhood.[283] Childhood starts at conception and ends for girls at puberty, around 9 years old, and for boys at around age 15.[284] It is a period of learning and acquiring skills to become a responsible member of the family, society and religion.[285] Children have entitlements and corresponding obligations to parents, society and the religion.[286] The boy and the girl child have differential treatment with respect to maturity, roles and responsibilities.[287]

Islam and traditional African communities seem to share similar conceptions of childhood. Both consider the beginning of childhood at conception. Both lay claim to strong moral and cultural value systems for the upbringing of children and both consider childhood a learning space. Therefore, the contribution of Islam to the conception of childhood in Africa was its ability

---

281 U Abd-Allah 'Islam and the cultural imperative' (2003) 8 *Journal of Islamic Law and Culture* 89.

282 The story is related in Bukhari and Muslim, Islam's most authoritative sources of the prophetic tradition; the concluding references is taken from *Musnad al-IU.umayd* quoted by U Abd-Allah 'Islam and the cultural imperative' (2003) 8 *Journal of Islamic Law and Culture* 89.

283 M Rajabi-Ardeshiri 'The rights of the child in the Islamic context: The challenges of the local and the global' (2009) 17 *International Journal of Children's Rights 475;* M Elahi 'The rights of the child under Islamic law: Prohibition of the child soldier' (1987-1988) 19 *Columbia Human Rights Law Review* 259; and D Olowu 'Children's rights, international human rights and the promise of Islamic legal theory' (2008) 12 *Law Democracy & Development* 62.

284 As above.

285 As above.

286 AS above.

287 As above.

to reinforce, legitimise and complement existing conceptions, whatever their virtues or vices.

3.3.2.2.2. Christianity

According to King Leopold II, 'evangelize the niggers so that they stay forever in submission to the white colonialists, so they never revolt against the restraints they are undergoing. Recite everyday: "Happy are those who are weeping because the kingdom of God is for them."'[288] Some scholars regard the relationship between Christianity and colonialism in this light;[289] they see Christian missionaries as the facilitators of colonialism while others consider them as the moral face of colonialism.[290] The commonality in history, culture and religion between Christian missionaries and the colonial officials further reinforces the perception of a common approach to Africa, and the impact of their policies on African societies. The colonial officials looked to the missionaries to support colonial structures and thinking, the missionaries looked to the colonial officials to promote and support their activities.

Christianity manifests the cultural values and practices of those who brought it to Africa.[291] Christianity's cultural values expressed in the 19th century place strong emphasis on the nuclear family, strong parental authority over the upbringing of children within that family structure, strong discipline as a basis for moral chastity, formal education as a hallmark of normal childhood, and strong responsibility of children towards their parents, among other

---

288 King Leopold II of Belgium to his missionaries in the Congo (1883) quoted in O Vengeyi*Aluta continua biblical hermeneutics for liberation: Interpreting biblical texts on slavery for liberation of Zimbabwean underclasses* (2013) 191.

289 For an elaborate historical account and details about these debates see generally E Isichei *A history of Christianity in Africa: From antiquity to the present* (1995) and R Elphick *et al Christianity in South Africa: A political, social and cultural history* (1998).

290 J Comaroff 'Christianity and colonialism in South Africa' (1986) 13 *American Anthropologist* 1 and R Gray 'Christianity, colonialism and communications in Sub-Saharan Africa' (1982) 13 *Journal of Black Studies* 59.

291 J Gerald & W Russello *Christianity and European culture: Selections from the work of Christopher Dawson* (2012) 46, 107.

things.[292] Christianity placed child welfare at the centre of good parenting.[293] This struck a familiar cord with the colonial officials:

> the quality of parenting directly affects numerous state interests including the civic virtue and citizenship of the rising generation and the future well-being of the nation. So the state has a profound interest in supporting good parenting and cultural institutions that help parents to cultivate virtues in their children.[294]

The great Enlightenment thinkers and political architects postulated a connection between the family, the state and the concept of childhood. According to Locke, 'parents have an obligation to preserve, nourish, and educate their children' during the imperfect state of childhood.[295] It was viewed 'to thrust and abandon [children] to a state as wretched,'[296] so parents had a responsibility to discipline children in ways they find 'most effectual to give such strength and health to their bodies, such vigour and rectitude to their minds, as may best fit his/their children to be most useful to themselves and others.'[297]

The family in traditional Africa was the essential unit of society that appropriated and propagated cultural norms through childrearing practices. Christianity's impact on childbearing and childrearing practices and, ultimately, on African traditional cultures was direct and immediate. Unlike Islam, Christianity was not accommodating to local cultures.[298] Christianity's approach to African traditional cultures was to replace traditional values that were incompatible with its teaching of Christian values.

---

292 L Wardle 'The jurisprudence of parenting and the influence of religion on effective parenting' (2011) 2 *International Journal of the Jurisprudence of the family* 437.

293 As above.

294 As above.

295 J Locke Second treatise on government, in two treatises on government § 58 (1690, gutenberg e-book, posted 2010), available at http://www.gutenberg. Org/files/7370/7370.

296 As above.

297 J Locke Second treatise on government, in two treatises on government § 58 (1690, gutenberg e-book, posted 2010), available at http://www.gutenberg.Org/files/7370/7370.

298 L Sanneh *West African Christianity* (1983) 227; L Sanneh *Piety and power between the world of Islam and that of the West* (1996) 3 and A Byaruhanga-Akiiki *Africa and Christianity: Domestication of Christian values in the African Church* (1993) 179.

Within the scope of this work, a major contribution of Christianity to the conception of childhood in Africa was its willingness and ability to make childhood a subject of public policy as well as a private concern of the family. That is to say childhood was a subject of public policy even as it was a private family space. As a public space, childhood was essential to governance and, thus, the responsibility of governments. As a private domain, parents had unrestricted rights and authority over the upbringing and education of their children.[299] Considering childhood as a public space opened it up to government regulation. The advent of Christianity and colonialism marked the elimination of the end for an active role for African culture in childhood and an increasing role for the law and state in childhood issues.

3.3.2.3. Poverty and HIV/AIDS

Poverty affects the construction of childhood in Africa in multiple ways. Poverty reduces the duration of childhood and weakens the social network of security that has sustained a healthy childhood in traditional African communities.[300] HIV/AIDS depletes the immediate support mechanism for children and, consequently, thrusts upon children in Africa roles and responsibilities that hereto belonged to adults alone.[301] The combined effect of poverty and HIV/AIDS is the fast transition of children in Africa from childhood to adult roles and responsibilities.

Poverty is difficult to define, and child poverty is even more problematic.[302] UNICEF describes child poverty as:

> a human condition, characterized by the sustained or chronic deprivation of the resources, capabilities, choices, security and power

---

299 See, generally, H Englund (ed) *Christianity and public culture in Africa* (2011).

300 UNICEF Childhood under threat: Why are millions of children losing out on their childhood? (2005) The Status of the World's Children Report available at: http://www.unicef.org/sowc05/english/index.html.

301 G Foster & J Williamson A review of current literature on the impact of HIV/AIDS on children in sub-Saharan Africa, AIDS, 14 (suppl. 3), 2000, S275–S284.

302 S Tsegaye *et al Child poverty in Africa: An overview* (2010) 8.

> necessary for the enjoyment of an adequate standard of living and other civil, cultural, economic, political and social rights.[303]

Poverty has a devastating impact on children and their experience of childhood. According to UNICEF,

> Children living in poverty experience deprivation of the material, spiritual and emotional resources needed to survive, develop and thrive, leaving them unable to enjoy their rights, achieve their full potential or participate as full and equal members of society.[304]

Even though poverty has been a challenge in Africa for a very long time, extended family and community support systems have always cushioned the effects of poverty on the vulnerable members of the community.[305] This 'shared management, caretaking, and socially distributed support'[306] system, called the extended family, provided children with alternative source of support and livelihood. However, the increasingly high rate of household poverty, the devastating effects of the HIV/AIDS pandemic, encroaching individualism and other societal pressures have steadily eroded these social support networks.[307]

---

303 UNICEF Childhood under threat: Why are millions of children losing out on their childhood? (2005) The Status of the World's Children Report available at: http://www.unicef.org/sowc05/english/index.html.

304 UNICEF Childhood under threat: Why are millions of children losing out on their childhood? (2005) The Status of the World's Children Report available at: http://www.unicef.org/sowc05/english/index.html.

305 L Callaghan 'Building on an African worldview' (1998) 89 *Early Childhood Matters* 30; S Harkness & C Super 'Shared child care in East Africa: Socio-cultural origins and developmental consequences' in M Lamb *et al* (eds) *Child care in Context: Socio-cultural perspectives* (1992) 441; B Kaye *Bringing up children in Ghana* (1992); R LeVine 'Challenging expert knowledge: Findings from an African book of infant care and development' in U Gielen & J Roopnarine (eds) *Childhood and adolescence: Cross-cultural perspectives and applications* (2004) 149; A Nsamenang *Human Development in cultural context: A Third World perspective* (1992); R Ohuche & B Otaala *The African child in his environment* (1981); T Weisner 'Support for children and the African family crisis' in T Weisner *et al* (eds) *African families and the crisis of social change* (1997) 20; N Uka (1966) *Growing up in Nigerian culture* (1966).

306 T Weisner 'Support for children and the African family crisis' in T Weisner *et al* (eds) *African families and the crisis of social change* (1997) 23.

307 M Skovdal & M Daniel 'Resilience through participation and coping-enabling social environments: The case of HIV-affected children in sub-Saharan Africa' (2012) 11 *African Journal of AIDS Book* 153; L Lee 'Youths navigating social networks and social support systems in settings of chronic crisis: The case of youth-headed households in Rwanda' (2012) 11 *African Journal of AIDS Book* 165'; R Evans 'Safeguarding inheritance and enhancing the resilience of orphaned young people living in child and youth-headed households in Tanzania and Uganda' (2012) 11 *African Journal of AIDS Book* 177; M Daniel & A Mathias 'Challenges and coping strategies of orphaned children in Tanzania who are not adequately cared for by adults' (2012) 11 *African Journal of AIDS Book* 191; L Wood at el 'Read me to resilience': Exploring the use of cultural stories to boost the positive adjustment of children orphaned by AIDS (2012) 11 *African Journal of AIDS Book* 225; M

The consequences of that erosion include the street children phenomenon, child headed households, a ready supply of children for trafficking, child soldiers and other forms of child abuse. These children, therefore, are forced to take up roles and responsibilities that had previously been the sole preserve of adults.[308] Gradually, poverty is earning itself a place among the factors that forcefully graduate a child from the status of childhood into adulthood.

The impact of poverty is exacerbated by the HIV/AIDS pandemic. HIV/AIDS kills society's most productive sector and its breadwinners; it increases dependency ratios and renders millions of children orphans.[309]

With many siblings to take care of and, in most cases, with no inheritance to enable them to discharge their new responsibilities, these children have to become breadwinners giving rise to the phenomenon called 'child-headed households', in many countries in Africa.[310]

Skovdal & V Ogutu 'Coping with hardship through friendship: The importance of peer social capital among children affected by HIV in Kenya' (2012) 11 *African Journal of AIDS Book* 241; M Van der Brug 'Strategies to bring about change: A longitudinal book on challenges and coping strategies of orphans and vulnerable children and adolescents in Namibia African' (2012) 11 *African Journal of AIDS Book* 273.

308 M Skovdal & M Daniel 'Resilience through participation and coping-enabling social environments: The case of HIV-affected children in sub-Saharan Africa' (2012) 11 *African Journal of AIDS Book* 153; L Lee 'Youths navigating social networks and social support systems in settings of chronic crisis: The case of youth-headed households in Rwanda' (2012) 11 *African Journal of AIDS Book* 165'; R Evans 'Safeguarding inheritance and enhancing the resilience of orphaned young people living in child and youth-headed households in Tanzania and Uganda' (2012) 11 *African Journal of AIDS Book* 177; M Daniel & A Mathias 'Challenges and coping strategies of orphaned children in Tanzania who are not adequately cared for by adults' (2012) 11 *African Journal of AIDS Book* 191; L Wood at el 'Read me to resilience': Exploring the use of cultural stories to boost the positive adjustment of children orphaned by AIDS (2012) 11 *African Journal of AIDS Book* 225; M Skovdal & V Ogutu 'Coping with hardship through friendship: The importance of peer social capital among children affected by HIV in Kenya' (2012) 11 *African Journal of AIDS Book* 241; M Van der Brug 'Strategies to bring about change: A longitudinal book on challenges and coping strategies of orphans and vulnerable children and adolescents in Namibia African' (2012) 11 *African Journal of AIDS Book* 273.

309 M Skovdal & M Daniel 'Resilience through participation and coping-enabling social environments: The case of HIV-affected children in sub-Saharan Africa' (2012) 11 *African Journal of AIDS Book* 153; L Lee 'Youths navigating social networks and social support systems in settings of chronic crisis: The case of youth-headed households in Rwanda' (2012) 11 *African Journal of AIDS Book* 165'; R Evans 'Safeguarding inheritance and enhancing the resilience of orphaned young people living in child and youth-headed households in Tanzania and Uganda' (2012) 11 *African Journal of AIDS Book* 177; M Daniel & A Mathias 'Challenges and coping strategies of orphaned children in Tanzania who are not adequately cared for by adults' (2012) 11 *African Journal of AIDS Book* 191; L Wood at el 'Read me to resilience': Exploring the use of cultural stories to boost the positive adjustment of children orphaned by AIDS (2012) 11 *African Journal of AIDS Book* 225; M Skovdal & V Ogutu 'Coping with hardship through friendship: The importance of peer social capital among children affected by HIV in Kenya' (2012) 11 *African Journal of AIDS Book* 241; M Van der Brug 'Strategies to bring about change: A longitudinal book on challenges and coping strategies of orphans and vulnerable children and adolescents in Namibia African' (2012) 11 *African Journal of AIDS Book* 273.

310 As above.

Far from making children in Africa powerless victims of overwhelming circumstances, as they are usually presented, the challenges presented by poverty, HIV and AIDS are bringing out in children coping strategies and a resilient spirit.[311] The question these struggling and surviving children pose to policy makers in Africa is: would the law be used to support or to stop children from gaining access to adult powers and privileges to enable them meet adult roles and responsibilities? Using laws to empower vulnerable children make ends meet seems to be the most appropriate response.

3.4. Conclusion

The question whether the different understanding of childhood in Africa can be distilled into common core features is a complex one. First, because there is a multiplicity of cultures and cultural experiences of children in Africa. Second, there is a scarcity of continental book materials on childhood in Africa that would facilitate such an exercise. Third, such an enterprise faces enormous methodological challenges, such as generating comparable data across countries, communities and cultures in Africa.

However, the fact that it is a difficult undertaking does not mean it is an impossible task. Although African culture was and remains diverse and varied, the chapter used discernible common trends and features of African cultures and common experiences of Africans as a framework to analyze and distil common core features of childhood in Africa. Using 'who is a child?', the autonomy rights of the child, best interests of the child, and child participation as analytical guides, the chapter outlines the key features of the image of childhood in Africa.

Traditional communities in Africa generally believe childhood starts at conception. African communities, in general, see and treat children as 'beings' in the making: as being in a preparatory period for responsible adulthood. It is a period to learn the core tenets of African culture - respect, reciprocity, responsibility, restraint and reproduction. The endpoint of childhood is

311 M Skovdal & M Daniel 'Resilience through participation and coping-enabling social environments: The case of HIV-affected children in sub-Saharan Africa' (2012) 11 *African Journal of AIDS Book* 153.

earned. The ability to demonstrate maturity, control over natural instincts, marriage, procreation and a successful passage through appropriate rituals, amongst other factors, transit a child into adulthood. It is possible today to add HIV/AIDS and poverty among the social factors that are graduating children into adulthood in Africa.

Even though some of the cultural values find a resemblance in human rights norms, there is no substantial evidence to support the notion that the relationship between children and adults in traditional African communities was rights-based. There were privileges, roles and responsibilities associated with childhood. Respect or disrespect of these privileges, roles and responsibilities was either rewarded or sanctioned by the community. The interests of children and the interests of the family and communities were deemed to be complementary. Almost all African cultures and traditions had mechanisms that enabled children to participate in societal decision- making.

Law and policy making in Africa have not significantly benefited from the positive cultural features of childhood in traditional African society. A reason for this state of affairs is that current law making or law reform on childhood in Africa is externally driven. The CRC Committee and the African Children's Committee are pushing African countries to enact laws or harmonize existing legislation with international human rights norms. Effective law reform must take cognizance of the fact that children in Africa also live their lives under cultural norms that are considered legitimate by their communities.

It is the contention of this chapter that there is a common core understanding of childhood in traditional communities in Africa. The African image of childhood has positive and negative features. Policy makers should benefit from the positive features while working with traditional communities to transform the negative features.

CHAPTER 4

THE IMAGE OF CHILDHOOD IN THE AFRICAN CHILDREN'S CHARTER

This chapter is divided into five parts. The first part outlines the reasons that motivated the drafting and adoption of the African Children's Charter. These reasons include the lack of meaningful participation in the drafting process of the CRC, the feeling that the CRC did not adequately reflect the conception of childhood in Africa, and the need to have greater and context-specific protection for children in Africa. It is argued that though these were valid concerns at the time of drafting the African Children's Charter, the CRC Committee has significantly addressed these concerns either through the adoption of Optional Protocols or through progressive interpretation of the CRC. Therefore, the need for the African Children's Charter in its current form no longer exists.

Part 2 discusses the effect of the increasingly blurred distinction between the CRC and the African Children's Charter. In addition to the fact that the CRC and the African Children's Charter are textually and normatively similar, the emerging jurisprudence of the CRC Committee and the African Children's Committee is also similar. It is argued in this section that two possible negative effects arise out of these similarities: First, there is the danger of the African Children's Charter duplicating the CRC. Second, because the African Children's Charter displays upward legitimacy based on the international human rights system rather than a downward legitimacy based on the cultural context of its operation, the African Children's Charter faces the same challenges of cultural legitimacy that the CRC faces in Africa, unless the African Children's Committee deliberately interprets the provisions of the African Children's Charter in a context-sensitive manner.

Parts 3 and 4 of the chapter examine the theoretical and practical challenges that might face the effective and efficient implementation of the African Children's Charter in many traditional communities in Africa. These sections juxtapose the conception of childhood in the African Children's Charter with the conception of childhood in traditional African communities as discussed in chapter three in order to illustrate the divergence between the African Children's Charter's interpretation and how communities in traditional African society still see and treat children. The point is not to approve the traditional perception of childhood, but to point out that it exists and that those interpreting the African Children's Charter need to take these views into consideration. A failure to accommodate a traditional understanding of childhood will continue to create a hybrid lived experience for children. Such a possibility further complicates the effective and efficient promotion and protection of children's rights and alienates families and communities.

The last part discusses what remains of the distinguishing or unique features of the African Children's Charter in contrast to the CRC and its Protocols. It is noted that the discussion around the duties of the child may be the only surviving feature of the African Children's Charter that the CRC does not cover.[1] With respect to the definition of the child, the CRC Committee, through its various general comments and concluding observations, has preferred 18 as the upper limit of defining who a child is,[2] and has ensured that the same standard of the 'best interests' of the child, as provided for in the African Children's Charter, is also recommended.[3] The higher standard of protection extended to the girl child and to children of imprisoned mothers offered in the African Children's Charter has been taken care of, in one form or the other, either by the Optional Protocols or through the general

1 See the discussion at page 104 to 106.

2 See the discussion at page 104 to 106.

3 See the discussion at page 104 to 106.

comments and the Day of General Discussion of the CRC Committee.[4] The section concludes that unless the African Children's Committee innovatively interprets the provisions of the African Children's Charter in such a way that they do not simply echo the CRC, it is likely that the African Children's Charter will become increasingly redundant. Essentially, the image of childhood in the African Children's Charter is substantially a reflection of the image of the child in the CRC.

4. Introduction

A number of process-related and substance-orientated reasons were put forward by academics and policy makers in Africa as to the desirability of Africa to adopt a regional treaty dealing with children's rights.[5] As to process, it has been argued that there was inadequate participation by many African states in the movement leading to, and the actual drafting and adoption of the CRC. Also, regarding substance, the CRC did not adequately include some of the challenges children in Africa face. Furthermore, the image of childhood in the CRC does not comprehensively reflect the understanding of childhood in Africa. Therefore, the CRC was considered as lacking an African cultural fingerprint. Arguably, there was a need for an African children's treaty rooted in the philosophical and cultural heritage of African communities.

Participation in treaty making is voluntary. It allows states to control the behaviour of other states in a common process in order to define and determine acceptable future behaviour within an area of discussion.[6] Participation in

---

4 See the discussion at page 104 to 106.

5 See F Viljoen 'Supra-national human rights instruments for the protection of children in the Africa: The Convention on the Rights of the Child and the African Charter on the Rights and Welfare of the Child' (1998) 31 *Comparative and International Law Journal of Southern Africa* 199; D Olowu 'Protecting children's rights in Africa: A critique of the African Charter on the Rights and Welfare of the Child' (2002) 10 *International Journal of Children's Rights* 127; D Chirwa 'The merits and demerits of the African Charter on the Rights and Welfare of the Child' (2002) 10 *International Journal of Children's Rights* 157; A Lloyd 'Evolution of the African Charter on the Rights and Welfare of the Child and the African Committee of Experts: Raising the gauntlet' (2002) 10 *International Journal of Children's Rights* 179; M Gose *The African Charter on the Rights and Welfare of the Child* (2002), J Sloth-Nielsen & B Mezmur 'The dutiful child: The implications of article 31 of the African's Children's Charter' (2008) 52 *Journal of African Law* 159; B Mezmur 'The African Children's Charter versus the United Nations Convention on the Rights of the Child: A zero-sum game? (2008) 23 *South Africa Public Law Journal* and T Kaime *The African Charter on the Rights and Welfare of the Child: A socio-legal perspective* (2009).

6 S Sitaraman *State participation in international treaty regimes* (2009) 3.

international treaty-making processes comes with political, monetary and sovereignty costs. Because of these cost implications for national policymaking, states sometime refuse to participate in the process. When states decide to participate in a treaty after it has been negotiated, either through ratification or accession, it should be assumed that they are satisfied with the content of the treaty. However, some scholars argue that not all states that ratify treaties genuinely consent to do so but are coerced or coaxed by various factors.[7] The argument is that strong states establish the regimes and weaker states are made either to follow suit or suffer consequences if they refuse.[8]

Only four African countries participated meaningfully in the drafting process of the CRC.[9] Therefore, it may be presumed that the minimal participation by African states resulted in an input of next to nothing in the drafting process. This situation probably was made worse by a powerful negotiating and lobbying bloc in the Working Group, such as the European Group. Why was Africa not adequately represented in the negotiating process? The question is pertinent in the light of the fact that many more African countries participated in the drafting process of the International Covenant on Civil and Political Rights and the International Covenant on Economic, Social and Cultural Rights, just a few years after most of them had gained independence, than did in the 1980s with regard to the CRC.[10] The apparently incongruent behaviour of African countries might be explained by the fact that the subject matter of the CRC was not accorded a high priority, at that time, by African states and for this reason they did not take their participation seriously.

---

7 A An-Na'im 'Cultural transformation and normative consensus on the best interests of the child' (1994) 8 *International Journal of Law and the Family* 62.

8 A Moravcsik 'Why is the U.S human rights policy so unilateral?' in S Patrick & S Forman (eds) *Multilateralism and U.S foreign policy: Ambivalent engagement* (2001) 345.

9 F Viljoen 'Supra-national human rights instruments for the protection of children in Africa: The Convention on the Rights of the Child and the African Charter on the Rights and Welfare of the Child' (1998) 31 *The Comparative and International Law Journal of Southern Africa* 199 citing R Barsh 'The draft Convention on the Rights of the Child: A case of eurocentrism in standard setting' (1989) 58 *Nordic Journal of International law* 24.

10 Z Arat 'Forging a global culture of human rights: Origins and prospects of the International Bill of Rights' (2006) 28 *Human Rights Quarterly* 416; See generally J Humphrey *Human rights & the United Nations: A great adventure* (1984); J Morsink *The Universal Declaration of Human Rights: Origins, drafting, and intent* (1999). Take for example, in the drafting of the International Bill of Rights the following countries from North Africa participated meaningfully: Algeria, Egypt, Libya, Mauritania, Morocco, Somalia, Sudan and Tunisia. See S Waltz 'Universal human rights: The contribution of Muslim states' (2004) 26 *Human Rights Quarterly* 799 for the extent of the contribution of these African countries.

Nevertheless, irrespective of the lack of meaningful participation by African states, the universal ratification of the CRC by African states should be indicative of the general acceptance of the image of childhood in the CRC by African states. Ratification, as a means of participation in the implementation of a treaty, is theoretically indicative of a state's intention to accept the terms and conditions of a treaty and to be bound by the provisions of that treaty. The explanation of a lack of meaningful participation in the drafting process of the CRC as a justification for the creation of an African Children's Charter is significantly weakened by the overwhelming subsequent ratification of the CRC by African states.

Even though the CRC is considered the most comprehensive treaty on children's rights, there are a number of issues that the CRC does not cover.[11] Those who drafted the African Children's Charter held the view that there were 'specific problems that African children confront'[12] that the CRC failed to provide for. These problems include internal displacement of children; apartheid; harmful cultural practices; the situation of children affected by armed conflict; which was thought to be inadequately provided for in the CRC, and the challenges facing the girl child, such as child marriage. Therefore, it was argued that there was a need for a regional children's rights framework in Africa to deal with these issues.[13] However, most of these challenges could have been addressed and, actually, have been progressively addressed through optional protocols and an expansive interpretation of the CRC by the CRC Committee.

The most credible justification for the adoption of the African Children's Charter, arguably, is the one concerning the nature and scope of the image or conception of childhood provided for in the CRC. The greatest challenge with respect to this justification is that the African Children's Charter does

11 Some of the issues included, for example, the girl child, responsibilities and duties of the child, the role of extended families, children and armed conflicts, internal displacement, children under apartheid, children of imprisoned mothers.

12 J Sloth-Nielsen & B Mezmur 'Surveying the book landscape to promote children's legal rights in an African context' (2007) 7 *African Human Rights Law Journal* 330.

13 See, generally, ANPPCAN 'The rights of the child selected proceedings of a workshop on the draft Convention on the Rights of the Child: An African perspective' (1988).

not provide for an alternative image of childhood. Even though at the time of drafting of the African Children's Charter there were differences between the CRC and the African Children's Charter, these differences were those of standards and not theoretical differences with respect to the conception of childhood. That is why, conceptually, the African Children's Charter is similar to the CRC. If one of the cases against the CRC is poor participation by African states and the lack of autochthony of its norms and standards in Africa, how participatory was the drafting of the African Children's Charter and how autochthonous is the conception of childhood in the African Children's Charter?

In the light of the similarities between the African Children's Charter and the CRC, there is a question if the African Children's Charter is a needful complement to the CRC or an unnecessary and burdensome duplication for state parties and other policy makers. Scholarly reaction to the question, so far, can be classified as abolitionist or retentionist. The abolitionists consider the African Children's Charter duplicative and an unwise use of time and scarce resources that otherwise could have been used to directly improve the wellbeing of children in Africa.[14] Their argument is that whatever additions the African Children's Charter introduces could effectively be taken care of within the framework of the CRC or, better still, within a protocol to the African Charter on Human and Peoples' Rights (ACHPR) akin to the Protocol to the African Charter on Human and Peoples' Rights on the Rights of Women in Africa. The protocol route is seen as the most effective and efficient option, by some of these scholars.[15] According to the same scholars, creating a whole treaty and its monitoring mechanism to effectively handle 'seven unique features' is not only costly for the AU and the African human rights system, but also for state parties that have to report on almost the same issues twice and to different bodies.

---

14 S Gutto 'The reform and the renewal of the African human and peoples' rights system' (2001) 2 *African Human Rights Law Journal* 175 bemoaning the duplication in the system and advocating for synergies; see, to some extent, D Olowu 'Protecting children's rights in Africa: A critique of the African Charter on the Rights and Welfare of the Child' (2002) 10 *International Journal on Children's Rights* 127.

15 D Olowu 'Protecting children's rights in Africa: A critique of the African Charter on the Rights and Welfare of the Child' (2002) 10 *International Journal on Children's Rights* 127.

Those who advocate for the retention of the African Children's Charter hold the view that it is never a waste to have an additional layer of human rights protection for the most vulnerable of society. Protecting human rights might be costly, but the implications of the failure to protect them are even more costly, it is argued. Even though, textually, the two instruments (the CRC and African Children's Charter) may be similar, the existence of the African Children's Charter provides room for possible innovative interpretations that might not only benefit children in Africa but might spark international conversations on the rights of children in different contexts.[16] For this group of scholars the question around the utility of the African Children's Charter is moot, and efforts should be directed towards making the best of the situation.[17] According to this group, the value of specific treaties is obvious and that is why different categories of vulnerable people continue to clamour for a specific treaty to better protect them.[18] For a category that makes up more than half of the population of the continent, it is worthwhile and commendable to offer children in Africa treaty-specific protection.

While there is a strong case for rationality in the architecture of the African human rights system, such rationalization should not be at the expense of effective protection of vulnerable groups in Africa. The fact that it has taken the ACHPR almost three decades to start to discharge its mandate effectively might be indicative of the fact that housing all the treaties within the African human rights system under the umbrella of the ACHPR may not be the most prudent way to have proceeded. Nevertheless, the question of streamlining, rationalising and harmonising the African human rights system should never be a moot question. Effective human rights systems continuously reinvent

---

16 See, for example, D Chirwa 'The merits and demerits of the African Charter on the Rights and Welfare of the Child' (2002) 10 *The International Journal of Children's Rights* 157 exploring how the complementary provisions as well as the distinctive provisions of the African Children's Charter could be enhanced to better offer protection for children's in Africa.

17 B Mezmur 'The African Children's Charter versus the United Nations Convention on the Rights of the Child: A zero-sum game?' (2008) 23 *South Africa Public Law Journal* 1 noting that emphasis should really be on the value adding of the African Children's Charter.

18 S Ebobrah 'Towards a positive application of complementarity in the African human rights system: Issues of functions and relations' (2011) 22 *European Journal of International Law* 663 highlighting the value adding of the quasi-judicial bodies within the African human rights with respect to investigating mass violations, amicable settlements etc.

themselves to meet different challenges.[19] It is possible that if the human and financial resources used to implement the African Children's Charter were all housed within the framework of ACHPR, it could perform better. Either way, however, the requirement is for the African Children's Committee to discharge its mandate creatively and innovatively[20] and to interpret the provisions of the African Children's Charter in such a way that validates its existence, adds value to the promotion and protection of children's rights in Africa, and reduces the potential of duplication and redundancy.

4.1. A historical overview of the African Children's Charter

There is no publicly available *travaux préparatoires* of the African Children's Charter. Any historical account of the drafting process of the African Children's Charter is a patchwork of the notes of surviving members of the drafting team and the work of scholars. In 1979, within the framework of the Organisation of African Unity (OAU), 'aware of the deep concern of African states about the future of African children as inheritors and keepers of African cultural heritage,'[21] African leaders adopted the Declaration on the Rights and Welfare of the Child (the OAU Declaration). This marked the first time that African countries at the highest level deliberated, agreed and declared that children in Africa are entitled to human rights, and their welfare is a subject of public policy at all levels. The OAU Declaration advanced a number of philosophical and conceptual arguments.

First, as its title suggests, the OAU Declaration advances the argument that the rights and welfare or wellbeing for children are not the same. Rights may result in the wellbeing of children but are not the only means to ensure

19 S Gutto 'The reform and the renewal of the African human and peoples' rights system' (2001) 2 *African Human Rights Law Journal* 175.

20 Creativity and innovation should not mean activism by the African Children's Committee. Since state parties and other stake holders might take issues with such an approach, a good example is the stand taken by the Family Policy in Russia with respect to the activities of the CRC which the centre deems *ultra vires*. See the publication by the Family Policy Centre entitled Ultra vires acts by the Committee on the Rights of the Child and the new Optional Protocol to UNCRC'. Available at http://www.familypolicy.ru/rep/int-12-034en-s.pdf.

21 Preamble to the Declaration on the Rights and Welfare of the Child (1979) para 6 available at: http://www.issafrica.org/AF/RegOrg/unity_to_union/pdfs/oau/hog/pHoGAssembly1979.pdf.

welfare. A right is a vehicle needed to secure a child's physical, economic, mental, spiritual, moral or social wellbeing.

Second, the drafters of the OAU Declaration promoted a hybrid approach in contemplating an African framework for children's rights and welfare. The idea postulated by the OAU Declaration seems to be that an African treaty on children must benefit from combining the best of two worlds, that is, it must incorporate internationally agreed values, norms and concepts and, at the same time, must benefit from the African cultural heritage.

Third, the drafters seem to have a minimalistic view of culture, as 'African arts, language and culture.'[22] They adopted a 'harmful' approach in dealing with culture; for example, the OAU Declaration states:

> Member States should thoroughly examine cultural legacies and practice that are harmful to normal growth and development of the child such as child marriage and female circumcision, and should take legal and educational measures to abolish them.[23]

Finally, the drafters envisaged the centrality of the family to the welfare of the child: the 'welfare of the African Child is inextricably bound up with that of its parents and other members of its family.'[24] For the first time in the Preamble, a concept in the title is singled out, probably for emphasis. Either the drafters envisaged that the welfare component of the OAU Declaration was a function of the family environment of the child or they did not conceive that rights could apply within the family environment. The emphasis on the vertical application of the rights of the child, that is to say that child's rights are held with respect to the state, is one of the legacies that the African Children's Charter inherited.

---

22 It is possible to consider the addition of the word culture to the list in paragraph 10 of the Declaration as an intention to adapt a broader view of culture. The difficulty with this view is the fact that language and arts are aspects of culture. To have mentioned these specifically would mean the exclusion of aspects that are not directly listed.

23 Para 3 of the Declaration. The expression 'such as' would imply the possibility of more additions to the list of specific cultural legacies and practices.

24 Preamble to the Declaration para 7.

The OAU considered the Declaration a first step in a process towards a regional binding- treaty on children's rights and welfare in Africa. Therefore, at the Monrovia Summit of 1979 the OAU directed the Secretary General to explore the possibilities of bringing to fruition such a binding national and regional treaty. In the mid-1980s the African Network for the Prevention and Protection of Children against Abuse and Neglect (ANPPCAN)[25] and UNICEF convened a meeting in Nairobi to discuss the draft Convention on the Rights of the Child and sought African input into that draft. In the course of the deliberations, participants agreed that although the draft CRC was comprehensive, it did not cover context-specific issues peculiar to Africa.[26] ANPPCAN and the OAU co-hosted a working group of experts to brainstorm and develop an African Charter on the Rights and Welfare of the Child.[27] After a number of meetings of the Working Group, a draft African Children's Charter was completed and presented to the OAU for adoption. The OAU deliberated on the draft African Children's Charter and, in 1990, adopted it, just over a year after the CRC had entered into force.

The drafting process of the African Children's Charter was non-state-actor-centered. Available records indicate that 57 representatives of national and international nongovernmental organizations, nine representatives of African governments and only one participant from the OAU took part in the discussions and drafting process of the African Children's Charter.[28] Comparatively, even though NGOs played a significant role in the negotiation and drafting process of the CRC (the process was primarily government proposed and led), the process that led to the drafting of the African Children's Charter was predominately led by civil society organizations. There is no record of participation by communities in Africa or other important

25 The African Network for the Prevention and Protection against Child Abuse and Neglect (ANPPCAN) is a pan African network that promotes child rights and child protection in Africa (http://www.anppcan.org/).

26 See, generally, ANPPCAN 'The rights of the child selected proceedings of a workshop on the draft Convention on the Rights of the Child: An African perspective' (1988).

27 See, generally, ANPPCAN 'The rights of the child selected proceedings of a workshop on the draft Convention on the Rights of the Child: An African perspective' (1988).

28 See ,generally, ANPPCAN 'The rights of the child selected proceedings of a workshop on the draft Convention on the Rights of the Child: An African perspective' (1988).

stakeholders. The processes that lead to the adoption of the African Children's Charter can best be described by adapting the words of Ibhawoh as follows:

> the African Children's Charter has merely been decreed from above through the OAU, while cultural orientations and attitudes have been expected to confirm by legislative fiat with this new image and understanding of childhood. Culture evolves, however, rather than transforms and the process of evolution is painstakingly gradual and complex.[29]

The lack of participation by key stakeholders in the drafting process of the African Children's Charter leads to the question whether the drafting of the African Children's Charter was an exercise in indigenous law making or a mere transplanting of legal norms and standards.

At the same time when African states were preparing for the drafting of a regional treaty on children's rights, there was an international effort to draw up a global child rights treaty. Though the UN Declaration called on states, through legislative measures, to recognize and enforce the statement of general principles in the Declaration, these were just principles and, therefore, legally non-binding. The need for an internationally binding treaty on children's rights was obvious. The UN Commission on Human Rights, during its 34th session in 1978, reinforced the concern over the plight of children around the world and agreed to work towards an international and legally binding treaty to protect children.

The 1959 Declaration had existed for 20 years, yet the UN General Assembly decided to designate 1979, the 20th anniversary of the UN Declaration, as the International Year of the Child. As part of the celebration, the General Assembly established a Working Group to elaborate the draft Convention submitted by Poland into an internationally acceptable treaty to protect and

29 This is the original expression 'In many African nations, human rights have merely been decreed from above through constitutional and other legal provisions, while cultural orientations and attitudes have been expected to conform by legislative fiat with these new human rights standards. Culture evolves however, rather than transforms and the process of evolution is painstakingly gradual and complex' in B Ibhawoh 'Between culture and constitution: Evaluating the cultural legitimacy of human rights in the African state (2000) 22 *Human Rights Quarterly* 838. The 'above' here would refer to the African Union that seems to assume cultural legitimacy on behalf of the communities in Africa.

promote the rights of children. The Working Group completed its work with the adoption of a draft Convention on the Rights of the Child in December 1988. On 20 November 1989 the General Assembly adopted the Convention, and it was opened for ratification on 26 January 1990. By 2 September 1990, the Convention had 20 ratifications – the minimum number needed for it to enter into force.[30]

Comparatively, whereas the process of the African Children's Charter was initiated by non-governmental organizations, the CRC process was started by a government and followed through by an intergovernmental organization. The process of negotiating the CRC started and remained within the UN arena, but in the case of the African Children's Charter it started outside the OAU and only the final product was handed over to the states. The UN process was fairly representative of a global interest; the same cannot be said of the process that resulted in the African Children's Charter.

It is possible to argue that the difficulty that the African Children's Charter faced with respect to ratification is rooted more in how the process started than the frequently cited reluctance of states parties to ratify the African Children's Charter. Consequently, even though the two processes, one leading to the adoption of the CRC and the other to the adoption of the African Children's Charter, started almost at the same time, state involvement in the UN process ensured that the UN treaty entered into force before its African counterpart.

4.2. The African Children's Charter as a transplant of the CRC

Policy makers involved in domestic law making either to establish new legal standards or reform existing ones to meet new challenges 'face a choice between two basic means of supplying new laws: indigenous law-making and transplantation of legal rules from other jurisdictions.'[31] Whatever the choice,

30 As of 30 October, 194 States and a Territory have ratified the CRC. Newest ratifications are from South Sudan and the State of Palestine.

31 P Grajzl & V Dimitrova-Grajzl 'The choice in the lawmaking process: Legal transplants vs. indigenous law' (2009) 5 *Review of Law and Economics* 615.

it will have implications for the implementation of the law. Research indicates that how a country or, in this case, a continent receives its 'laws is a much more important determinant of the current effectiveness of its legal institutions than the particular legal family that it adopted.'[32] Legal transferability comes in degrees. The legal norms more 'resistant to transplantation' are those that 'organise constitutional, legislative, administrative or judicial institutions and procedures' and are meant to 'allocate power, rulemaking, decision making, above all policy making powers.'[33] In situations where 'legal borrowings are incompatible with host country's [culture], they are likely to be rejected ... as alien or imposed.'[34] International law makers face similar challenges to those faced by policy makers at the domestic level. Therefore, the concept of indigenous law making and the transplantation of norms through law making apply with respect to treaty making.

Going the route of indigenous law making might avoid challenges around the 'illegitimacy, incompleteness, ineffectiveness and exclusion'[35] of the outcome of the law-making process. Indigenous efforts at law making might also result in an 'accumulation of knowledge' due to 'an incremental and practical process of trial and error', and the engagement of a wider constituency in the debate and law making process. Consequently, such a process and resultant law are more likely to reflect and respond to the state's or continent's 'own history, process, and context, constantly evolving and adapting in response to its own challenges internal or external', and nourished by 'its own culture, institutions, and nationalist mythology.'[36] It would seem that the drafters of the African Children's Charter opted out of an indigenous law-making process in favour of the transplantation of international norms and standards into Africa.

32 M Amos 'Transplanting human rights norms: The case of the United Kingdom's Human Rights Act' (2013) 35 *Human Rights Quarterly* 386 citing D Berkowitz *et al* 'Economic development, legality and the transplant effect' (2003) 51 *American Journal of Comparative Law* 163.

33 M Amos 'Transplanting human rights norms: The case of the United Kingdom's Human Rights Act' (2013) 35 *Human Rights Quarterly* 386 citing C de Secondat & B de Montesquieu *The spirit of law* (1748) Series 6.

34 J Gillespie, 'Transplanted company law: An ideological and cultural analysis of market-entry in Vietnam' (2002) 51 *International and Comparative Law Quarterly* 650.

35 M Mutua 'Standard setting in human rights: Critique and prognosis' (2007) 29 *Human Rights Quarterly* 547.

36 A An-Na'im *African constitutionalism and the rule of Islam* (2006) 171.

4.3. How 'African' is the African Children's Charter?

One of the arguments for the regionalisation of international human rights and international human rights laws is that the impact of human rights law depends, as do all laws, on changing the local consciousness of rights and relationships.[37] In order for human rights ideas to be effective they need to be translated into local terms and resonate favourably within local contexts of power and meaning. In the field of human rights, regionalism and regionalisation were supposed to narrow the gap between people and international human rights norms and mechanisms. It is believed that with a shared history, geography and, in some cases, language and religion, as well as a commonality of values, regions will best meet the human rights yearning of their people as well as the aspirations of the international human rights system.[38]

It was the desire to bring the benefits of international human rights closer to Africans, as well as to temper these benefits with the context-specific realities of the continent that resulted in the adoption of a regional human rights system. Other reasons that motivated the OAU, and its legal successor, the AU, to put in place human rights treaties and mechanisms that reflect and respond to the specific needs of the continent include the absence of participation by Africans in determining the concepts and content of the international human rights norms and standards, as well as specific political, economic and cultural needs in Africa.

The human rights system was conceived to perform at least a two-fold function. First, it should provide the first port of call when something fundamental goes wrong at the country level and the country has failed to address it adequately; and, second, it ought to provide a common minimum human right standard specific to the region.[39] As mentioned above, regional

---

37 H Steiner & P Alston *International human rights in context: Law, politics and morals* (2005) 369.

38 C Cerna 'Universality of human rights and cultural diversity: Implementation of human rights in different socio-cultural contexts' (1994) 16 *Human Rights Quarterly* 740.

39 M Cerna 'Universality of human rights and cultural diversity: Implementation of human rights in different socio-cultural contexts' (1994) 16 *Human Rights Quarterly* 740.

specificity and a context-specific nature of human rights systems are among the virtues of regional human rights systems.

Context and cultural specificities of regional human rights norms and institutions are critical in the area of children's rights and welfare.[40] Even though African cultures tend to share core common values and an understanding of childhood, there are significant differences within and among countries in Africa. Two of the drafters of the African Children's Charter have publicly stated that cultural specificities and the benefits of regionalisation drove the desire to adopt a regional treaty on children's rights. Muthoga, one of the drafters of the African Children's Charter, noted that the motivation to draft the African Children's Charter 'originated from a desire to address certain peculiarly African problems.'[41] Wako, who is credited with the preparation of the first draft of the African Children's Charter,[42] for his part, predicated the African move to adopt the African Children's Charter on the fact that 'each region, with its unique culture, traditions and history, is best placed to handle and resolve its human rights situation.'[43]

These assertions have been taken at face value by some scholars and commentators without subjecting the African Children's Charter to a context-specific critical analysis to ascertain their validity.[44] Most analysis and critique of the African Children's Charter have been done by means of a comparison with the CRC or the international human rights system. This section will attempt a critique of the African Children's Charter with reference to the image of childhood in traditional African communities with regard to four

40 B Rwezaura 'Competing 'images' of childhood in social and legal systems of contemporary sub Saharan Africa' (1998) 12 *International Journal of law, Policy and the Family* 255; see generally P Veerman *The rights of the child and the changing image of childhood* (1992).

41 L Muthoga 'Analysis of international instruments for the protection of the rights of the child' in Community Law Centre (ed) *International Conference on the Rights of the Child: Papers and reports of a conference convened by the Community Law Centre* (1992) 123.

42 T Kaime 'The foundations of rights in the African Charter on the Rights and Welfare of the Child: A historical and philosophical account' (2009) 3 *African Journal of Legal Studies* 120.

43 S Wako 'Towards an African Charter on the Rights of the Child' paper delivered at the Workshop on the Draft Convention on the Rights of the Child, Nairobi, 9-11 May 1988 cited in T Kaime 'The foundations of rights in the African Charter on the Rights and Welfare of the Child: A historical and philosophical account' (2009) 3 *African Journal of Legal Studies* 120.

44 T Kaime 'The foundations of rights in the African Charter on the Rights and Welfare of the Child: A historical and philosophical account' (2009) 3 *African Journal of Legal Studies* 120.

main themes: 'Who is a child?', the autonomy rights of the child, the best interests of the child, and child participation.

4.3.1. Who is a child?

4.3.1.1. The starting point of childhood

Article 2 of the African Children's Charter provides that 'for the purposes of this Charter, a child means every human being below the age of 18 years', which position is a deviation from the flexible position taken in article 1 of the CRC.[45] By placing the age of majority for all purposes at 18, the African Children's Charter sets a very high and uniform standard of protection for all children in Africa, under all circumstances, thereby avoiding one of the criticisms against the CRC. The question that the drafters of the African Children's Charter did not answer is whether 'below the age of 18' includes the unborn child.

Even though human rights are entitlements accruing on the basis of membership of the human family, there is no agreement among human rights scholars, scientists and philosophers as to the exact qualification and entry point into this family.[46] At the centre of the scholarly debate is the question: At what stage do the unborn have life and, therefore, qualify for the protection of that life? Some people hold the view that since the 'unborn child is not literally a person whose rights could already be protected', the reference to 'human being' in article 1 of the CRC cannot include the unborn,[47] whereas others have argued for an 'inclusive meaning' of the term 'child' to encompass unborn children.[48]

---

45 Article 1 of the Convention on the Rights of the Child provides that a child is any human being below the age of 18 unless majority is attained earlier in accordance with national laws applicable to the child. This provision allows for some margin of flexibility for national authorities to determine the upper limit of childhood.

46 See generally R Joseph *Human rights and the unborn Child* (2009); R Copelon *et al* 'Human rights begin at birth: International law and the claim of fetal rights' (2005) 13 *Reproductive Health Matters* 120; and L Glenn 'A legal perspective on humanity, personhood, and species boundaries' (2003) 3 *The American Journal of Bioethics* 27.

47 For more details see L LeBlanc T*he Convention on the Rights of the Child: United Nations lawmaking on human rights* (1995) 65-72.

48 See, generally, R Joseph *Human rights and the unborn child* (2009).

Those who support and those who are against the inclusion of the unborn within the meaning of article 1 of the CRC and, by implication, article 2 of the African Children's Charter predicate their positions on the different provisions and interpretations of international human rights treaties. The position of the pro-unborn[49] children movement seems to be based mainly on the teleology of the provisions of human rights treaties, whereas the anti-unborn[50] movement adapts a realistic approach in interpreting the provisions.

Philip Alston summarizes the position in relation to the recognition of the right to life of the un-born when he observes, in the context of the CRC:

> [t] he acceptance of a preambular paragraph recognizing that 'the child . . . needs special safeguards and care, including appropriate legal protection, before as well as after birth' cannot be interpreted as an indirect reversal of that explicit rejection [of proposals to recognize the right to life of the unborn]. To do so would be to attribute to the preamble an importance considerably in excess of that which may reasonably be accorded to such broad policy pronouncements.[51]

He continues:

> Neither the text of the Convention itself, nor any of the relevant circumstances surrounding its adoption, lend support, either of a legal or other nature, to the suggestion that the Convention requires legislators to recognize and protect the right to life of the fetus.[52]

In spite of Alston's view that there is an 'explicit rejection', the CRC Committee seems to entertain the view that the plight of the unborn falls within its mandate. In its 2006 General Comment, the CRC Committee used the phrase 'the child before birth'[53] in relation to the unborn. In addition, the

49 This refers to scholars, human rights activities and philosophers who hold the opinion that life starts before birth and should be protected right from the womb.

50 This refers to scholars, human rights activities and philosophers who hold the opinion that life starts at birth and should be protected only once the child is born.

51 P Alston 'The unborn child and abortion under the draft Convention on the Rights of the Child' (1990) 12 *Human Rights Quarterly* 156.

52 As above.

53 See R Joseph *Human rights and the unborn child* (2009) as cited in S Yoshihara 'Human rights and the

CRC Committee has admonished state parties to address 'discriminatory laws on abortion affecting disabled children…',[54] and urged states to book 'factors which lead to practices such as female infanticide and selective abortions, and to develop strategies to address them.'[55] It would seem from the utterances of the CRC Committee,[56] that it considers the unborn as persons possessing life worthy of protection and, secondly, as children within the meaning of the CRC.

Some members of the CRC Committee might get support for their views from the broader pro-unborn movement. These activists hold the view that one does not acquire life or humanness upon birth. Life is inherent and, thus, one is born already a living being and was therefore living even before birth. Proceeding on this generous premise, pro-unborn activists appropriate to the unborn the 'equal and inalienable rights of all members of the human family to the right to life, recognition and equality before law without discrimination.'[57] The prohibition that a 'sentence of death shall not be carried out on pregnant women'[58] is seen as protection by the law of the unborn. This proposition is not without basis. According to William Schabas, 'with respect to the exclusion [from execution] of pregnant women, the Secretary-General's Annotations suggest that the provision was added out of "consideration for the interests of the unborn child"'.[59]

Schabas reports that 'many delegations to the United Nations would have preferred some mention that the right to life began "from conception," thereby protecting the foetus.'[60] The mention in the Preamble to the Declaration on

---

unborn child by R Joseph: Book review' (2011) *The National Catholic Bioethics Quarterly* 599.

54 Cited in M Nowak *Commentary on the United Nations Convention on the Rights of the Child, Article 6: the right to life, survival and development* (2005) 29.

55 As above.

56 It should be noted though that the CRC Committee utterance with respect to the unborn child is mainly discussed within the framework of non-discrimination and not right to life. However, either way, it implies some level of protection and thus recognition of the unborn child.

57 Para 1 of the preamble to the Universal Declaration of Human Rights.

58 Article 6(5) of the International Convention on Civil and Political Rights.

59 W Schabas *The abolition of the death penalty in international law* (1997) 25.

60 As above.

the Rights of the Child and the incorporation of the phrase 'appropriate legal protection, before as well as after birth'[61] in the Preamble of the CRC have been seen as recognition of the rights of the unborn child. The understanding is, unlike the *travaux préparatoires*, which is a 'supplementary means of interpretation to be used in limited circumstances,'[62] that the Preamble is part of the treaty itself.

Regional courts have also grappled with the issue of whether human rights are premised upon birth. The European Court of Human Rights (the Court) has entertained two important cases relevant to the discussion: *Open Door and Dublin Well Women v Ireland*[63] and *Odievre v France*.[64] In both cases the Court regarded the efforts of member states to protect the foetus to be a 'legitimate aim.'[65]

An examination of the reasoning in the second case is illustrative. In this case the Court tried to compartmentalise humanness into stages. According to the Court:

> Since the unborn has the capacity to become a person and in some states is protected, it requires 'protection in the name of human dignity,' without making it a 'person' with the 'right to life' for the purposes of Article 2.[66]

The approach of the Court resulted in divergent and dissenting opinion among the judges of the Court. For example, in a separate opinion, Judge Costa contended that the difficulties with defining what a person is in a philosophical sense should not prevent the law from attempting its own definition. He asserts that it is the mandate of judges to interpret the words

61 Para 3 of the Preamble to the Declaration of the Rights of the Child 1959.

62 U Linderfalk *On the interpretation of treaties: The modern international law as expressed in the 1969 Vienna Convention on the Law of Treaties* (2007) 238.

63 (14234/88) [1992] ECHR 68 (29 October 1992).

64 [2003] 1 FCR 621 EctHR.

65 *Open Door Counseling & Dublin Well Women Centers*, App. No. 14234/88 at Para. 63; Odievre, App. No. 42326/98 at para 3 (2003).

66 R Scott 'The English fetus and the right to life' (2004) 11 *European Journal of Health Law* 352.

and provisions in relevant legal treaties.[67] Judge Ress, in a dissenting opinion, observed that 'everyone,' as used in international human rights treaties, includes 'human being before birth and, above all, the notion of "life" as covering all human life commencing with conception, that is to say from the moment an independent existence develops until it ends with death, birth being but a stage in that development.'[68] Concurring, Judge Mularoni held that 'although legal personality is only acquired at birth, this does not to my mind mean that there must be no recognition or protection of "everyone's right to life" before birth.'[69]

Though there is no record of a direct case before the Inter-American Commission on Human Rights dealing with foetal rights, it would seem that the Inter-American human rights system's protection of humanness and right to life does not exclude the unborn child.[70] This impression is based on the opinion the Commission rendered in 1981 in *United States and Commonwealth of Massachusetts* against the reversal of a conviction of a doctor who performed an abortion. In that case the Commission held that 'every person has the right to have his life respected. This right shall be protected by law and, in general, *from the moment of conception*.[71] No one shall be arbitrarily deprived of his life.'[72]

Within the African human rights system there are signs of a tendency to include the unborn for the purpose of human rights protection. Though there is also no record of a case before any of the treaty monitoring mechanisms in the African human rights system, the protection of the unborn can be inferred from the Protocol to the African Charter on Human and Peoples' Right on the Rights of Women in Africa (Women's Protocol). A generous interpretation

67 Quoted in J Pichon 'Does the unborn child have a right to life? The insufficient answer of the European Court of Human Rights in the judgment Vo v. France' (2007) 7 *Germany Law Journal* 433.

68 A Mowbray 'Institutional developments and recent Strasbourg cases' (2005) 5 *Human Rights Law Review* 176.

69 As above, 77.

70 See generally R Joseph *Human rights and the unborn child* (2009).

71 Emphasis is supplied.

72 Article 4(1) of the American Convention on Human Rights adopted in Costa Rica (22 November 1969).

of article 14(2) (c) encompasses this possibility. According to article 14(2) (c) of the Women's Protocol:

> Protect the reproductive rights of women by authorising medical abortion in cases of sexual assault, rape, incest, and where the continued pregnancy endangers the mental and physical health of the mother or the *life of the mother or the foetus.*[73]

By referring to the 'life of the...foetus' in the context of protection, it is possible to impute a view among the drafters of life before birth and they made a conscious balancing decision in favour of the life of the mother. Thus, a medical abortion becomes an exception to the absolute right to life.

There is mounting evidence of a momentum towards including unborn children within the meaning of 'human being' as provided for in article 1 of the CRC and article 2 of the African Children's Charter.[74] The position of the African countries that participated in the drafting process of the CRC, Algeria, Morocco and Senegal, was that the CRC should protect life 'from the moment of conception,'[75] because 'it was only logical to guarantee the right to life from the moment life began.'[76] This position is consonant with the views of communities in traditional African societies, as well as Islamic customary law and practices in Africa.[77]

It is possible to anticipate that when the African Children's Committee has an opportunity to expound on the ambit of article 2 of the African Children's Charter, it will interpret it to include the unborn child. However, it is difficult to understand why, when the African position is clear that life starts upon conception, an African children's treaty should fail to engage with the

73 Protocol to the African Charter on Human and Peoples' Rights on the Rights of Women in Africa. Emphasis is mine.

74 It should be noted that by arriving at this conclusion the author is not in any way taking this conclusion as his position or recommendation that this should be the right interpretation of an African position. The point being made here is that the drafters of the African Children's Charter could have benefited from the debate in coming up with an African specific treaty.

75 See generally L LeBlanc *The Convention on the Rights of the Child: United Nations lawmaking on human rights* (1995) special at page 68 and S Detrick *The United Nations Convention on the Rights of the Child: A guide to the 'travaux préparatoires'* (1992).

76 L LeBlanc *The Convention on the Rights of the Child: United Nations lawmaking on human rights* (1995) 67.

77 See chapter three above for more details on the conception of childhood in traditional African communities.

question directly. The African representatives at the drafting process of the CRC unfailingly tried to include their specific conception into the CRC. If the purpose of drafting the African Children's Charter was to provide for the elucidation of African specific values around childhood, the beginning of life should have been given due consideration.

4.3.1.2. The end point of childhood

In addition to the starting point of childhood, another area where article 2 of the African Children's Charter fails to take cognizance of African cultural values and heritage is in its strict prescription with respect to the endpoint of childhood. The idea that a child, by some magic, turns into an adult on attaining 18 is at odds with the way African traditional cultural heritage and philosophy of life treats the transition from childhood to adulthood. In African philosophy a child's transition from childhood to adulthood is a function of demonstrated physical, mental and emotional maturity.[78]

The 'straight 18' position of the African Children's Charter has also become a source of legal tension between the African Children's Charter and the African Youth Charter. For example, the rights and freedoms provided for in the African Youth Charter accrue to 'minors' as well as well as to 'youth' or young people. The African Youth Charter defines 'minors' 'as young people aged 15 to 17 years, subject to each country's laws;' and the 'youth' as 'every person between the ages of 15 and 35 years.'[79] The sense of flexibility with respect to the conception of young people in Africa, though commendable, is achieved at the cost of lumping children together with young people - different categories with divergent needs. In international law, specific treaties should take precedence over general treaties, and the provisions of treaties that offer more protection should normally prevail over those providing less protection.[80] In this case, both treaties are specific treaties and the question of which one offers more protection is largely a context-specific question.

---

78 B Rwezaura 'Competing 'images' of childhood in social and legal systems of contemporary sub-Saharan Africa' (1998) 12 *International Journal of Law, Policy and the Family* 255.

79 See the definition section to the African Youth Charter.

80 See, for example, article 41 of the Convention on the Rights of the Child.

Upper age limits serve to clarify the nature of the relationship between the state and the child in question. Therefore, it is an important tool to ensure protection for vulnerable children. However, vulnerability and immaturity differ and vary from context to context, from child to child and from one moment in time to another. Therefore, using a uniform shield of protection based only on age to offer all children protection might not be useful in all cases.[81] For instance, strict age delineation could disempower rather than protect certain categories of children, such as the breadwinners of child-headed households – a new phenomenon in the African context. In such situations, an age requirement could be more effective when it is flexible and sensitive to context. Allowing these children to engage in income generating activities, for example, could serve a higher goal than using age to limit them.

The question that arises is: If article 2 of the African Children's Charter does not reflect the African context of childhood, where did it come from? The closest to the definition of the child in the African Children's Charter was the proposal by Finland in the Working Group, which discussed the draft article 1 of the CRC. This proposal provided: 'For the purpose of the present Convention, a child means every human being *who has not attained* the age of 18 years.' The drafters of the African Children's Charter perhaps deleted the highlighted phrase and replaced it with *below*, with the result being: 'for the purposes of this Charter, a child means every human being below the age of 18 years.' Alternatively, the drafters of the African Children's Charter simply deleted the exception *"unless under the law applicable to the child, majority is attained earlier"* provided for in article 1 of the CRC states.

The image of childhood articulated in the African Children's Charter is closer to that proposed by Finland than it is to the understanding of childhood in traditional African values. The drafters of the African Children's Charter deleted the only factor introduced in the CRC, in order to reflect the

81 K Cheney 'Conflicting protectionist and participation models of children's rights: Their consequences for Uganda's orphans and vulnerable children' in A Imoh & N Ansell (eds) *Children's lives in an era of children's rights: The progress of the Convention on the Rights of the Child in Africa* (2014) 17; A Norman 'Children's rights in the time of AIDS in KwaZulu-Natal, South Africa' in A Imoh & N Ansell (eds) *Children's lives in an era of children's rights: The progress of the Convention on the Rights of the Child in Africa* (2014) 34; S Okyere 'Children's participation in prohibited work in Ghana and its implications for the Convention on the Rights of the Child' in A Imoh & N Ansell (eds) *Children's lives in an era of children's rights: The progress of the Convention on the Rights of the Child in Africa* (2014) 92.

diversities of understanding of childhood in the world - making the image of the child in article 2 of the African Children's Charter even stricter than the so-called 'Western' conception of childhood child under article 1 of the CRC.

4.3.2. Autonomy rights of the child

The African Children's Charter confers upon children the right and freedom to think, talk, choose, meet and share, in public and private, whatever they are capable of conceptualizing and communicating. These rights and freedoms are limited only by the ability and willingness of the child, the law and, in some instances, the reasonable supervision of parents. The following rights epitomise the nature and spirit of the autonomy rights provided for children in Africa under the African Children's Charter: freedom of expression,[82] freedom of association,[83] freedom of thought, conscience and religion,[84] and the protection of privacy.[85]

These four rights provided for in the African Children's Charter are probably its most radical, potentially empowering and transformative provisions. However, the efficacy of these provisions depends on whether they reflect and respond to the way African families, communities and states understand childhood. To simply transplant such rights and freedoms from other contexts without adapting them to local realities is problematic. The way a society sees and treats children is a subset of the way that society sees and treats itself. A brief sketch of the broader debate on whether human rights, as codified in different treaties, are alien or not appropriate in Africa is provided below.

There is no consensus among scholars writing on Africa as to whether human rights, as codified in international human rights treaties, are indigenous to Africa.[86] There seems to be a level of agreement among scholars across the

---

82 Article 7.

83 Article 8.

84 Article 9.

85 Article 10.

86 For a general discussion of this see I Shivji *The concept of human rights in Africa* (1989); J Donnelly 'Human rights and human dignity: An analytic critique of non-Western conceptions of human rights '(1982) 76 *American Political Science Review* 303; M Goodhart 'Origins and universality in the human rights debates: Cultural essentialism and the challenge of globalization' (2003) 25 *Human Rights Quarterly* 935; J Donnelly

divide that human rights, as codified in the international human rights treaties, have their roots in the particular thinking, history and circumstances of the West.[87] Within the broad consensus there are variations of position. There are those who are of the view that even though what is codified in the human rights treaties may have originated in the West, it does not mean that there are no corresponding values that serve the purpose that human rights serve in the West, in non-western cultures, including Africa.[88] Others hold that 'there is no specifically African concept of human rights.'[89]

In the opinion of some scholars, human rights, regardless of their historical and philosophical origins, should apply universally.[90] This is because the conditions, institutions and structures that gave rise to human rights in the Western society are prevalent in different parts of the world. Human rights norms that emerged as a result of these developments also apply to these parts of the world, including Africa.[91] Others insist that the presence of externally imposed circumstances, institutions and structures should not be used to justify the application of external values and norms, such as human rights, to non-western societies.[92]

The debate about the 'Africanness' of human rights has implications for the rights of children in Africa. The rights of children operate within the broader human rights framework. If the nature, scope and identity of the broader human rights framework in Africa are a subject of scholarly debate, it is reasonable to expect that the nature and scope of children's rights, as a subset of this larger framework, will be subject to a similar debate. Examining

---

'The relative universality of human rights' (2007) 29 *Human Rights Quarterly* 281.

87 I Shivji *The concept of human rights in Africa* (1989) 10.

88 See L Marasingle 'Traditional conceptions of human rights in Africa' in C Welch & R Meltzer (eds) *Human rights and development in Africa* (1984) 32; C Welch 'Human rights as a problem in contemporary Africa' in C Welch & R Meltzer (eds) *Human rights and development in Africa* (1984) 11.

89 R Howard *Human rights in Commonwealth Africa* (1986) 23.

90 J Donnelly 'Human rights and human dignity: An analytic critique of non-Western conceptions of human rights' (1982) 76 *American Political Science Review* 303; M Goodhart 'Origins and universality in the human rights debates: Cultural essentialism and the challenge of globalization' (2003) 25 *Human Rights Quarterly* 935; J Donnelly 'The relative universality of human rights' (2007) 29 *Human Rights Quarterly* 281.

91 J Donnelly 'The relative universality of human rights' (2007) 29 *Human Rights Quarterly* 281.

92 G van Bueren *The international law on the rights of the child* (1998) 131.

the content of the autonomy rights of children as outlined in the African Children's Charter and juxtaposing this with the traditional understanding of childhood as outlined above, is necessary in order to reveal any tension between the human rights conception of childhood and the traditional understanding of childhood in Africa.

The freedoms of expression, association and religion are interrelated. The CRC Committee has treated them as such.[93] In the absence of any practice by the African Children's Committee to the contrary, the provisions for these rights under the African Children's Charter will be analyzed with this understanding in mind. The African Children's Charter assures every child who is capable of communicating his or her views the right to express and disseminate those views freely, subject only to lawful restrictions. Further, every child is granted the right to free association and peaceful assembly in conformity with the law. The freedom of thought, conscience and religion concretize and reinforce the legal autonomy and individualized agency of the child in the African context.

In the absence of travaux *préparatoires*[94] and an interpretation of these provisions by the African Children's Committee, this section will use interpretations of similar provisions at the international level, the practice of the CRC Committee and academic opinion to analyze these articles and speculate on their possible application and implications in Africa. Thus, the first level of analysis will be upward – using the international framework to attempt to interpret these provisions; the second level will be downward - investigating their application and implications in a traditional African context.

At the international level, the freedom of expression, association and assembly were not considered appropriate for children until the CRC, and, by implication, the African Children's Charter incorporated article 19 of the ICCPR and rendered it explicitly applicable to children.[95] There

---

93 A MacLeod 'Liberal theory of freedom of expression for children' (2004) 79 *Chicago-Kent Law Review* 55.

94 With the exception of the selected proceeding report of the Workshops organised during the discussions leading to the drafting of the African Charter on the Rights and Welfare of the Child, there is no proceeding report of the actual drafting process that is publicly available.

95 G van Bueren *The international law on the rights of the child* (1998) 131.

were a number of reasons why it was thought that granting these rights to children was not in their best interests. First, it was believed that 'to confer the full range of choice rights on a child is also to confer the burdens and responsibilities of adult legal status, which necessarily removes the protection rights of childhood'.[96] Second, granting autonomy and choice rights to children without any claw-back clauses and with no lower age limit was thought to be problematic because 'young children . . . seem to have virtually no direct expressive, deliberative or informational interests that are served by freedom of expression.'[97] It would be understandable if autonomy rights granted to children allow the nature and scope of autonomy and choice rights to increase with age. Third, children's autonomy is not a uniform experience that takes place at the same time for all children across time and space. It is rather a 'child-specific element and not merely an aspect of children's general "personhood" because it is gradual, depending upon children's maturity and their evolving capacities.'[98] For these reasons, a number of scholars, before the adoption of the CRC, held the view that article 19 of the ICCPR should not be extended to children.[99]

Article 19 of the ICCPR epitomizes classic freedom of expression as an autonomy right. According to the Human Rights Committee, the freedom of expression includes not only freedom to 'impart information and ideas of all kinds,' but also freedom to 'seek' and 'receive' them 'regardless of frontiers,' and in whatever medium, 'either orally, in writing or in print, in the form of art, or through any other media of his choice.'[100] Naturally, it includes 'every communicable type of subjective idea and opinion, of value-neutral news

96 B Hafen & J Hafen 'Abandoning children to their autonomy: The United Nations Convention on the Rights of the Child' (1996) 37 *Harvard International Law Journal* 461.

97 A MacLeod 'Liberal theory of freedom of expression for children' (2004) 79 *Chicago-Kent Law Review* 55.

98 E Brems 'Children's rights and universality' in J Willems (ed) *Developmental and autonomy rights of children: Empowering children, caregivers and communities* (2007) 11 cited in S Langlaude 'On how to build a positive understanding of the child's right to freedom of expression' (2010) 10 *Human Rights Law Review* 33.

99 G van Bueren *The international law on the rights of the child* (1998) 139; S Langlaude 'On how to build a positive understanding of the child's right to freedom of expression' (2010) 10 *Human Rights Law Review* 33.

100 Human Rights Committee, General Comment 10, Article 19 (Nineteenth session, 1983), Compilation of General Comments and General Recommendations Adopted by Human Rights Treaty Bodies, U.N. Doc. HRI/GEN/1/Rev.1 at 11 (1994).

and information, of commercial advertising, art works, political commentary regardless of how critical, pornography.'[101] Granting children such enormous verbal and non-verbal expression rights was considered detrimental to children's wellbeing because this will likely make any effort intended 'to close out undesirable contents, such as pornography or blasphemy,'[102] extremely difficult. The drafters of the CRC and the African Children's Charter thought differently. The fact that the provision was lifted *verbatim* from the ICCPR is probably indicative of the CRC's and African Children's Charter's vision of children – as autonomous individuals whose rights and freedoms are equal to those of adults.

There are a number of reasons why children are conferred with autonomy rights under the CRC and, by implication, the African Children's Charter. In the case of children, some scholars hold the view that freedom of expression cultivates 'deliberative capacities and can stimulate critical reflection on a range of options' and, thus, develops more 'reflective and mature individuals and so benefiting society as a whole.'[103] It protects children's development, fulfillment, participation in society, and the imparting of information. There seems to be an inverse relationship between the child's right to freedom of expression and parental guidance; the nature and scope of the rights expand as the child matures, whereas parental ability and freedom to provide appropriate direction and guidance diminish.[104] Thus,

> as children develop cognitive, emotional, and moral capacities, the range of material from which they need to be protected diminishes. Similarly, as children mature, the scope and content of their rights to expression increase.[105]

---

101 M Nowak *CCPR Commentary* (1993) 358. However, these rights and freedoms are limited in the interest of public, health, order and safety.

102 M Nowak *CCPR Commentary* (1993) 341.

103 T Campbell 'Rationales for freedom of communication' in T Campbell & W Sadurski (eds) *Freedom of communication* (1994) 33.

104 A MacLeod 'Liberal theory of freedom of expression for children' (2004) 79 *Chicago-Kent Law Review* 55.

105 As above.

That is why freedom of expression is considered as a developmental right as well as an autonomy right.[106] The obligation to ensure that children enjoy these developmental rights rests with states. According to the CRC Committee, it is states parties that must 'refrain from interference in the expression of those views, or in access to information, while protecting the right of access to means of communication and public dialogue.'[107]

It would seem that the CRC Committee considers the right to freedom of expression as mainly creating a vertical obligation between the child and the state.[108] The CRC Committee takes a formalistic view of this right and the process of realising it. According to the CRC Committee, freedom of expression imposes positive and negative obligations. Positively, the state must create structures, mechanisms and proceedings through which children can express their views freely in all matters affecting them and ensure that children's views are given due weight in accordance with their age and maturity.[109] Some scholars express concern over imposing positive obligations on states. The reason for the criticism is that it is 'unrealistic [because of] the financial costs of ensuring that everyone'[110] can exercise these rights. UNICEF holds the view that the scope of the right to freedom of expression is wide enough to include the family environment.[111]

There is concern over the way the right to freedom of expression is crafted in the CRC and the African Children's Charter: First, on a general note, the concept and content of the right to freedom of expression demonstrate the tension among autonomy rights, developmental rights, protection rights and relational rights. The tension reflects a clash of visions, philosophies and ideologies that are struggling to colonise and control the childhood space. On the one hand, children need protection from the negative effects of the rights

106 J Eekelaar 'The emergence of children's rights' (1986) 6 *Oxford Journal of Legal Studies* 161.

107 See CRC Committee General Comment 12: *The right of the child to be heard*, 1 July 2009, CRC/C/GC/ para 81.

108 S Langlaude 'On how to build a positive understanding of the child's right to freedom of expression' (2010) 10 *Human Rights Law Review* 33.

109 As above.

110 E Barendt *Freedom of speech* (2005) 104.

111 R Hodgkin & P Newell *Implementation handbook for the Convention on the Rights of the Child* (2007) 140.

and privileges of the adult world. On the other, children need all the rights to live, survive and develop. To strike a balance is not easy for policy makers because each child is unique and lives in a unique set of circumstances.

Second, the evidence of this tension is demonstrated when the drafters of the CRC and the African Children's Charter divert from their trademark of age restrictions to a customised and an individualised approach in determining maturity or evolving capacities when discussing these rights and freedoms.[112] On the one hand, this flexibility is commendable in the sense that, for once, the drafters of the CRC and the African Children's Charter acknowledge that it is virtually impossible to capture the diversities within the structural space called childhood through an age-based classification system; on the other, this concession complicates the situation for children and policy makers. The reliance on capabilities and maturity as a minimum threshold for the exercise of these rights is problematic. The concept of maturity as used in the CRC is already 'hopelessly complex and subjective.'[113] It makes 'customized findings of maturity,'[114] as anticipated within the parameters of the right to freedom of expression, inherently difficult. Firstly, because of the nature of maturity itself; and secondly, because of the non - existing 'reasoned generality - and, hence, the lack of neutrality-in subjective decisions' which might affect the quality of decisions about maturity.[115]

The right to freedom of association flows naturally from and complements the right to freedom of expression. Association is a means as it is an end right. It enables the child to express views, contribute to debate, and form alliances for the purpose of realising other rights. There is a close link between the components of freedom of association and participation. In discussing participation below, issues around freedom of association will be touched upon again.

112 See article 5 of the Convention on the Rights of the Child and article 9(2) of the African Charter on the Rights and Welfare of the Child.

113 B Hafen & J Hafen 'Abandoning children to their autonomy: The United Nations Convention on the Rights of the Child' (1996) 37 *Harvard International Law Journal* 461.

114 As above.

115 As above.

The right to freedom of thought, conscience and religion is 'far-reaching and profound'.[116] It confers on an individual 'freedom of thought on all matters.'[117] It is *jus cogens* and, thus, non derogable 'even in time of public emergency.'[118] The right holder is at liberty to manifest his or her freedoms 'individually or in community with others and in public or private.'[119] The freedom is limited only by law enacted to protect public safety, order, health or morals (such morality should not derive exclusively from a single tradition),[120] or the fundamental rights of others. These rights and freedoms enable an individual to hold, develop, refine and, ultimately, change his or her thoughts, conscience and religion without any form of interference or anyone compelling him or her 'to reveal his thoughts or adherence to a religion or belief'.[121] The rights and freedoms place on the state a positive and negative obligation to refrain from interfering with the protected rights as well as to take active steps to put in place a favourable environment for the exercise of these rights and freedoms.

The codification of these rights and freedoms in the CRC and the African Children's Charter was done within the spirit of similar provisions in the ICCPR.[122] The implication is that the rights and freedoms apply to children as they would apply to adults. However, the CRC introduces an additional limitation with respect to children that is not provided for under the ICCPR. This limitation provides for 'direction to the child in the exercise of his or her right in a manner consistent with the evolving capacities of the child.'[123]

---

116 Human Rights Committee, General Comment 22, Article 18 (Forty-eighth session, 1993) Compilation of General Comments and General Recommendations Adopted by Human Rights Treaty Bodies, U.N. Doc. HRI/GEN/1/Rev.1 at 35 (1994).

117 As above.

118 As above.

119 As above.

120 As above.

121 As above.

122 L LeBlanc *The Convention on the Rights of the Child: United Nations lawmaking on human rights* (1995) 68 and S Detrick *The United Nations Convention on the Rights of the Child: A guide to the 'travaux préparatoires'* (1992) 45.

123 Article 14(2) of the Convention on the Rights of the Child.

The CRC Committee has not adequately clarified the nature, scope and content of 'the rights and duties of parents' and under what circumstances they are 'applicable' to 'provide direction' in the manifestation of these rights and freedoms. It would seem from the text that parental rights and duties are limited to reasonable supervision and guidance with diminishing scope, as the capacities of the child to take reasonable decisions increase.

From the analysis so far, it could be argued that the understanding of autonomy rights provided in the CRC and, by implication, the African Children's Charter is compatible with the liberal and individualistic conception of personhood and society. The direct applicability of this view of children's autonomy rights in societies yet to develop a mature liberal and individualist based societal structure is bound to be an uphill task. Traditional communities in Africa are more or less communitarian in their conception of society and their worldview including the role of individuals in society.[124] The image of the child whose interests, rights and freedoms must trump societal interest is uncommon in these societies.

The reason the African Children's Charter by implication has been related to the provisions of the CRC throughout this section is because, even though textually the provisions within the African Children's Charter with respect to freedom of expression, freedom of association, freedom of thought, conscience and religion are not the same as corresponding provisions in the CRC, substantively these provisions mirror the image and understanding of childhood and liberty rights, as anticipated in the CRC. Article 7 confers freedom of expression on a child 'who is capable of communicating his or her own views' and subjects the exercise of this right and freedom to 'such restrictions as are prescribed by laws.' This is not to say that there are no minor differences; for instance, the use of 'capable of communicating' is different from a similar provision in the CRC. The African Children's Charter's version of the corresponding provision in the CRC has been criticised as

---

124 J Mbiti *African religions and philosophy* (1990) 102; R Zimba 'Indigenous conceptions of childhood development and social realities in southern Africa' in R Zimba *Between culture and biology: Perspectives on ontogentic development* (2002) 98; A Shutte *Philosophy for Africa* (1993) 46; I Menkiti 'Person and community in African traditional thought' in R Wright (ed) *African philosophy* (1984) 171; J Mbiti *African religions and philosophy* (1969) 109.

excluding children who may not be able to communicate their opinion.[125] It is reasonable to presume that capability could be defined broadly as including both verbal and nonverbal abilities. In addition, capability could be seen not only as an objective test but also as a minimum threshold, thus ruling out infants and younger children who may not be able to benefit meaningfully from the expectations of this right and freedom.

In addition, the deference to national law can be interpreted as some level of flexibility, allowing for a margin of appreciation the role for state parties. However, not qualifying this law by introducing an expression such as 'reasonable or acceptable in a democratic society' means that the margin is wide enough to include just about any 'law.' The provisions of the African Children's Charter cannot be interpreted in isolation, though; other provisions relating to the best interests of the child might come into play. But the reference to law alone might give the impression that childhood in Africa is the sole responsibility of law. Except for children who stay in urban centres, a majority of children in Africa live their lives outside the reach of formal law.

Furthermore, the rendition of the freedom of expression in the African Children's Charter is not clear as to the scope of this right and freedom. Who should assure that the child who is capable of communicating his view actually does so? Is it the state alone or also the family? It would seem, like the CRC, that the African Children's Charter was conceived primarily to create a vertical obligation between the child and the state. The African Children's Committee's Guidelines on Initial State Party Report as well as the Guidelines on Periodic State Party Report give credence to the presumption that the African Children's Charter anticipates the application of rights and freedoms in a formalistic manner.[126] In addition, in discussing the right to freedom of expression, the African Children's Committee in its concluding observations on Uganda's State Report commended the constitutional rights in Uganda that 'allow children to express their points of view, *outside the family boundaries.*'[127]

---

125 R Sillah & T Chibanda 'Assessing the African Charter on the Rights and Welfare of the Child (African Children's Charter) as a blueprint towards the attainment of children's rights in Africa' (2013) 11 *IOSR Journal of Humanities and Social Science* 50.

126 See http://African Children's Committee.org/state-reports/.

127 The African Committee of Experts on the Rights and Welfare of the Child Concluding Observation to the

Even though there is evidence to suggest that children in traditional communities in Africa express themselves in various ways, there is not sufficient evidence to suggest that they do so as a matter of rights.[128] This provision, therefore, is more a reflection of development within an international human rights system that is overly driven by liberal and individualistic motivations, than it is a reflection of the traditional value system around child upbringing and participation in traditional African communities.

Additionally, the provision of the right to freedoms of thought, conscience and religion in the African Children's Charter is textually and substantively similar to the CRC provision, which in turn is similar to the provisions in the ICCPR. However, the African Children's Charter introduces the element of the best interests of the child as a possible limiting factor in the consideration of the nature and scope of the enjoyment of this right and freedom by a child. It is the only place in the text where the drafters used the concept of 'best interests' of the child without the usual qualifications of 'a' paramount or 'the' paramount prefix.[129] It is not clear what the intention of the drafters is, but it might mean that 'best interests' is not the only consideration, but one consideration. It is similar to the implication of using 'a' to prefix the 'best interests' concept in the CRC. It can be argued that by requesting that parents and legal guardians provide 'guidance and direction in the exercise of these rights having regard to the evolving capacities, and best interests of the child', that the 'best interests' principle here is just one consideration.

There are concerns with regard to the contextualization of the right to freedoms of thought, conscience and religion for children in Africa, in the African Children's Charter. The first is that in traditional African communities,

---

Republic of Uganda available at: http://African Children's Committee.org/state-reports/.

128 C Ngara 'African ways of knowing and pedagogy revisited' (2007) 2 *Journal of Contemporary Issues in Education* 7; I Goduka 'Indigenous epistemologies - Ways of knowing: Affirming our legacy' (1999) 13 *South African Journal of Higher Education* 26; and see generally M Runco 'Creativity as an extracognitive phenomenon' in L Shavinina & M Ferrari (eds) *Beyond knowledge: Extracognitive aspects of developing high ability* (2004); C Himonga 'The rights of the child to participate in decision making: A perspective from Zambia in W Ncube *Law, culture, tradition and children's rights in East and Southern Africa* (1998) 115.

129 See D Chirwa 'The merits and demerits of the African Charter on the Rights and Welfare of the Child' (2002) 10 *International Journal of Children's Rights* 157 for the slight difference between using the indefinite article 'a' and the definite article 'the' to qualify the best interests of the child.

religion is a way of life rather than a specific belief or a practice.[130] Thus, the question of choice may not even arise. The relevant question might be that of change of religion and this would be relevant in communities where there are alternative religious beliefs. The second concern is that the text of the limitation is problematic. The African Children's Charter anticipates that only 'parents, and where applicable, legal guardians'[131] play a role in the life of a child. In traditional communities in Africa, there are more actors in the life of a child than anticipated here. The CRC's provision is more accommodating to traditional family arrangements in Africa than the African Children's Charter. Article 5 of the CRC reads:

> States Parties shall respect the responsibilities, rights and duties of *parents or, where applicable, the members of the extended family or community as provided for by local custom, legal guardians or other persons legally responsible for the child,* to provide, in a manner consistent with the evolving capacities of the child, appropriate direction and guidance in the exercise by the child of the rights recognized in the present Convention.[132]

Those who step in to take care of children in many traditional African communities do not necessarily do so in accordance with the law. The emphasis on legal guardianship may not adequately reflect the context in which the African Children's Charter is meant to be implemented.

The third concern is that it is difficult to understand the imposition of 'a duty to provide guidance and direction' without a corresponding right or mechanism for enforcing such a duty if, indeed, it is a legal duty. The appropriateness of the language of rights and duties for some of the responsibilities parents and communities discharge affectionately in traditional community is debatable. Parents provide guidance and direction to their children not necessarily because it is a duty imposed by law but because it is the right thing to do, and

130 See, generally, J Mbiti *African religions and philosophy* (1990).

131 See, for example, article 9(3) of the African Charter on the Rights and Welfare of the Child.

132 Article 5 of the Convention on the Rights of the Child.

the community expects it of them. They do it because it is thought to be in the best interests of their children, an issue to which this book now turns.

4.3.3. The best interests of the child

The African Children's Charter refers at least four times to the concept of the 'best interests.' First, as an overarching principle;[133] second, relating to the freedom of thought, conscience and religion;[134] third, with respect to parental responsibilities;[135] and, finally, relating to alternative family care.[136] However, the concept is not defined anywhere in the African Children's Charter. Nevertheless, there is much literature on the best interests of the child.[137] Reviewing this body of knowledge does not add a new dimension to the book; what is attempted is a textual analysis of article 4 of the African Children's Charter, which is the main provision in the African Children's Charter dealing with the best interests of the child, as an overarching principle. Reference will be made to literature on the concept of the best interests of the child at the international level, when necessary.

Children and their interests are at the centre of African philosophy, culture, religion, families and communities.[138] It would be difficult to argue that traditional communities in Africa did not put the interests of the child first. The difficulty is with the use of the adjective 'best' qualifying that interest. What is best for a child is child, family and community-specific; first and foremost, it differs and varies across groups of children, across families and contexts, as well as over a period of time. In addition, the adjective is value

133 Article 4(1) of the African Charter on the Rights and Welfare of the Child.

134 Article 9(2) of the African Charter on the Rights and Welfare of the Child.

135 Article 20(a) of the African Charter on the Rights and Welfare of the Child.

136 Article 25(3) of the African Charter on the Rights and Welfare of the Child.

137 P Alston (ed) *The best interests of the child: reconciling culture and human rights* (1994) 17; for a detailed discussion see P Alston & B Gilmour-Walsh *The best interests of the child: Towards a synbook of children's rights and cultural values* (1996); S Parker 'The best interests of the child: principles and problems' (1994) 8 *International Journal of Law and the Family* 26; s Parker 'The best interests of the child: Principles and problems' in P Alston (ed) *The best interests of the child: Reconciling culture and human rights* (1994) 27; S Parker 'The best interests of the child: Principles and problems' (1994) 8 *International Journal of Law and the Family* 78; A An'im ' cultural transformation and normative consensus on the best interests of the child' (1994) 8 *International Journal of Law and the Family* 62.

138 See the discussion in chapter three about the best interests of the child in traditional African communities.

laden. Values are cultural products. All cultures are equal partners in the development of a common humanity. It is possible to imagine that some of the interests considered best in one part of the world may not be so in other parts of the world. Therefore, putting children's wellbeing first is a common aspiration for all cultures; how this is to be done should, as much as possible, be left to each culture to determine. This is probably why the concept of the best interests of the child have not been defined or prescribed in the CRC or in the African Children's Charter though the practice of the monitoring bodies might sometimes seem to indicate that there is a pre-determined content to the concept.[139]

Article 4 of the African Children's Charter expects the best interests of the child to be protected 'in all actions' by 'any person or authority'. What is meant by the reference to 'all actions'? Are the actions contemplated legal or non-legal actions?

It is, therefore, useful to examine the nature and scope of the actions that must take the best interests of the child into consideration. The Black's Law Dictionary defines 'action' as:

> [a]n ordinary proceeding in a court of justice, by which one party prosecutes another party for the enforcement or protection of a right, the redress or prevention of a wrong, or the punishment of a public offense.[140]

In this sense, action is synonymous with lawsuit. If it is what the drafters of the African Children's Charter intended, then it means that the African Children's Charter guarantees children's best interests only in and through a formal process. Examples of such formal processes include custody and divorce proceedings, foster care and adoption, medical decisions, dispute settlement or other formal decisions. The emphasis seems to be on law, policies, legislative or administrative remedies or interventions. This state-centred, legally focussed and formalistic approach to ascertaining and determining

139 See the next chapter for a discussion on the tendencies of treaty bodies to interpret this concept from a right based approach only.

140 Black's Law Dictionary 9th edition.

the best interests of the child seems to be the primary emphasis of the CRC Committee. According to the CRC Committee, the 'best interests' principle

> requires active measures throughout Government, parliament and the judiciary. Every legislative, administrative and judicial body or institution is required to apply the best interests principle by systematically considering how children's rights and interests are or will be affected by their decisions and actions.[141]

However, taking such a restrictive approach to defining the expression 'all actions' cannot be in the best interests of all children especially in Africa where the majority of children spend their childhood in rural areas beyond the meaningful reach of the state.[142] It is, therefore, possible to understand 'all actions' in a wider and broader sense. The CRC Committee takes a broader view with respect to what constitute 'acts.' According to the CRC Committee: 'The word "action" does not only include decisions, but also all acts, conduct, proposals, services, procedures and other measures. Inaction or failure to take action and omissions are also 'actions.'[143]

The Oxford Dictionary of English defines 'action' as 'the fact or process of doing something, typically to achieve an aim.'[144] In this sense, the best interests of the child should encompass any process that involves children or targets them, for whatever purpose, to ensure that the wellbeing of children is the first aim.

The CRC Committee, in some instances, has employed the concept of the 'best interests' of the child in this sense. For example, the CRC Committee noted as follows: 'All decision-making concerning a child's care, health, education, etc. must take account of the 'best interests' principle, *including*

141 General Comments CRC/GC/2003/5 03/10/2003 General Comment 5 (2003): General Measures of Implementation of the Convention on the Rights of the Child para 12.

142 UNICEF 'Children in an Urban World' The State of the world's Children 2012 where it is noted that although majority of children still leave in the rural areas, the number of children living in the urban areas mainly live in slums most of which are not in touch with state services available at http://www.unicef.org/sowc2012/pdfs/SOWC%202012-Main%20Report_EN_13Mar2012.pdf.

143 See paragraphs 17 and 18 of the General Comment 14 of the CRC Committee.

144 Oxford University Press, 2013.

decisions by parents,[145] professionals and others responsible for children.'[146] Since the African Children's Charter refers to 'any person or authority', it is reasonable to presume a wider intention. This is because a 'person' in law is 'any being whom the law regards as capable of rights and duties,'[147] and 'authority', as used in this provision, might mean an entity that 'has the right or permission to act legally on another's behalf.'[148] Therefore, it is legally possible that the scope of this provision includes the actions of natural and artificial persons if their actions concern children. If this is the intention of the drafters of the African Children's Charter, it would seem that the nature and scope of the obligation primarily to take cognisance of children's best interests in all actions is wider under the African Children's Charter than the CRC. The CRC seems to anticipate only the actions 'undertaken by public or private social welfare institutions, courts of law, administrative authorities or legislative bodies.'[149]

Even though, theoretically, the phrasing of the best interests' provisions under the African Children's Charter is plausible, translating such an aspiration into policy and enforcing such policy are fraught with challenges. The reference in article 4(2) to 'all judicial or administrative proceedings affecting a child' may be a reality check on the overly aspirational nature of article 4(1) and, therefore, a necessary narrowing of the scope of the 'best interests' of the child' obligation under article 4 of the African Children's Charter.

Whatever the interpretation, there are a number of concerns with the concept of the best interests of the child as provided for in the African Children's Charter. The legalistic approach to the concept of the best interests of the child in the African context is likely to be exclusionary. Many children in Africa live their childhood beyond the scope of formal law. In addition, the fact that the approach is so state centric is limiting because a number of states

145 CRC Committee, General Comment 7, Children's Rights in Juvenile Justice 2005, CRC/C/GC/7/Rev.1, para. 13). Emphasis added.

146 CRC Committee, General Comment 7, Children's Rights in Juvenile Justice 2005, CRC/C/GC/7/Rev.1, para. 13).

147 Black's Law Dictionary 9th edition.

148 Black's Law Dictionary 9th edition.

149 See article 3(1) of the Convention on the Rights of the Child, for an example.

in Africa are either weak or at different stages of formation and, thus, though some might be willing to promote and protect children's best interests, they might simply not be able to. As a result, a significant number of children in Africa might complete their childhood experience without meaningful contact with the state. Furthermore, the African Children's Charter's reference to any 'person or authority' is too wide and, at best, aspirational and, therefore, is in conflict with its legalistic tendencies. Finally, the African Children's Charter seems, explicitly, to anticipate a child's contribution to determining his or her best interests mainly in judicial and administrative proceedings. Because the African Children's Charter provision of a 'child who is capable of communicating his or her own views' is tied to judicial and administrative proceedings. Children's participation in determining their interests should not be limited to judicial, administrative or formal proceedings but be allowed in all actions that affect children.

4.3.4. Children's participation rights

For children, participation rights are multi-faceted and could 'include a wide range of activities that differ in form and style when children are at different ages.'[150] Langlaude is of the opinion that participation 'of the child in society enables the child to be heard, to be informed about public affairs and to play a role in the life of the country.'[151] The African Children's Charter directly mentions the word 'participation' only twice: The first reference is to the participation rights of children with disability, and the second reference is to the meaningful participation of nongovernmental organisations.[152] The African Children's Committee has not been sufficiently engaged in clarifying the conceptual implication of this right within the African Children's Charter. However, the reference in article 4(2) to 'provide for the views of the child' could be interpreted as giving children the rights to participate in the determination of their interests. The reference to 'judicial or administrative

150 UNICEF, The participation rights of adolescents: A strategic approach (2001) 11 a working paper quoted in S Langlaude 'On how to build a positive understanding of the child's right to freedom of expression' (2010) 10 *Human Rights Law Review* 33.

151 S Langlaude 'On how to build a positive understanding of the child's right to freedom of expression' (2010) 10 *Human Rights Law Review* 33.

152 See articles 13(1) and 14(i) of the African Charter on the Rights and Welfare of the Child.

proceedings' gives the impression that participation, in this context, is expected to happen outside private settings. Such a restrictive rendition arguably is sensitive to the traditional context in Africa.

In traditional African communities children, as part of the family and community, participate in family and community processes.[153] However, there is insufficient evidence to suggest that such participation is a matter of right. What is evident among many traditional communities in Africa is that rights to participation are determined by the position of the person in the social hierarchy. For instance, the ability of a child to participate in decision-making within the family is affected by his or her social status as a child and also by the hierarchical position of that child among his or her siblings. In the context of West Africa it has been said that 'as long as one's parents are alive a child is always a child' and must come under 'some sphere of parental authority even vicariously.'[154] Such parental authority determines a child's level, method and approach to participation. This is because this authority demands respect in return. Pellow states that in some cases it is possible that 'respect for one's elders, when carried to extreme, rules out any chance of exercising one's free will.'[155] In fact, it has been said that traditional African family 'expects 'childhood' .... to be a continuous period of self-effacing obedience to traditional authority.'[156] Conceptualising child participation as a matter of rights within the family setting is bound to be challenging in traditional communities in Africa.

Article 12(2) of the CRC, which provides that the child 'be heard in any judicial and administrative proceedings', has been the subject of intensive debate. A child's right to participation is one of the 'most debated and examined aspects'[157] of the CRC. The manner in which article 12 of the

---

153 C Chimonga 'African customary law and children's rights: Intersections and domains in a new era' in J Sloth-Nielsen (ed) *Children's rights in Africa: A legal perspective* (2008) 71.

154 A Nsamenang *Human development in cultural context: A Third World perspective* (1992) 151.

155 D Pellow *Women in Accra: Options for autonomy* (1977) 56.

156 W Ncube 'The African cultural fingerprints: The changing concept of childhood' in W Ncube (eds) *Law, culture, tradition and children's rights* (1998) 19.

157 G Lansdown 'The realisation of children's participation rights: Critical reflection' in B Percy-Smith & N Thomas (eds) *A handbook of children and young people's participation: Perspective from theory and practice* (2010) 11.

CRC deals with what constitutes participation when participation should be considered as a right, how participation should take place, where and why the child should participate constitutes part of the reason for this debate. According to article 12 of the CRC and article 4(2) of the African Children's Charter the right to participate accrues to 'the child' who is 'capable of forming … views', in the case of the CRC, and 'capable of communicating … views' in the case of the African Children's Charter.

These provisions can be interpreted to mean, first, that this right accrues to a child on an individual basis and not to a group of children.[158] If so, it makes the right to participation more of a private than a public experience for children. Second, these provisions can be interpreted in a broader manner to support public and collective forms of participation for children.[159]

The first interpretation seems to be faithful to the texts of the CRC, while the second interpretation is more to the purpose. The drafters of the CRC used different expressions to convey their intention to individualise rights to children. These included 'a child',[160] 'each child',[161] 'every child'[162] and 'the child.'[163] The first three expressions are used mainly within the context of the CRC to confer rights, and the last expression is used mainly to denote a specific application of the conferred rights.[164] The use of 'the child' in article 12 conforms to the general trend. Therefore, it is reasonable to conclude that within the meaning of article 12, participation is more an individual right of a child than a collective right for children. The child's right to participation is further limited to the expression of 'views' on issues that affect the child only. It is debatable if this right is wide enough to include the involvement of

158 N Thomas & B Percy-Smith 'Introduction' in in B Percy-Smith & N Thomas (eds) *A handbook of children and young people's participation: Perspective from theory and practice* (2010) 2 citing Nigel Cantwell.

159 G Lansdown 'The realisation of children's participation rights: Critical reflection' in B Percy-Smith & N Thomas (eds) *A handbook of children and young people's participation: Perspective from theory and practice* (2010) 12.

160 See article 1 of the Convention on the Rights of the Child.

161 See article 2(1) of the Convention on the Rights of the Child.

162 See article 6(1) of the Convention on the Rights of the Child.

163 See article 12(1) of the Convention on the Rights of the Child.

164 Compare for example the usage in article 1 of the Convention on the Rights of the Child. Similar pattern is followed in many articles of the CRC.

children in different forms of collective social action and whether the views referred to here are on public or private issues.

The challenge with interpreting article 12 of the CRC and, by implication, article 4(2) of the African Children's Charter as conferring private participatory rights on children is that this provision places a public obligation on states to ensure the realisation of this right. Governments are obliged, at domestic level, to make this right a legal entitlement, to make efforts to systematically provide the child with means that facilitate meaningful participation, raise local awareness and provide well-resourced mechanisms for children to influence public decisions at all levels.[165] The CRC Committee expects that such participation enabling mechanisms should facilitate consultative participation, collaborative participation, and child-led participation in the public spheres.[166] A participation right envisages a situation wherein children should be empowered to determine the process as well as the outcome of decision-making.

As stated previously, participation in the private and public spheres in different cultures provokes 'different concerns and approaches.'[167] In traditional African communities children, as part of the family and community, participate in family and community processes and there is insufficient evidence to suggest that such participation is a matter of right. The right to participation is determined by the position of the person in the social hierarchy.

Interpreted as sensitivity to the feelings and views of children by families and communities, child participation is a less problematic concept in traditional communities in Africa. The purposive interpretation of article 12 of the CRC and article 4(2) of the African Children's Charter to include collective rights to participation as a matter of rights is equally not problematic when considered in the context of a vertical relationship between citizens and their

---

165 G Lansdown 'The realisation of children's participation rights: Critical reflection' in B Percy-Smith & N Thomas (eds) *A handbook of children and young people's participation: Perspective from theory and practice* (2010) 14.

166 G Lansdown 'The realisation of children's participation rights: Critical reflection' in B Percy-Smith & N Thomas (eds) *A handbook of children and young people's participation: Perspective from theory and practice* (2010) 20.

167 Editorial: 'International child book: Promise and challenge' (1997) 4 *Childhood* 147.

governments. On the other hand, such an interpretation would be difficult to implement horizontally within family and communal settings in traditional Africa. The African Children's Committee seems to suggest that participation as provided for in the African Children's Charter differs from such traditional understandings. The African Children's Committee expects of state parties 'advocacy in families, communities and traditional settings'[168] to ensure that children participate in decision making. The reference to 'advocacy in families, communities and traditional settings'[169] in this respect would suggest at least two things: First, that the African Children's Committee is of the opinion that child participation is alien to families, communities and traditional settings in Africa and, therefore, governments need to spend resources to instil this virtue in traditional communities in Africa. Second, the reference may suggest that the African Children's Committee holds the view that it has a far better brand of child participation that it wants governments to instil in families and communities in Africa and, thus, needs effort and resources to cultivate these new techniques of child participation in their communities.

The CRC Committee holds the view that states have a positive obligation to facilitate the participation of children in all actions that affect them and that state parties are expected to 'continue to assist children when they want to establish organizations with the goal of promoting and protecting their rights.'[170] As a component of this obligation, state parties should provide children with 'information, support and favourable conditions in order to participate appropriately and in a way that enhances their dignity and self-esteem.'[171] Since the 'circle' of participation closest to children, where they

168 See Concluding Recommendations by the African Committee of Experts on the Rights and Welfare of The Child (African Children's Committee) on the Republic of Tanzania Report on The Status of implementation of The African Charter on The Rights and Welfare of The Child available at http://www.African Children's Committee.org/wp-content/uploads/2011/03/African Children's CommitteE-Recommendations-Tanzania-initial-English.pdf.

169 See Concluding Recommendations by the African Committee of Experts on the Rights and Welfare of The Child (African Children's Committee) on the Republic of Tanzania Report on The Status of implementation of The African Charter on The Rights and Welfare of The Child available at http://www.African Children's Committee.org/wp-content/uploads/2011/03/African Children's Committee-Recommendations-Tanzania-initial-English.pdf.

170 See for example CRC, Concluding Observations regarding the Dominican Republic, 11 February 2008, CRC/C/ DOM/CO/2 para 34.

171 UNICEF 'circles of participation' The State of the World's Children (2003) 3. Available at http://www.unicef.org/sowc03/contents/pdf/SOWC03-eng.pdf.

impart information and their views, is the family, within the framework of the CRC children's participation rights are expected to be respected within the family environment too. From the above analysis with respect to article 4(2), the African Children's Charter is more substantively, normatively and textually akin to article 12(2) of the CRC than it is relevant to the African context it was supposed to reflect and respond to.

If issues such as the definition of a child, what the rights of children are, what the interests of the child entail, and how and where the child should participate in the African Children's Charter are firmly rooted in the understanding of childhood in the CRC, how legitimate and culturally and philosophically friendly is the African Children's Charter to the African context?

4.4. Cultural legitimacy as a challenge to the implementation of the African Children's Charter

The continued inability of human rights norms and standards to effectively end impunity is forcing international and national policy makers to shift the policy battlefront to issues surrounding the implementation of human rights. By implementation is meant the ability to translate and transfer the values and norms embodied in human rights treaties to enhance the quality of life and dignity of every human being.[172] There is a direct correlation between the effectiveness of the methods and mechanisms used to implement human rights norms and values, and the acceptance of these norms and values by their beneficiaries.[173]

Acceptance is easy to measure at a formal level. The voluntary ratification of a human rights treaty by a state and its willingness and ability to domesticate that treaty suffices as an indicator of acceptance of the treaty norms and their implications. Unfortunately, formal acceptance is an insufficient indicator of acceptance because ratification, as an exercise of state volition, is a multivocal

172 C Heyns & F Viljoen 'The impact of the United Nations human rights treaties on the domestic level' (2001) 23 *Human Rights Quarterly* 2483.

173 See L Keith 'National constitutions and human rights protection: Regional differences and colonial influences' in S Carey & S Poe *Understanding human rights violations* (2004) 162; L Ogundele 'Legal systems and constitutionalism in Sub-Saharan Africa: An empirical examination of colonial influences on human rights' (2007) 29 *Human Rights Quarterly* 1065.

undertaking - it may be genuine, hypocritical or utterly false.[174] Consequently, 'ratification in itself [could] largely [be] a formal, and in some cases an empty, gesture.'[175]

In addition, ratification is state-centred. This is problematic, at least in an African context, because the nature, intention and the scope of the state are subjects of academic debate. Some scholars argue that the states in Africa, as colonial projects, were created 'to be totalitarian, oppressive, and exploitative.'[176] As a result, states are not 'necessarily the most reliable [representatives] of the people whom they govern.'[177] In addition, it has been claimed that in Africa 'power ... radiates outward from the core political areas and tends to diminish over distance.'[178] As a result, the 'state plays only a limited role in the daily lives of many Africans.'[179]

Furthermore, there are concerns that ratification by weaker and small states may not be genuinely voluntarily. Powerful and richer states use 'a form of coercion by intellectual means [in addition] to the use of "soft power" par excellence,'[180] to ensure ratification by small and weaker states. According to An Na'im, 'it is misleading to assume genuine representation of popular perceptions and attitudes towards human rights in our countries from the formal representation of "our delegates" to international fora.'[181] Instead, 'popular acceptance' by families and communities is crucial to the cost effective implementation of human rights. Therefore, in the debate of what should constitute commonly agreed standards of human rights and how these standards should be implemented, it is imperative that the values and voices

---

174 B Simmons *Mobilizing for human rights: International law in domestic politics* (2009) 58.

175 C Heyns & F Viljoen 'The impact of the United Nations human rights treaties on the domestic level' (2001) 23 *Human Rights Quarterly* 2483.

176 M Mutua 'Justice under siege: The rule of law and judicial subservience in Kenya' (2001) 23 *Human Rights Quarterly* 96.

177 M Freeman 'Human rights and real cultures: Towards a dialogue on "Asian values"' (1998) 16 *Netherlands Quarterly of Human Rights* 26.

178 J Herbst *States and power in Africa: Comparative lessons in authority and control* (2000) 251.

179 J Herbst *States and power in Africa: Comparative lessons in authority and control* (2000) 272.

180 L Bell *et al Negotiating culture and human rights* (2001) 242.

181 A An-Na'im Human right *in cross-cultural perspectives: A quest for consensus* (1995) 427.

of local families and communities ought not to be neglected, dismissed or discounted.

Whatever implementation strategy is adopted, it is important to note that the cultural values, needs, opinion and expectation of the recipient communities are crucial building blocks for, or stumbling blocks to implementation. Empirical book, academic admonition and states admissions all bear witness to the powerful role that culture plays in the human rights dialogue, as well as implementation.[182] The influence of culture gets stronger as human rights norms get closer to the basic unit of society: family and children. Therefore, the implementation of human rights norms that impact on the lives of families and children should be sensitive to cultural context. For instance, a book of the implementation of the CRC in three South American countries concluded that the level of implementation was 'conditioned by the interface between understandings of rights and broader questions of politics, cultures and institutions.'[183]

Similarly, in the African context, states, academic institutions and non-governmental organisations have identified socio-cultural contexts as posing significant challenges to the effective and efficient implementation of children's rights in Africa.[184] Perceptions around how culturally legitimate the provisions of treaties dealing with children rights are in an African context are at the core of these implementation challenges.[185] A number of state parties to the CRC and, in few instances, the African Children's Charter[186] have stated that culture and traditions in their own countries presented the greatest challenge to their efforts to implement children's rights.[187]

---

182 See the discussions on the role culture plays in the implementation of human rights in S Harris-Short 'International human rights law: Imperialist, inept and ineffective? Cultural relativism and the UN Convention on the Rights of the Child' (2003) 25 *Human Rights Quarterly* 130.

183 J Grugel & E Peruzzotti 'The domestic politics of international human rights law: Implementing the Convention on the Rights of the Child in Ecuador, Chile, and Argentina' (2012) 34 *Human Rights Quarterly* 178.

184 http://www.odi.org.uk/sites/odi.org.uk/files/odi-assets/publications-opinion-files/6050.pdf.

185 T Kaime *The African Charter on the Rights and Welfare of the Child: A socio-legal perspective* (2009) 36, 53.

186 See for example the Initial State Report of the Republic of Senegal to the African Children's Committee.

187 S Harris-Short 'International human rights law: Imperialist, inept and ineffective? Cultural relativism and the UN Convention on the Rights of the Child' (2003) 25 *Human Rights Quarterly* 130.

The acceptance and effective implementation of the CRC and, by implication, the African Children's Charter (in the light of the textually, normative and substantive similarities between the two treaties) in Africa have been hampered by their perceived lack of cultural legitimacy.[188] At the level of formal acceptance some states have significantly minimised the extent of their obligations under the CRC and the African Children's Charter[189] through reservations citing religious and cultural factors.[190] Some states in Africa base their willingness to implement article 18 of the CRC, for example, on the condition that it will be interpreted and 'implemented in accordance with the Islamic law.'[191] Or, more generally, 'the Government of Djibouti shall not consider itself bound by any provisions or articles that are incompatible with its religion and its traditional values.'[192] It is difficult to imagine which principle or provision of the CRC falls outside this blanket reservation.

State reports to the CRC Committee have also attributed implementation challenges with respect to the CRC to communities differing cultural values and norms. According to the Democratic Republic of Congo,

> Africa is moving towards a form of modernity, which nevertheless retains 'authentic' aspects; these should be taken into account and safeguarded. For this reason, legislation which is too advanced in relation to mental, social, economic and cultural structures is sometimes more dangerous than an outdated legal system.[193]

Advancing the same argument, that law is a blunt tool to address entrenched cultural values and practices, the Malian delegation said in the context of FGM that it is 'impossible to legislate against voluntary excision.'[194] Things

188 As above.

189 The Republic of Egypt, Botswana, and Sudan among others have entered reservation to the African Children's Charter.

190 Harris-Short, n 187.

191 See for example the reservation of Algeria to the CRC.

192 Reservation entered by Djibouti to the CRC. Mauritania entered similar reservation to the CRC.

193 See the addendum to the Initial Report of the Congo (U.N. Doc. CRC/C/3/Add 57 209) as cited in S Harris-Short International human rights law: Imperialist, inept and ineffective? Cultural relativism and the UN Convention on the Rights of the Child' (2003) 25 *Human Rights Quarterly* 130.

194 Summary Record of the 571st Meeting of the CRC Committee: Mali, UN CRC Committee, U.N. Doc.

are made more difficult because of the 'perception among the local population that the general civil and criminal law, as opposed to customary law and practice, enshrines "alien ideas" that have been forcibly imposed on them by more powerful outsiders.'[195] Chad has admitted that the 'weight of custom and tradition' has made 'it difficult to implement some provisions' of the CRC.[196] The implementation of the 'foreign' nature of the values codified in the CRC standards

> comes up against the enormous complexity of the concrete realities of nations, such as inter alia, ethnic particularism and cultural diversities....these factors...mean that implementation of the provisions of the Convention is somewhat relative and variable depending on the country.[197]

Because of cultural hurdles to implementing the provisions of the CRC and in light of the similarities between it and the African Children's Charter, state parties are forced 'to steer a course between the desirable and the feasible.'[198] Perhaps 'the entire Convention was not suited to the realities of African life'[199] or the state could not 'force its citizens to abide by ideas and principles that were alien to them and there would be no point in adopting laws that could

---

CRC/C/SR.571 (1999) 26 as cited in S Harris-Short International human rights law: Imperialist, inept and ineffective? Cultural relativism and the UN Convention on the Rights of the Child' (2003) 25 *Human Rights Quarterly* 130.

195 According to the delegation of the Republic of Uganda while referring to the successes the state has recorded in its efforts to eliminate FGM. See Summary Record of the 409th Meeting: Uganda, U.N. CRC Committee, U.N. Doc. CRC/C/SR.409 (1997) 55 as cited in S Harris-Short International human rights law: Imperialist, inept and ineffective? Cultural relativism and the UN Convention on the Rights of the Child' (2003) 25 *Human Rights Quarterly* 130.

196 See the summary records of the meeting of the CRC Committee on the initial report of the Republic of Chad U.N. Doc. CRC/C/3/Add 50 (1997) 35.

197 Initial Reports of The Republic of Guinea Addendum: Guinea, U.N. CRC Committee, U.N. Doc. CRC/C/3/Add 48, (1996) 164 cited in S Harris-Short International human rights law: Imperialist, inept and ineffective? Cultural relativism and the UN Convention on the Rights of the Child' (2003) 25 *Human Rights Quarterly* 130.

198 Summary Record of the 136th Meeting: Burkina Faso, U.N. CRC Committee, U.N. Doc. CRC/C/SR.1 36 (1995) 31 as cited in S Harris-Short International human rights law: Imperialist, inept and ineffective? Cultural relativism and the UN Convention on the Rights of the Child' (2003) 25 *Human Rights Quarterly* 130.

199 Summary Record of the 420th Meeting: Togo, CRC Committee, U.N. Doc. CRC/C/SR.420, (1997) 46 as cited in S Harris-Short International human rights law: Imperialist, inept and ineffective? Cultural relativism and the UN Convention on the Rights of the Child' (2003) 25 *Human Rights Quarterly* 130.

not be enforced'[200] or simply because of the conceptual difficulties involved in implementing the CRC:

> Traditionally, the law developed in the wake of social changes and changes in the ways of thinking. In the case of the Convention, however, the contrary would appear to be the case in the Sudan, where changes in attitudes and in the organisation of institutions were apparently supposed to follow in the wake of the law.[201]

There is increasing evidence seen in the state reports submitted by states in Africa that the challenges they face with respect to implementing the provisions of children's rights are partly rooted in the differences in the cultural values and image of childhood in the CRC and, by implication, the African Children's Charter and in traditional African communities.

In the words of the Congolese state report:

> Traditional African culture in general and Congolese culture in particular makes for conformity in behaviour, the notion of collective responsibility and the principle of linear authority – of the father over the son and the elder over the younger. Respect in traditional society is more than a rule for living; it designates each individual's place and role.[202]

The point emerging from the reporting exercise is that states claim they are willing to implement their obligations under the CRC but effectively are unable to do so because 'the weight of tradition [was] extremely heavy,'[203]

200 Comments from the delegation of the Republic of Benin see Summary Record of the 543rd Meeting: Benin, U.N. CRC Committee, U.N. Doc. CRC/C/SR.543 (1999) 58 as cited in S Harris-Short International human rights law: Imperialist, inept and ineffective? Cultural relativism and the UN Convention on the Rights of the Child' (2003) 25 *Human Rights Quarterly* 130.

201 *Summary Record of the 69th Meeting of the CRC Committee: Sudan*, U.N. Doc. CRC/ C/SR.69 (Sudan) 40 as cited in in S Harris-Short International human rights law: Imperialist, inept and ineffective? Cultural relativism and the UN Convention on the Rights of the Child' (2003) 25 *Human Rights Quarterly* 130.

202 Initial Reports of States Parties Due in 1992: Addendum: Democratic Republic of Congo, U.N. CRC Committee, U.N. Doc. CRC/C/3/Add. 57, p. 50 as cited in in S Harris-Short International human rights law: Imperialist, inept and ineffective? Cultural relativism and the UN Convention on the Rights of the Child' (2003) 25 *Human Rights Quarterly* 130.

203 *Summary Record of the 89th Meeting: Sudan*, U.N. CRC Committee, U.N. Doc. CRC/C/SR.89 (1994) 18 as cited in in S Harris-Short International human rights law: Imperialist, inept and ineffective? Cultural relativism and the UN Convention on the Rights of the Child' (2003) 25 *Human Rights Quarterly* 130.

due to the 'social and cultural backwardness'[204] of their people or, generally, because their people consider the childrearing values of the CRC as alien to theirs.

Some scholars have cautioned against this victim-like attitude of states. It has been argued that putting the blame on 'entrenched cultural practices'[205] for ineffective implementation provides useful excuses for inaction, thereby allowing governments 'to get the benefits of international legitimacy without the "inconvenience" of compliance with human rights standards.'[206] Submissions by state parties before human rights treaty bodies should be thoroughly examined for 'dangers of distortion, political manipulation and unfounded appeals to a mythical past.'[207] Some states simply engage in 'self-serving opportunistic' efforts to 'invoke conjured traditions to justify economic, social and political repressions.'[208] These critics advise that those who are the victims of the abuses should rather be consulted 'to determine whether those who are subordinated, excluded and or marginalised regard their situation as culturally legitimate.'[209]

These arguments are not without merit. Conceptually, they are inherently self-defeating. First, to accuse the states of not being the authoritative and authentic representative of the values of their people is to legitimise the perception that these same states do not know their people and, thus, have no

---

204 Summary Record of the 657th Meeting: Central African Republic, U.N. Committee on the Rights of the Child, U.N. Doc. CRC/C/SR.657 (2000) 46 as cited in in S Harris-Short International human rights law: Imperialist, inept and ineffective? Cultural relativism and the UN Convention on the Rights of the Child' (2003) 25 *Human Rights Quarterly* 130.

205 A An-Na'im 'Human rights and Islamic identity in France and Uzbekistan: Mediation of the local and global' (2000) 22 *Human Rights Quarterly* 906.

206 As above.

207 S Harris-Short International human rights law: Imperialist, inept and ineffective? Cultural relativism and the UN Convention on the Rights of the Child' (2003) 25 *Human Rights Quarterly* 130 citing A Pollis 'Towards a new universalism; reconstruction and dialogue' (1998) 16 *Netherlands Quarterly of Human Rights* 17; J Donnelly 'Cultural relativism and universal human rights' in J Donnelly *Human rights in theory and practice* (1989) 118; R Howard 'Cultural absolutism and the nostalgia for community' (1993) 15 *Human Rights Quarterly* 315.

208 A Pollis 'Towards a new universalism; reconstruction and dialogue' (1998) 16 *Netherlands Quarterly of Human Rights* 17.

209 M Freeman 'Human rights and real cultures: Towards a dialogue on "Asian Values"' (1998) 16 *Netherlands Quarterly of Human Rights* 26.

mandate in the first place to negotiate international human rights treaties on their behalf. Therefore,

> If state elites are not faithfully representing the culturally rooted views, attitudes and opinions of the people whom they govern, the norms enshrined within the UN Convention on the Rights of the Child, despite near-universal ratification, lose their claim to cultural legitimacy.[210]

If the policy value of human rights is dependant and determined by its translatability and transferability into lived realities through implementation, and implementation, in turn, relies on the formal and cultural acceptability of the human rights norms, it is reasonable to assume that the gap between human rights values and the cultural norms of the beneficiaries is a determining factor for effective implementation. Therefore, since there is a conceptual and cultural gap between the image of childhood in the CRC and the understanding of childhood in traditional communities in Africa, its implementation in Africa will continue to be challenging until the CRC either creates an African culture in its own image or the CRC is Africanised in its implementation.

A reason why state parties to the CRC ratified the African Children's Charter may have been because they were fearful that the implementation of the CRC in their countries might be difficult and because these states perceived the African Children's Charter to be 'more responsive to traditional African values and concerns'[211] relating to childhood. It has been demonstrated in this work that the African Children's Charter is but an 'edited' version of the CRC and that its textual, conceptual and substantive similarities are not coincidental. So, it is reasonable to presume that the implementation of the African Children's Charter will face the same challenges that its mother treaty, the CRC, is facing in Africa and elsewhere. Since the normative commonality

210 S Harris-Short International human rights law: Imperialist, inept and ineffective? Cultural relativism and the UN Convention on the Rights of the Child' (2003) 25 *Human Rights Quarterly* 130.

211 Initial Reports of States Parties Due in 1992: Addendum: Uganda, U.N. CRC Committee, U.N. Doc. CRC/C/3/Add 40, (1996) 18 cited in S Harris-Short International human rights law: Imperialist, inept and ineffective? Cultural relativism and the UN Convention on the Rights of the Child' (2003) 25 *Human Rights Quarterly* 130.

between the African Children's Charter and the CRC calls into question the autochthony of the former, it is better to regard and treat the relationship between the CRC and the African Children's Charter simply as an act of legal transplantation.

4.5. The unique features of the African Children's Charter

The African Children's Charter is not in all respects a copy of the CRC. It differs from and improves upon the provisions of the CRC in a number of areas. For the purpose of this work, they will be grouped into two broad categories:

First, there are those provisions that, theoretically, offer a higher and broader standard of protection for children in Africa. These are provisions dealing with the definition of who a child is,[212] provisions dealing with primacy of the provisions of the African Children's Charter over harmful cultural practices,[213] children in armed conflicts,[214] children of imprisoned mothers,[215] internally displaced children, specific protection for the girl child, children who were living under apartheid, and a broader mandate and power for its monitoring body, the African Children's Committee.[216] These provisions address African specific challenges that either were not sufficiently dealt with under the CRC or that did not offer a sufficiently high threshold of protection to children in Africa.[217]

212 Article 2 of the African Charter on the Rights and Welfare of the Child.

213 Article 21 of the African Charter on the Rights and Welfare of the Child.

214 Article 22 of the African Charter on the Rights and Welfare of the Child.

215 Article 30 of the African Charter on the Rights and Welfare of the Child.

216 Articles 21(2), 23, 32 of the African Charter on the Rights and Welfare of the Child.

217 However, article 1 of the Optional Protocol on the Involvement of Children in Armed Conflict; reflects the provisions of article 22(2) of the African Children's Charter. In addition, the Optional Protocol on the Sale of Children, Child prostitution and Pornography has extended and expanded the nature and scope of the protection available under the CRC to the girl child. In 2011, the CRC Committee hosted a General Day of Discussion on the Children of Incarcerated Parents something that is provided for only in the African Children's Charter. In its General Comment No.14 the Committee defines the child as any human being below the age of 18 without immediate reference to the exception in article 1. See paragraph 21 that states *'the term "children" refers to all persons under the age of 18 within the jurisdiction of a State party*, without discrimination of any kind, in line with articles 1 and 2 of the Convention.

The second category of provisions deals with an African-specific philosophy and cultural heritage. Article 31 of the African Children's Charter, conferring duties and responsibilities on children, falls under this category. This provision amplifies the traditional understanding of childhood, that it is a period of learning and preparation for responsible adulthood, as well as a reciprocal societal care and goodwill. The other African specific provision provided for in the African Charter on Human and Peoples' Rights, collective rights, is omitted from the African Children's Charter. The rights granted children in the African Children's Charter can be enjoyed only individually.

There have been a number of concerns with respect to burdening children with duties and responsibilities under the African Children's Charter, but Julia-Sloth Nielsen and Benyam Mezmur adequately address these concerns.[218] According to these authors, article 31 makes a valuable contribution to international human rights law. A purposeful interpretation of this article provides a complement to the concept of 'rights of child' and thus allows children to play positive roles in society in accordance with their age as they mature. Since maturity is a process, allowing children to play responsible roles in families and society should equip children with livelihood skills and make out of them responsible citizens.

The question this section seeks to answer is whether these 'unique' features are sufficient enough to meet the threshold for a new regional treaty for children. In other words, could these African specific challenges be effectively addressed through interpretations and, possibly, through the Optional Protocols to the CRC? With the benefit of hindsight, the answer to this question is positive. For example, the three Optional Protocols to the CRC have significantly addressed the African concerns around higher definitional standards for children in

218 See generally J Sloth-Nielsen & B Mezmur 'A dutiful child: The implications of Article 31 of the African Children's Charter' (2008) 52 *Journal of African Law* 159.

armed conflict,[219] trafficking,[220] and a communication mechanism,[221] (which was one major contribution of the African system but is now established under the CRC). Also, a number of General Comments and Days of General Discussions have paid attention to some of the shortcomings of the CRC, including issues around children of imprisoned mothers.

In the light of the fact that many of the once unique features of the African Children's Charter have been addressed through the CRC, or could still be addressed within that framework, is the African Children's Charter redundant? The answer is no. Firstly, the 18 members of the CRC Committee, the extremely limited resources at its disposal, the enormous amount of work that still needs to be done globally on children make an additional support and protective layer for children a worthwhile venture.

The CRC Committee is inundated with work and will need a significant number of years to exhaust its backlog of state reports due for consideration, for example.[222] The addition of a communication procedure will simply exacerbate an already bad situation for the CRC Committee. Therefore, it is unreasonable to expect that the CRC Committee has the requisite capacity, time and resources to attend to the plight of all children around the world and in a timely manner. Thus, a regional mechanism such as the African Children's Committee with a mandate similar to that of the CRC Committee should be a welcome relief to children's rights policy makers and activists, especially in Africa.

Secondly, textual and substantive similarities in a human rights treaty do not necessarily translate into the same interpretation and reasoning by the monitoring bodies. Interpretation of treaties or laws, in general, is not a

219 For example, article 1 of the Optional Protocol to the Convention on the Rights of the Child on the involvement of children in armed conflict has significantly enhance the protection of children within the context of armed conflict.

220 For example, article 1 of Optional Protocol to the Convention on the Rights of the Child on the sale of children, child prostitution and child pornography places a blanket prohibition on all forms of trafficking in children.

221 For Optional Protocol to the Convention on the Rights of the Child on a Communications Procedure, which has just entered into force.

222 See the Report of the CRC Committee, General Assemble fifty-ninth session, Supplementary no 41(A59/41).

formulaic or mechanical exercise with predictable outcomes. Two judges sitting in the same courts and reading from the same treaty could end up with different interpretations. Even if the texts of the CRC and the African Children's Charter are similar, and the mandates of the CRC Committee and the African Children's Committee are the same, it is possible to anticipate innovative interpretation by the African Children's Committee that could situate those texts in the context of their implementation. It is possible that the approaches of the two treaty bodies may not be exactly the same. In such a situation, it is possible that the two treaty bodies could engender constructive dialogue around child's rights and welfare in Africa.

4.6. Conclusion

The African Children's Charter was conceived to address African specific challenges facing children, as well as to reflect and respond to an African philosophy of childhood and cultural heritage. The African Children's Charter has addressed these African-specific challenges and offers children in Africa a higher threshold of protection. However, textually and substantively, the African Children's Charter does not adequately reflect and respond to an African understanding of childhood and to an African cultural heritage. Even if the African Children's Charter in its Preamble expresses its intention to be culturally and context-specific, textually and substantively it is a mere transplant of the CRC. The CRC, whose focus is global, in some instances is more flexible and more attuned to or aligned with the African cultural context than the African Children's Charter with communities in Africa as its primary audience and whose cultural norms, practices and aspirations for childhood it is meant to reflect.

What the drafters of the African Children's Charter denied Africa of by their decision to transplant the CRC is Africa's ability to preserve its 'entitlement of historical communities to maintain a local connection with their laws as a legitimate vector of cultural identity.'[223] The possible result of this decision is that the African Children's Charter, unless interpreted contextually, threatens

223 P Legrand 'On the unbearable localness of the law: Academic failures and unreasonable observations' (2002) 10 *European Review of Private Law* 63.

to deprive the continent of an African conception of childhood that is 'historically, sociologically, economically and politically' African. What the drafters of the African Children's Charter have achieved, instead, is to expose the African Children's Charter to the same conceptual and normative defects inherent in the CRC and, consequently, to subject the implementation of the African Children's Charter to the same cultural legitimacy challenges confronting the CRC. The new image of the child and vision of the family and its role in the upbringing of the child introduced by the African Children's Charter is more deeply rooted in the CRC than in the cultural practices and values of its member states.

The failure of the African Children's Charter to promote and portray an African understanding of childhood exposes it to the same accusation of a lack of cultural legitimacy that the CRC faces and makes it suffer from the same defects inherent in the CRC. It is reasonable to ask if there is any value in retaining two duplicative treaties and if it is efficient to fund two processes to arrive at the same goal. The way in which the African Children's Committee interprets and applies the provisions of the African Children's Charter is a determinant in answering this question. The fact that two treaties are similar textually, normatively and substantively in itself does not guarantee that the two treaty bodies monitoring such treaties inherently will interpret and apply the provisions of those treaties in a similar manner. Therefore, if the African Children's Committee interprets the African Children's Charter through the lens of an African philosophy of childhood and cultural heritage, the African Children's Charter will be a value added. However, if it interprets and applies the provisions of the African Children's Charter according to the liberal and universalist approach of the CRC Committee, it will be difficult to justify the usefulness of retaining the African Children's Charter.

CHAPTER 5

THE AFRICAN CHILDREN'S COMMITTEE: A PROPOSITION FOR A CONTEXT-SENSITIVE INTERPRETATION OF THE AFRICAN CHILDREN'S CHARTER

The chapter is divided into five parts and a conclusion. The first part situates the discussion of the African Children's Committee within the broader challenge of weak institutional frameworks for the implementation of human rights.

The second part reviews the strengths and weaknesses of the working methods of human rights treaty bodies, in general, in light of the similarities between the working methods of the African Children's Committee and those of other human rights treaty bodies. This part argues that international human rights treaty bodies discharge their mandates within a universalist paradigm of human rights. It is suggested that a major advantage the African Children's Committee could leverage in applying its mandate is to complement the universalism of human rights as a theoretical framework with the universal pluralist paradigm for the interpretation of the African Children's Charter.

The third part examines how the African Children's Committee has interpreted its mandate and the provisions of the African Children's Charter. It is argued that so far there has been a tendency on the part of the African Children's Committee to rely mainly on a universal human rights paradigm in discharging its mandate. This assertion will be substantiated through examination of the African Children's Committee's approach to considering state party reports and its interpretation of the provisions of the African Children's Charter. will be examined. It is argued that state parties to the African Children's Charter have highlighted the duality[1] of the lived experience of children in their countries. The challenge of the duality of childhood experience is a reason why the African Children's Committee should not operate within a universal human rights' theoretical framework only.

The fourth part demonstrates other challenges that the African Children's Committee might encounter if it continues to carry out its mandate within the framework of universalism. These challenges include the high likelihood of merely echoing and duplicating the voice and mandate of the CRC Committee in an African context. If the African Children's Committee cannot substantially and procedurally be distinguished from the CRC Committee, it would increasingly be difficult to avoid the conclusion that the African Children's Charter is more of a duplication of the CRC than a complement. To avoid the African Children's Charter becoming redundant, it is recommended that the African Children's Committee should complement the discharging of its mandate with a pluralistic universalist theoretical framework. A mixed theoretical framework will assist the African Children's Committee to discharge its mandate effectively and efficiently.

5. Introduction

At the beginning of the 21st century it seemed 'clear that the concept of human rights [was] widely accepted as the 'idea of our time,'[2] probably because human rights norms, values and standards had increased substantially in the 20th century. The next challenge is to strengthen institutional frameworks in order to better implementation of the body of human rights norms and standards. The main challenge facing the realisation of human

1 Children in African countries live their lives governed by the ethos of their cultures and also the norms and standards of the CRC and the African Children's Charter. It is this experience of living constantly under two different legal regimes that is referred to in this work as duality or hybridity.

2 C Heyns & F Viljoen 'The impact of the United Nations human rights treaties on the domestic level' (2001) 23 *Human Rights Quarterly* 483.

rights has been that of implementation.[3] Already there are sufficient norms and standards; the argument is that what is needed 'are not new standards and procedures, but rather efficient mechanisms to enforce existing standards and recommendations of monitoring bodies and to prevent the occurrence of future human rights violations.'[4]

The human rights movement has a history of strong standard setting but a weak institutional framework for the implementation of these standards. This assertion is demonstrated by the fact that of the three core issues the UN was established to handle (peace and security, development, and human rights) it is only human rights that lacks an effective institutional framework for its monitoring and implementation. The UN Security Council was established to ensure global peace and security. The United Nations Development Program was set up to oversee the development agenda of the United Nations. However, initially, the Human Rights Commission created within ECOSOC, but with no real powers on its own, had a mandate to oversee the implementation of human rights.

Historically, the failure to put in place robust institutional mechanisms to implement human rights was not due to a lack of ideas on how best to implement human rights. In fact, a number of proposals were made with a view to enhancing the institutional frameworks for monitoring and implementing human rights. These included the proposal to establish a World Court of Human Rights, first made in 1947 and repeated in June 2009,[5] and the creation of the office of the World's Attorney General for human rights. So far, these remain mere aspirations. Less radical proposals were made in the early 1950s aimed, primarily, at giving the Human Rights Commission fact-finding powers and the authority to initiate inquiries into alleged violations of human rights. These efforts too faced numerous challenges.[6] Substantially,

3 M Mutua 'Looking past the Human Rights Committee: An argument for de-marginalizing enforcement' (1998) 4 *Buffalo Human Rights Law Review* 211; see also M Nowak 'A roundtable: On the creation of World Court of Human Rights' (2012) 259.

4 M Nowak 'Proposals for improving the UN human rights programme' (1993) 11 *Netherlands Quarterly Human Rights* 153.

5 M Nowak 'A roundtable: On the creation of World Court of Human Rights' (2012) 259; see also http://www.udhr60.ch/report/hrCourt_scheinin0609.pdf.

6 M Mutua 'Looking past the Human Rights Committee: An argument for de-marginalizing enforcement'

the Human Rights Commission's only compulsory mandates were to 'book the reports submitted by states parties' and to 'transmit its reports, and such general comments as it may consider appropriate' to state parties, in general, through ECOSOC.[7]

Opinion is divided as to why states are reluctant in drafting human rights treaties to put in place a strong, functioning and effective institutional framework to oversee the implementation of human rights. Some scholars are of the opinion that weak human rights monitoring mechanisms are in the best interests of universal human rights norms;[8] that anchoring human rights norms in strong institutions 'raises the cost of joining' human rights regimes. Since human rights 'institutions with real power cut to the bone of sovereignty,'[9] these scholars argue that strong human rights institutions are a deterrent to universal ratification of human rights norms.

They argue, 'rather than push for a more effective universal supervision and enforcement regime, a noble but an unrealizable goal;'[10] it is more useful to have more states on board with weaker institutions than to have fewer states on board with a stronger institutional framework for enforcement.[11] The argument is that a weaker institutional framework for the implementation of human rights is faithful to the original intention of the states when they negotiated and ratified human rights treaties. According to these scholars, states understand human rights as a system of norms the 'objective of [which] was to avoid evaluation at all costs.'[12] Human rights treaty bodies are intended

(1998) 4 *Buffalo Human Rights Law Review* 211.

7 Art. 40 of the International Covenant on Civil and Political Rights GA. Res. 2200A (XX), U.N. GAOR, 21 st Sess., Supp. No. 16, at 52, U.N. Doc. AN6316 (1966), 999 U.N.T.S. 171.

8 M Mutua 'Looking past the Human Rights Committee: An argument for de-marginalizing enforcement' (1998) 4 *Buffalo Human Rights Law Review* 211; see also generally H Steiner 'Individual claims in a world of massive violation: What role for Human Rights Committee?' in P Alston & J Crawford (eds) *The future of human rights treaty monitoring* (2000) 15.

9 H Steiner 'Individual claims in a world of massive violation: What role for Human Rights Committee?' in P Alston & J Crawford (eds) *The future of human rights treaty monitoring* (2000) 25.

10 M Mutua 'Looking past the Human Rights Committee: An argument for de-marginalizing enforcement' (1998) 4 *Buffalo Human Rights Law Review* 211.

11 H Steiner 'Individual claims in a world of massive violation: What role for Human Rights Committee?' in P Alston & J Crawford (eds) *The future of human rights treaty monitoring* (2000) 25.

12 P Alston 'The Committee on Economic, Social and Cultural Rights' in P Alston (ed) *The United Nations and human rights: A critical appraisal* (1992) 507.

to facilitate the exchange of information and experience among states through constructive dialogue that 'should have no conclusion.'[13]

This position may not be representative of all states. Human rights standard-setting are the preserve of states. States make proposals, negotiate those proposals and agree to them. It is difficult to imagine that there are no states that support the effective implementation and enforcement of human rights. It can further be argued, since human rights are natural entitlements of all human beings, that the only reason states want to codify them in a treaty is to render them enforceable. In addition, rendering human rights weak to 'sell' them to a wider market could end up making human rights, in general, ineffective in attending to the plight of those whose rights are violated. Therefore, compromising the rights of those who are abused and violated in exchange for the consent of state parties can hardly be a noble venture.

Other scholars disagree with the proponents of weak institutional mechanisms for the implementation of human rights. They are of the opinion that the concept of a right entails a right holder and a duty bearer; if a duty bearer fails to honour his or her obligation then the right holder is entitled to an enforceable remedy. Therefore, monitoring mechanisms that are not 'inquisitorial nor accusative and [whose ends are] neither condemnation nor approbation'[14] are incompatible with the very concept of human rights. Having human rights norms without able and willing institutions to enforce the norms is against the object and purpose of the whole enterprise of human rights. Over a period of time, there has been progress in the implementation of human rights norms, but this is due more to the resilience of some of the human rights treaty bodies and the activism of non-state actors[15] than it is to the willingness of states.

It would be inaccurate to blame states alone for structural, institutional, organizational and operational deficits inherent in the design and functioning

---

13 P Alston 'The Committee on Economic, Social and Cultural Rights' in P Alston (ed) *The United Nations and human rights: A Critical appraisal* (1992) 507.

14 D McGoldrick *The Human Rights Committee: Its role in the development of the International Covenant on Civil and Political Rights* (1991) 89.

15 A Boyle & C Chinkin *The making of international law* (2007) 41.

of human rights treaty bodies. Some factors contributing to the weaknesses in the functioning of human rights treaty bodies are internal to the human rights treaty bodies, and other factors are simply beyond the control of states.[16] For example, it is safe to assume that the structure, mandate, composition, powers and legal status of the findings of a human rights treaty body are factors within the control of states. But the extent of independence, style and quality of outputs of the monitoring bodies are within the control of a treaty monitoring body. Neither treaty bodies nor states have significant influence and control over the cultural norms and standards of states.[17]

A combination of states' unwillingness to grant sufficient powers to human rights treaty monitoring bodies and concerns around the style and quality of the outputs of human rights treaty monitoring bodies are contributing factors responsible for the implementation challenges facing human rights norms. In addition, cultural norms and identities of countries play a significant role in the implementation challenges human rights norms face at national levels.[18]

Some human rights treaty-monitoring bodies have innovatively enhanced their mandate and powers through creative interpretations of the treaty setting them up.[19] Over a period of time, the style and quality of reasoning of the monitoring bodies also have been improving.[20] However, a significant number of human rights monitoring bodies still struggle to find a correct balance between protecting the rights of vulnerable groups from the negative aspects of cultural practices, on the one hand, and promoting and protecting the positive cultural values of all people, on the other.[21]

---

16 L Helfer & A Slaughter 'Towards a theory of effective supranational adjudication' (1997) 107 *Yale Law Journal* 273.

17 L Helfer & A Slaughter 'Towards a theory of effective supranational adjudication' (1997) 107 *Yale Law Journal* 273.

18 T Zwart 'Using local culture to further the implementation of international human rights: The receptor approach' (2012) 34 *Human Rights Quarterly* 546.

19 K Mechlem 'Treaty bodies and interpretation of human rights' (2009) 42 *Vanderbilt Journal of Transnational Law* 905.

20 M Mutua 'Looking past the Human Rights Committee: An argument for de-marginalizing enforcement' (1998) 4 *Buffalo Human Rights Law Review* 211; and H Steiner 'Individual claims in a world of massive violation: What role for Human Rights Committee?' in P Alston & J Crawford (eds) *The future of human rights treaty monitoring* (2000) 25.

21 S Harris-Short 'International human rights law: Imperialist, inept and ineffective? Cultural relativism and

Whilst culture is a force for the promotion and protection of human rights norms, it is also an important factor in the violation and abuses of human rights. Cultures in different parts of the world are local receptors for human rights norms that facilitate the assimilation of human rights norms into local practices. The current approach of looking at culture solely from a 'harm' perspective is one sided. Children live most of their lives within a cultural environment and many of these culture norms and practices are not harmful to the life, survival and development of children. Interpreting universal norms from a context relevant perspective is beneficial for the effective implementation of human rights. Such a context-friendly approach to interpreting and applying human rights standards will ensure that universal norms speak to and through local values and norms. The context-specific application of universal human rights norms will reduce resistance, facilitate acceptance and ensure the realisation of human rights.

5.1. International human rights treaty bodies: Mandates and methods

The treaty-based system of human rights within the UN has its roots in the Charter-based system of human rights. Before examining the treaty-based system, it would be apt to briefly look at how the Charter-based system operated before the advent of the treaty-based system of human rights within the UN. Article 68 of the UN Charter provides that 'the Economic and Social Council shall set up commissions... for the promotion of human rights.' One such commission was the Commission on Human Rights (CHR), whose mandate included:

> [s]ubmitting proposals, recommendations and reports to the Council regarding :(a) an international bill of rights; (b) international declarations or conventions on civil liberties, the status of women, freedom of information and similar matters; (c) the protection of

the UN Convention on the Rights of the Child' (2003) 25 *Human Rights Quarterly* 130.

> minorities; (d) the prevention of discrimination on grounds of race, sex, language or religion.[22]

It was agreed not to confer the CHR with a protective mandate despite the recommendation of the Preparatory Commission to the effect that the work of CHR should be directed 'towards ... any matters within the field of human rights...'[23] Upon a request from the CHR, the ECOSOC added functions to the term of reference of the CHR to the effect that it could submit reports and recommendations or proposal on 'any other matter concerning human rights.'[24] However, ECOSOC was not prepared to empower the CHR to assist it in its role by identifying 'cases where violation of human rights committed in one country may, by its gravity, its frequency, or its systematic nature, constitute a threat to [world] peace.'[25]

It is not an exaggeration to state that from the outset of the development of human rights, political and national interests prevailed most of the time over the need for effective implementation. This is due to the following reasons:

> The subject of international human rights has almost from the very beginning been dominated by the politician, who has been the true midwife of virtually all innovation in this field. But as politicians, they have inevitably followed the political standards set in the political arena, where the national interest and national traditions are the limiting conditions of diplomatic flexibility. They have put a premium on prudence, gradualism, continuity and incremental improvement.[26]

In spite of its limited mandate, the CHR proceeded to facilitate the elaboration of the most comprehensive human rights standards within the UN system –

---

22 J Morsink *The Universal Declaration of Human Rights: Origins, drafting and intent* (1999) 13.

23 F Coomans *et al* (eds) *Human rights from exclusion to inclusion; principles and practice: An anthropology from the work of Theo van Boven* (2000) 119.

24 As above.

25 B Lepard *Rethinking humanitarian intervention: A fresh legal approach based on fundamental ethical principles in international law and world religion* (2002) 152.

26 F Coomans *et al* (eds) *Human rights from exclusion to inclusion; principles and practice: An anthropology from the work of Theo van Boven* (2000) 121.

the International Bill of Rights.[27] In addition, it developed for itself working methods and tools that have left an indelible mark on the working methods of other human rights bodies.[28] The legacy of the CHR includes considering state reports and issuing of recommendations, issuing general comments, receiving and considering complaints, the appointment of special rapporteurs and the establishment of working groups.

As a result of its advocacy, innovative interpretation and opportune circumstances, the CHR developed some powers. Despite these innovations, there was a limitation inherent to the working methods of the CHR, which is the tendency of the CHR to see and treat human rights as universal norms that must be implemented, irrespective of culture and context.[29] This approach limited the ability of the CHR to engage in the context-specific and sensitive application of human rights norms through its working methods. A possible explanation for this approach is that the UDHR itself is predicated on the universality of human rights and that factor influenced the work of the CHR. The UDHR conceptualises human rights as 'a common standard of achievement for all peoples and all nations,'[30] and 'the equal and inalienable rights of all members of the human family.'[31] The CHR was replaced in 2006 with the Human Rights Council (HRC).

In addition to setting standards in the field of international human rights, another major legacy of the CHR was to lay the foundation for the creation of a treaty-based system of human rights promotion and protection within the UN system.

---

27 M Mutua 'Looking past the Human Rights Committee: An argument for de-marginalizing enforcement' (1998) 4 *Buffalo Human Rights Law Review 211.*

28 M Mutua 'Looking past the Human Rights Committee: An argument for de-marginalizing enforcement' (1998) 4 *Buffalo Human Rights Law Review* 211; and H Steiner 'Individual claims in a world of massive violation: What role for Human Rights Committee?' in P Alston & J Crawford (eds) *The future of human rights treaty monitoring* (2000) 25.

29 see M Mutua 'Looking past the Human Rights Committee: An argument for de-marginalizing enforcement' (1998) 4 *Buffalo Human Rights Law Review* 211 and M Addo 'Practice of United Nations human rights treaty bodies in the reconciliation of cultural diversity with universal respect for human rights' (2010) 32 *Human Rights Quarterly* 601.

30 Para 8 of the Preamble to the Universal Declaration of Human Rights.

31 Para 1 of the Preamble to the Universal Declaration of Human Rights.

Within the UN human rights system, at present, there are ten treaty-based human rights mechanisms.[32] Every member state of the UN is a party to at least one of the human rights treaties constituting the UN treaty-based human rights system. A body of independent experts monitors the implementation of each of these human rights treaty bodies. All state parties are required periodically to submit state reports on the extent of their conformity of domestic standards and practices with the provisions of the treaty under consideration. These state party reports are then reviewed, usually in the presence of state party delegations. At the end of the review process, the monitoring body issues concluding observations on the adequacy of the progress made by a state party towards the implementation of the provisions of a given human rights treaty.

In addition to receiving reports, eight of the ten treaty bodies within the UN treaty based human rights system receive individual communications.[33] These complaints are brought by parties asking a treaty body to give a finding as to the violation of a protected treaty right. In addition, some treaty monitoring

32 Human Rights Committee (CCPR), Committee on Economic, Social and Cultural Rights (CESCR), Committee on the Elimination of Racial Discrimination (CERD), Committee on the Elimination of Discrimination against Women (CEDAW), Committee against Torture (CAT), Subcommittee on Prevention of Torture (SPT), CRC Committee (CRC), Committee on Migrant Workers (CMW), Committee on the Rights of Persons with Disabilities (CRPD) Committee on Enforced Disappearances (CED). Nine of these ten bodies monitor the implementation of core human rights treaties while the tenth SPT monitors places of dentition.

33 Currently, 8 of the human rights treaty bodies (CCPR, CERD, CAT, CEDAW, CRPD, CED, CESCR and CRC) may, under certain conditions, receive and consider individual complaints or communications from individuals: The Human Rights Committee (CCPR) may consider individual communications alleging violations of the rights set forth in the International Covenant on Civil and Political Rights by States parties to the First Optional Protocol to the International Covenant on Civil and Political Rights; The Committee on Elimination of Discrimination against Women (CEDAW) may consider individual communications alleging violations of the Convention on the Elimination of All Forms of Discrimination against Women by States parties to the Optional Protocol to the Convention on the Elimination of Discrimination against Women; The Committee against Torture (CAT) may consider individual complaints alleging violations of the rights set out in the Convention against Torture and Other Cruel, Inhuman or Degrading Treatment or Punishment by States parties who have made the necessary declaration under article 22 of the Convention; The Committee on the Elimination of Racial Discrimination (CERD) may consider individual petitions alleging violations of the International Convention on the Elimination of All Forms of Racial Discrimination by States parties who have made the necessary declaration under article 14 of the Convention; The Committee on the Rights of Persons with Disabilities (CRPD) may consider individual communications alleging violations of the Convention on the Rights of Persons with Disabilities by States parties to the Optional Protocol to the Convention; The Committee on Enforced Disappearances (CED) may consider individual communications alleging violations of the International Convention for the Protection of All Persons from Enforced Disappearance by States parties who have made the necessary declaration under article 31 of the Convention. The Committee on Economic, Social and Cultural Rights (CESCR) may consider individual communications alleging violations of the International Covenant on Economic, Social and Cultural Rights by States parties to the Optional Protocol to the International Covenant on Economic, Social and Cultural Rights.

bodies have an inquiry procedure.[34] For example, under article 20 of the Convention against Torture, the Committee Against Torture has a mandate to carry out a confidential inquiry based on a reasonable indication of the systematic practice of torture by a state party, in the context of alleged systematic or gross violations of treaty rights. The inquiry procedure can be used within the context of a communication or outside a formal complaint mechanism.

Human rights treaty monitoring bodies significantly contribute to the development and understanding of international human rights norms. These treaty bodies adopt general comments to elucidate the nature and content of the different obligations associated with treaty rights and freedoms. The commentaries upon the provisions of the treaty play an important role in enabling the implementation of human rights treaties. There are now a little over 100 of these general comments within the UN human rights system.[35]

Most human rights treaty bodies at the international level operate a dual mandate regime – a promotional and protective mandate.[36] The African Children's Committee borrows its working methods mainly from these international models. It would be prudent to examine how the mandates of the human rights treaties operate before discussing them with respect to the African Children's Committee. The working methods of the human rights treaty bodies at the international level will be grouped and discussed under their promotional and protective methods of work.

5.1.1. Promotional mandate

A promotional mandate includes 'information and education functions, a quasi-legislative function, an institutional co-operation function, and a function in the examination of state reports.'[37] The examination of state party

34 Committee against Torture (CAT), Committee on the Elimination of Discrimination against Women (CEDAW), and the CRC Committee (CRC).

35 See http://www2.ohchr.org/english/bodies/treaty/comments.htm.

36 Until recently, it was only the CRC that did not have a protection mechanism.

37 S A Yeshanew 'Utilising the promotional mandate of the African Commission on Human and Peoples' Rights to promote human rights education in Africa' (2007) *African Human Rights Law Journal* 191.

reports and the quasi-legislative functions take the bulk of the promotional mandate of human rights treaty bodies. These two mandates, in addition to quasi-legislative functions, will be examined here.

5.1.1.1. Receiving and considering state party reports

It has been said that the reporting process 'is a lecture in the anatomy of [the implementation of] human rights.'[38] The reporting mechanism, 'through the interrelated process of introspection and inspection,'[39] enables and provides states with an opportunity 'to take stock of its achievements and failures'[40] in implementing the provisions of a human rights treaty.

The reporting mechanism was envisaged to function as a periodic and a comprehensive review and exchange of information on the legislation, policies and programmes, administrative rules and procedures, and practices that the state party has put in place to facilitate the actual enjoyment of rights provided for in a human rights treaty. In addition, it is intended to ascertain progress made, and foster a better understanding of the problems and shortcomings encountered in the implementation of human rights obligations. It is expected that reporting will facilitate principled and targeted policy-making as well as public scrutiny and involvement in the formulation, implementation and review of the relevant human rights related policies of the government.[41]

The practical application of the reporting mechanism increasingly renders this working method one of the 'weakest in the range of implementation techniques' for the realisation of human rights.[42] The texts of the different mandates that empower the human rights treaty bodies to receive and consider state party reports tend to confirm this impression. First, the different

38 Joaquim Fonseca quoted by A Devereux & C Anderson 'Reporting under international human rights treaties: Perspectives from Timor Leste's experience of the reformed process' (2008) 8 *Human Rights Law Review* 69.

39 F Viljoen *International human rights in Africa* (2012) 349.

40 As above.

41 See generally General Comment 1 of the Committee on Economic, Social and Cultural Rights Report on the 3rd session E/1989/22 E/C.12/1989/5.

42 F Gaer 'First fruits: Reporting by states under the African Charter on Human and Peoples' Rights' (1992) 10 *Netherlands Quarterly of Human Rights* 29.

provisions of the treaties that confer powers on treaty bodies do not empower these treaty bodies to proactively consider the situation of human rights in the territory of a state party in the absence of a state report. The passive mandate granted to treaty bodies with respect to reporting has

> compelled treaty bodies to behave, in situations where allegations of massive human rights violations were made, as if nothing has happened and wait for years until the time for the submission of the report was due.[43]

Second, in addition to textual ambiguities, the challenges of the reporting mechanism are that its efficacy depends on the political honesty of a state party; on the quality of the report; on available, reliable and independent information; on the quality of participation of other stakeholders in the reporting process; and, finally, on the functionality and efficiency of follow-up mechanisms. A treaty body has no control over most of these factors.

Third, the difficulty with the current reporting mechanism is that state parties tend to consider it a 'mere game.' A member of one of the treaty bodies presented this alarming reflection:

> I think that they [states with bad human rights records] have now learned how to "play the game". They, and other countries, seem mainly concerned now with "treading water" during the dialogue, simply with "getting through" the two or three days of examination, so that these matters can be shelved again for another few years.[44]

This attitude is found not only among states with dubious human rights records but also among liberal democracies. In an empirical book of why state parties comply with their reporting obligations, LeBlanc and others note, though government 'effectiveness is the most important variable affecting state compliance with reporting requirements,' that, surprisingly, 'compliance by

43 A Bloed *et al* (eds) *Monitoring human rights in Europe: Comparing international procedures and mechanisms* (1993) 15.

44 R Higgins 'Opinion: Ten years on the UN Human Rights Committee: Some thoughts upon parting' (1996) 6 *European Human Rights Law Review* 581.

liberal democracies has significantly declined in the last decade.'[45] According to the authors of the book, 'within the period covered, liberal democracies are also less likely to comply with reporting requirements than are other regime types.'[46] In addition:

> officials entrusted with reporting responsibilities often admit privately that they are much more concerned with fulfilling as quickly as possible, and with the least possible effort, the unwanted, boring and burdensome task of reporting than they are with using the reporting process as a means of determining treaty compliance and working towards improvement.[47]

Since the success of reporting as a monitoring tool depends, primarily, on 'the goodwill and good intentions of reporting states' it is possible for a report to be a 'good report' while the situation of human rights on the ground may not be as good as reported.[48] Alluding to this possibility, Viljoen notes that it is possible for a human rights treaty body to be 'blinded by the comparatively good quality of the report and lose sight of the inherently poor human rights record of the country in question.'[49]

Nevertheless, 'reduced to its core', ratification of a human rights treaty is indicative of a state party's intention to 'give effect' to its provisions.[50] State reporting of progress and challenges in implementation remain 'the backbone' of the work of treaty bodies. To make the reporting mechanism more meaningful, human rights treaty bodies, as 'legal bodies,'[51] engaging in 'norm-to-fact decision making'[52] through interpretation have improved the human

45 L LeBanca *et al* 'Compliance with the reporting requirements of human rights conventions' (2010) 14 *The International Journal of Human Rights* 789.

46 As above.

47 P Alston & J Crawford (eds) *The future of human rights treaty monitoring* (2000) 131.

48 J Donnelly *International human rights* (1998) 80.

49 F Viljoen 'Review of the African Commission on Human and peoples' Rights: 21 October 1986 to 1 January 1997' in C Heyns (ed) *Human rights law in Africa* (1999) 95.

50 F Viljoen *International human rights in Africa* (2012) 349.

51 H Steiner 'Individual claims in a world of massive violation: What role for Human Rights Committee?' in P Alston & J Crawford (eds) *The future of human rights treaty monitoring* (2000) 49.

52 H Steiner 'Individual claims in a world of massive violation: What role for Human Rights Committee?' in P

rights treaty regime. For instance, these human rights treaty bodies have turned a reporting system that was intended 'neither to be inquisitorial nor accusative' with an end that 'was neither condemnation nor approbation'[53] into a constructive dialogue emanating in conclusions.

The bold move by human rights treaty bodies purposefully to interpret their mandates with respect to reporting more generously has been praised and criticised. Pedone and Kloster regard the expansive interpretation of human rights treaty provisions by treaty bodies as a usurpation of power by treaty bodies and, as such, a negation of the principle of good faith.[54] According to these critics, when states ratify a human right treaty, they do so with a particular understanding which, in the opinion of these scholars, does not include reporting in the form and format it has evolved into. They argue that law has to be certain and predictable. The interpretation of the law must be faithful to the intention of the drafters and of those who ratify these laws. A faithful interpretation of the mandate of treaty bodies in respect of reporting translates into the following:

> a spectrum of powers between neutrally summarizing the reports, making collective suggestions in consideration of the reports, issuing non-State party specific comments on procedural matters, and issuing suggestions and recommendations for specific states parties.[55]

Those who see the activist posture of the treaty bodies as well-meaning insist that 'on the one hand, the law ought to be a comprehensive whole, closed and complete; and yet, on the other hand, the need for further determinations is continual.'[56] According to them, it is because of this kind of creativity by the different human rights treaty bodies that the reporting mechanism

---

Alston & J Crawford (eds) *The future of human rights treaty monitoring* (2000) 49.

53 D McGoldrick *The Human Rights Committee: Its role in the development of the International Covenant on Civil and Political Rights* (1991) 89.

54 J Pedone & A Kloster 'New proposals for human rights treaty body reform' (2013) 22 *Journal of Transnational Law and Policy* 29.

55 As above.

56 N Pavel 'Defining the concept of human rights in the light of juridical value theory' (2012) 4 *Contemporary Readings in Law and Social Justice* 502 citing G Hegel.

> may prove to be an effective means to develop a universal culture of rights, one in which the actual meaning of rights and their implementations for specific individuals and groups are commonly understood and internalized by governments and civil society alike.[57]

One reason for praising the reporting mechanism is the role concluding observations play in advancing the implementation of human rights law. It is not yet settled in international human rights law what the exact legal status of concluding observations is, but some scholars argue that 'a statement of an authoritative body performing an important supervisory function cannot remain without consequences.'[58]

An examination of the concluding observations of the CRC Committee, for the purpose of this work, suggests that this treaty body approaches its reporting mandate within a universalist paradigm of human rights. In an assessment of the practices of state parties under the CRC, Harris-Short arrived at a similar conclusion.[59] Human rights treaty bodies tend to operate within the universalist theory of human rights. They accommodate cultural diversity only to the extent that diversity affects minority groups, women and mainly the individual rights to cultural life.[60]

Those human rights treaty bodies that have dealt with cultural issues mainly pronounced themselves with respect to cultural practices that were 'callous', 'stupid', 'archaic' or a 'barbarity that could not be condoned.'[61] This negative and harmful approach to cultural practices might eventually dilute the essence

---

57 J Karp 'Reporting and the CRC Committee' in A Bayefsky (ed) *The human rights system in the 21st century* (2000) 37.

58 V Dimitrijevic 'State reports' in G Alfredsson *et al* (eds) *International human rights monitoring mechanisms: Essays in honour of Jakob Th. Moiler* (2001) 198.

59 S Harris-Short 'International human rights law: Imperialist, inept and ineffective? Cultural relativism and the UN Convention on the Rights of the Child' (2003) 25 *Human Rights Quarterly* 130; see also M Addo 'Practice of United Nations human rights treaty bodies in the reconciliation of cultural diversity with universal respect for human rights' (2010) 32 *Human Rights Quarterly* 601.

60 M Addo 'Practice of United Nations human rights treaty bodies in the reconciliation of cultural diversity with universal respect for human rights' (2010) 32 *Human Rights Quarterly* 601.

61 S Harris-Short 'International human rights law: Imperialist, inept and ineffective? Cultural relativism and the UN Convention on the Rights of the Child' (2003) 25 *Human Rights Quarterly* 130 and M Addo 'Practice of United Nations human rights treaty bodies in the reconciliation of cultural diversity with universal respect for human rights' (2010) 32 *Human Rights Quarterly* 601.

of the 'constructive dialogue' originally intended by the reporting mechanism. Increasingly, it appears that human rights treaty bodies hand out instructions to governments regarding what they should do about the 'backward culture'[62] of their people without taking into account any lessons that some of these state parties might want to communicate about cultural practices within their jurisdictions.

What informs the approach that human rights treaty bodies take when they consider state party reports? It would seem from the positions and practices of the treaty bodies that most of them adopt a strictly legal approach to discharging what, essentially, is a socio-legal mandate.[63] The socio-legal mandate of the human rights treaty bodies was designed to provide these 'quasi-judicial bodies [with] sufficient flexibility' to draw 'inspiration from both the political approaches of inter-governmental entities as well as the strictly legal approaches of the judicial institutions.'[64] A flexible understanding of the mandate is needed if the human rights treaty bodies are to promote a balanced, positive and complementary view of culture as well as to highlight the harm that culture has caused. It might be helpful if human rights treaty bodies in the discharge of their global mandate keep in mind, in some instances, that 'to assert a human right as a justification for law reform, against law reform, or for a particular interpretation of law, is essentially a political claim.'[65]

It is possible that the positions held by human rights treaty bodies with respect to culture have their roots in the texts of the treaties setting them up. The UDHR for instance, expects everyone 'to participate in the cultural life of the community.'[66] The use of the definite article ('the') to qualify culture gives the impression that there is a single, identifiable culture that everyone

---

62 S Harris-Short 'International human rights law: Imperialist, inept and ineffective? Cultural relativism and the UN Convention on the Rights of the Child' (2003) 25 *Human Rights Quarterly* 130.

63 M Addo 'Practice of United Nations human rights treaty bodies in the reconciliation of cultural diversity with universal respect for human rights' (2010) 32 *Human Rights Quarterly* 601.

64 As above.

65 L McNamara *Human rights controversies: The impact of legal form* (2007) *Kindle edition loc* 486.

66 See article 27(1) of the Universal Declaration of Human Rights.

is supposed to take part in.[67] Such a 'view of cultural life stands in contrast to the reality of diversity and pluralism that characterizes modern cultures.'[68] The improvement provided by the ICCPR, that persons belonging to ethnic, religious, or linguistic minorities 'shall not be denied the right, in community with the other members of their group, to enjoy their own culture'[69] may be interpreted to place on state parties a negative rather than a positive obligation in this respect. In addition, this provision of the ICCPR might be interpreted to refer only to the possible tension between a dominant and a minority culture. It is argued that the same energy and passion that human rights treaty bodies have admirably displayed to expose, condemn and confront the ills of culture should be used to interpret purposively these textual provisions to promote context-specificity on cultural issues. Such a balanced approach would enhance the quality of the constructive dialogue as well as the promotion and protection of human rights at domestic levels.

5.1.1.2. Quasi-legislative mandate of human rights treaty bodies

Almost all international human rights treaties with monitoring bodies provide for an interpretative function as part of the mandate of the monitoring mechanism. One of the ways in which human rights treaty bodies have sought to carry out this function and, in the process, hope to modify the conduct of state parties is through a purposeful and targeted interpretation of the treaty provisions. Many treaty bodies now use general comments as interpretative tools to clarify and specify the nature, content and scope of obligations undertaken by state parties, to rectify ambiguities, to resolve potential conflicts in implementation, and to strengthen normative weaknesses in the treaties they supervise.

---

67 M Addo 'Practice of United Nations human rights treaty bodies in the reconciliation of cultural diversity with universal respect for human rights' (2010) 32 *Human Rights Quarterly* 601.

68 As above.

69 See article 27 of the International Covenant on Civil and Political Rights Adopted and opened for signature, ratification and accession by General Assembly resolution 2200A (XXI) of 16 December 1966 entry into force 23 March 1976, in accordance with Article 49.

There has been some concern with respect to the legal basis and status of these general comments.[70] Other concerns relate to the quality of the general comments.[71] The question whether general comments have binding legal status divides scholars. On the one hand, some scholars hold the view that general comments, together with concluding observations, are by nature non-binding interpretation of a binding treaty.[72] One of the reasons for this view is that human rights treaty bodies are generally quasi-judicial bodies without binding powers. Some national courts and state parties also take the view that general comments are non-binding interpretations.[73] On the other hand, other scholars hold the view that even though general comments are not purely legal documents, they however, as the authoritative interpretation of binding legal treaties, have some level of binding nature.[74] According to Steiner and Alston, scholars

> seek to portray them as authoritative interpretations of the relevant treaty norms, though others see them as a *de facto* equivalent of advisory opinions which are to be treated with seriousness but no more, to highly critical approaches that classify them as broad, unsystematic statements which are not always well founded, and are not deserving of being accorded any particular weight in legal settings.[75]

The fixation on the binding nature of the general comments of the treaty bodies is probably overstated. As useful as the binding force of decisions and

70 D McGoldrick *The Human Rights Committee: Its role in the development of the International Covenant on Civil and Political Rights* (1991) 89.

71 J Pedone & A Kloster 'New proposals for human rights treaty body reform' (2013) 22 *Journal of Transnational Law and Policy* 29.

72 C Blake, 'Normative instruments in international human rights law: Locating the general comment' (Working Paper No 17, Centre for Human Rights and Global Justice, New York University School of Law, 2008) 6–7. For a more detailed discussion of the legal status of general comments see P Gerber *et al* 'General Comment 16 on state obligations regarding the impact of the business sector on children's rights: What is its standing, meaning and effect?' (2013) 14 *Melbourne Journal of International Law* 1.

73 See for example the Irish Supreme Court decision in *Kavanagh v The Governor of Mount Joy Prison* [2002] IESC 11

74 V Dimitrijevic 'State reports' in G Alfredsson *et al* (eds) *International human rights monitoring mechanisms: Essays in honour of Jakob Th. Moiler* (2001) 178.

75 H Steiner & P Alston *International law in context: Law, politics and morals* (2008) 731.

judgements might be, commentators should not lose sight of that fact that human rights treaty bodies perform other important roles. For instance, they serve as a global conscience whose influence is based on moral persuasion and chastisement.

Whether a binding authority on human rights norms or as a global conscience, it is important that their role is not the expression of a particular version of morality or culturally specific norms. Unfortunately, as in the case of the reporting process discussed above, human rights treaty bodies' interpretations of the provisions of the different treaties tend to follow a universalist paradigm of human rights. Addo, analysing the various concluding observations and decisions arrived at a similar conclusion.[76] One area of work where human rights treaty bodies exercise a level of binding authority is when they are called upon to adjudicate individual complaints,[77] to which the author now turns.

5.1.2. Protective mandate: Quasi-judicial bodies and adjudication of complaints

A number of human rights treaty bodies have a protective mandate.[78] One method used to ensure protection of the rights and to remedy alleged violations is the complaint or communication mechanism. An individual or a state party can bring these communications alleging violations of a provision of a treaty to which the country alleged to have violated a right is a party. Within the UN system, the complaint mechanisms have assisted in clarifying the normative content of human rights and have provided concrete relief to individuals whose rights have been violated.[79] Communication procedures were meant to serve several purposes, including: clarifying the content and

---

76 M Addo 'Practice of United Nations human rights treaty bodies in the reconciliation of cultural diversity with universal respect for human rights' (2010) 32 *Human Rights Quarterly* 601

77 M Mutua 'Looking past the Human Rights Committee: An argument for de-marginalizing enforcement' (1998) 4 *Buffalo Human Rights Law Review* 211; and H Steiner 'Individual claims in a world of massive violation: What role for Human Rights Committee?' in P Alston & J Crawford (eds) *The future of human rights treaty monitoring* (2000) 25.

78 These are treaty bodies that receive communication either from individuals or State parties.

79 M Mutua 'Looking past the Human Rights Committee: An argument for de-marginalizing enforcement' (1998) 4 *Buffalo Human Rights Law Review* 211; and H Steiner 'Individual claims in a world of massive violation: What role for Human Rights Committee?' in P Alston & J Crawford (eds) *The future of human rights treaty monitoring* (2000) 25.

object of the rights in the human rights treaties, delivery of individual justice to victims of human rights violations, and inculcating in states a culture of respect for the rights provided for in human rights treaties to which a state is a party.[80] These purposes have been described as 'unrealizable as [they are] noble.'[81]

The observation is predicated on a number of concerns. Some of the reasons are external to the treaty bodies, while some are internal. Externally, the states that negotiated and ratified these treaties seem reluctant to concede such powers to human rights treaty bodies. In addition, some of the evasive and euphemistic language, such as 'communication' rather than 'petition', 'views' rather than 'decisions', might have been calculated to 'deny [these human rights treaty bodies] the properties of a judicial or an adjudicatory body, such as a national court or an international tribunal.'[82]

Internally, the fact that the composition of the human rights treaty bodies is multidisciplinary instead of only consisting of legal practitioners, may affect the quality of legal reasoning within these bodies and, thus, their legal authority.[83] Some of the consequences of these qualitative deficits include the 'traditionally formulaic presentations of ... views which have been user-unfriendly, rigidly structured, disjunctive and difficult to read, and lack sharp legal argumentation and reasoning.'[84] Consequently, the body of knowledge that communication procedures have generated within the UN system have failed to make a 'significant contribution to the normative development of the

---

80 M Mutua 'Looking past the Human Rights Committee: An argument for de-marginalizing enforcement' (1998) 4 *Buffalo Human Rights Law Review* 211; and H Steiner 'Individual claims in a world of massive violation: What role for Human Rights Committee?' in P Alston & J Crawford (eds) *The future of human rights treaty monitoring* (2000) 25.

81 H Steiner 'Individual claims in a world of massive violation: What role for Human Rights Committee?' in P Alston & J Crawford (eds) *The future of human rights treaty monitoring* (2000) 25.

82 M Mutua 'Looking past the Human Rights Committee: An argument for de-marginalizing enforcement' (1998) 4 *Buffalo Human Rights Law Review* 211.

83 H Steiner 'Individual claims in a world of massive violation: What role for Human Rights Committee?' in P Alston & J Crawford (eds) *The future of human rights treaty monitoring* (2000) 76, see also M Mutua 'Looking past the Human Rights Committee: An argument for de-marginalizing enforcement' (1998) 4 *Buffalo Human Rights Law Review* 211.

84 M Mutua 'Looking past the Human Rights Committee: An argument for de-marginalizing enforcement' (1998) 4 *Buffalo Human Rights Law Review* 211.

human rights movement'[85] and 'hardly summon the human rights community to debate and dialogue. They fail to educate their readership adequately about the [rights and obligations in the human rights treaties] in particular or about human rights in general.'[86]

Unfortunately, the views given in individual communications are hardly referred to in a domestic legal setting or used widely as a basis of policy making.[87] It is possible, however, to argue that the continuous addition to the number of complaint mechanisms within the UN human rights system points to the fact that there is some value to the global human rights system of these complaints mechanisms.

The African Children's Committee have similar working tools. Articles 42-45 of the African Children's Charter mandate the African Children's Committee to receive state party reports, consider communications, and interpret the provisions of the African Children's Rights Charter.

5.2. The African Committee of Experts on the Rights and Welfare of the Child

A virtue of the African Children's Charter is that it established the African Children's Committee to monitor its implementation. Established under article 32 of the African Children's Charter, the African Children's Committee has a dual mandate of promoting and protecting the rights and welfare of the child. The African Children's Charter came into force in 1999; it was not until 10 July 2001 that the African Children's Committee was finally established. The African Children's Committee was inaugurated at its first meeting in Addis Ababa, Ethiopia, from 29 April to 2 May 2002. The African Children's Committee is a body of 11 independent members 'of high moral standing, integrity, impartiality and competence in matters of the rights and welfare of the child, serving in their personal capacity.' Unlike some UN human rights

85 H Steiner 'Individual claims in a world of massive violation: What role for Human Rights Committee?' in P Alston & J Crawford (eds) *The future of human rights treaty monitoring* (2000) 17.

86 As above, 21.

87 As above.

treaties that require that some of the members must be lawyers, there is no such requirement in the African Children's Charter.

Article 42 of the African Children's Charter provides the African Children's Committee with a mandate to promote and protect the rights and welfare of children in Africa. In carrying out this broad mandate, the African Children's Charter expects the African Children's Committee, alone or in collaboration with others, to monitor the implementation of the African Children's Charter. In addition, the African Children's Committee is mandated to ensure the protection of the rights and welfare of the children provided for in the African Children's Charter. Moreover, the African Children's Committee is empowered to interpret the provisions of the African Children's Charter, generate and document information about the status of children's rights and welfare in Africa. The African Children's Charter expects the African Children's Committee to give its views, make recommendations to governments, and formulate and lay down principles and rules aimed at protecting the rights and welfare of children in Africa.[88] Theoretically, at least, the African Children's Charter has provided for a 'progressive and action-orientated enforcement mechanism.'[89]

At the time of its drafting and until recently, the mandate of the African Children's Committee was broader and more robust than that of its counterpart at the UN level.[90] After almost 20 years of discharging its

88 For a comprehensive discussion of the mandate of the African Children's Committee and how the African Children's Committee has discharged its mandate see B Mezmur 'The African Committee of Experts on the Rights and Welfare of the Child: An update' (2006) 6 *African Human Rights Journal* 549; B Mezmur 'Still an infant or now a toddler? The work of the African Committee of Experts on the Rights and Welfare of the Child and its 8th ordinary session' (2007) 7 *African Human Rights Law Journal* 258; B Mezmur 'The 19th ordinary session of the African Committee of Experts on the Rights and Welfare of the Child: Looking back to look head' (2007) 7 *African Human Rights Journal* 545; J Sloth-Nielsen & B Mezmur 'Win some, lose some: The 10th ordinary session of the African Committee of Experts on the Rights and Welfare of the Child' (2008) 8 *African Human Rights Law Journal* 207; B Mezmur & J Sloth-Nielsen 'An ice-breaker: State party reports and the 11th session of the African Committee of Experts on the Rights and Welfare of the Child' (2008) 8 *African Human Rights Law Journal* 596; J Sloth-Nielsen & B Mezmur 'Out of the starting blocks: The 12th and 13th sessions of the African Committee of Experts on the Rights and Welfare of the Child' (2009) 9 *African Human Rights Law Journal* 336 and J Sloth-Nielsen & B Mezmur 'Like running on a treadmill? The 14th and 15th sessions of the African Committee of Experts on the Rights and Welfare of the Child' (2010) 10 *African Human Rights Law Journal* 534.

89 A Lloyd 'How to guarantee credence: Recommendations and proposals for the African Committee of Experts on the Rights and Welfare of the Child' (2004) 12 *The International Journal of Children's Rights* 21.

90 The CRC Committee had only a promotional mandate. But with the adaptation of the 3rd Optional Protocol adding a protection mandate to the CRC Committee, it cannot any longer be correct to say that

mandate and 37 sessions held so far by the African Children's Committee, it is possible to glean some sense or indication of how the African Children's Committee perceives its mandate and intends to proceed with the function of promoting and protecting children's rights in Africa.[91] This preliminary assessment will focus on the monitoring and enforcement mechanisms of the African Children's Committee.

5.2.1. Promotional mandate of the African Children's Committee

5.2.1.1. Receiving and considering state party reports

The African Children's Charter confers on the African Children's Committee the mandate 'to monitor the implementation'[92] of the rights provided for in the African Children's Charter. One main tool that the African Children's Charter provides the African Children's Committee with, in this regard, is the receiving of state party reports. Article 43 of the African Children's Charter provides that:

> [every] State party to the present Charter shall undertake to submit to the Committee through the Secretary-General of the Organization of African Unity, reports on the measures they have adopted which give effect to the provisions of this Charter and on the progress made in the enjoyment of these rights.

The African Children's Charter provides for the submission of initial reports 'within two years of the entry into force of the Charter for the state party concerned'[93] and periodic reporting is expected 'thereafter, every three years.'[94] Such reports should contain 'sufficient information'[95] on the implementation

---

the mandate of the African Children's Committee is broader than that of the CRC Committee.

91 The African Committee of Experts on the Rights and Welfare of the Child held its 22 session in November 2013.

92 See article 42 (b) of the African Charter on the Rights and Welfare of the Child.

93 Article 43 (a) of the African Charter on the Rights and welfare of the Child.

94 Article 43 (b) of the African Charter on the Rights and welfare of the Child.

95 Article 43 (2) (a) of the African Charter on the Rights and welfare of the Child.

of the African Children's Charter and such information should be sufficient enough to give the African Children's Committee a 'comprehensive understanding of the implementation'[96] of the rights in the African Children's Charter in the territory of the state party. In addition, the state report 'shall indicate factors and difficulties, if any, affecting the fulfilment of the obligations contained in the Charter.'[97]

Even though the reporting provision is modelled after that of the CRC, the African Children's Charter differs from the CRC in a number of ways: First, even though the period for the initial report is the same as in the CRC, unlike the CRC, the timeframe for periodic reports is 3 years, while under the CRC it is 5 years.[98] Second, the CRC expects that only difficulties that affect 'the *degree* of fulfilment of the obligations' should be provided for in the report.[99] The provision under the African Children's Charter omits the word 'degree.' Therefore, theoretically speaking, whereas it is not possible to report under the CRC a lack of fulfilment of obligations but only the degree of fulfilment, it is possible to report under the African Children's Charter the difficulties that hamper fulfilment of the obligation in its entirety. However, since state parties are supposed to 'report on the measures they have adopted which give effect to the provisions of this Charter and on the *progress* made in the enjoyment of these rights,'[100] it is possible to argue that the idea of degree of implementation is already captured in the word 'progress.'

Third, textually, the CRC provides the CRC Committee with the possibility 'to request from state parties further information'[101] that could assist it to assess the degree of implementation in the jurisdiction of a state party. This possibility is not provided for in the African Children's Charter. Finally, the CRC expects state parties to 'make their reports widely available to the

96 Article 43 (2) (a) of the African Charter on the Rights and welfare of the Child.

97 Article 43 (2) (b) of the African Charter on the Rights and welfare of the Child.

98 See article 44(b) of the Convention on the Rights of the Child.

99 See article 44(2) of the Convention on the Rights of the Child.

100 See article 43(1) of the African Charter on the Rights and Welfare of the Child.

101 See article 44(4) of the Convention on the Rights of the Child.

public'[102] in their countries, but that is not a requirement under the African Children's Charter.

Some of the normative limitations of the other provisions of the African Children's Charter discussed earlier on in chapter 4 equally affect the reporting mandate of the African Children's Committee. Article 43 of the African Children's Charter mandates the African Children's Committee to receive reports from state parties but is silent on what the African Children's Committee should do with that report. It is possible for a state party to argue that complementary reports, the invitation of state delegations, and the concluding observations of the African Children's Committee have no legal basis in the African Children's Charter. The practice of inviting complementary reports from civil society organisations, conducting pre-sessions and inviting state delegations to the meeting of the African Children's Committee, as well as issuing concluding observations are provided for only in the Rules of Procedures of the African Children's Committee. Article 38(1) empowers the African Children's Committee to adopt its own rules, thus it is possible to argue that in adopting the rules relating to the process of considering a state party report, the African Children's Committee is simply exercising its powers under article 38(1).

In addition, the requirement of submitting state party reports every three years, if followed through thoroughly by all state parties, may prove to be cumbersome to the state parties and the African Children's Committee. First, state parties are required to produce and submit reports to the ACHPR, the African Children's Committee and the APRM, in addition to the nine UN treaty bodies, making a total of 12 reports: one for every month of the year.[103] Second, if state parties had submitted their reports to date, the African Children's Committee would have 68 outstanding initial reports and 113 periodic reports submitted.[104] The total of outstanding reports as of 2014 was already 111. To receive and consider these overdue reports, the African

102 See article 44(6) of the Convention on the Rights of the Child.

103 Nine because SPT does not receive reports from State parties but rather visits places of detentions.

104 This is according to the report of the evaluation of the African Committee of Experts on the Rights and Welfare of the Child, that was carried out in 2010. A copy of the report is on file with the author.

Children's Committee will need 21 years if it were to consider 10 reports every session (to complete the backlog). Further additional reports will be ready and become overdue within those 21 years. The African Children's Committee certainly does not have the resources and capacity to meaningfully consider all these reports on time.

The African Children's Committee, through its Rules of Procedure and Guidelines for Initial Reports of State Parties, has tried to reduce the burden on state parties with regards to their reporting obligations. In order to avoid duplication and reduce the reporting burden of African states, the Committee has asked state parties if and when they submit reports to the CRC, to submit the same report to it with a supplementary report on the African Children's Charter's specific provisions.[105] This innovation, commendable as it is, is not far-reaching enough. It does not address however the African Children's Committee's burden; it only addresses the reporting burden of state parties. If all the state reports submitted to the CRC Committee are submitted to the African Children's Committee in addition to state party reports that might be submitted directly to the African Children's Committee, in the long run the consideration of the reports submitted will become a burdensome exercise for the African Children's Committee. In addition, why should a state be 'cross examined' on the same facts twice, especially when reporting takes time and resources.

Unlike the provisions of UN treaties,[106] the provision of the African Children's Charter does not include other AU organs or agencies in the reporting cycle. This omission deprives the reporting system under the African Children's Charter of at least two useful channels. First, it robs the reporting mechanism of an opportunity to bring documented and gross abuses of human rights to the attention of states and non-governmental organizations in a formalized setting. Second, it robs the reporting mechanism under the African Children's Charter of a forum to submit the investigated incidence of gross abuses of

105 See Rule 20 of the African Committee of Experts on the Rights and Welfare of the child's Procedures for the Consideration of State party Reports available at http://African Children's Committee.org/wp-content/uploads/2011/03/African Children's CommitteE-Procedure-for-State-reports-English.pdf.

106 See for example article 45 of the Convention on the Rights of the Child.

human rights to inter-governmental fora that should discuss them with a view to passing resolutions and recommendations to the state party concerned.

5.2.1.2. Quasi-legislative mandate of the African Children's Committee

The African Children's Committee uses mainly general comments as its protective interpretative tools. This is an area of its mandate in which the African Children's Committee demonstrates interpretative boldness and a context sensitive interpretation and application of the African Children's Charter. The African Children's Committee in November 2013 adopted its first General Comment on Article 30 of the Charter. This article is a unique feature of the African Children's Charter; it outlines provisions for the 'special treatment' of mothers who are in conflict with the law.

The General Comment establishes some key principles for states when implementing Article 30. It states that all primary caregivers, male or female, fall within the ambit of this article. It does not simply consider children living in prison with their mothers but considers the impact of stigma and separation caused by arrest and detention. The General Comment applies the four general principles of life, survival and development, non-discrimination, best interests of the child, child participation when taking decisions regarding a parent's arrest, pre-trial measures, trial and sentencing, imprisonment, release and reintegration into the community.

The General Comment sets out the legal, policy and administrative measures that state parties need to undertake in order to better implement the provisions of the African Children's Charter. These include preference for non-custodial sentences of primary caregivers; placement of children in appropriate alternative care when custodial sentencing is inevitable; alternatives to pre-trail detentions, such as bail and notice to appear in court; the provision of specialised care and services to accommodate children and their caregivers in prison in circumstances where this is unavoidable; no death sentence for pregnant women; and regular contact between primary caregivers and their children.

In its *General Comment No. 1 (Article 30 of the African Charter on the Rights and Welfare of the Child) on "Children of Incarcerated and Imprisoned Parents and Primary Caregivers" 2013* the African Children's Committee interpreted the word 'mother' in article 30 of the African Children's Charter to include

> 'parents' and 'caregivers' who may include a grandparent, a relative, or a member of the extended family who, according to certain prevailing circumstances like death or illness of the child's parents, becomes the primary caregiver or main supporter of the child.[107]

This is a significant improvement on the position of the African Children's Charter which limits the circle of care of the child to 'parents or legal guardians' of the child.[108] This expansive interpretation of the provisions of the Children's Charter by the African Children's Committee is in tune with the specific context of children in Africa where caregiving is a communal responsibility.

The second General Comment is on article 6 of the African Children's Charter. The General Comment discusses the legal and contextual basis, the general nature of state obligations and key principles underlying the implementation of article 6. These principles are the best interests of the children, non-discrimination, survival, development and protection, and the participation of children. It discusses the interdependence and indivisibility of the rights within Article 6 and within the African Children's Charter, in general. The General Comment situates the rights within the framework of justice for children, the prevention of harmful practices, rights to education, health and social welfare, the right to parental care and protection, the right to inherit parental property, and the right to official documentation.

It discusses the content of the right to a name to include birth registration. The features of the right to birth registration should be universal; by this the Committee means it should be inclusive of children living with disabilities, parents with a disability, children born to refugees, internally displaced persons or asylum seekers, and children of undocumented migrants, children

107 Paragraph 13(1).

108 See for example article 3, article 9(2) and article 10.

born to indigenous parents, and children of imprisoned mothers. The General Comment recommends that the birth registration system should be free and accessible, immediately after birth.

The second part of the General Comment deals with the right to acquire a nationality. It interprets this right without discrimination as it relates to the nationality and the gender of the parent, nationality and children born to indigenous people, nationality and children with disabilities, nationality and foundlings and abandoned children, nationality and adopted children and those in similar situations, nationality of a child in case of change of status of his or her parents. The General Comment provides for remedies and recommends a pro-active role of states in implementing article 6, coordination, sensitization and capacity building.

An innovation in the General Comment is how the African Children's Committee defines what constitutes harmful cultural practices in the African context to include

> all practices that imperil the life of the child, undermine his/her dignity or are prejudicial to his/her health, to his/her mental or physical integrity, or to his/her growth and development regardless of their being condoned by a society, culture, religion, or tradition.[109]

By this definition the African Children's Committee locates the harm not in the culture *per se* but in certain practices that might or might not be condoned by culture that imperil, undermine or are prejudicial to the life, dignity, growth and development of the child.

These are encouraging signs that the African Children's Committee appreciates the needs to interpret and apply the text of the African Children's Charter in a flexible way so as to ensure better implementation and protection of children's rights. However, the African Children's Committee can do more to give prominence to the cultural heritage of Africans and their philosophical understanding of childhood. Examples of how the African Children's

109 See paragraph 30 of the draft General Comment on article 6 of the African Charter on the Rights and welfare of the Child on the Rights of the Child to a Name and Nationality.

Committee might consider furthering such an approach are provided throughout this book.

One of the African Children's Charter's African-specific features is that it places responsibilities and duties on children towards their families, communities, societies and Africa. *The General Comment on Article 31 of the African Charter on the Rights and Welfare of the Child on "The Responsibilities of the Child"* interprets this unique feature of a regional child rights treaty. According to the African Children's Committee, placing responsibilities and duties on children shows the value placed on children's role as active participants and contributors to society's greater good, right from childhood. It is recognition of children and young people as citizens who contribute to society in the here and now, not only in the future.[110]

According to the African Children's Committee, cchildhood in the African context is not a period of total dependence. Children bear responsibilities towards the family or household from age or time to function independently. Children should take part in productive activities for the family's sustenance, such as being viewed as an opportunity to learn, grow, and develop the capacity to assume greater responsibilities in the larger society. Thus, children taking responsibility for family and communal life are considered an element of children's care and protection.[111] These responsibilities and duties entail the child working to cohesion the family cuts across all three dimensions. Thus, children should be able to provide moral or emotional support to other members when due, actively take part in social functions, affairs, or involvements of the family and contribute economically to the family unit's sustenance. [112]

Ensuring that children "respect parents, elders and superiors," is essential to protecting the "role of kinship and kinship networks in building family cohesion, contributing to the upbringing and

---

110 https://www.acerwc.africa/wp-content/uploads/2018/04/Website_version_GC_Booklet_General_Comment_ACERWC_ART31_2018.pdf para 11.

111 Paras 28 & 58.

112 Para 60.

socialisation of children and in reducing or providing support against family vulnerabilities. Also, "By supporting the family unit, therefore, children contribute towards protecting the means for their survival by securing the survival of the group (family structure) which they rely upon or need for their wellbeing. The 'family' includes "parents, siblings, the elderly, and other members of the extended family…"[113]

5.2.2. The quasi-judicial mandate of the African Children's Committee

Rights without remedies are mere aspirational guides. That is one reason why the African Children's Charter has been praised for providing for a complaint procedure under article 44. Judicial bodies have a mandate to provide remedies in the case of violations of rights. However, the mandate of quasi-judicial bodies to provide effective remedies are sometimes not so explicit and, in some cases, depend on interpretation and the political will of member states to comply with decisions or recommendations of quasi-judicial bodies.

It is debatable whether article 44 of the African Children's Charter explicitly confers the power to consider communications on the African Children's Committee. Article 44 provides:

1) The African Children's Committee may receive communication, from any person, group or nongovernmental organization recognized by the Organization of African Unity, by a member state, or the United Nations relating to any matter covered by this Charter.
2) Every communication to the African Children's Committee shall contain the name and address of the author and shall be treated in confidence.

The provision seems only to empower the African Children's Committee to receive communications but is silent on what the African Children's Committee should do with communications. If article 44 is the only legal basis for receiving and considering communications by the African Children's Committee, then it would seem that the explicit mandate is weak indeed.

113 Para 61.

However, it is possible to locate a legal basis for receiving and considering communications outside of article 44. Article 42(a) (ii) confers the African Children's Committee with powers 'to formulate and lay down principles and rules aimed at protecting the rights and welfare of children in Africa.' In the same vein, article 42(c) empowers the African Children's Committee with interpretative powers at the request of the parties mentioned therein. Article 46 empowers the African Children's Committee to draw inspiration from international human rights law. The combination of these powers can imply a quasi-judicial interpretative function.

Furthermore, article 44(b) mandates the African Children's Committee to 'ensure protection of the rights enshrined in the Charter'. The word 'ensure' has been defined to mean to 'make certain, guarantee [or even] make inevitable'. Interpreted in this way, article 44(b) mandates the African Children's Committee to adopt relevant and effective measures to remedy violations of children's rights. In addition, article 45, which authorizes the African Children's Committee to 'resort to any appropriate method of investigation', is another strand in the legal basis for it to exercise its contentious jurisdiction to interrogate alleged violations of children's rights. Despite the normative weaknesses of article 44, it can be said that a teleological construction could still endow the African Children's Committee with remedial powers. However, the strength of law lies in its certainty; it is important that the powers of the African Children's Committee in contentious areas like communications be 'given' to it rather than be 'taken' by it.

Rule 74 of the Rules of Procedure of the Committee read together with article 1 of the Guidelines on Communication is a significant improvement on article 44 of the African Children's Charter. In clear terms, it empowers the African Children's Committee to receive, consider and define communications. In addition, the requirement for *locus standi* is so broad that it can be said there is no standing requirement before the African Children's Committee. Anybody can bring a communication with or without the consent of the victim as long as the complainant can prove it is in the best interests of the child. The Guidelines, too, fill the gap in article 44 of the African Children's Charter by providing for more or less the same admissibility requirements under similar treaty bodies.

The African Children's Committee has received sixteen complaints. It has decided on ten and six are pending. Therefore, it is difficult discuss all of the cases received in order to assess the full implication of this mechanism under the African Children's Charter. Nonetheless, one of the earlier cases to be decided by the African Children's Committee will be assessed. The communication *Institute for Human Rights and Development in Africa (IHRDA) and Open Society Justice Initiative on Behalf of Children of Nubian Descent in Kenya v The Government of Kenya* (the Nubian case) will be used to illustrate the points being made.[114] In the Nubian case, the complainants, the Nubians, are descendants of the Sudanese Nubian ethnic group who were members of the British colonial forces in East Africa, known as the King's African Rifles. When World War II ended, the British ignored the request of the Nubians for repatriation and instead allocated a piece of land to them in Kibera near Nairobi, the capital of Kenya, without issuing them with a formal title deed.

Because the Nubian ethnic group cannot lay a formal claim to land in Kenya, successive governments in Kenya have refused to recognise them as citizens and have denied them of the rights that flow from citizenship. After repeated and failed attempts to claim their rights to citizenship using the Kenyan national judicial systems, the Institute for Human Rights and Democracy in Africa and the Open Society Initiative jointly filed a communication with the African Children's Committee on behalf of the Nubian children. The communication claimed the rights of the Nubians to Kenyan citizenship and all the benefits of that citizenship.

In its decision, the African Children's Committee, in affirming the right of the people of Nubian descent to Kenyan nationality, significantly contributed to the jurisprudence of the African human rights system. First, the African Children's Committee held that the best interests of children serves as an exception to the rule on the exhaustion of local remedies. Second, the African Children's Committee reaffirmed the indivisibility and interdependence and

114 Available at http://www.African Children's Committee.org/wp-content/uploads/2011/09/002-09-IHRDA-OSJI-Nubian-children-v-Kenya-Eng.pdf.

interrelatedness of the human rights of children.[115] According to the African Children's Committee, there was a direct link between the violation of the civil and political rights to nationality and the socio-economic rights to health and education; the two generations of rights could not be separated. The decision of the African Children's Committee in the African human rights system is already

> having considerable potential to offer redress to victims of human rights violations, to prevent future violations in Africa, and to contribute to a better understanding of the content of the rights and obligations in question.[116]

Therefore, there is evidence of a willingness on the part of the African Children's Committee to interpret the African Children's Charter in a context-sensitive manner. The rigidity of the provisions in the African Children's Charter might be a factor hindering the extent to which the African Children's Committee might want to innovate in discharging its mandate.

5.3. The practice of state reporting under the African Children's Charter

So far, Algeria, Angola, Benin, Burkina Faso, Burundi, Cameron, Chad, Comoros, Côte d'Ivoire, Egypt, Eritrea, eSwathini, Ethiopia, Gabon, Ghana, Guinea Bissau, Guinea, Kenya, Lesotho, Liberia, Libya, Madagascar, Malawi, Mali, Mauritania, Namibia, Niger, Nigeria, Rwanda, Senegal, Seychelles, Sierra Leone, South Africa, Tanzania, Togo, Uganda, Zambia and Zimbabwe,[117] have submitted state reports to the African Children's Committee. Some of these state reports will be examined to ascertain the nature and scope of the constructive conversations between state parties and the African Children's Committee. Emphasis will be placed on understanding

115 E Durojaye & E Foley 'Making a first impression: An assessment of the decision of the Committee of Experts of the African Children's Charter in the Nubian children communication' (2012) 12 *African Human Rights Law Journal* 564.

116 R Murray & E Mottershaw 'The mechanisms for the implementation of the decisions of the African Commission on Human and Peoples' Rights' (2014) 36 *Human Rights Quarterly* 349.

117 See https://www.acerwc.africa/initial-and-periodic-reports/ for more details.

who is a child, autonomy rights of children, the best interests of the child, and child participation. Where relevant, the African Children's Committee's unique African features will be examined as they play out in the reports and concluding observations of the African Children's Committee.

5.3.1. State party reporting and 'who is a child?' under the African Children's Charter

A review of state party reports submitted to the African Children's Committee so far reveals the duality of the conception of childhood and confirms the hybridity of the policy environment in Africa in which children live every day. This duality exists between the way traditional communities and customary laws see and treat childhood and how statutory and human rights laws conceptualise childhood. For instance, after listing a plethora of laws and policies – laws that could compete favourably with other international practices governing childhood, Senegal's State report noted:

> Traditional values that are deeply welded into highly dissuasive taboos… constitute the foundations of and perpetuate the solidarity of the Senegalese community at large. These values are the springboard of a protection system from which the promotion of the rights of the child can find the basis for its launch and justification.[118]

Not all traditional values around childhood are compatible with the statutory understanding of childhood in Senegal.[119] But children and the family live their lives under both systems that sometimes are complementary and at other times, contradictory.

In its report, the Government of Tanzania admits that 'Tanzania has diverse definitions of a child and is not yet in compliance with the definition of the child according to Article 2 of the African Charter.'[120] This diversity in

118 See page 26 of the Initial, first and second State Report of the Republic of Senegal 1998-2009 submitted to the African Committee of experts on the Rights and Welfare of the child in 2009.

119 See page 26 of the Initial, first and second State Report of the Republic of Senegal 1998-2009 submitted to the African Committee of experts on the Rights and Welfare of the child in 2009.

120 See page 10 of the Initial State Report of Tanzania submitted to the African Committee of Experts on the Rights and Welfare of the Child in 2006.

the conceptions of childhood exists because 'under Customary, Islamic and Hindu Law ... the age of majority is considered to be puberty.'[121] In Uganda, traditionally, 'any person who is still under the care of their parent is considered a child,'[122] and 'children who marry or have children early are usually considered and treated as adults.'[123]

Other state parties to the African Children's Charter try to cope with the duality and hybridity of childhood experience through the introduction of exceptions or claw-back provisions. For example, in Mali, according to Article 2 of the Child Protection Code 'a child shall be any person aged less than 18 years and who *has not yet reached majority age by special provisions.*'[124] In that country 'the majority age is not uniform. It varies between 18 and 21 years depending on the subject: criminal, civil, social or political.'[125] In Sudan, the Child Act, 2010, 'contains a number of other child definitions, depending on the circumstances in which a child lives.'[126]

The approach of the African Children's Committee to the challenge of the duality and hybridity of childhood in Africa is the same as that of the CRC Committee - harmonization.[127] The Concluding Observations of the African Children's Committee urge state parties to harmonise traditional understanding with the conception of childhood in the African Children's Charter.[128] The message is that states should abandon their traditions and

121 See page 11 of the Initial State Report of Tanzania submitted to the African Committee of Experts on the Rights and Welfare of the Child in 2006.

122 See page 12 of the Initial Report of the Republic of Uganda submitted to the African Committee of experts on the rights and Welfare of the Child in 2007.

123 See page 12 of the Initial Report of the Republic of Uganda submitted to the African Committee of experts on the rights and Welfare of the Child in 2007.

124 See page 10 of the Initial Report of the Republic of Mali 1999-2006 submitted to the African Committee of Experts on the Rights and Welfare of the Child in 2007.

125 See page 10 of the Initial Report of the Republic of Mali 1999-2006 submitted to the African Committee of Experts on the Rights and Welfare of the Child in 2007.

126 See page 18 of the Initial Report of the Republic of Sudan submitted to the African Committee of Experts on the Rights and Welfare of the Child in 2009.

127 In a number of concluding observations of the CRC Committee and the few seen by the writer from the African Committee of Experts on the Rights and Welfare of the Child the approach to issues of variation in upper age limits is to recommend harmonisation of different ages of maturity with the provisions of the two instruments.

128 See for example the concluding observation of the African Committee of Experts on the Rights and Welfare of the Child to the Republic of Tanzania.

embrace human rights thinking and perceptions of childhood. By the same token that traditional value around childhood in Africa are expected to accommodate human rights values and norms, it is reasonable to accept that human rights norms and values should be malleable to local values, which are the 'basis for its launch and justification.'[129] In that case, the message of the African Children's Committee or the CRC Committee would be that of mutual accommodation.

The concept of accommodation refers to a process wherein different value systems or norms acknowledge, recognise and tolerate differences to facilitate harmony and mutual co-existence.[130] According to Angle, for any relationship between values to account as accommodation, such a relationship must meet at least two conditions. First, there should be significant and persistent disagreement. Second, there should be willingness as well as the desirability and inevitability of interaction.[131] The willingness to compromise is intrinsic to such a relationship. One advantage of an accommodative relationship is a legitimate commitment from the parties to the relationship.[132] This commitment is as a result of the existence of agreement on the 'norms of accommodation.'[133] The difference between the concept of accommodation and harmonisation is that in the latter the 'lesser values' are expected to conform in form and content to 'superior values', whereas the former envisages a norm-to-norm relationship that is mutually beneficial.

It is argued that this framework facilitates the implementation of human rights norms without dislodging local values. Thus, accommodation, rather than harmonisation of laws on childhood with the CRC, will engender dialogue, facilitate value-to-value and norm-to-norm conversation between traditional African value systems on childhood and the international human rights norms on childhood. Such tolerance of a diversity of norms with

129 See page 26 of the Initial, first and second State Report of the Republic of Senegal 1998-2009 submitted to the African Committee of experts on the Rights and Welfare of the child in 2009.

130 A Gibbard *Wise choices, apt feelings: A theory of normative judgement* (1990) 244.

131 S Angle *Human rights in Chinese thought: A cross-cultural inquiry* (2002) 62.

132 As above.

133 As above, 63.

respect to the child should facilitate a complementarity of norms and reduce the complexities of duality and hybridity with respect to the lived experience of children in Africa.

5.3.2. State party reporting and the best interests of the child under the African Children' Charter

The Guidelines on Initial State Party Reporting require state parties to report on measures put in place to ensure the promotion and protection of the best interests of the child.[134] The responses of state parties to these guidelines concerning the best interests of the child demonstrate a limited and legalistic approach to the concept. In the absence of clear guidance on the concept and the probable constituent elements of the best interests of the child, it is difficult to assess the quality of reporting of state parties to the African Children's Charter in this regard.

The most comprehensive guidance to state parties and policy makers about the meaning of the best interests of the child is from the CRC Committee in its General Comments number 14 on the best interests of the child.[135] According to General Comment 14, the best interests of the child is a substantive right, a 'fundamental, interpretative legal principal' and a rule of procedure.[136] Substantively, it is the 'right of the child to have his or her best interests assessed and taken as a primary consideration when different interests are being considered.'[137] As an interpretative legal rule, 'if a legal provision is open to more than one interpretation, the interpretation which most effectively serves the child's best interests should be chosen.'[138] As a procedural guarantee, whenever any decision is to be taken that will likely affect a child or group of children, 'the decision-making process must include

134 See Guidelines number 10(b) of the Guidelines for Initial Reports of States Parties (Prepared by the African Committee of Experts on the Rights and Welfare of the Child pursuant to the Provision of article 43 of The African Charter on the Rights and Welfare of the Child) African Children's Charter/2 II. Rev2.

135 Available at http://www2.ohchr.org/English/bodies/crc/docs/GC/CRC_C_GC_14_ENG.pdf.

136 See para 6(b) of General Comment number 14 of the CRC Committee.

137 See para 6(a) of General Comment number 14 of the CRC Committee.

138 See para 6(b) of General Comment number 14 of the CRC Committee.

an evaluation of the possible (positive or negative) impact of the decision on the child or children concerned.'[139]

As helpful as the elaboration may be to judges, translating it into clear indicators for reporting purposes may be daunting. The difficulty is compounded by the fact that 'the concept of the child's best interests is complex and its content must be determined on a case-by-case basis.'[140] In addition, the concept of the child's best interests 'is flexible and adaptable.'[141] Therefore, it should be 'adjusted and defined on an individual basis, according to the specific situation of the child or children concerned.'[142] Furthermore, the best interests of the child principle is 'a dynamic concept that requires an assessment appropriate to the specific context.'[143] It is, therefore, difficult to cover the ramifications of the concept of the best interests of the child through a reporting mechanism as provided for under the African Children's Charter.

That is probably why state parties to the African Children's Charter report mainly on laws, policies and institutions mandated to protect the best interests of the child or completely omit discussing the concept in their state reports.[144] Senegal reports that 'legal and social protection measures with appropriate legal standards have been taken in favour of the child,'[145] as measures taken to ensure the best interests of the child. In Tanzania, the best interests of the child, or child welfare, is 'a guiding principle of child related legislation.'[146] In Togo, the best interests of the child mean 'all that is beneficial to the latter for his mental, moral, physical and material well-being.'[147] Despite this broad

139 See para 6(c) of General Comment number 14 of the CRC Committee.

140 See para 32 of General Comment number 14 of the CRC Committee.

141 See para 32 of General Comment number 14 of the CRC Committee.

142 See para 32 of General Comment number 14 of the CRC Committee.

143 See para 1 of General Comment number 14 of the CRC Committee.

144 For example, the state report of Uganda preferred to discuss the best interests in line with other issues while Egypt omits a separate discussion on the best interests of the child principle it's in state report.

145 Senegal tends to mix the best interests of the child and actions that are taken in favour of the child for example.

146 Tanzania seemed to have limited the understanding of the best interests of the child principles to legislative principles. See page 11 of the Initial State Report of Tanzania submitted to the African Committee of Experts on the Rights and Welfare of the Child in 2006.

147 See page 14 of the Initial Report of the Republic of Togo submitted to the African Committee of Experts on

definition, the report of Togo adopts a very legalistic approach to the best interests of the child.

Not many of the state party reports to the African Children's Committee engage with African cultural values and practices as positive contributing factors to promoting and protecting the best interests of the child. Rather, the reports that do discuss culture mainly see culture from a negative and harmful perspective with respect to the best interests of the child. For instance, Senegal sees one of its major challenges in implementing children's rights as follows:

> The ever-persistent traditional perception of the child, whereby, for the majority of the country's population, the child is not a subject of law, does not facilitate the change of mentality and comportment to promote the full development of the child within the framework of his/her rights.[148]

In Tanzania, the laws of the country require 'courts to take customs into consideration when determining the best interests of the child;'[149] however, non-governmental organisations consider the 'customs of the community [as] outdated and may act against the best interests of the child.'[150] Tanzania did not report whether there are positive cultural features in that country that could enhance the promotion and protection of children's rights. When state parties do not engage with positive cultural norms in their countries through the reporting process, it is difficult to blame human rights treaty bodies for not sufficiently dealing with positive cultural norms in Africa. It would seem that the state reports examined simply list national legislation and policies that perfectly reproduce the wording of either the CRC or the African Children's Charter on the subject of the best interests of the child. As a result, countries fail to adequately engage with the flexibility and adaptability of the concept of best interests of the child from a cultural angle.

---

the Rights and Welfare of the Child in 2009.

148 See page 41 of the Initial, first and second State Report of the Republic of Senegal 1998-2009 submitted to the African Committee of experts on the Rights and Welfare of the child in 2009.

149 See page 13 of the Initial State Report of Tanzania submitted to the African Committee of Experts on the Rights and Welfare of the Child in 2006.

150 See page 13 of the Initial State Report of Tanzania submitted to the African Committee of Experts on the Rights and Welfare of the Child in 2006.

Togo's state report is an exception. The country has a ministry that has a 'policy of promoting the values, traditions and positive cultural practices.'[151] The policy of promoting positive cultural practices has yielded positive results. It has resulted in the modification of the period of 'initiation rites of traditional Voodoo practice' from three years to a few weeks.[152] In addition:

> The Ministry undertook public awareness campaigns on the promotion of traditional mechanisms for the protection of young girls in communities. Hence, traditional practices of the Bassar community (dance of the virgins) and Kabyè (akpéma) have been promoted. Today, many are young girls who abstain until marriage. The promotion of these traditional values and cultural practices aims for the protection of children from early and forced marriage and from STD / HIV-AIDS.[153]

As debatable as the point made by the Togolese government is, the point the government of Togo is making is that allowing traditional cultures to adjust through internal mechanisms to the modern needs of a society is more efficacious than externally imposed transformation. This internal process of transformation is painfully slow. Nevertheless, in some cases, it is in the long-term interest of the effective implementation of human rights that the slow pace of change is accommodated and, in fact, encouraged.

5.3.3. State party reporting and autonomy rights of children in Africa

An additional area state parties struggle when reporting under the African Children's Charter relates to the autonomy rights of children. Conceptually, state parties' reports examined for the purpose of this book do not distinguish between how autonomy rights apply to children and to adults. As a result, state parties simply list general constitutional and statutory provisions that

151 See page 5 of the Initial Report of the Republic of Togo submitted to the African Committee of Experts on the Rights and Welfare of the Child in 2009.

152 See page 6 of the Initial Report of the Republic of Togo submitted to the African Committee of Experts on the Rights and Welfare of the Child in 2009.

153 See page 6 of the Initial Report of the Republic of Togo submitted to the African Committee of Experts on the Rights and Welfare of the Child in 2009.

guarantee autonomy rights and imply children's autonomy rights from these provisions. These state reports do not state in clear terms how these general provisions, which in many cases are a recitation of similar provisions in international and regional human rights treaties, have been applied to children or used by children.

However, state parties do convey the challenges of duality and hybridity that confront the implementation of the African Children's Charter in their countries. With respect to freedom of religion, for example, Tanzania, after listing all the legal provisions that guarantee freedom of religion, thought and conscience, reports:

> Customarily children conform to the religion of their parents. Under the Local Customary Law Order of 1963 children belong to the father. When parents have different religions the child automatically adopts the father's religion.[154]

This is an example of the duality of children's lived experience in Tanzania. Under customary law children's autonomy rights relating to choosing a religion are restricted, whereas the African Children's Charter provides children without unfettered autonomy rights in this regard. So, in the public space children have autonomy rights, yet in the family space they do not have any of the dimensions of such rights.

In interpreting articles 7, 8 and 9 of the African Children's Charter dealing with freedom of expression, Egypt submits that these articles 'aimed at putting in place the required balance between the role of the family, the school and the society in developing the personality, properties and capacities of the child based on his freedom of expression of his ideas.'[155] Mali, on its own, admits that 'despite this provision of the Constitution, traditionally parents closely supervise children on the exercise of these freedoms, without leaving much room for manoeuvre.'[156]

154 See page 20 of the Initial State Report of Tanzania submitted to the African Committee of Experts on the Rights and Welfare of the Child in 2006.

155 See page 39 of the Initial Report of Arab Republic of Egypt to the African Committee on Experts on the Rights and Welfare of the Child, 2003.

156 See page 5 of the Initial Report of the Republic of Togo submitted to the African Committee of Experts on

Though the reporting practice under the African Children's Charter is still in its infancy and it is difficult to measure its ability to ensure constructive dialogue as well as its efficacy in facilitating the implementation of the African Children's Charter, the emerging trend is that this mechanism suffers from the same limitations noticed at the UN level. Inadequacy of the guidance sent to state parties, inability or unwillingness of state parties to deeply engage with the content of the rights in the African Children's Charter and the complexity involved in capturing and accurately reporting the interaction between the modern and traditional experience of children, their families and communities further exacerbate these limitations in Africa.

The reporting practice under the African Children's Charter is beginning to appear more like a mechanism for an exchange of information by state parties in return for experience, expertise and guidance from the African Children's Committee, and not a constructive dialogue. When the African Children's Committee develops its interpretative mandate fully,[157] it may be able to provide more guidance to state parties with respect to their reporting mandate. For now, the only guidance is that which is provided by the guidelines for Initial State Party Reporting, which is grossly inadequate for the purpose of periodic reports.

5.3.4. State party reporting and child participation

There is no indication of substantial child participation in the reporting process before the African Children's Committee. The state party reports examined for the purpose of this book do not make mention of the mechanism put in place to ensure that children participate meaningfully in the preparation, submission and presentation of the state party reports to the African Children's Committee.

the Rights and Welfare of the Child in 2009.

157 See page 29 of the Initial Report of the Republic of Mali 1999-2006 submitted to the African Committee of Experts on the Rights and Welfare of the Child in 2007.

5.4. An assessment of the African Children's Committee

The African Children's Committee is a treaty body in the African human rights system that has exerted significant effort, against all odds, to discharge its mandate.[158] According to an external evaluation of the activities of the African Children's Committee in 2010, a number of external and internal challenges negatively affected the ability of the African Children's Committee to maximise its mandate.[159] Externally, the effective and efficient performance records of the African Children's Committee were limited by the inherent overall weaknesses of the African human rights system:

Normative deficits: Like other human rights treaty bodies within the African human rights system, the African Children's Committee has an overly promotional mandate. Even though the African Children's Charter provides for a protective mandate, the wording of the mandate leaves much to be desired.

Coordination and poor complementarity: The mandate of the African Children's Committee is not normatively or functionally connected to that of the African Charter and that of the African Court on Human and Peoples' Rights. This lack of a substantive relationship between the treaties weakens the possibility for complementarity.

---

158 For a year by year progress report and assessment of the performance of the African Committee of Experts on the Rights and Welfare of the Child please see For a comprehensive discussion of the mandate of the African Children's Committee and how the African Children's Committee has discharged its mandate see B Mezmur 'The African Committee of Experts on the Rights and Welfare of the Child: An update' (2006) 6 *African Human Rights Journal* 549; B Mezmur 'Still an infant or now a toddler? The work of the African Committee of Experts on the Rights and Welfare of the Child and its 8th ordinary session' (2007) 7 *African Human Rights Law Journal* 258; B Mezmur 'The 19th ordinary session of the African Committee of Experts on the Rights and Welfare of the Child: Looking back to look head' (2007) 7 *African Human Rights Journal* 545; J Sloth-Nielsen & B Mezmur 'Win some, lose some: The 10th ordinary session of the African Committee of Experts on the Rights and Welfare of the Child' (2008) 8 *African Human Rights Law Journal* 207; B Mezmur & J Sloth-Nielsen 'An ice-breaker: State party reports and the 11th session of the African Committee of Experts on the Rights and Welfare of the Child' (2008) 8 *African Human Rights Law Journal* 596; J Sloth-Nielsen & B Mezmur 'Out of the starting blocks: The 12th and 13th sessions of the African Committee of Experts on the Rights and Welfare of the Child' (2009) 9 *African Human Rights Law Journal* 336 and J Sloth-Nielsen & B Mezmur 'Like running on a treadmill? The 14th and 15th sessions of the African Committee of Experts on the Rights and Welfare of the Child' (2010) 10 *African Human Rights Law Journal* 534.

159 The Report of the Evaluation of the activities of the African Committee on Experts on the Rights and Welfare of the Child conducted by Remember Miamingi in 2010 is on file with the author.

Funding and governance challenges: The African Children's Committee has operated on a budget of about 80,000 United States Dollars per year.[160] Trying to implement human rights within limited resources on a continent without a fully developed culture of human rights and rule of law at the national level is a difficult task.

Internal weakness: Internally, a lack of appropriate expertise among the members of the African Children's Committee, as well as, initially, the poor quality of the analysis and legal reasoning combined to slow the work of the African Children's Committee during the initial stages.

In spite of these challenges the African Children's Committee has managed to spearhead the campaign for universal ratification of the African Children's Charter by African countries.[161] The number of states parties reporting to the African Children's Committee is increasing. The number of communications the African Children's Committee is receiving across the continent is also increasing.[162] Importantly, the turnaround time for the consideration of state party reports, the issuing of concluding observations and consideration of communications by the African Children's Committee is improving considerably. Increased donor support, as well as engagement by civil society organisations, has resulted in an increased profiling of the work of the African Children's Committee.

However, the greater challenge facing the African Children's Committee is that of a voice and an identity. The textual similarities between the CRC and the African Children's Charter, as well as the similarities of the working methods of the CRC Committee and these of the African Children's Committee might turn the African Children's Committee into an echo of the voice of the CRC Committee. What was the unique African feature of the African Children's

160 See the Report of the evaluation of the African Children's Committee. A copy is on file with the author. According to the report of the second evaluation of the African Children's Committee, the African Children's Committee 'received approximately 36% of the budget indicated in the Strategic Plan. Of this about one-third was provided by Member States and two-thirds by Development Partners'. See Evaluation Report of the African Children's Committee 2014 at page 12.

161 There are about 47 ratifications of the African Charter on the Rights and Welfare of the Child. There are only 7 more ratifications and the African Children's Charter will attend universal ratification in Africa.

162 According to the Secretariat of the African Committee of Experts on the Rights and Welfare of the Child it has already received 16 communications.

Charter, to an extent, is reflected in the Optional Protocols to the CRC and the general comments of the CRC Committee. Therefore, it is the quality and direction of the jurisprudence of the African Children's Committee and the effectiveness of its working methods that will set it apart from the presence of the CRC Committee on human rights in Africa. The African Children's Committee relies more on the jurisprudence of the African Commission on Human and Peoples' Rights and, to some extent, on the interpretation of the provisions of the CRC by the CRC Committee, in discharging its mandate.[163]

An examination of the concluding observations of the African Children's Committee, the first General Comment of the African Children's Committee, as well as the first decision of the African Children's Committee on a communication indicates a tendency by the African Children's Committee to approach its mandate within the paradigm of universal human rights. For instance, in its Concluding Observation on the State Report of Tanzania, the Committee recommended:

> The Committee urges the State party to undertake its *obligations under international children's rights standards* to ensure that the legislative and programmatic measures taken are implemented and sustained and that they remain effective to also ensure that the sale and traffic in children is curtailed and eventually eliminated.[164]

In an effort to serve as a follow-up mechanism for the Concluding Observations of the CRC Committee, the African Children's Committee directs the attention of state parties to the Concluding Observations of the CRC Committee. If it is done with respect to provisions of the African Children's Charter that are different or provide better protection and without

163 A good example will be the decisions of the African Committee on the Rights and Welfare of the Child in the Nubian case. In that case the African Children's Committee mainly appropriated the jurisprudence of the African Commission on Human and Peoples' Rights and available international legal reasoning to the situation of children of Nubian decent in Kenya. Of course, there is no need to reinvent the wheel when available jurisprudence suffices. Nonetheless, for a treaty body that is still trying to find its feet; it has more room to innovate and 'experiment'. Another demonstration of this point is the General Comment 1 of the African Committee on the Rights and Welfare of the Child that relies mainly on the jurisprudence of these two bodies to explain the content of the right in the African Children's Charter.

164 See the Concluding Observation of the Committee of Experts on the Rights and Welfare of the Child to the Republic of Tanzania available at http://Www.African Children's Committee.Org/Wp-Content/Uploads/2011/03/African Children's Committee-Recommendations-Tanzania-initial-English.pdf. Emphasis is mine.

further elaboration, it could be counterproductive. For example, with respect to the juvenile justice system in Tanzania the African Children's Committee directs the state party to 'work on the Concluding Observations made by the UN CRC Committee aimed at improving the state of juvenile justice in its jurisdiction.'[165] As useful as this advice is, it indicates deference in an area in which the African Children's Committee could develop context-specific interpretation, despite the normative limitation with respect to this subject in the African Children's Charter.

Whenever the African Children's Committee does not rely on the universal human rights paradigm within the UN system, it uses the same paradigm from the decisions of the African Commission on Human and Peoples' Rights. For example, in the communication *Institute for Human Rights and Development in Africa (IHRDA) and Open Society Justice Initiative on Behalf of Children of Nubian Descent in Kenya v The Government of Kenya*[166] the African Children's Committee relied heavily on the jurisprudence of the African Commission. As mentioned, it is one of the progressive decisions in the African human rights system. However, in its efforts to use 'international human rights principles and standards', the African Children's Committee may have overly relied on universal standards that might not have sufficiently addressed context-specific issues such as the structural dynamics between boys and girls.[167] The African Children's Committee relied on jurisprudence from the African Commission, but equally these decisions are rooted in universal standards.[168] As useful as this practice is for the complementarity

165 See the Concluding Observation of the Committee of Experts on the Rights and Welfare of the Child to the Republic of Tanzania available at http://www.African Children's Committee.org/wp-content/uploads/2011/03/African Children's Committee-Recommendations-Tanzania-Initial-English.Pdf. Emphasis is mine.

166 Available here http://www.African Children's Committee.org/wp-content/uploads/2011/09/002-09-IHRDA-OSJI-Nubian-children-v-Kenya-Eng.pdf.

167 E Durojaye & E Foley 'Making a first impression: An assessment of the decision of the Committee of Experts of the African Children's Charter in the Nubian children communication' (2012) 12 *African Human Rights Law Journal* 564.

168 In the course of this decision, the African Children's Committee relied on the following decisions from the Commission: *Free Legal Assistance Group and Others v Zaire*, Communications No. 25/89, 47/90, 56/91, 100/93, *SERAC v Federal Republic of Nigeria*, Communication No. 155/96, *Purohit and Moore v The Gambia*, Communication 241/2001, *Free Legal Assistance Group and Others v Zaire*, Communications No. 25/89, 47/90, 56/91, 100/93, *Legal Resources Foundation v Zambia*, Communication No. 211/98, *Civil Liberties Organization v Nigeria*, Communication No. 45/90, *Anwak Justice Council v Ethiopia*, Communication No. 299/2005, *Dawda Jawara v The Gambia*, Communication Nos. 147/95 and 149/96, *Constitutional Rights*

of the African human rights system, the danger with respect to the African Children's Committee is that the African Commission's use of the universal paradigm of human rights to interpret the provisions of the ACHPR might reduce the African Children's Committee's contribution to the development of African jurisprudence on children's rights;[169] the CRC Committee is already operating within a universalist human rights theoretical framework in Africa. The African Children's Committee will be duplicating the CRC Committee if it interprets the African Children's Charter from a universal paradigm of human rights in the light of the textual and substantive similarities between the CRC and the African Children's Charter.

In order to avoid redundancy and duplication, the African Children's Committee cannot continue to echo and legitimise the international image of childhood without significantly contributing to the discourse around it. The CRC Committee, comparatively, has enormous resources and years of developing jurisprudence, so it is a challenge as well as an opportunity to fill in gaps and break new ground. Therefore, one of the questions that the African Children's Committee will have to answer is how it can discharge its context-specific mandate in a way that complements the mandate of the CRC Committee without compromising the African philosophy of childhood and cultural heritage. Some of the answers to this question, partly, depend on the philosophical and theoretical orientation underlying the work that the African Children's Committee does. It is suggested in this work that the African Children's Committee should adopt pluralistic universalism as a philosophical and theoretical framework within which to discharge its mandate.

Project [CRP] v Nigeria, Communication No. 60/91. These are decisions the Commission mostly relied on article 61 of the ACHPR and borrowed freely from international principles.

169 This is because the African Commission is not in a position where it is discharging a similar mandate with another human rights treaty body at universal level within Africa. The mandate of the Human Rights Council and the human rights instruments that it interprets and monitor could be substantially differentiated from the ACHPR. The same cannot be said about the CRC and the African Children's Charter.

5.4. Pluralistic universalism: Application and implication

5.4.1. Application of pluralistic universalism

Human rights are as much universal minimum procedural safeguards as they are normative standards or values. Standards as well as value systems are a direct result of social practices: to consider something, as a value is to 'implicitly affirm that there is or there has been a social practice supporting that something.'[170] Human rights are theoretical postulations that are rooted in social practices that are either specific to a particular time or place or to all times and places depending on one's philosophical standpoint. Explicitly or implicitly, therefore, the acts of interpreting and or adjudicating human rights norms are from a certain philosophical or theoretical orientation.

As has been argued, human rights treaty bodies at the international level mainly operate from the platform of a universalist human rights paradigm. Predominantly, the texts, as well as the consistent interpretations of these texts, tend to support this position of the human rights treaty monitoring bodies at the international level. Even though it has been argued in this work that the African Children's Charter is textually, substantively and normatively very similar to the CRC, it is further contended that the *raison d'être* of the African Children's Charter, the spirit in which it was designed to be interpreted and the context of its implementation cannot fit neatly within a universalist paradigm of human rights.

The African Children's Charter, unlike other regional human rights treaties in other parts of the world, is intended to be interpreted by taking into account:

> [t]he virtues of [the African] cultural heritage, historical background and the values of the African civilization, which should inspire and characterize their reflection on the concept of the rights and welfare of the child.[171]

170 C Corradetti *Relativism and human rights: A theory of pluralistic universalism* (2009) x.

171 Preamble to the African Charter on the Rights and Welfare of the Child.

Inherent, therefore, in the adoption of the African Children's Charter is the understanding that universal norms with respect to childhood, as much as possible, should validate local moral principles and claims with respect to childhood in Africa. If the African Children's Committee wants to be true to the object and purpose of the drafters of the African Children's Charter, it must operate within a theoretical framework that facilitates accommodation between universal norms on childhood in Africa and cultural particularism.

There are three theoretical options the African Children's Committee could choose from: universalism,[172] relativism[173] and the mixed positions.[174] These mixed positions include relative universalism,[175] pluralistic relativism,[176] and pluralistic universalism.[177] Common to these is a desire to accommodate some level of contextualisation within a universalist paradigm, or some universalism within a relativist world. The difference within the positions lies in the extent of deference shown either to universal norms over local norms or to local norms over universal values.

According to classical relativists there are fundamental and divergent values unique to different communities. These values are so core to the value system of these communities that no inter-communal agreement can bridge the difference in values and norms between different communities.[178] For example, classical relativists suggest:

1) Cultures are the moral sources for individual actions, so what is morally right is culturally context-dependent.
2) One must act in accordance with his or her own cultural context.

---

172 J Donnelly *Universal human rights in theory and in practice* (2003) 22.

173 D Wong 'Relativism' in P Singer (ed) *A companion to ethics* (1995) 442; see D Wong *Moral Relativity* (1986) 443; T Scanlon 'Fear of relativism' in P Moser & L Carson (eds) *Moral relativism* (2001) 142.

174 These are positions that merge either some elements of relativism and universalism or some pluralistic features with either relativism or universalism.

175 M Nussbaum 'Non-relative values: An Aristotelian approach' in M Nussbaum & A Sen (eds) *The quality of life* (1993) 242.

176 D Wong *Natural moralities: A defence of pluralistic relativism* (2006) 29.

177 C Corradetti *Relativism and human rights: A theory of pluralistic universalism* (2009) 106.

178 As above, 6.

3) Therefore, it is wrong to defend the principle of universality of moral principle.[179]

The combined effect of (b) and (c) above is that cultural values apply universally. An individual has rights within the context of his or her own culture; other cultures around the world must act in respect of this right of the individual. Ironically, according to this opinion, 'the tolerance of moral diversity is the only value or norm for which there are good objective moral reasons of universal application.'[180]

The position of the classical relativists is predicated upon two main hypotheses: the 'standard-related' and the 'non-neutrality' hypotheses.[181] According to the 'standard-related' hypotheses 'any proportional truth (p) can be formulated only according to some standards 's1', s2' etc.; whereas 'non-neutrality'[182] maintains, in the light of a multiplicity of standards, that 'there is no privileged neutral point of observation for evaluating the superiority of one standard in respect to the other.'[183] In short, for the classical relativist there are no superior cultural values or norms and, thus, no room for culture-to-culture judgements.

In failing to allow a space for some cross-cultural norms and values, this school of thought fails to capture the reality of transferability of norms across culture and time. In the case of children who are helplessly vulnerable to some very harmful cultural practices, the classical relativists offer no hope.

The 'mixed' relativist position combines the elements of both classical relativism and universalism. The strength of the mixed positions is that they bridge the gap. Wong's pluralistic relativism represents the thinking within this position, which holds, even though it is true, that

179 As above, 37.

180 J Nickel & D Reidy 'Relativism, self-determination and human rights' in D Chatterjee (ed) *Democracy in global world: A human rights and political participation in the 21st century* (2008) 3.

181 T Moesteller *Relativism in contemporary American philosophy* (2006) 2.

182 A Macintyre 'Practical rationalities as forms of social structures' in *The MacIntrye Reader* (1998) 121.

183 C Corradetti *Relativism and human rights: A theory of pluralistic universalism* (2009) 13 citing H Siegel Relativism refuted: A critique of contemporary epistemological relativism (1987) 6.

> [c]ertain judgements can be either true or false based on certain circumstances, there exist other kinds of judgement which, independently from given circumstances, do indeed maintain their truth validity in a universal way.[184]

However, they are careful to make sure that universal moral values should be seen and treated only as a 'skeleton of morality, insufficiently rich in content to be action guiding.'[185] For them, action related priorities 'must be established by local criteria within the truth condition for moral judgement.'[186]

The classic universalist maintains, conceptually and substantively, that human rights are, or should be held universally by all human beings, irrespective of their context or culture. This position seems logical at a conceptual level, but the implementation of human rights depends, to an extent, on local norms, institutions and structures influenced, largely, not by international values and standards. In addition, in the realm of children's rights, universalism of children's rights causes them to be difficult to implement. Children live most of their lives within the family, and in Africa a significant number of children live in minimal contact with state structures. The cultural values of the family influence their childbearing and childrearing practices. Thus, for realistic implementation of children's rights, there must be some yielding that allows for variation and contextualisation at different levels.

A 'mixed' position among universalists accommodates or 'concedes a certain degree of variations at different levels'[187] without undermining universal and mutually agreed safeguards. A mixed position in this class is pluralistic universalism. The difference between the 'mixed' position of the relativists and the pluralistic universalists is that the former concedes that 'the truth-conditions of certain judgements are independent from universally valid procedural constraints;'[188] the latter maintain that 'only truth-conditions

184 C Corradetti *Relativism and human rights: A theory of pluralistic universalism* (2009) 59.

185 D Wong *Natural moralities: A defence of pluralistic relativism* (2006) 81.

186 As above.

187 C Corradetti *Relativism and human rights: A theory of pluralistic universalism* (2009) 75.

188 As above, 61.

that satisfy mutually agreed procedural validity'[189] should be deferred to by universal norms such as human rights. It is this constrained flexibility that commends this theory for consideration in the work of the African Children's Committee. How is validity to be determined? It is suggested that Habermas' proposition should be the starting point. According to Habermas:

> [a] norm is valid when the foreseeable consequences and the side effects of its general observance for the interests and value-orientations of each individual could be jointly accepted by all concerned without coercion.[190]

Pluralist universalism is flexible enough to guarantee the concept of 'best interests', child participation, and non-discrimination, leaving the actual content of these principles and values to local considerations if they are not repugnant to universal safeguards.

Adopting a pluralistic universalist approach to its work as a theoretical framework in examining a state report, for instance, means that the African Children's Committee's starting point and endpoint is the context in which children spend their childhood. The provisions of the African Children's Charter are deployed to enhance a local framework of protection of childhood and resolve tension between the local values and the best interests of the child. The current reporting practices under the African Children's Charter are mainly a legal conversation between the laws and policies of the state party and the legal provisions of the African Children's Charter. It is possible for such a conversation to continue for a long time without impacting significantly on the lives of children who live under the radar of the law. A pluralistic universalist approach ensures that reporting is a constructive dialogue, not between the African Children's Committee and the government, but with the state.[191] The state includes different actors whose values and activities have a direct bearing on the rights and welfare of the child.

---

189 As above.

190 J Habermas 'A genealogical analysis of the cognitive content of morality' in J Habermas *The inclusion of the other: Studies in political theory* (1998) 42.

191 Government is an agent of the state. Therefore, the state includes government and non-government actors.

Equally, in its interpretative mandate, the African Children's Committee should interpret the provisions of the African Children's Charter in a way that promotes the African philosophy of childhood and cultural heritage. In order to do this, the universal image of childhood embedded in the African Children's Charter should be considered as a procedural safeguard that concedes to local variations whenever desirable and improves wherever needed the ability of local norms to better promote and protect the best interests, autonomy and participatory rights of children. Highlighting, acknowledging and strengthening local norms and values around childhood, while interpreting an African children's rights treaty that is firmly rooted in the universalist paradigm of human rights, such as the African Children's Charter, should enable the African Children's Committee to meaningfully complement the activities of the CRC Committee, enhance the African Children's Committee's voice and identity, and reduce redundancy. This book will attempt to demonstrate the possible application of pluralistic universalism by the African Children's Committee using the definition of the child, corporal punishment, child labour, and child marriage.

5.4.1.1. Pluralistic universalism and the definition of childhood

The definition of childhood from a pluralistic universalist perspective will take as its point of departure that there are many and equally valid starting points and endpoints of childhood, and that these markers are not and cannot be arbitrarily determined. Different markers, such as maturity, age or any other culturally specific means of determining maturity, provide an equally valid approximation of the evolving capacities of children. Since maturity is child-specific, gender specific, context-specific and culture specific, setting a uniform entry point and exit from childhood for all children may disempower other children.

Individualisation of the definition of the child should take into consideration the specific circumstances of the child and views of the childhood. For example, from this vantage point, it may be argued that a child heading a household and who desires to get married to another child in order to effectively manage the affairs of the household should not be denied such an opportunity on the basis of an arbitrary determination based on a rigid counting of the number of years. Another example is that of an orphaned child who is 15 or 16 years old with no one to care for him or her, but who is willing and able to be gainfully employed. Arguably, such a child should not be denied the vital means of livelihood by virtue of some universalist age-based category.

What should be universal in the definition of childhood is the desire to protect children from the possible negative consequences of their immaturity putting them at risk of the predatory behaviour in the adult world. In addition, defining childhood should be a tool to empower children to live meaningful lives now and to be well prepared for future roles and responsibilities. What should be pluralistic are the mechanisms for attaining this protection and empowerment. Although article 1 of the CRC embodies the spirit of flexibility, it still excludes other sources and mechanisms for determining childhood apart from the law applicable to the child.

The African Children's Committee is limited by the rigidity of article 2 of the African Children's Charter. This inflexibility has been praised based on its perceived potential to offer a high threshold of protection to children. It is possible to argue that such rigidity is, in fact, a double-edged sword that protects children, on one hand, while on the other, disempowers children and thereby exposes them to other forms of vulnerability. If article 2 of the African Children's Charter does not provide adequate protection to children, any other law or treaty that offers better protection should be read into article 2 pending the possible amendment of the African Children's Charter.[192]

5.4.1.2. Pluralistic universalism and the best interests of the child

Applying the 'best interests' principle from a universal pluralistic perspective entails considering the principle as an 'empty universal' concept. In the light of the fact that there are different societal conceptions of what is in the best interests of a child, a treaty body, determining what is in the best interests of a

192 See article 1(2) of the African Charter on the Rights and Welfare of the Child.

child, should take into account 'the importance of the traditions and cultural values of each people for the protection and harmonious development of the child'.[193] A universal pluralistic approach will encourage a 'reconciliation of the best interests principle with cultural norms'[194] rather than a reconstruction of cultural values based solely on the norms of the CRC. This is certainly difficult but not impossible if applied on a case by case, child, norm and context-specific basis. Such an approach will avoid an 'extreme stance of cultural relativism'[195] as well as the extreme form of human rights exceptionalism. This book will test how a child's best interests could be secured within the pluralistic universalism using the contentious issues of child marriage, child labour and corporal punishment.

5.4.1.2.1. Pluralistic universalism and child marriage

Marriage is a universal phenomenon. How, why and when people get married differs from culture to culture, community to community and from a period to another. The need to protect children from the burdens of marriage can be effective only if it is child specific. In many cultures readiness for sex is equated with readiness to be married. In formal law, the age of sexual consent does not necessarily translate to the age to give free and informed consent to marriage. In traditional communities, there is the understanding that sex is practiced exclusively within the confines of marriage. In cultures that equate readiness for sex to readiness to undertake the responsibilities and consequences of sex, such as marriage, it is arguable that allowing children to engage in sexual behaviour as early as 12, while permitting children to be eligible for marriage only at 18, is not protective of all children.

Adopting a pluralistic universalist approach to evaluating child marriage, the African Children's Committee could approach the universal concept of marriage from a context and child specific position. Children of a certain age who want to marry other children could be treated differently from a situation in which adults want to take advantage of children and abuse them in the

193 See para 11 of the Preamble to the Convention on the Rights of the Child.

194 M Freeman 'Culture, childhood and rights' (2011) 5 *The Family in Law* 15.

195 G Van Bueren *The international law on the rights of the child* (1995) 47.

name of marriage. Age, maturity, the specific circumstance of the child should all have roles in arriving at the decision of whether a particular marriage arrangement is in the best interests of a particular child in a particular community. These assessments could be carried out by a judicial officer, a government official, a traditional ruler, or other religious leaders.

5.4.1.2.2. Pluralistic universalism and corporal punishment

The African Children's Charter provides for 'domestic discipline' as part of the duties and obligations of parents and other persons in charge of the child. Such discipline must be administered without compromising the inherent dignity of the child.[196] The provision in the African Children's Charter, without an exact counterpart in the CRC, indicates an intention on the part of the drafters of the African Children's Charter to balance African cultural practices of domestic discipline with the requirements of human rights. The concept of discipline has a cultural dimension: imposing a single model of discipline on all cultures is problematic.

Article 20 of the African Children's Charter guarantees the cultural particularism of the African continent without compromising the universal requirement of respect for human dignity in line with the theoretical framework of pluralistic universalism. In interpreting this provision, the African Children's Committee in this light ensures that families', communities' and cultures' right to determine what constitutes discipline for a child is not lost. The role of the African Children's Committee is to ensure that whatever discipline is applied to children must be consistent with respecting their dignity. Dignity, though a universal value, has varying manifestations from culture to culture and from time to time. In subjecting discipline to the test of dignity, the African Children's Committee must ensure that it is context-sensitive.

196 See article 20(1) (c) of the African Children's Charter.

5.4.1.2.3. Pluralistic universalism and child labour

In rural communities in Africa every member of the family is expected to contribute to family wellbeing, according to his or her capacity. As a result, children have worked to ensure family survival. Such work was in accordance with the evolving capacity of children. Work and labour have a cultural and context-specific meaning and application: the capacity to engage in work differs from one person to another and varies even within the same age group.

In interpreting its mandate to protect children from engaging in hazardous labour, the African Children's Committee has to take into consideration the context and child-specific circumstances. For example, in some communities in Africa children in rural areas are sent to stay with family members in the urban areas.[197] These children engage in different forms of labour to help the family they are staying with. In turn, the children of the relatives are sent to school. The practice has a serious potential for abuse, but it is equally a useful mechanism for children to access education. Applying a pluralistic universalist theoretical framework will enable the African Committee to encourage the positive element and provide guidance to minimise the chance of abuse.

5.4.1.3. Pluralistic universalism and autonomy rights of children

This book has argued that autonomy rights, as provided for in the CRC, are not norms commonly shared by traditional communities in Africa. This is not denying the fact that there are proxy traditional values that serve some of the purposes of human rights and complement human rights. It is equally true that there are traditional values that are not harmful to children, without exact counterparts in the human rights regime. These differences make for conflict or tension between these two frameworks of value systems. In such circumstances, 'the greater the capacity to form links between competing frameworks, the greater the possibility of claiming validity across

197 E Omike 'In the best interests of the child: The case of child domestic workers in Ghana and Nigeria' in A Imoh & N Ansell (eds) (2014) *Children's lives in an era of children's rights: The progress of the Convention on the Rights of the Child in Africa.*

communities'[198] by the universal human rights. Pluralistic universalism provides the bridge that enhances cross-cultural validity of norms that protect children.

5.4.1.4. Pluralistic universalism and participation rights

From a pluralistic universalism perspective, child participation in decision-making is a universal phenomenon. The outcome should be universal - children taking part in decisions that affect their lives. However, how children should participate and what should constitute participation should be context-specific.

5.4.2. Implications of pluralistic universalism on the promotion and protection of children's rights in Africa

According to the International Centre 'for Book on Women (ICRWC) 'the highest prevalence of child marriage is concentrated in Western and Sub-Saharan Africa,'[199] child marriage is associated with fatal consequences for the girl child. 'Girls younger than 15 are five times more likely to die in childbirth than women in their 20s. Pregnancy is consistently among the leading causes of death for girls ages 15 to 19 worldwide.'[200] According to UNICEF, 'poverty, the perception that marriage will provide 'protection', family honour, social norms, customary or religious laws that condone the practice, an inadequate legislative framework and the state of a country's civil registration system'[201] are contributing factors to the high prevalence of child marriage.

---

198 M Freeman 'Culture, childhood and rights' (2011) 5 *Family in Law* 16.

199 http://www.icrw.org/child-marriage-facts-and-figures.

200 http://data.unicef.org/corecode/uploads/document6/uploaded_pdfs/corecode/Child-Marriage-Brochure-HR_164.pdf.

201 http://data.unicef.org/corecode/uploads/document6/uploaded_pdfs/corecode/Child-Marriage-Brochure-HR_164.pdf. Sometimes, there is a tendency to blur the differences between cultural practices and practices that are becoming cultural. While the former is a core component of a culture, the latter are practices introduced in a culture by external factors and usually embraced not by everyone practicing a practical cultural belief. A good example of the difference by two is what Kaime discusses in T Kaime 'The struggle for context in the protection of children's rights: Understanding the core concepts of the African Children's Charter' (2008) 58 *Journal of Legal Pluralism* 33.

According to the International Labour Organisation, 48 million children in sub-Saharan Africa are engaged in child labour.[202] Significant numbers of these children engage in the worst form of child labour.[203] These children are exposed to accidents and other injuries at work, sexual and physical abuse, emotional and physical neglect, serious health and developmental consequences.[204] One of the main causes of child labour is cultural values.[205]

According to the Global Initiative to End all Corporal Punishment of Children, the prevalence of corporal punishment of children in Africa is still one of the highest globally.[206] Cultural values are some of the contributing factors to the prevalence of corporal punishment in Africa.[207]

In the light of these enormous challenges facing children in Africa and the negative role culture is said to play in exacerbating these challenges, a call for more prominence of cultural values and context-specific considerations in the protection of children rights could easily be misconstrued as a licence for more abuse of children. Such concerns are not without justification. Abuses of children have resulted from cultural practices that have impacted negatively on the wellbeing of children in Africa.[208] Unbounded flexibility in the interpretation and application of children's rights could only compound an already precarious situation for children's rights in Africa.

---

202 ILO defines child labour as all forms of work by children under the age laid down in ILO standards (normally 15 years or the age of completion of compulsory schooling subject to some exceptions. See http://www.ilo.org/wcmsp5/groups/public/---ed_norm/---declaration/documents/publication/wcms_decl_fs_37_en.pdf.

203 According to ILO, worst forms of child labour include slavery, debt bondage, prostitution, pornography, forced recruitment of children for use in armed conflict, use of children in drug trafficking and other illicit activities, and all other work likely to be harmful or hazardous to the health, safety or morals of girls and boys under 18 years of age. See http://www.ilo.org/wcmsp5/groups/public/---ed_norm/---declaration/documents/publication/wcms_decl_fs_37_en.pdf.

204 http://www.ilo.org/ipec/Regionsandcountries/Africa/WCMS_101161/lang--en/index.htm.

205 http://www.ilo.org/ipec/Regionsandcountries/Africa/WCMS_101161/lang--en/index.htm.

http://www.ilo.org/ipec/Regionsandcountries/Africa/WCMS_101161/lang--en/index.htm.

206 http://www.endcorporalpunishment.org/pages/pdfs/reports/Report-AllAfrica.pdf.

207 http://www.endcorporalpunishment.org/pages/pdfs/reports/Report-AllAfrica.pdf.

208 P Welbourne 'Culture, children's rights and child protection' (2002) 11 *Child Abuse Review* 345; W Ncube Law, *culture, tradition and children's rights in East and Southern Africa* (1998) 18; M Freeman 'Culture, childhood and rights' (2011) 5 *The Family in Law* 21; D Engel 'Law, culture and children with disabilities: Educational rights and the construction of difference' (1991) 166 *Law, Culture & Disability* 166.

Nonetheless, the abuse of culture, which in turn results into abuses of children's rights and wellbeing, is not an indictment on culture and its usefulness as a tool to promote and protect the wellbeing of children in Africa. It is an indictment of abuses. It is these abuses that article 1(3) of the African Children's Charter addresses. However, there are aspects of cultures that do not result into abuses of children's rights, but that are nonetheless in conflict with the children's rights regime. Article 10 of the African Children's Charter providing for the right to privacy to all persons below the age of 18 and subject only to reasonable supervisions by parents, is one such example.[209] Another example is participation rights as espoused in the CRC.[210] It has been said that the traditional African family 'expects 'childhood' .... to be a continuous period of self-effacing obedience to traditional authority;' [211] child labour, child marriage and corporal punishment are some extreme examples already discussed in the course of this work that generate tensions at different levels.

The argument of this book is that when two valid norms governing behaviour - in this case, children's rights and cultural norms are regulating children's behaviour - clash, the tension should not necessarily be resolved always in favour of children's rights framework.[212] A child-case and context-specific approach that is in the best interests of that child should be used.[213] The assumption should not be that respect for children's rights as espoused in the African Children's Charter is in the best interests of the child in all circumstances; nor are cultural norms.

5.5. Conclusion

In addition to textual, substantive and normative similarities between the CRC and the African Children's Charter, the mandate and the working methods

209 P Nyaundi 'Circumcision and the rights of the Kenyan boy-child' (2005) a *African Human Rights Journal* 171; compare with paragraph 29 of the Committee on the Rights of the Child, General Comment No. 3, HIV/AIDS and the right of the child, U.N. Doc. CRC/GC/2003/3 (2003).

210 See the discussion on pages 175-179 of this book.

211 W Ncube *The African cultural fingerprint? The changing concept of childhood* (1998)18.

212 See the discussion in page 22, and 115-126 of this book.

213 For more details, see the discussion on pages 266 -270 and 291 -292.

of the African Children's Committee and those of the CRC Committee are similar. Also, the two treaty bodies have interpreted their mandates and the provisions of the treaty each of them monitors in a similar manner. Both treaty bodies address the same issues from almost the same theoretical and philosophical standpoint. If this trend continues, questions around the value added or the usefulness of the African Children's Committee will be increasingly asked. And, from an effectiveness and efficiency point of view, the voice of those calling for the abolition of the African Children's Committee or a complete reconfiguration of its mandate will grow louder and louder.

Before the three Optional Protocols to the CRC were adopted and entered into force, the explicit value of the African Children's Charter laid in its higher standard with respect to the definition of the child, its position regarding the roles of children in armed conflict, protection against harmful cultural practices, its provisions for effective protection of internally displaced children and children of imprisoned mothers, the girl child, and unequivocal standards with respect to the best interests of the child. Either through the Optional Protocols regime or through a progressive interpretation of the provisions of the CRC, the CRC Committee's jurisprudence covers almost all of these unique features of the African Children's Charter. It might not be possible to strongly defend the existence of the mandate of the African Children's Committee on the basis of these unique features since they no longer are truly 'unique'.

In order to interpret the African Children's Charter in accordance with the object and purpose of the drafters, the African Children's Committee need to adopt a flexible approach to discharging its mandate. The African Children's Charter empowers the African Children's Committee in discharging its mandate to take cognizance of the philosophical and cultural heritage of communities in Africa. Inherent in the preambular statement of the African Children's Charter is an understanding that African countries want a context-specific promotion and protection of children's rights and welfare. However, interpreting the African Children's Charter in such a context-specific manner should not mean that children in Africa do not benefit from the safeguards provided for in international human rights. What it means is that children in Africa should live, survive and develop in a positive atmosphere of African culture and traditions while benefiting from the positive norms of child upbringing in other parts of the world.

Unlike the CRC Committee, which presides over a universalist-inclined treaty, the African Children's Committee oversees a treaty that is universal but which, at the same time, defers to pluralistic tendencies in the rearing and upbringing of children. It is advisable that the African Children's Committee in discharging its duties operates within a framework that allows for universalist values to be mediated through local norms relating to children. The pluralistic universalism theoretical platform affords the African Children's Committee with the necessary flexibility to carry out its work in such a manner. Such an approach allows the African Children's Committee to develop a voice that is familiar to its constituency and an identity that fosters a constructive complementarity between the CRC and the African Children's Charter, as well as between the CRC Committee and the African Children's Committee.

CHAPTER 6

CONCLUSION AND RECOMMENDATIONS

6. Introduction

This chapter is divided into two parts. The first part outlines the findings of this book. It sketches the conceptions of childhood in the CRC and the African Children's Charter. The main finding of this part is that the image of children in the CRC and the African Children's Charter differs in some fundamental regards from the understanding of childhood by different communities in Africa. These differences in the conception of childhood create tension.

The second part makes recommendation. It recommends the review of some of the provisions of the African Children's Charter in order to incorporate some context-specific understanding of childhood in Africa. With respect to the mandate of the African Children's Committee, the book recommends several institutional and operational changes to the mandate of the African Children's Committee. In addition, it is recommended that the African Children's Committee adopts 'pluralistic universalism' as a philosophical framework that provides guidance to the African Children's Committee in its interpretation and application of the African Children's Charter.

6.1. Conclusion

6.1.1. The conception of childhood in the CRC

One of the greatest achievements of the CRC is the fact that it has universalised and legalised a uniform image of childhood for all countries and cultures. The CRC provides an overarching definition of who a child is, what should be considered to be or not to be in the best interests of the child, how society should see and treat children, what rights and autonomy children have and how children's voices should be received and treated. The CRC places obligations of conduct as well as obligations of results on state parties to ensure that children enjoy all the rights and privileges provided to them in the CRC. In addition, all state parties are expected to report on a regular basis about the progress they are making to ensure compliance with their obligations. The entry into force of the Optional Protocol on a Communications Procedure means that if state parties fail to comply with their obligations, children in the state parties that have become party to this Protocol have recourse to enforceable legal remedies at the international level.

The image of the child in the CRC could be summarised as follows:

1) A child is a human being below the age of 18 years.
2) A child is an autonomous, rights bearing, talking, thinking and deciding individual.
3) A child is an active citizen participating in all decisions affecting her or him.
4) A child's interest is paramount to all other considerations. Therefore, the family, communities and states should be organised to serve those interests.

This conception of childhood is in line with centuries of philosophical and political development in Western Europe and North America (these two geopolitical entities have been loosely referred to in the course of this book as the 'West') around the conception of personhood and the place of the individual in society. These philosophers and political scientists substantively agree with the judgment of Margaret Thatcher, the former Prime Minister of Great Britain, when she declared that 'there is no such thing as society. There are individual men and women, and there are families.'[1] In this context, society is seen as a mere voluntary association of individuals pursuing self-

1 Prime Minister Margaret Thatcher, talking to Women's Own Magazine October 31 1987 available at http://briandeer.com/social/thatcher-society.htm.

centred interests. For such an association of individuals to work, its constituent members must be autonomous in order to meaningfully contribute to the wellbeing of the association. In addition, it is logical that each member of the association should possess rights 'enforceable' against the association and should be in a position to participate in all the undertakings of the association on an equal footing with all other members. It would be illogical for children, as legitimate members of this association, not to be granted all the rights and privileges other members enjoy. The only distinction granted children by virtue of their vulnerability within this association of autonomous and self-focussed individuals, is to shield them against the burdens arising from such a societal arrangement wherein every individual is at liberty to pursue his or her welfare.

Societies organised on the basis of the equal autonomy, equal rights and equal liberty of all its members, irrespective of age, do not exist in all parts of the world. Nevertheless, it is such a society that is anticipated by the CRC. Therefore, by situating its image and understanding of childhood within a liberal tradition not commonly shared by all cultures and traditions, the CRC's conception of childhood excludes other images of childhood not compliant with or contradicting the CRC's own understanding of childhood. Where and when local understanding of childhood diverges from the conception of childhood in the CRC, the CRC Committee insists that state parties harmonise their local laws and values with the CRC. Harmonisation is used as a mechanism to transform local understandings of childhood by ensuring that the way local communities see and treat children conforms to the expectations in the CRC. The successful implementation of the CRC entails, to an extent, the elimination of local norms and values around childhood that are inconsistent with the CRC, and the substitution of those local values and norms with the CRC's values and norms.

6.1.2. The conception of childhood in traditional communities in Africa

There is substantial evidence to support the assertion that there exists a cross-cultural and trans-communal common core understanding of childhood in Africa. This common core understanding of childhood is not entirely incompatible with human rights but varies in a significant sense from the image of childhood in the CRC. The following common features are representative of the conception of childhood in traditional communities in Africa:

In traditional communities in Africa childhood starts at conception and ends at any time when the child demonstrates maturity, control over natural instincts or is able to marry and procreate. A child is generally considered to be a person-in-the-making. Thus, childhood is perceived as a journey of nurture and learning to become a complete or a full person.

In traditional communities in Africa children are conceptualised as semi-autonomous but dependant beings. On one hand, children are seen and treated as separate beings with interests that must be promoted and protected by everyone in the community. On the other, it is the duty of everyone in the community to mould the personhood of the child in line with the core communal values of respect, reciprocity, responsibility, restraint and reproduction of family lineage.

Children are active participants producing and reproducing cultural norms in traditional communities in Africa. However, they must participate in a culturally acceptable manner. This delicate balance allows children to think only within culturally acceptable confines, to talk only as permitted by custom, and participate only through acceptable customary means and modes of communication.

There is insufficient evidence to suggest that families in traditional Africa bring up children on the basis that children's best interests are paramount. There is evidence to suggest that families and traditional communities operate on the basis of a deferral of interest. By this is meant that when families and communities in traditional societies consider a course of action or inaction to be in the best interests of children, they defer to children's interest. If it is decided that certain actions or inactions are thought not to be in the immediate or medium term best interests of children, but necessary in the long term interest of children, families and communities, the child's best interests is subservient to the broader family or communal interest.

Some of these cultural values might be found to resemble human rights norms, but there is no substantial evidence to support the notion that the relationship between children and adults in traditional African communities is rights-based. There are privileges, roles and responsibilities associated with childhood. Respect for or disrespect of these privileges, roles and responsibilities will be either rewarded or sanctioned by the community. The interests of children and the interests of the family and communities are not clearly demarcated. Almost all African cultures and traditions have mechanisms that enable children to participate in societal decision-making, but their participation is not as a matter of rights, as it is understood by the CRC.

The aspects of childhood in traditional African communities that correspond to the features of childhood in the CRC, do not pose policy and implementation challenges in Africa. The challenge arises where there are divergences. As the book illustrates, there are divergences between the CRC and an African philosophical and cultural understanding of childhood. The perceived difference in the way the CRC conceptualises childhood and how childhood is understood in traditional communities was one of the reasons why the African Children's Charter was adopted.

6.1.3. The conception of childhood in the African Children's Charter

The adoption of the African Children's Charter was predicated on the limitations of the CRC and on the understanding that there were differences in the way childhood is seen and treated in traditional African communities and how it is portrayed in the CRC. For instance, in traditional African societies, childhood is understood to start from conception but does not have a definite endpoint. Childhood ends as soon as a child practically can demonstrate maturity or can take on mature roles and responsibilities, rather than measured by a numerical age.

In addition, the term 'child' or 'childhood' has biological and social connotations in traditional communities in Africa that differ from the meaning these terms have elsewhere. Sociologically, they refer to a perpetual relationship of mutual dependence between parents and their offspring, irrespective of age and maturity. Socially, if an individual, for instance, fails to start a family or undergo certain rituals, that person is considered in some communities in Africa to remain a 'child' irrespective of age or status. The practical implication is that a person is a 'child' as long as he or she lives, behaves, thinks and feels like a 'child'. On the other hand, an individual is considered mature enough to be an adult once he or she is physically strong, emotionally stable, and socially responsible, ready for, or actually married.

For many reasons, the definition of a 'child' in traditional African communities is more complex than the image of childhood presented in the CRC. In a number of communities in Africa, the prerogative to declare a human being either a child or an adult is vested in the traditions and customs of the community. This determination of status is not based on the number of years one has lived, but on the demonstrated evidence of maturity. Whether a human being is a baby, a child, a 'youth', an adult or an elder is determined in traditional African societies on the basis of biology, physical development, ability and status. With the exception perhaps of babyhood, each milestone entails special protection, privileges as well as roles and obligations. A ritual is performed to mark an exit from one stage of development and to qualify an individual for entry into the next developmental phase.

The African Children's Charter was intended to be a potential harmoniser of conflicting values that could assimilate the relevant values from the CRC and at the same time promote and protect an African philosophy of childhood and cultural heritage. The drafters of the African Children's Charter, however, did not adequately reflect an African philosophical and cultural heritage in the African Children's Charter. The adoption of the African Children's Charter addressed African-specific challenges facing children in Africa and offered them a higher threshold of protection. However, textually and substantively, the African Children's Charter does not adequately reflect and respond to an African understanding of childhood rooted in an African cultural heritage and philosophy of life. Though, in its Preamble, the African Children's Charter expresses its intention to be culturally and context-specific, in many respects it is predominantly a mere transplant of the CRC.

The conception of childhood in the African Children's Charter is in line with that encapsulated in the CRC. For instance, in the African Children's Charter, childhood is understood as follows:

1) A child is a human being below the age of 18 years.
2) A child is an autonomous, rights bearing, talking, thinking and deciding individual.
3) A child is an active citizen participating in all decisions affecting her or him.
4) A child's interest is the primary consideration.

6.1.4. The implication of the differences in the conception of childhood between the CRC and African Children's Charter, on one hand, and traditional communities in Africa, on the other

The implementation of human rights norms and values is less troublesome when local communities perceive them as being closer or relevant to their local values. The difference in the conception of childhood between the CRC and the African Children's Charter, on one hand, and the conception of childhood by traditional communities in Africa, on the other, is a difference in form and content. The consequence of such a significant divergence of views on the effective and efficient implementation of children's rights is considerable. The CRC and the African Children's Charter intend to modify local values, norms and practices around child rearing and upbringing, in Africa, through assimilation by harmonisation.

It has been argued in this book that underpinning the concept of harmonisation is the premise that the successful implementation of the provisions of the CRC, and by extension the African Children's Charter, in contexts that do not conform in their understanding of childhood to the image of childhood in the CRC and the African Children's Charter, entails a reformulation of socio-political, socio-economic and socio-cultural norms, values and institutions of the host communities in order to conform to the expectations of the CRC and the African Children's Charter. The conception of childhood and the underlying values in the CRC and the African Children's Charter constitute a new cultural conception of childhood and a new norm and set of values on how children should be seen and treated, which are alienated from those that exist among various cultures, specifically, in Africa.

Since childhood, family and culture are interrelated, the new cultural conception of childhood introduced by the CRC and the African Children's Charter has implications for the nature and forms of family structures in cultures different from the neoliberal socio-political context of rights-based treaties. For most children, childhood is experienced in a family environment. The successful implementation of the conception of childhood, as it is envisaged in the CRC and the African Children's Charter, will require neoliberal family values and structures to be implemented as a first step towards creating a sustaining local context to support the understanding of childhood. By implication, the nature, structure, roles and responsibilities of the family must change in order to facilitate a transformation in the fundamental nature of adult-child relationships that is needed to support the new concept of childhood. Such a change is fundamental because the family setting envisaged in the CRC and the African Children's Charter is such that the rights parents have, with respect to their children are essentially functional: they serve the best interests of the child. In this functional sense, children are in charge of their own lives, and take rational decisions. This form of family structure is not common to all societies.

The successful implementation of the CRC and the African Children's Charter is dependent on a process of societal transformation that results in a new cultural value system. The task of embedding the conception of childhood in the CRC and the African Children's Charter in Africa is a monumental, time consuming and expensive undertaking. First, it is not easy for families and communities to alter age-old family values and patterns and to embrace new ones. Second, as a result of the efforts to replace local values with new ones, time and resources that could have been used to improve the wellbeing of children are used to promote and protect a particular image of childhood and to transform societal values to reflect this particular understanding of childhood.

For the transformative mission of the CRC and the African Children's Charter to succeed, policy makers must empower children to claim these rights against every contextual odd and, at the same time, empower communities to change the way in which they understand childhood. Children in traditional African communities could adapt perhaps quickly to how the CRC and the African Children's Charter conceptualise them, their roles and relationship with a wider society. If the societies in which the children live are slow to accept or adapt to the new conception of childhood and the roles of children, it could result in an inter-generational clash. Such an eventuality could have a serious impact on the harmonious existence of families and societies in Africa. In such a scenario the CRC's and the African Children's Charter's image of childhood might, albeit indirectly and unintentionally, in traditional societies, fossilise the social context in which children live. At least in this sense, children's rights as provided for in the CRC and the African Children's Charter divorces children from the local context wherein childhood is spent on a daily basis and replace it with international child rearing norms and practices. If care is not taken, such an approach will weaken parent-society-child ties and, ultimately, may not be in the best interests of children.

Conceptualising childhood, as the CRC and the African Children's Charter do, in a manner incompatible with the norms and values of family structures in traditional communities in Africa endangers the institution whose health and harmonious cohesion is essential to the life, survival and development of the child. The prototype of the universal child espoused in the CRC and the African Children's Charter is not incompatible with family values and norms in some parts of the world and, to some extent, in urban settings in Africa. If the *grundnorm* that informs the conception of childhood in the CRC and the African Children's Charter is incompatible with how traditional communities in Africa understand childhood; it is desirable that these communities must adjust their cultural norms and embrace the new culture of childhood proposed in the CRC and the African Children's Charter or the ground impact of these treaties will significantly become compromised.

The danger inherent in the conception of childhood in the CRC and the African Children's Charter lies not only in the possible fracture of harmonious societal relationships, but also in the possible distortion of the nature of childhood. Children inherently are dependent persons - a natural, not a legal fact. Placing children and their parents on the same footing as co-autonomous persons in their relationship with the state and insisting that parents and people with the responsibility to take care of children should acknowledge children's autonomy and let them speak for themselves and decide their needs, the CRC and the African Children's Charter, indirectly and unintentionally, could be seen by some communities as trying to push children to assume adult responsibilities and roles too early. In the absence of a mature and strong state and institutional infrastructure in such a situation, the child might be endangered.

For the transformative image of childhood in the CRC and the African Children's Charter to function effectively and efficiently, certain preconditions must be met. These are: A strong and reliable state infrastructure; a good governance culture; and a flexible cultural and traditional context. The existence of these preconditions is not exclusively within the ability of the CRC and the African Children's Charter to create. Furthermore, using the instrumentality of law to force a social transformation considered alien might not be without negative social side effects for children, their families and communities. As mentioned, the possible challenges that could result from such an approach include a multi-layered childhood experience as a result of the duality of culture and a hybridity of expectations; dysfunctional child to family relationships; and the weakening of the social fabric that sustains child-rearing practices.

The argument is not that the conception of childhood in the CRC and the African Children's Charter is wrong, but that the understanding of childhood in the CRC and the African Children's Charter is problematic if divorced from the context that produced the image of childhood and if implemented in non-similar contexts. The history of childhood vulnerability and abuse, the great insights of the Enlightenment period, the economic prosperity of Western society, the various agitations for equality, autonomy and liberty by slaves, blacks and women, and the individualisation of citizens in the West influenced those who conceptualised the child in the CRC and later in the African Children's Charter.

Not all societies have undergone that transformation or acquired the competencies and built the institutions and mechanisms that allow such competencies to thrive. Not all societies value the competencies, institutions and mechanisms that have emerged in the West as a result of its historical, political and economic peculiarities. For instance, what an individual brought up in an individualistic society holds in high regard might be different from the values of an individual from a communitarian society. An individual's needs are met by the state in a neoliberal context; the family is the essential institution in communities without strong state institutions. Someone from a neoliberal society is comfortable with state authority over children and unworried about parental rights and authority, whereas a person from communities with fragile and non-state infrastructure might prefer parental authority over children to that of the state.

Autonomous childhood and responsible parenting are not and should not be mutually exclusive. What is problematic in non-liberal societies is the CRC's and the African Children's Charter's effort to elevate the child and his or her interest above that of the family. In traditional communities in Africa the family interest is equated with the child's interest. In addition, the CRC's and the African Children's Charter's attempt to link the child directly to the state, thereby introducing the state's presence into every family, may be problematic for communities where the state is a distant presence. Replacing parental paternalism with state paternalism is not only unrealistic in these communities; but it is also difficult to understand how state paternalism, in and of itself, confers children with autonomy and liberty.

An additional point is that enforcing a particular image of childhood on other parts of the world runs the risk of not adequately meeting all the childbearing and childrearing needs of communities in other contexts. Societies invent and reinvent themselves to meet and accommodate changing needs and circumstances. For these processes to be comprehensive they must be internally driven and must involve all sectors of the community. The transformation anticipated within the framework of the CRC is perceived by communities and sometimes by state parties as alien to local values and norms in Africa.

6.1.5. Specific implications of the differences in the conception of childhood in the African Children's Charter and traditional communities in Africa

The first specific challenge that the African Children's Charter faces revolves around its legitimacy. The failure of the African Children's Charter to promote and portray an African understanding of childhood exposes it to the accusation of a lack of cultural legitimacy. In some instances, the CRC is more flexible and accommodating to the unique features of child rearing in traditional communities in Africa than the African Children's Charter. For example, article 5 of the CRC is wider in its anticipation of circles of care for a child and more in tune with childcare practices in Africa than the African Children's Charter.

The second specific challenge is that the similarity between the CRC and the African Children's Charter makes the latter look like an unnecessary duplication of the former. In addition to normative similarities between the CRC and the African Children's Charter, the mandate and working methods of the African Children's Committee and those of the CRC Committee are similar. So far, there has been little difference in how the two treaty bodies interpret their mandates and the provisions of the treaty each of them monitors. Both treaty bodies largely address the same issues from the same theoretical and philosophical standpoints. If this trend continues, questions around the need for an African Children's Charter and the African Children's Committee increasingly will be asked. From an efficiency point of view, the voice of those calling for the abolition of the African Children's Charter and the African Children's Committee or for a complete reconfiguration of the mandate of the African Children's Committee will be strengthened.

At the time of its adoption the African Children's Charter had a number of features, which distinguished it from the CRC. Before the three Optional Protocols to the CRC were adopted and entered into force, the explicit value of the African Children's Charter were in its high standards with respect to the definition of the child , its categorical position regarding the roles of children in armed conflict, its protection against harmful cultural practices, its recognition and protection of internally displaced children and children of imprisoned mothers, its specific protection of the girl child, and unequivocal standard with respect to the best interests of the child. However, the combined effect of the three Optional Protocols to the CRC and the very progressive interpretation of the provisions of the CRC by the CRC Committee mean that almost all of the unique features of the African Children's Charter have been subsumed under the CRC regime. It might no longer be possible to defend the existence of the mandate of the African Children's Committee on the basis of these unique features if they no longer are as 'unique' as they used to be. Unless the African Children's Committee innovatively interprets its mandate in a way that fills in the gaps in the manner in which the CRC Committee discharges its mandate, its role may be called into question.

6.1.6. The role of the African Children's Committee in narrowing the gap between the conceptions of childhood in the CRC and the African Children's Charter and the understanding of childhood by communities in Africa

As demonstrated in the book, the divergence in the conception of childhood in Africa is not merely an academic creation. These differences in the understanding of childhood impact daily on the lived experience of children. Children daily fluctuate between different regimes governing their childhood experiences. For instance, in school and in public places they might be considered children within the meaning of the CRC and the African Children's Charter, but at home or participating in the culture of their communities they might be seen and treated as adults. There is a role for the African Children's Committee to mitigate this sense of duality or hybridity in which children in Africa live their childhood.

The African Children's Committee occupies a privileged position as the only regional child rights mechanism that has been established to protect children within the framework of a regional philosophy of human rights and cultural heritage. Inherent in this move by countries in Africa to adopt a culturally specific human rights treaty on children is an understanding that state parties wanted an African context-specific application of children's rights. These countries wanted to allow children in Africa to benefits from the 'best' of both worlds. African countries want children to be brought up in accordance with the cultural traditions of their communities and also to be allowed to benefit from other cultural norms that might have been crystallised through the CRC.

Unlike the CRC Committee, that presides over a universal children's rights treaty, the African Children's Committee oversees a treaty that is universal but which, if flexibly interpreted, at the same time, should concede to pluralistic tendencies in the rearing and upbringing of children in different African communities. It is advisable that in the discharge of its duties, the African Children's Committee operates within a framework that allows for universal values to be mediated through local norms relating to children. The 'pluralistic universalism' theoretical platform should afford the African Children's Committee the necessary flexibility to carry out its work in such a manner. Such an approach will allow the African Children's Committee to develop a voice that is familiar to its constituency and an identity that fosters a constructive complementarity between the CRC and the African Children's Charter as well as between the CRC Committee and the African Children's Committee. It is against that background that the following recommendations are made.

6.2. Recommendations

6.2.1. A review of the African Children's Charter

The African Children's Charter in its current form is a duplication of the CRC. After the adoption of the Optional Protocols, it is no longer distinguishable normatively from the CRC as amended. In addition, the African Children's Charter has not, in a meaningful way, inculcated an African philosophical and cultural understanding of childhood into the promotion and protection of children's rights and welfare in Africa. Retaining the African Children's Charter in its current form is not a cost-effective way for the continent to promote and protect the rights of its children. In the absence of any significant difference between the CRC and the African Children's Charter, reporting under the two treaties as well as funding the effective functioning of the African Children's Committee increases the procedural cost of guaranteeing the rights and welfare of children in a continent struggling to raise resources to meet basic needs.

To enhance the ability of the African Children's Charter to offer a better and holistic protection of children in Africa, it is recommended that the African Children's Charter should be reviewed to benefit from the positive aspects of African philosophical and cultural understandings of childhood, some of which have been highlighted in this book and include articulating a context sensitive definition of childhood and cultural norms that encourage collective and social intelligence.

Specifically, it is recommended that the following provisions relevant to the discussion in this book should be amended.

6.2.1.1. Definition of the child

Article 2 of the African Children's Charter states 'for the purposes of this Charter a child means every human being below the age of 18 years.' It is recommended that this article should read:

(1) For the purposes of this Charter, a child means every human being below the age of eighteen years unless under the law, customs and tradition of a people applicable to the child, majority is attained earlier.

(2) *Any decision to grant majority earlier than 18 years and in accordance with national laws, customs and traditions, should take cognisance of the best interests of the child.*[2]

By introducing the concepts of 'a people', 'customs' and 'traditions' in defining who a child is in Africa, the proposed amendment takes cognisance of the cultural and philosophical heritage of the child in Africa. The danger inherent in a flexible definition of childhood is potential abuse, especially of the girl child. Many African countries are struggling to eliminate child marriage. A

2 The words in italics are those proposed for insertion into the existing article.

flexible and opened-ended definition of childhood indirectly encourages the harmful practice of child marriage in Africa.

Arguably, the risk of abuse inherent in a flexible and context-specific application of children's rights norms is not insurmountable. Three approaches are suggested here that could minimise the chance of abuse:

First, an individualised and case-by-case approach should be adopted when categorising children for the purpose of protection. For example, it might be harmful for a girl child below 16 years of age to be married; preventing a girl of 17 years from getting married to her lover does not serve the same protective purpose.

Second, in determining whether a context-specific value or norm should be allowed to apply to children, the litmus test of harmfulness introduced by the African Children's Committee in its draft General Comment 2 should be used. According to the African Children's Committee, a practice condoned by culture is said to be harmful if such a practice is capable of imperilling, undermining or prejudicing the life, dignity, growth and development of the child. The burden of demonstrating that a cultural practice is detrimental to child wellbeing is on the government.

Third, in order to minimise the chances of abuse, it is recommended that the concept of the 'best interests' of the child be introduced to validate definitions by national laws, customs and traditions. It is up to the African Children's Committee in constructive conversations with state parties to give a context-specific content to the concept of the 'best interests' of the child.

6.2.1.2. The best interests of the child

The current provision of article 4 of the African Children's Charter reads:

> 1. In all actions concerning the child undertaken by any person or authority the best interests of the child shall be the primary consideration.
>
> 2. In all judicial or administrative proceedings affecting a child who is capable of communicating his/her own views, an opportunity shall

> be provided for the views of the child to be heard either directly or through an impartial representative as a party to the proceedings, and those views shall be taken into consideration by the relevant authority in accordance with the provisions of appropriate law.

It is recommended that article 4 of the African Children's Charter be reviewed to read as follows:

1. In all *decisions* and actions concerning the child undertaken by any person or authority either in the formal or *customary settings* the best interests of the child shall be the primary consideration.

2. In all judicial, administrative and *other proceedings* affecting a child who is capable of communicating his/her own views an opportunity shall be provided for the views of the child to be heard either directly or through an impartial representative as a party to the proceedings, and those views shall be taken into consideration by the relevant authority in accordance with the provisions of appropriate law *or custom.*[3]

It has been argued in the course of this book that 'actions' as used in article 4 of the African Children's Charter gives the impression that the determination process of the best interests of the child is an overly legal process. Including 'decisions' in article 4 of the African Children's Charter will widen the scope of the provision to include non-legal and non-formal processes that affect children. The intention to include children living in traditional settings and governed by traditional norms is reinforced by the insertion of 'customary setting, or custom.' So also, the expression 'other proceedings' is intended to cover customary law and traditional processes that might affect children but fall outside the 'judicial' and 'administrative' proceedings provided for in article 4 of the African Children's Committee.

6.2.1.3. Autonomy and liberty rights

Articles 7, 8, 9 and 10 of the African Children's Charter express autonomy and liberty rights provisions. These provisions situate autonomy and liberty as

3 The italics words are the suggested amendments.

legal concepts devoid of cultural dimensions. It has been argued in the course of this work that agency, which is at the root of autonomy and liberty rights, is a legal and a cultural construct. Therefore, the inclusion of the cultural dimension of autonomy and liberty within the ambit of articles 7-10 of the African Children's Charter will be theoretically appropriate and in line with the object and purpose of the African Children's Charter as stated in the Preamble. One of such object and purpose is to ensure that African philosophy and cultural heritage be infused in the interpretation of the African Children's Charter.

Therefore, it is recommended that articles 7 to 10 of the African Children's Charter be amended as follows:

The current article 7 reads:

> Every child who is capable of communicating his or her own views shall be assured the rights to express his opinions freely in all matters and to disseminate his opinions subject to such restrictions as are prescribed by laws.

It is proposed that article 7 should read:

Every child who is capable of communicating his or her own views shall be assured the rights to express his opinions freely in all matters and to disseminate his opinions subject to such restrictions as are prescribed by laws, *custom and tradition.*[4]

The current article 8 reads:

> Every child shall have the right to free association and freedom of peaceful assembly in conformity with the law.

The proposed article 8 should read:

Every child shall have the right to free association and freedom of peaceful assembly in conformity with the law, *customs and tradition.*[5]

---

4 Italics indicate the words that should be added to the current provisions in the course of an amendment.

5 Italics indicate the words that should be added to the current provisions in the course of an amendment.

The current article 9 reads:

> 1. Every child shall have the right to freedom of thought conscience and religion.
>
> 2. Parents, and where applicable, legal guardians shall have a duty to provide guidance and direction in the exercise of these rights having regard to the evolving capacities, and best interests of the child.
>
> 3. States Parties shall respect the duty of parents and where applicable, legal guardians to provide guidance and direction in the enjoyment of these rights subject to the national laws and policies.

The proposed article 9 should read:

1. Every child shall have the right to freedom of thought conscience and religion.

2. Parents, and where applicable, legal guardians and *extended family members with responsibility of care for the child*, shall have a duty to provide guidance and direction in the exercise of these rights having regard to the evolving capacities, *cultural values and norms that are in the* best interests of the child.[6]

3. States Parties shall respect the duty of parents and where applicable, legal guardians *and other caregivers* to provide guidance and direction in the enjoyment of these rights subject to the national laws and policies, *cultural norms and tradition.*[7]

The current article 10 reads:

> No child shall be subject to arbitrary or unlawful interference with his privacy, family home or correspondence, or to the attacks upon his honour or reputation, provided that parents or legal guardians shall have the right to exercise reasonable supervision over the conduct of their children. The child has the right to the protection of the law against such interference or attacks.

6 Italics indicate the words that should be added to the current provisions in the course of an amendment.

7 Italics indicate the words that should be added to the current provisions in the course of an amendment.

The proposed article 10 should read:

No child shall be subject to arbitrary or unlawful interference with his privacy, family home or correspondence, or to the attacks upon his honour or reputation, provided that parents or legal guardians *and other caregivers* shall have the right to exercise reasonable supervision over the conduct of their children in accordance *with law, cultural norms and tradition*. The child has the right to the protection of the law against such interference or attacks.[8]

The cultural norms and traditions provided for in these recommendations are those that are in the best interests of the child. What is in the best interests of children should be determined in a context-specific and case-by-case basis.

6.2.1.4. Child participation

Child participation is a right as it is a means of achieving other rights: it underpins all the rights in the African Children's Charter. The specific provision in the African Children's Charter that captures the right to participation is article 4(2) that reads:

> In all judicial or administrative proceedings affecting a child who is capable of communicating his/her own views, an opportunity shall be provided for the views of the child to be heard either directly or through an impartial representative as a party to the proceedings, and those views shall be taken into consideration by the relevant authority in accordance with the provisions of appropriate law.

It is recommended that this provision should read:

In all judicial or administrative *or other* proceedings affecting a child who is capable of communicating his/her own views, an opportunity shall be provided for the views of the child to be heard either directly or through an impartial representative as a party to the proceedings, and those views shall be taken into consideration by the relevant authority in accordance with the provisions of appropriate law, *cultural norms and values and tradition*.

---

8 Italics indicate the words that should be added to the current provisions in the course of an amendment.

Including cultural norms, values and tradition in this provision will ensure that traditional and cultural practices around child participation in traditional communities in Africa are not neglected.

6.2.2. Institutional reform of the African Children's Charter

In the light of the similarities between the African Children's Charter and the CRC, the African Children's Charter could be seen to be duplicative and an unwise use of time and scarce resources that could otherwise be utilized directly to improve the wellbeing of children in Africa. Carried to its logical conclusion, viewing the African Children's Charter as an 'echo chamber' of the CRC could lead to legitimate questions about the utility of a standalone regional treaty on children in Africa. In the absence of a strong counterargument, a proposal to re-enact the provisions of the African Children's Charter as a protocol to the ACHPR akin to the Protocol to the African Charter on Human and Peoples' Rights on the Rights of Women in Africa maybe plausible. Such a move could facilitate rationality and effective complementarity in the architecture of the African human rights system and reduce operational costs: the promotional and protective mandates in the African human rights system would be streamlined, rationalised and harmonised.

A srong argument could be made for a need to retain the African Children's Charter as it stands. An additional layer of human rights protection for the most vulnerable of society is desirable. Protecting human rights may be costly, but the implications of a failure to protect them are even more costly. In addition, even though textually two treaties may be similar, it does not automatically mean that the supervising treaty mechanisms will interpret the treaties in similar ways. Furthermore, the value of a specific treaty is obvious and that is why various categories of vulnerable people continue to clamour for an interest group specific treaty to better protect them. For a category that makes up more than half of the population of the continent, it is worthwhile and commendable to offer children in Africa treaty-specific protection.

However, multiplicities of human rights treaty bodies do not necessarily translate into effective promotion and protection of children's rights. Ideally, it is a commendable undertaking for Africa to have a regional children's rights treaty. However, unless if the African Children's Committee finds its unique voice on children's rights and foster a distinctive, credible but complementary identity, retaining it in its current configuration in the long run may not be, pragmatically, sustainable. First, there are funding constraints; and second, there is a possibility of eventuality of state apathy as a result of the multiple obligations arising under the different treaties within the African human rights system. Consolidating promotional mandates in one institution should not automatically lead to marginalisation of different categories of vulnerable groups. The experience of the African Commission on Human and Peoples' Rights tends to indicate that different vulnerable groups such as women and indigenous people are receiving attention.[9]

The longer it takes for the African Children's Committee to justify its existence, not in contradiction to the CRC Committee but in how the African Children's Committee extents and expands context-specific promotion and protection of children's rights in Africa, the stronger the case will be for the African Children's Charter to be re-enacted as a Protocol to the African Charter on Human and Peoples' Rights on the Rights and Welfare of Children in Africa. This could be done within the framework of article 18(3) of the ACHPR. The number of Commissioners on the African Commission on Human and Peoples' Rights could be increased to accommodate Commissioners with children's rights and welfare expertise. Such additional number of Commissioners should be significant enough to constitute a Chamber of the African Commission on Human and Peoples' Rights dealing with children's rights issues, such as monitoring, investigation of gross, systematic and systemic violations of children's rights and possible referrals to the African Court.

Bringing the African Children's Charter within the framework of the ACHPR and merging the two monitoring bodies should strengthen the promotion and protection of children's rights and welfare in Africa. It would ensure that children's rights and welfare not only are positioned in the mainstream

9 The African Commission on Human and Peoples' Rights have established a Working Group on Indigenous People, have established a Special Rapporteur on Women's Rights and facilitated the process of adopting and reporting under the Women's Protocol.

through the work of the African Commission, but also receive specific attention within the Chamber on children's rights. It would also ensure that the promotion and protection of children's rights benefit from the decades of institutional learning in the African Commission. More broadly, the re-enactment of the African Children's Charter as a Protocol to the ACHPR will streamline human rights promotion within the African human rights system and reduce the cost of the operation.

6.2.3. Operational reform of the African Children's Charter

Since a proposition to re-enact the African Children's Charter as a Protocol to the ACHPR at the moment maybe premature and radical, an alternative is for State Parties to carry out the following operational improvements to the mandate and functions of the African Children's Committee:

6.2.3.1. Receiving and consideration of state party reports

The comparative advantage of quasi-judicial over judicial bodies lies in the ability of the former to monitor the day-to-day implementation and compliance with human rights norms and standards in the absence of a complaint. Therefore, it is recommended that the mandate of the African Children's Committee to receive and consider state party reports with respect to the progress being made in the implementation of the provisions of the African Children's Charter be maintained. However, maintaining the mandate in its current form will not address the concerns around duplication and redundancy of procedures. The timeframe and the nature of reporting provided within the African Children's Charter should be changed.

With respect to the timeframe for reporting, expecting state parties to submit reports every three years will be burdensome and discourage compliance by state parties with respect to their reporting obligations or affect the quality of reports that are submitted. Equally, the frequency of reporting affects the ability of the African Children's Committee, composed entirely of part-time members who meet only for a limited number of days in a year, to thoroughly consider and issue specific, targeted and functional concluding observations every three years. In a bid to reduce the backlog and be seen to be efficient, the African Children's Committee might resort to formulaic methods of disposing of reports that will not enhance the promotion and the protection of the rights and welfare of children in Africa. It is, therefore, recommended that the reporting timeframe be extended, at least, to a five year-cycle.

Relating to the nature of the report itself, it is recommended that the current reporting format that requires state parties to report on all the provisions of the African Children's Charter be reviewed. To report on all the measures taken to promote and protect children's rights is a massive undertaking: hardly any measure or combination of measures conceivably doesn't have a direct or indirect implication for the realisation of the rights and welfare of children in the short, medium and long term. In a bid to guide state parties to report on everything, state party guidelines from the African Children's Committee in the past have been extremely generic. On the part of the states, in their efforts to report on everything, state parties usually end up submitting shallow reports, which omit important dimensions of their intervention on children's rights and welfare issues.

Therefore, it is recommended that an à *la carte* approach to reporting by state parties be adopted by the African Children's Committee. Under such an arrangement, the African Children's Committee will provide guidance to a state party with respect to which article or group of articles such a state party should report on. This approach will facilitate a comprehensive review of the records of the state party on specific issues pertinent to that country. Because the reporting requirement is tailor-made to address the most serious challenges facing children in a given state party, it is easy to recommend a targeted intervention, follow up that intervention and encourage an incremental improvement in the promotion and protection of rights and welfare of children in the territory of a state party.

Furthermore, such an arrangement will place the burden of requesting a report on the African Children's Committee thereby making the African Children's Charter reporting mechanism more proactive than the wait-to-receive regime that operates now. In the event of state parties failing to submit a requested report, the African Children's Committee could solicit information specific to the issues they are interested in from other stakeholders. The African Children's

Committee could also activate its mandate to investigate and report on the specific issue. Thematic reporting could ensure that the overarching principles of the African Children's Charter be highlighted in every single article and issue reviewed or reported on.

6.2.3.2. The protective mandate of the African Children's Committee

Adjudicating individual communications is not an effective means of promoting and protecting the rights and welfare of children by a quasi-judicial body. In Africa, where the record of compliance even with judicial decisions is low, adjudicating alleged violations of children's rights by the African Children's Committee made more sense when Africa, as a region, did not have a regional judicial body. The advent of the African Court on Human and Peoples' Rights may mean that the African Children's Committee should invest less of its resources in its communication function and more into other forms of protection mandate including the power to carry out investigative missions into alleged violations and when it deems it necessary to refer such allegations of massive and systematic violation of children's rights and welfare to the African Court. In any decision given by the Court in a case referred to the Court by the African Children's Committee, the African Court could mandate the African Children's Committee to monitor the implementation of such a decision.

To facilitate this innovation, article 44 of the African Children's Charter mandating the African Children's Committee to receive communications should be amended to give an express mandate to the African Court to receive complaints on the violation of children's rights through the African Children's Committee. A provision similar to article 27 of the Protocol to the African Charter on Human and Peoples' Rights on the Rights of Women in Africa should be inserted in the place of the current article 44 of the African Children's Charter. Under such an arrangement, the African Children's Committee's main assignment with respect to communication would be processing it and defending it before the African Court, together with or on behalf of the victim(s).

In order for the African Children's Committee effectively and efficiently to process complaints and defend them before the African Court, it is pertinent that some members of the African Children's Committee should be lawyers. Therefore, it is recommended that sub paragraph 4 be inserted into article 33 of the African Children's Charter to the effect that at least 3 members of the African Children's Committee shall be lawyers or have legal training.

Two concerns arise as a result of this recommendation: The first concern relates to the possible impact of this recommendation on access to justice. The second arises with respect to the possibility of inundating the African Court with cases, which might eventually lead to children's rights not receiving the appropriate attention before the African Court. With respect to the first concern, enabling children to access justice from the African Court rather than from the African Children's Committee should not negatively affect access to justice for children. The prospect of rich and binding jurisprudence from the African Court on children's rights issues in Africa should aid the cause of justice for children and not hinder it.

The second concern is a capacity concern on the part of the African Court to handle all the cases that might come before it. Failure is a real possibility. However, there are mechanisms in place in international law to minimise such a risk. First, complaints are not supposed to reach the African Children's Committee and, through the African Children's Committee, the African Court if available remedy at the local level has not been exhausted. Second, the African Children's Committee in its guidelines could decide which communications merit to be transferred to the African Court. Third, should the African Court become inundated with cases, there are mechanisms that could be put in place either to appoint full time judges, as in the European human rights system, increase the number of judges or establish new chambers to deal with these issues.

6.2.4. A change in the philosophical and theoretical inclination of the African Children's Committee

A review, in the context of this book, of how the African Children's Committee has discharged its mandate reveals an inclination to operate within a purely universal human rights paradigm. This philosophical and theoretical disposition should not pose a problem if the provisions of the African Children's Charter were purely predicated on universal human rights thinking. What is clear from the Preamble and some of the substantive provisions of the African Children's Charter is that the drafters of the African Children's Charter intended a treaty that marries universalism with cultural and philosophical particularism in Africa. In practice, the African Children's Committee should discharge its mandates in a manner that sees and treats universal images of childhood through African cultural and philosophical lenses. The mandate of the African Children's Committee stands at the intersection between a universal understanding of who a child is, what is in a child's best interests, what rights should be accorded children and how children should participate in social decision-making and implementation processes, on one hand, and African philosophical and cultural norms, on the other.

To successfully carry out this dual and delicate balancing mandate, the African Children's Committee needs to adopt and place centrally a theoretical position that provides a justification for how the African Children's Committee discharges its mandate. There are a number of mixed theoretical postulations for the African Children's Committee to select from. As indicated in the course of this book, the most appropriate theoretical framework that effectively accommodates the dual nature of the mandate of the African Children's Committee is the 'universal pluralistic' theory. This theory permits a variation of universal norms to accommodate local contexts that satisfy commonly agreed standards.

This theoretical framework will ensure that the African Children's Committee in the discharge of its mandate ameliorates the challenges children and state parties face in Africa with respect to the duality of the lived experience of children. It will also facilitate the documentation of and highlight positive cultural values and norms around childhood in Africa. Eventually, it may result in a constructive conversation on children's wellbeing between the African Children's Committee and the CRC Committee, on one hand, and among cultures and traditions in Africa, on the other. The African Children's Committee has a mandate to promote, protect and project the best in Africa's child rearing norms and values as it also inserts into the continent the best norms and values from other parts of the world.

Bibliography

Books, chapter in books and articles

Abd-Allah U 'Islam and the cultural imperative' (2003) 8 *Journal of Islamic Law and Culture* 89

Abebe T & Tefera T 'Earning rights: Discourses on children's rights and proper childhood in Ethiopia' in Imoh A & Ansell N (eds) (2014) *Children's lives in an era of children's rights: The progress of the Convention on the Rights of the Child in Africa* Routledge: Oxon

Achebe C (1994) *Things fall apart* New Jersey: Book and Education Association

Addo M 'Practice of United Nations human rights treaty bodies in the reconciliation of cultural diversity with universal respect for human rights' (2010) 32 *Human Rights Quarterly* 601

Aguilar M (1998) *The politics of age and gerontocracy in Africa* Trenton: Africa World Press

Aiken W & LaFollette H (eds) (1980) *Whose child? Parental rights, parental authority and state power* Totowa: Rowman and Littlefield

Aitken S 'Global crises of childhood: Rights, justice and the unchildlike child' (2001) 33 *Area* 119

Alanen L 'Gender and generation: Feminisms and the 'child question' in Qvortrup J *et al* (eds) (1994) *Childhood matters* Aldershot: Avebury

Alanen L 'Rethinking childhood' (1988) 31 *Acta Socioligica* 53

Alston P & Crawford J (eds) (2000) *The future of human rights treaty monitoring* Cambridge: Cambridge University Press

Alston P & Gilmour-Walsh B (1996) *The best interests of the child: Towards a synbook of children's rights and cultural values* (Innocenti Studies, UNICEF International Child Development Centre)

Alston P (ed) (1994) *The best interests of the child: Reconciling culture and human rights* Oxford: Oxford University Press

Alston P 'The legal framework of the Convention on the Rights of the Child' (1992) 2 *Bulletin of Human Rights* 9

Alston P 'The unborn child and abortion under the draft Convention on the Rights of the Child' (1990) 12 *Human Rights Quarterly* 156

Alston P 'The Committee on Economic, Social and Cultural Rights' in Alston P (ed) (1992) *The United Nations and human rights: A critical appraisal* Oxford: Clarendon

Alstott A 'Is the family at odds with equality? The legal implications of equality for children' (2008) 82 *South California Law Review* 1

Amos M 'Transplanting human rights norms: The case of the United Kingdom's Human Rights Act' (2013) 35 *Human Rights Quarterly* 386

An Nawawi A 'Islam cultural and the imperative' (2003) 8 *Journal of Islamic Law and Culture* 89

Anderson C 'Reporting under international human rights treaties: Perspectives from Timor Leste's experience of the reformed process' (2008) 8 *Human Rights Law Review* 69

Anderson J (2005) *Conjure in African American Society* Baton Rouge: Louisiana State University Press

André C & Godin M 'Children's rights in the Democratic Republic of Congo and neoliberal reform: The case of mines in the province of Kitanga' in Imoh A & Ansell N (eds) (2014) *Children's lives in an era of children's rights: The progress of the Convention on the Rights of the Child in Africa* Routledge: Oxon

Ang F *et al* (2006) *Participation rights of children* Antwerp and Oxford: Intersentia

Angle S (2002) *Human rights in Chinese thought: A cross-cultural inquiry* Cambridge: Cambridge University Press

An-Magritt J 'Pluralization of family forms' in Qvortrup J *et al* (2009) *the Palgrave handbook of childhood studies* Basingstoke: Palgrave

An-na'im A (2006) *African constitutionalism and the rule of Islam* Philadelphia: University of Pennsylvania Press

An-Na'im A 'Cultural transformation and normative consensus on the best interests of the child' (1994) 8 *International Journal of Law and the Family* 62

An-Na'im A (1995) *Human rights in cross-cultural perspectives: A quest for consensus* Pennsylvania: University of Pennsylvania Press

An-Na'im A 'Human rights and Islamic identity in France and Uzbekistan: Mediation of the local and global' (2000) 22 *Human Rights Quarterly* 906

Ansell N 'The Convention on the Rights of the Child: Advancing social justice for African children? in Imoh A & Ansell N (eds) (2014) *Children's lives in an era of children's rights: The progress of the Convention on the Rights of the Child in Africa* Routledge: Oxon

Appell A 'The pre-political child of child-cantered jurisprudence' (2009-10) 46 *Houston Law Review* 703

Appiah A (1992) *In my father's house: Africa in the philosophy of culture* New York: Oxford University Press

Arat Z 'Forging a global culture of human rights: Origins and prospects of the International Bill of Rights' (2006) 28 Human *Rights Quarterly* 416

Arblaster A (1984) *The rise and decline of Western liberalism* Oxford: Basil Blackwell

Archambault C 'Ethnographic empathy and the social context of rights: "Rescuing" Maasai girls from early marriage' (2011) 113 *American Anthropologist* 632

Archard D (2004) *Children: Rights and childhood* Routledge: London

Aries P (1962) *Centuries of childhood: A history of family life* New York: Alfred A. Knopf

Armstrong A *et al* 'Towards a cultural understanding of the interplay between children's and women's rights: An Eastern and Southern African perspective' (1995) 3 *International Journal of Children's Rights* 333

Austin C (1989) *Human embryos* Oxford: Oxford University Press

Baderin M & Ssenyojo M	(2010) *International human rights law: Six decades after the UDHR and beyond* Burlington: Ashgate
Bair J	(2005) *The International Covenant on Civil and Political Rights and its (first) Optional Protocol: A short commentary* Frankfurt/Berlin: Peter Lang
Barendt E	(2005) *Freedom of speech* Oxford: Oxford University Press
Barsh R	'The draft Convention on the Rights of the Child: A case of eurocentrism in standard setting' (1989) 58 *Nordic Journal of International law* 24
Bartholet E	'Ratification by the United States of the Convention on the Rights of the Child: Prons and cons from a child's rights perspective' (2011) 633 *The ANNAls of the American Academy of Political and Social Science* 80
Beck U	'Democratisation of the family' (1997) 4 *Childhood* 151
Bell L *et al*	(2001) *Negotiating culture and human rights* New York: Columbia University Press
Bennett T	(1999) *Human rights and African customary law under the South African Constitution* Cape Town: Juta
Benporath S	'Autonomy and vulnerability: On just relations between adults and children' (2003) 37 *Journal of Philosophy of Education* 127
Berkowitz D *et al*	'The transplant effect' (2003) 51 *American Journal of Comparative Law* 163
Berry J	'Cultural relations in plural societies: Alternatives to separation and their socio-psychological implications' in N Miller & M Brewer (eds) (1984) *Groups in contact: The psychology of desegregation* New York Academic Press
Bhabha H	'Signs taken for wonders: Questions of ambivalence and authority under a tree outside Delhi, May 1817 (1985) 12 *Critical Inquiry* 144
Blanchfield L	'The United Nations Convention on the Rights of the Child: Background and policy issues' (2009) *Congressional Book Service Report for Congress*

Bledsoe C (1980) *Women and marriage in Kpelle society* Stanford: Stanford University Press

Bloed A *et al* (eds) (1993) *Monitoring human rights in Europe: Comparing international procedures and mechanisms* Dordrecht: Kluwer Academic Publishers

Blustein J (1982) *Parents and children: The ethics of the family* New York: Oxford University Press

Boakye-Boaten A 'Changes in the concept of childhood: Implications on children in Ghana' (2010) 3 *The Journal of International Social Book* 105

Boateng F 'African traditional education: A method of dissemination cultural values' (1983) 3 *Journal of Black Studies* 335

Bossuyt M (1987) *Guide to the 'travaux Préparatoires' of the International Covenant on Civil and Political Rights* Dordrecht: Martinus Nijhoff Publishers

Bourdillon M & Musvosvi E 'What can children's rights mean when children are struggling to survive? The case of Chiweshe, Zimbabwe' in Imoh A & Ansell N (eds) (2014) *Children's lives in an era of children's rights: The progress of the Convention on the Rights of the Child in Africa* Routledge: Oxon

Bowden B (2009) *The empire of civilization: The evolution of an imperial idea* Chicago: University of Chicago Press

Boylan J & Ing P "Seen but not heard': Young people's experience of advocacy' (2005) 14 *International Journal of Social Welfare* 2

Boyle A & Chinkin C (2007) *The making of international law* Oxford: Oxford University Press

Brems E 'Children's rights and universality' in Willems J (ed) (2007) *Developmental and autonomy rights of children: Empowering children, caregivers and communities* Antwerp: Intersentia

Brennan S & Noggle R 'The moral status of children: Children's rights, parents' rights, and family justice' (1997) 23 *Social Theory and Practice* 1

Brighouse H 'What rights (if any) do children have?' in Archard D & Macleod C (eds) (2002) *The moral and political status of children* Oxford: Oxford University Press

Brown W & Halley J (eds) (2002) *Left legalism/left criticism* Durham: Duke University Press

Bruce C & Hafen J 'Abandoning children to their rights' (1995) *First things First* 9

Burman E 'Innocents abroad: Western fantasies of childhood and the iconography of emergencies' (1994) 18 *Disasters* 241

Busia K (1962) *The challenge of Africa* New York: Praeger

Byaruhanga-Akiiki A 'An Africa and Christianity: Domestication of Christian values in the African Church' in Olupona J & Nyang S (eds) (1993) *Religious plurality: Essays in honour of John S Mbiti* New York: Mouton de Gruyter

Callaghan L 'Building on an African worldview' (1998) 89 *Early Childhood Matters* 30

Campbell T 'Rationales for freedom of communication' in Campbell T & Sadurski W (eds) (1994) *Freedom of communication* Sydney: Dartmouth

Cannella G & Radhika V 'Childhood and cultural studies: Introduction' in Cannella G & Radhika V (2004) *Childhood and postcolonialisation: Power, education, and contemporary practice* New York: Routledge

Carey S (1985) *Conceptual change in childhood* Cambridge: Bradford Books, MIT Press

Cerna M 'Universality of human rights and cultural diversity: Implementation of human rights in different socio-cultural Contexts' (1994) 16 *Human Rights Quarterly* 740

Cheney K 'Conflicting protectionist and participation models of children's rights: Their consequences for Uganda's orphans and vulnerable children' in Imoh A & Ansell N (eds) (2014) *Children's lives in an era of children's rights: The progress of the Convention on the Rights of the Child in Africa* Routledge: Oxon

Chimonga C 'African customary law and children's rights: Intersections and domains in a new era' in Sloth-Nielsen J (ed) (2008) *Children's rights in Africa: A legal perspective* Aldershot: Ashgate Publishing Limited

Chirwa D 'The merits and demerits of the African Charter on the Rights and Welfare of the Child' (2002) 10 *International Journal of Children's Rights* 157

Cobbah J 'African values and human rights debate: An African perspective' (1987) 9 *Human Rights Quarterly* 309

Cockburn T 'Children and the feminist ethic of care' (2005) 12 *Childhood* 71
Cohen H (1980) *Equal rights for children* Totawa: Littlefield Adams

Cohen W 'The colonized as child: British and French colonial rule' (1970) 3 *African Historical Studies* 107

Coomans F *et al* (eds) (2000) *Human rights from exclusion to inclusion; principles and practice: An anthropology from the work of Theo van Boven* The Hague: Kluwer Law International

Coons J *et al* 'Puzzling over children's rights' (1991) *Brigham Young University Law Review* 307

Cooper L (1962) *Rousseau nature: The problem of the good life* University Park: Pennsylvania State University Press

Copelon R *et al* 'Human rights begin at birth: International law and the claim of fetal rights' (2005) 13 *Reproductive Health Matters* 120

Cornides J 'Human rights pitted against man' (2008) 12 *International Journal of Human Rights* 107

Corradetti C (2009) *Relativism and human rights: A theory of pluralistic universalism* Dordrecht: Springer

Corsaro W (2005) *The sociology of childhood* California: Pine Forge Press

Courlander H (1975) *A treasury of African folklore: The oral literature, traditions, myths, legends, epics, tales, recollections, wisdom, sayings and humor of Africa* New York: Crown Publishers

Croquet N 'The International Criminal Court and the treatment of defence rights: A mirror of the European Court of Human Rights jurisprudence?' (2011) 11 *Human Rights Review* 91

Cunningham H (1995) *Children and childhood in Western society since 1500* Singapore: Longman and Singapore Publishers

Cunningham H	'Children's changing lives from 1800-2000' in Maybin J & Woodhead M (Eds) (2003) *Childhoods in context* Chichester: Open University Press
Dahl R	'Adolescent brain development: A period of vulnerabilities and opportunities '(2004) 1021 *ANNALS New York Academy of Science* 12
Daniel M & Mathias A	'Challenges and coping strategies of orphaned children in Tanzania who are not adequately cared for by adults' (2012) 11 *African Journal of AIDS Book* 191
Dawes A	(1999) *Images of childhood in cultural perspective: Challenges to theory and practice* Cardiff: Cardiff Academic Press
De Haan M & Gunnar M	(2009) *Handbook of developmental social neuroscience* New York: The Guilford Press
de Jouvenal B	(1963) *The pure theory of politics* New Haven: Yale University Press
De Mause L	(ed) (1976) *The history of childhood* London: Souvenir Press
Degler C	(1980) *At odds: Women and the family in America from the revolution to the present* New York: Oxford University Press
Descartes R Cottingham J *et al*	(trans.) [PW] (1985) *The philosophical writings of Descartes* New York: Cambridge University Press
Detrick S	(1992) *The United Nations Convention on the Rights of the Child: A guide to the 'travaux préparatoires'* Dordrecht: Martinus Nijhoff Publishers
Detrick S	'Family rights' under the United Nations Convention on the Rights of the Child' in Lowe N & Douglas G (eds) (1996) *Families across frontiers* The Hague: Kluwer Law International
Detrick S	*(1999) Commentary on the United Nations Convention on the Rights of the Child* The Hague: Martinus Nijhoff Publishers
Deveaux M	(2000) *Cultural pluralism and the dilemmas of justice* Ithaca: Cornell University Press
Dewey J	'Experience and nature' in Boydston J (ed) (1988) *The later works* Carbondale: Southern Illinois University Press

Dimitrijevic V	'State reports' in Alfredsson G *et al* (eds) (2001) *International human rights monitoring mechanisms: Essays in honour of Jakob Th. Moiler* Leiden: Martinus Nijhoff (The Raoul Wallenberg Institute Human Rights Library)
Diptee A & Klein A	'African childhoods and the colonial project' (2009) 20 *Journal of Family History* 1
Diptee A	'African children in the British slave trade during the late eighteenth century' (2006) 27 *Slavery & Abolition* 183
Dolgin J	'Transforming childhood: Apprenticeship in American law' (1996-97) 31 *New England Law Review* 1113
Donnelly J	(1998) *International human rights* Boulder: Westview Press
Donnelly J	(2003) *Universal human rights in theory and in practice* Ithaca: Cornell University Press
Donnelly J	'Cultural relativism and universal human rights' in J Donnelly (1989) *Human rights in theory and practice* Ithaca: Cornell University Press
Donnelly J	'Human rights and human dignity: An analytic critique of non-Western conceptions of human rights' (1982) 76 *American Political Science Review* 303
Donnelly J	'The relative universality of human rights' (2007) 29 *Human Rights Quarterly* 281
Durkheim E	'Childhood' in Pickering W (ed) (1911) *Durkheim: Essays on morals and education* London: Routledge
Ebobrah S	'Towards a positive application of complementarity in the African human rights system: Issues of functions and relations' (2011) 22 *European Journal of International Law* 663
Eekelaar J	'The emergence of children's rights' (1986) 6 *Oxford Journal of Legal Studies* 161
Eekelaar J	'Children between cultures' (2004) 18 *International Journal of Law, Policy and the Family* 178
Eekelaar J	'The emergence of children's rights' (1986) 6 *Oxford Journal of Legal Studies* 161

Ehrlich B	(1975) *The fundamental principles of the sociology of law* New York: Russell & Russell
Elahi M	'The rights of the child under Islamic law: Prohibition of the child soldier' (1987-1988) 19 *Columbia Human Rights Law Review* 259
Ellis G	'Islam as a factor in Western African culture' (1911) 2 *The Journal of Race Development* 105
Ellis J	(1996) *Literature lost: Social agendas and the corruption of the humanities* Philadelphia: Temple University Press
Ellis J	'Different conceptions of a child's needs: Some implications of social work for Western African children and their parents' (1977) 7 *British Journal of Social Work* 155
Elphick R *et al*	(1998) *Christianity in South Africa: A political, social and cultural history* California: University of California Press
Englund H	H (ed*)* (2011) *Christianity and public culture in Africa* Athens: Ohio University Press
Ennew J	'Outside childhood: Street children's rights' in Franklin B (ed) (1995) *The handbook of children's rights* London: Routledge
Erny P	(1973) *Childhood and cosmos: The social psychology of black African child* New York: New Perspectives
Erny P	'First steps in the life of a black African child: Birth and early childhood' in Nsamenang A (1992) *Human development in a cultural context: A third world perspective* Newbury Park: Sage publications
Esposito J	(1999) *Oxford history of Islam* Oxford: Oxford University Press
Esposito J	(2002) *What everyone needs to know about Islam* Oxford: Oxford University Press
Esposito J	(2005) *Islam the straight path* Oxford: Oxford University Press
Evans R	'Safeguarding inheritance and enhancing the resilience of orphaned young people living in child and youth-headed households in Tanzania and Uganda' (2012) 11 *African Journal of AIDS Book* 177
Evensen J	'Working methods and procedures in the 3rd UNCLOS' (1986-iv) 199 Recueil Des Cours 425 cited in Boyle A & C Chinkin (eds) (2007) *The making of international law*

Fass P & Grossberg M (eds) (2012) *Reinventing childhood after World War II* Philadelphia: University of Pennsylvania

Fass P & Mason M (eds) (2000) *Childhood in America* New York: New York University Press

Federle K 'Rights flow downhill' (1994) 2 *International Journal of Children's Rights* 343

Feldman I & Ticktin M (2010) *In the name of humanity: The government of threat and care* Durham: Duke University Press

Fernández & A Fogli 'Culture: An empirical investigation of beliefs, work, and fertility' (2006a) *NBER Working Paper* No. 11268

Fernando J 'Children's rights: Beyond the impasse' *(2001)575 Annals of the American Academy of Political and Social Science 8*

Fionda J 'Legal concepts of childhood: An introduction' in Fionda J (2001) *Legal concepts of adulthood* Oxford and Portland: Hart Publishing

Fortes M (1957) *The web of Kinship among the Tallensi. The second part of an analysis of the social structure of a transvolta tribe* London: Oxford University Press

Foster G & Williamson J

Fox G 'Right to political participation in international law' (1992) 17 *Yale Journal of International Law* 539

Freeman M (ed) (2011) *Law and neuroscience* Oxford: Oxford University Press

Freeman M 'Human rights and real cultures: Towards a dialogue on "Asian values"' (1998) 16 *Netherlands Quarterly of Human Rights* 26

Freeman M 'The best interests of the child? Is the best interests of the child in the best interests of children?' (1997) 11 *International Journal of Law, Policy and the Family* 360

Freeman M 'The sociology of childhood and children's rights' (1998) 6 *The International Journal of Children's Rights* 433

Frug G (1999) *City making: Building communities without building walls* Princeton: Princeton University Press

Gaer F	'First fruits: Reporting by states under the African Charter on Human and Peoples' Rights' (1992) 10 *Netherlands Quarterly of Human Rights* 29
Garner B	(ed) (2009) *Black's Law Dictionary* St. Paul: West Group
Geertz C	(1983) *Local knowledge: Further essays in interpretive anthropology* New York: Basic Books
Gerald J & Russello W	(2012) *Christianity and European culture: Selections from the work of Christopher Dawson* Michigan: Catholic University of America Press
Gerber P *et al*	'General Comment 16 on state obligations regarding the impact of the business sector on children's rights: What is its standing, meaning and effect?' (2013) 14 *Melbourne Journal of International Law* 1
Gessner V & Thomas J	'Socio-legal book and policy studies: A review of the issues' (1988) 10 *Law and Policy* 85
Gibbard A	(1990) *Wise choices, apt feelings: A theory of normative judgement* Cambridge: Harvard University Press
Gillespie J	'Transplanted company law: An ideological and cultural analysis of market-entry in Vietnam' (2002) 51 *International and Comparative Law Quarterly* 650
Gillis J	'Transitions to modernity' in Qvortrup J *at el* (2002) *The Palgrave handbook of childhood studies* Basingstoke: Palgrave Macmillan
Glenn L	'A legal perspective on humanity, personhood, and species boundaries' (2003) 3 *The American Journal of Bioethics* 27
Goddard J	(2005) *The politics of childhood: International perspectives, contemporary development* Hampshire: Palgrave Macmillan
Goduka I	'Indigenous epistemologies - Ways of knowing, affirming our legacy' (1999) 13 *South African Journal of Higher Education* 26
Gonzalez-Mena J	(1997) *Multicultural issues in child care* Mountain View: Mayfield
Goodale M	'Introduction to anthropology and human rights in a new key' (2006) 108 *American Anthropologist* 1

Goodhart M 'Origins and universality in the human rights debates: Cultural essentialism and the challenge of globalization' (2003) 25 *Human Rights Quarterly* 935

Gose M (2002) *The African Charter on the Rights and Welfare of the Child* Community Law Centre: Bellville

Gottlieb A (2004) *The afterlife is where we come from: The culture of infancy in West Africa* Chicago: University of Chicago Press

Grajzl P & Dimitrova-Grajzl V 'The choice in the lawmaking process: Legal transplants vs. indigenous law' (2009) 5 *Review of Law and Economic* 615

Gray J (1995) *Enlightenment's wake: Politics and culture at the close of modern age* Park Square: Routledge

Gray J (2000) *Two faces of liberalism* New York: The New Press

Gray R 'Christianity, colonialism and communications in Sub-Saharan Africa' (1982) 13 *Journal of Black Studies* 59

Greif A (2005) *Institutions: Theory and history. Comparative and historical institutional analysis* Cambridge: Cambridge University Press

Greif A 'Cultural beliefs, and the organization of society: A historical and theoretical reflection on collectivist and individualist societies' (1994) 102 *Journal of Political Economy* 912

Grier B (2006) *Invisible hands: Child Labor and the State in colonial Zimbabwe* Portsmouth: Heinemann

Griffin J 'Do children have rights?' in Archard D & Macleod C (eds) (2002) *The moral and political status of children: New essays* Oxford: Oxford University Press

Griffin J 'First steps in an account of human rights' (2001) 9 *European Journal of Philosophy* 311

Gross B & Gross R (1977) *The children's rights movement: Overcoming the oppression of young people* New York: Anchor Press/Doubleday

Grugel J & Peruzzotti E 'The domestic politics of international human rights law: Implementing the Convention on the Rights of the Child in Ecuador, Chile, and Argentina' (2012) 34 *Human Rights Quarterly* 178

Grylls D (1978) *Guardians and angels: Parents and children in nineteen century literature* London: Faber & Faber

Guggenheim M (2005) *What's wrong with children's rights*? Cambridge: Harvard University Press

Guiso L *et al* 'Does culture affect economic outcomes' (2006) 20 *Journal of Economic Perspectives* 23

Gutmann A (ed) (1994) *Multiculturalism: Examining the politics of recognition* Princeton: Princeton University Press

Gutto S 'The reform and the renewal of the African human and peoples' rights system'(2001) 2 *African Human Rights Law Journal* 175

Gyekye K (1988) *The unexamined life: Philosophy and the African experience* Accra: Ghana Universities Press

Gyekye K (1995) *An essay on African philosophical thought: The Akan conceptual scheme* Cambridge: Cambridge University Press

Hadley J 'Introduction to Roman law in twelve academical lectures' (1973) *Wisconsin Magazine of History*

Hafen B & Hafen J 'Abandoning children to their autonomy: The United Nations Convention on the Rights of the Child' (1996) 37 *Harvard International Law Journals* 449

Hafen B 'Children's liberation and the new egalitarianism: Some reservations about abandoning youth to their 'rights' (1976) 605 *Brigham Young University Law Review* 644

Hall C (2000) *Cultures of the empire: Colonizers in Britain and the empire in the twentieth centuries* Manchester: Manchester University Press

Hammel E 'Meeting the minotaur' (1994) 35 *Anthropology Newsletter* 48

Harkness S & Super C 'Shared childcare in East Africa: Socio-cultural origins and developmental consequences' in Lamb M *et al* (eds) (1992) *Child care in context: Socio-cultural perspectives* Hillsdale: Erlbaum

Harris-Short S 'International human rights law: Imperialist, inept and ineffective? Cultural relativism and the UN Convention on the Rights of the Child' (2003) 25 *Human Rights Quarterly* 130

Hart H 'Bentham on legal rights' in Simpson A (ed) (1973) *Oxford essays in jurisprudence* Oxford: Clarendon Press

Hart R — (1992) *Children's participation: From tokenism to citizenship* Florence: UNICEF Innocenti Book Centre

Hart S — 'From property to person status: Historical perspective on children's rights' (1991) 46 *American Psychologist* 53

Heap S — 'Their days are spent in gambling and loafing, pimping for prostitutes, and picking pockets': Male juvenile delinquents on Lagos Island, 1920s-1960s' (2010) 35 *Journal of Family History* 48

Hegal G — (1820) *The philosophy of rights* 1820, translated. Oxford University Press; First Published: by Clarendon Press 1952, (translated: with notes by T M Knox)

Helfer L & Slaughter A — 'Towards a theory of effective supranational adjudication' (1997) 107 *Yale Law Journal* 273

Hemrica J & Heyting F — 'Tacit notions of childhood: An analysis of discourse about child participation in decision-making regarding arrangements in the case of parental divorce' (2004) 4 *Childhood* 449

Henddrick H — 'The evolution of childhood in Western Europe c.1400-c.1750' in Freeman M (ed) (2012) *Law and childhood studies: Current legal issues volume 14*

Hendrick H — 'Constructions and reconstructions of British childhood: An interpretative survey, 1800 to the present' in James A & Prout A (1997) *Constructing and reconstructing childhood: Contemporary issues in the sociological book of childhood* London: Falmer Press

Henkin L — (1990) *The age of rights* New York: Columbia University Press

Herbst J — (2000) *States and power in Africa: Comparative lessons in authority and control* Princeton: Princeton University Press

Herbst J — 'International laws of war and the African child: Norms, compliance, and sovereignty' in Doyle M *et al* (eds) (2004) *International law and organisation: Closing the compliance gap* Landham: Rowman & Littlefield Publishers

Herdt G — (1982) *Rituals of manhood: Male initiation in Papua New Guinea* New Brunswick: Transaction Publishers

Hermandez-Truyol B & Rush S — 'Culture, nationhood and human rights ideal' (2000) 5 *Michigan Journal of Race and the Law* 817

Hermandez-Truyol B (ed) (2002) *Moral imperialism: A critical anthropology* New York: New York University Press

Herring J 'Vulnerability, children, and the law' in Freeman M (ed) (2012) *Law and childhood studies: Current legal issues 2011* Oxford: Oxford University Press

Heyns C & Viljoen F 'The impact of the United Nations human rights treaties on the domestic level' (2001) 23 *Human Rights Quarterly* 2483

Heywood C (2001) *A history of childhood: Children and childhood in the West from medieval to modern times* Cambridge: Polity Press

Higgins R 'Opinion: Ten years on the UN Human Rights Committee- some thoughts upon parting' (1996) 6 *European Human Rights Law Review* 581

Himonga C 'The rights of the child to participate in decision making: A perspective from Zambia' in Ncube W (1998) *Law, culture, tradition and children's rights in East and Southern Africa* Aldershot and Brookfield: Ashgate

Hiner N & Hawes J (eds) (1985) *Growing up in America: Children in historical perspective* Urbana: University of Illinois Press

Hobbes T *Of man, being the first part of Leviathan: Of the first and second natural laws, and of contract (1588-1679) XIV The Harvard Classics* 1909

Hodgkin R & Newell P (2007) *Implementation handbook for the Convention on the Rights of the Child* Ginebra*: UNICEF*

Hodgson D 'The international legal protections of the child's right to a legal identity and the problem of statelessness' (1993) 7 *International Journal of Law, Policy and the Family* 255

Hoffman M 'The development of prosocial motivation: Empathy and guilt' in Eisenberg N (ed) (1982) *The development of prosocial behaviour* New York: Academic Press

Holland P (1992) *What is a child? Popular images of childhood* London: Virago

Holt J (1975) *Escape from childhood: The needs and rights of children* Boston: E. P. Dutton

Howard R (1986) *Human rights in Commonwealth Africa* Totowa: Rowman & Littlefield

Howard R 'Cultural absolutism and the nostalgia for community' (1993) 15 *Human Rights Quarterly* 315

Humphrey J (1984) *Human rights & the United Nations: A great adventure* New York: Transnational Publishers

Hwang C *et al* (1996) *Images of childhood* Mahwah: Lawrence Erlbaum Associates

Ibhawoh B Cultural relativism and human rights: Reconsidering the Africanist discourse' (2001) 19 *Netherlands Quarterly of Human Rights* 43

Ikuenobe P 'The idea of personhood in Chinau Achebe's things fall apart' (2006) 9 *Philosopia Africana* 117

Illick J (2002) *American childhoods* Philadelphia: University of Pennsylvania Press

Imoh A 'Realizing children's rights in Africa: An introduction' in Imoh A & Ansell N (eds) (2014) *Children's lives in an era of children's rights: The progress of the Convention on the Rights of the Child in Africa* Routledge: Oxon

Isichei E (1995) *A history of Christianity in Africa: From antiquity to the present* Grand Rapids: W.B. Eerdmans Publishing Company

James A & James L (2004) *Constructing childhood: Theory, policy and social practice* Basingstoke: Palgrave Macmillan

James A & Prout A (1997) *Constructing and reconstructing childhood: Contemporary issues in the sociological book of childhood* London: Routledge

James A & Prout A (eds) (1990) *Constructing and reconstructing childhood: Contemporary issues in the sociological studies* London: Falmer Press

James A *et al* (1998) *Theorizing childhood* New York: Teachers College Press

James A *et al* *(2002) Theorizing childhood* Cambridge: Polity Press

James *et al* 'Care and control in the construction of children's citizenship' in Invernizzi A & Williams J (eds) (2008) *Children and citizenship* London: Sage

Jenks C (1996) *Childhood* London: Routledge

Jenks C (1999) *Childhood* New York: Aldine De Gruyter

Jenks C (2005) *Childhood* London: Routledge

Jenks C (ed) (1982) *The sociology of childhood: Essential readings* London: Batsford Academic and Educational

Jenks C Editorial: 'Many childhoods' (2004) *11 Childhood* 5

Jewei C 'Evaluation of agency: A fundamental question for social and political philosophy' (2011) 42 *Metaphilosophy* 261

Joseph F (2011) *Children's books in England: Five centuries of social life* Cambridge: Cambridge University Press

Joseph R (2009) *Human rights and the unborn Child* Leiden: Martinus Nijhoff Publishers

Kagan J (1984) *The nature of the child* New York: Basic Books

Kaime T (2009) *The African Charter on the Rights and Welfare of the Child: A socio-legal perspective* Pretoria: PULP

Kaime T (2011) *The Convention on the Rights of the Child: A cultural legitimacy critique* Groningen: Europa Law Publishing

Kaime T "Vernacularising' the Convention on the Rights of the Child: rights and culture as analytic tools' (2010) 18 *International Journal of Children's Rights* 637

Kaime T 'Socio-legal approaches to children's rights under the African Charter on the Rights and Welfare of the Child: A discussion of methodology' in Atkin B (ed) (2009) *The International Survey of Family Law* Bristol: Family Law

Kaime T 'The African Children's Charter: Does it represent a relevant vision of childhood and children's rights?' (2009) 29 *Children's Legal Rights Journal* 15

Kaime T 'The foundations of rights in the African Charter on the Rights and Welfare of the Child: A historical and philosophical account' (2009) 3 *African Journal of Legal Studies* 120

Kaime T 'Culture or children's rights ... or both?' (2003) 50 *Children First* 15

Kaime T 'The Convention on the Rights of the Child and the cultural legitimacy of children's rights in Africa: Some reflections' (2005) 5 *African Human Rights Law Journal* 221

Kaime T 'The foundations of rights in the African Charter on the Rights and Welfare of the Child: A historical and philosophical account' (2009) 3 *African Journal of Legal Studies* 119

Kaime T 'The struggle for context in the protection of children's rights: Understanding the core concepts of the African Children's Charter'(2009) 58 *Journal of Legal Pluralism and Unofficial Law* 33

Kamenka E 'Thinking and teaching about human rights' in Kamenka E & Erh-soon T (eds) (1978) *Human rights* London: Edward Arnold Publishers

Kanu Y 'Tradition and educational reconstruction in Africa in post-colonial and global times: The case of Sierra Leone' (2007) 9 *African Studies Quarterly* 187

Kaphagawani D

Karp J 'Reporting and the CRC Committee' in Bayefsky A (ed) (2000) *The human rights system in the 21st century* The Hague: Kluwer Law International

Kaufman N & Rizzini I 'Closing the gap between rights and realities of children's lives' in Qvortrup J *et al* (eds) (2009) *The Palgrave handbook of child studies* Basingstoke: Palgrave

Kaye B (1992) *Bringing up Children in Ghana: An impressionist survey* London: Allen & Unwin.

Keith L & Ogundele A 'Legal systems and constitutionalism in Sub-Saharan Africa: An empirical examination of colonial influences on human rights' (2007) 29 *Human Rights Quarterly* 1065

Keith L 'National constitutions and human rights protection: Regional differences and colonial influences' in Carey S & Poe S (2004) *Understanding human rights violations* Aldershot: Ashgate

Kelly F 'Conceptualising the child through an "ethic of care": Lessons for family law' (2004) 4 *International Journal of Law in Context* 375

Kelly G & Philip G (1984) *Introduction 'The four faces of colonialism' education and colonial experience* New Brunswick: Transaction

Kelly P (2002) *Multiculturalism reconsidered: Culture and equality and its critics* Cambridge: Polity Press

Kociumbas J	'Childhood history as ideology' (1984) 47 *Labor history* 1
Kohlberg L	(1981) *Essays on moral development Vol 1 the philosophy of moral development* San Francisco: Harper San Francisco
Kohlberg L	(1984) *Essays on moral development Vol 1 the philosophy of moral development* San Francisco: Harper San Francisco
Koller M & Ritchie O	(1964) *Sociology of childhood* New York: Meredith Publishing
Kopelman L	'Children and bioethics: Uses and abuses of the best-interests standard' (1997) 22 *The Journal of Medicine and Philosophy* 213
Kramer M	'Rights without trimmings' in Kramer M *et al* (1998) *A debate over rights, philosophical enquiries* Oxford: Clarendon Press
LaFave L	'Origins of the evolution of "the best interests of the child" standard' (1989) 34 *South Dakota Law Review* 459
Langlaude S	'On how to build a positive understanding of the child's right to freedom of expression' (2010) 10 *Human Rights Law Review* 33
Langlois A	'The narrative metaphysics of human rights' (2005) 9 *The International Journal of Human Rights* 369
Lansdown G	'The realisation of children's participation rights: Critical reflection' in Percy-Smith B & Thomas N (eds) (2010) *A handbook of children and young people's participation: Perspective from theory and practice* London: Routledge
Larzelere R *et al*	'Do nonphysical punishments reduce antisocial behavior more than spanking? A comparison using the strongest previous causal evidence against spanking' (2010) 10 *BMC Paediatrics* 10
Lassiter J	'African culture and personality: Bad social science, effective social activism, or a call to reinvent ethnology?' (2000) 3 *African Studies Quarterly* 1
lbhawoh B	'Between culture and constitution: Evaluating the cultural legitimacy of human rights in the African state' (2000) 22 *Human Rights Quarterly* 838
LeBlanc L	(1995) T*he Convention on the Rights of the Child: United Nations lawmaking on human rights* Lincoln: University of Nebraska Press

LeBlanc L *et al*	'Compliance with the reporting requirements of human rights conventions' (2010) 14 *The International Journal of Human Rights* 789
Lee D	(1959) *Freedom and culture* Englewood Cliffs, NJ: Prentice-Hall
Lee L	'Youths navigating social networks and social support systems in settings of chronic crisis: The case of youth-headed households in Rwanda' (2012) 11 *African Journal of AIDS Book* 165
Lee N	'The challenge of childhood: Distributions of childhood's ambiguity in adult institutions' (1999) 6 *Childhood* 455
Legrand P	'On the unbearable localness of the law: Academic failures and unreasonable observations' (2002) 10 *European Review of Private Law* 63
Lepard B	(2002) *Rethinking humanitarian intervention: A fresh legal approach based on fundamental ethical principles in international law and world religion* Pennsylvania: Pennsylvania State University Press
LeVine R	'Challenging expert knowledge: Findings from an African book of infant care and development' in Gielen U & Roopnarine J (Eds) (2004) *Childhood and adolescence: Cross-cultural perspectives and applications* Westport: Praeger
Liao S	'The right of children to be loved' (2006) 14 *The Journal of Political Philosophy* 420
Linderfalk U	
Lindsey B	'An early judge of the Denver Juvenile Court cited in Scott E Legal construction of childhood' in Rosenheim M *et al* (eds) (2002) *A century of juvenile justice* Chicago: University of Chicago Press
Lloyd A	'Evolution of the African Charter on the Rights and Welfare of the Child and the African Committee of Experts: Raising the gauntlet' (2002) 10 *International Journal of Children's Rights* 179
Lloyd A	'How to guarantee credence: Recommendations and proposals for the African Committee of Experts on the Rights and Welfare of the Child' (2004) 12 *International Journal of Children's Rights* 21
Locke J	(1959) *An essay concerning human understanding* (collated and annotated by A Praser) Toronto: General Publishing Company

Locke J (2005) *Two treaties of government and a letter concerning toleration* Stilwell: Digireads.com Publishing

Lücker-Babel M 'The right of the child to express views to be heard: An attempt to interpret article 12 of the UN Convention on the Rights of the Child' (1995) 3 *International Journal of Children's Rights* 391

Lurie A 'Representing the child-client: Kids are people too an analysis of the role of the legal counsel to minor' (1993) 11 *New York Law School Journal of Human Rights* 205

MacCormick N 'Children's rights: A test case' in MacCormick N (1982) *Legal rights and social democracy* Oxford: Clarendon Press

Machery E *et al* 'Semantics, cross cultural style' (2004) 92 *Cognition* B1

Macintyre A (1998) 'Practical rationalities as forms of social structures' in *The MacIntrye Reader* Notre Dame: University of Notre Dame Press

MacLeod A 'Liberal theory of freedom of expression for children' (2004) 79 *Chicago-Kent Law Review* 55

Mailath G & Postlewaite A 'The social context of economic decisions' (2003) 1 *Journal of the European Economic Association* 354

Mairead N *et al* (2010) *Cultural diversity, heritage and human rights intersection in theory and practice* Boston: Martinus Nijhoff Publishers

Makgoba M (1997) *Mokoko, the makgoba affair: A reflection on transformation* Florida Hills: Vivlia Publishers and Booksellers

Makinde M (1988) *African philosophy, culture and traditional medicine* Athen: Ohio University Press

Makinde M 'A philosophical analysis of the Yuruba concepts of ori and human destiny' (1985) 17 *International Studies in Philosophy* 53

Manfred N 'Proposals for improving the UN human rights programme' (1993)11 *Netherlands Quarterly Human Rights* 153

Marasingle L 'Traditional conceptions of human rights in Africa' in Welch C & Meltzer R (eds) (1984) *Human rights and development in Africa* Albany: State University of New York Press

Maroney T	'Adolescent brain science and juvenile justice' in Freeman M (ed) (2011) *Law and neuroscience* Oxford: Oxford University Press
Martin F *et al*	(2006) *International human rights and humanitarian law: Treaties, cases & analysis* Cambridge: Cambridge University Press
Martin J & Gillespie G	'A neomeadian approach to human agency: Relating the social and the psychological in the ontogenesis of perspective coordinating persons' (2010) 44 *Integrative Psychological and Behavioral Science* 252
Martin J *et al*	'Taking and coordinating perspectives: From prereflective interactivity, through reflective intersubjectivity, to metareflective sociality' (2008) 58 *Human Development* 294
Mason M	'From father's property to children's rights' in Kermit L *et al* (1994) *The Oxford Companion to American Law*
Mathews G	'Getting beyond the deficit conception of childhood: Thinking philosophically with children' in Hand M & Stanley C (eds) (2008) *Philosophy in schools* London: Continuum
Matthews G	'Philosophy and developmental psychology: Outgrowing the deficit conception of childhood' in Siegel H (ed) (2009) *The Oxford handbook of philosophy of education* Oxford: Oxford University Press
Matos N	'The nature of learning, teaching and book in higher education' in Higgs P *et al* (eds) (2000) *African voices in education* Cape Town: Juta
Mayall B	(2002) *Towards a sociology for childhood* Philadelphia: Open University Press
Mayall B	'The sociology of childhood in relation to children's rights' (2000) 8 *International Journal of Children's Rights* 243
Mbikusita–Lewanika I	(1979) *Pre–school education in Zambia: A survey analysis and evaluation* Lusaka: University of Zambia
Mbiti J	(1969) *African religions and philosophy* London: Heinemann Educational Publishers
Mbiti J	(1970) *African religions and philosophy* Oxford: Heinemann Educational Publishers

Mbiti J	(1990) *African religions and philosophy* Oxford: Heinemann Educational Publishers
McGoldrick D	(1991) *The Human Rights Committee: Its role in the development of the International Covenant on Civil and Political Rights* Oxford: Clarendon Press
McNamara L	(2007) *Human rights controversies: The impact of legal form* Abingdon & New York: Routledge-Cavendish
McNee L	'The languages of childhood: The distinctive construction of childhood and colonial policy in French West Africa' (2004) 7 *African Studies Quarterly* 7
Mead J	'The social self' in Morris C (ed) (1934) *Mind, self and society from the standpoint of social behaviourist* Chicago: University of Chicago Press
Mead M & Wolfenstein M	(1954) *Childhood in contemporary cultures* London: Phoenix Books
Mead M	(1967) *An investigation of the thought of primitive children, with special reference to animism, personalities and cultures* New York: Natural History Press
Mechlem K	'Treaty bodies and interpretation of human rights' (2009) 42 *Vanderbilt Journal of Transnational Law* 905
Melton G	'The child's right to a family environment: Why children's rights and family values are compatible' (1996) 51 *American Psychologist* 1234
Menkel-Meadow C	'Durkheimian epiphanies: The importance of engaged socio science in legal studies' (1990-1991) 18 *Florida State University Law Review* 91
Menkiti I	'Person and community in African traditional thought' in Wright R (ed) (1984) *African philosophy* Lanham: University Press of America
Merry S	'Human rights and demonization of culture' (2003) 26 *Political and Legal Anthropology Review* 55
Mezmur B & Sloth-Nielsen J	'An ice-breaker: State party reports and the 11th session of the African Committee of Experts on the Rights and Welfare of the Child' (2008) 8 *African Human Rights Law Journal* 596

Mezmur B 'Still an infant or now a toddler? The work of the African Committee of Experts on the Rights and Welfare of the Child and its 8th ordinary session' (2007) 7 *African Human Rights Law Journal* 258

Mezmur B 'The 19th ordinary session of the African Committee of Experts on the Rights and Welfare of the Child: Looking back to look head' (2007) 7 *African Human Rights Journal* 545

Mezmur B The African Children's Charter versus the United Nations Convention on the Rights of the Child: A zero-sum game? (2008) 23 *South Africa Public law Journal*

Mezmur B 'The African Committee of Experts on the Rights and Welfare of the Child: An update' (2006) 6 *African Human Rights Journal* 549

Mills J 'On liberty' (1860) *Harvard Classics* 25 New York: Bartleby.com

Mintz S (2004) *Huck's part: A history of American childhood* Cambridge: Belknap Press

Moesteller T (2006) *Relativism in contemporary American philosophy* London: Continuum

Moqvist I 'Constructing a parent' in Bloch M *et al* (eds) (2003) *Governing children, families and education: Reconstructing a welfare state* New York: Palgrave Macmillan

Moravcsik A 'Why is the U.S human rights policy so unilateral?' in Patrick S & Forman S (eds) (2001) *Multilateralism and U.S foreign policy: Ambivalent engagement* Colorado: Lynne Rienner Publishers

Morris B (2000) *Animals and ancestors: An ethnography* Oxford: Berg

Morsink J (1999) *The Universal Declaration of Human Rights: Origins, drafting, and intent* Philadelphia: University of Pennsylvania Press

Mowbray A 'Institutional developments and recent Strasbourg cases' (2005) 5 *Human Rights Law Review* 176

Mugambi M 'Forget your past, thank colonialism' (1998) *The People's Digest* 111

Muncie J 'Governing young people: Coherence and contradictions in contemporary youth justice' (2006) 26 *Critical Social Policy* 770

Mutua M (2002) *Human rights: A political and cultural critique* Philadelphia: University of Pennsylvania Press

Mutua M	'Justice under siege: The rule of law and judicial subservience in Kenya' (2001) 23 *Human Rights Quarterly* 96
Mutua M	'Looking past the Human Rights Committee: An argument for de-marginalizing enforcement' (1998) 4 *Buffalo Human Rights Law Review* 211
Mutua M	'Standard setting in human rights: Critique and prognosis (2007) 29 *Human Rights Quarterly* 547
Mwambene L & Sloth-Nielsen J	'Benign accommodation? Ukuthwala, 'forced marriage' and the South African Children's Act' (2011) 11 *African Human Rights Law Journal* 1
Nasiniyu–Wasike A	'Polygamy: A feminist critique' in Oduyoye M & Kanyoro M (eds) (1992) *The will to rise* Maryknoll: Orbis
Ncube W	(1989) *Law, culture, tradition and children's rights in East and Southern Africa* Aldershot: Dartmouth Publishing Company
Ncube W	'The African cultural fingerprints: The changing concept of childhood' in Ncube W (eds) (1998) *Law, culture, tradition and children's rights* Aldershot: Dartmouth Publishing Company
Neisser U & Jopling D	(1997) *The conceptual self in context: Culture, experience, and self-understanding* Cambridge: Cambridge University Press
Ngara C	'African ways of knowing and pedagogy revisited' (2007) 2 *Journal of Contemporary Issues in Education* 7
Ngugi W	(1986) *Decolonizing the mind: The politics of language in African literature* New Hampshire: Heinemann
Nickel J & Reidy D	'Relativism, self-determination and human rights' in Chatterjee D (ed) (2008) *Democracy in global world: A human rights and political participation in the 21st century* Lanham: Rowman & Littlefield
Norman A	'Children's rights in the time of AIDS in KwaZulu-Natal, South Africa' in Imoh A & Ansell N (eds) (2014) *Children's lives in an era of children's rights: The progress of the Convention on the Rights of the Child in Africa* Routledge: Oxon
Nowak M	(1993) *CCPR Commentary* Strasbourg: NP Engel
Nowak M	'Article 6: The right to life, survival and development' in Alen A *et al* (eds) (2005) *Commentary on the UN Convention on the Rights of the Child* Leiden/Boston: Martinus Nijhoff

Nsamenang A (1992) *Human development in cultural context: A third world perspective* Newbury Park: Sage Publications

Nussbaum M 'Non-relative values: An Aristotelian approach' in Nussbaum M & Sen A (eds) (1993) *The quality of life* Oxford: Clarendon Press

Nwanosike F & Onyije E 'Colonialism and education' (2011) *Proceedings of the International Conference on Teaching, Learning and Change* 624

Nyasani J J (1997) *The African psyche* Nairobi: University of Nairobi and Theological Printing Press

Oba A 'Islamic law as customary law: The changing perspective in Nigeria' (2002) 51 *International Comparative Law Quarterly* 817

Ochaita E & Espinosa M 'Children's participation in family and school life: A psychological and development Approach' (1997) 5 *International Journal of Children's Rights* 279

O'Flaherty M 'The concluding observations of United Nations human rights treaty bodies' (2006) 6 *Human Rights Law Review* 27

Ohuche R & Otaala B (1981) *The African child in his environment* Oxford: Pergamon

Okere T 'African culture: The past and the present as an indivisible whole' in Okere T (1996) *Identity and change: Nigerian philosophical studies* Washington DC: Paideia Publishers

Okyere S 'Children's participation in prohibited work in Ghana and its implications for the Convention on the Rights of the Child' in Imoh A & Ansell N (eds) (2014) *Children's lives in an era of children's rights: The progress of the Convention on the Rights of the Child in Africa* Routledge: Oxon

Olowu D 'Children's rights, international human rights and the promise of Islamic legal theory' (2008) 12 *Law Democracy & Development* 62

Olowu D 'Protecting children's rights in Africa: A critique of the African Charter on the Rights and Welfare of the Child' (2002) 10 *International Journal on Children's Rights* 127

Omike E 'In the best interests of the child: The case of child domestic workers in Ghana and Nigeria' in Imoh A & Ansell N (eds) (2014) *Children's lives in an era of children's rights: The progress of the Convention on the Rights of the Child in Africa Routledge: Oxon*

O'Neill O & Ruddick W (eds) (1979) *Having children: philosophical and legal reflections on parenthood* New York: Oxford University Press

Onwauchi P (1972) *African identity and black liberation* New York: Black Academy Press

Orchardson I (1961) *The Kipsigis* Nairobi: East African Literature Bureau

Ottino A (2000) *The universe within a Balinese village through its ritual practices* Paris: Karthala Editions

Panikkar R 'Is the notion of human rights a Western concept?' (1982) 30 *Diogenes* 75

Parekh B (2000) *Rethinking multiculturalism: Cultural diversity and political theory* Basingstoke: Macmillan Press

Parekh B 'Non-ethnocentric universalism' in Dunne T & Wheeler N (eds) (1999) *Human rights in global politics* Cambridge: Cambridge University Press

Parker S 'The best interests of the child: Principles and problems' (1994) 8 *International Journal of Law and the Family* 26

Parker S

Pavel N 'Defining the concept of human rights in the light of juridical value theory' (2012) 4 *Contemporary Readings in Law and Social Justice* 502

Pedone J & Kloster A 'New proposals for human rights treaty body reform' (2013) 22 *Journal of Transnational Law and Policy* 29

Pellow D (1977) *Women in Accra: Options for autonomy* Chicago: Algonac, Mich: Reference Publications

Percy-Smith B (2010) *A handbook of children and young people's participation: Perspectives from theory and practice* London: Routledge

Pichon J 'Does the unborn child have a right to life? The insufficient answer of the European Court of Human Rights in the judgment Vo v. France' (2007) 7 *Germany Law Journal* 433

Pollis A 'A new universalism' in Pollis A & Schwad P (eds) (2000) *Human rights: New perspectives, new realities* Boulder: Lynne Rienner Publishers

Pollis A 'Towards a new universalism; reconstruction and dialogue' (1998) 16 *Netherlands Quarterly of Human Rights* 17

Pollock L (1983) *forgotten children: Parent-child relations from 1500 to 1900* Cambridge: Cambridge University Press

Postman N (1994) *The disappearance of childhood* New York: Vintage Books

Prout A & James A 'A new paradigm for the sociology of childhood: Provenance, problems and problems' in James A & Prout A (eds) (1997) *Constructing and reconstructing childhood. Contemporary issues in the sociological book of childhood* London: Falmer Press

Prout A

Pupavac V 'Misanthropy without borders: The international children's rights regime' (2001) 25 *Disasters 95*

Purdy L (1992) *In their best interests? The case against equal rights for children* Ithaca: Cornell University Press

Qvortrup J (2005) *The little's' and the prospects for generational childhood studies. Booking childhood and welfare: Perspectives and challenges* conference paper: International Conference Childhoods June 29 – July 3, 2005, Oslo

Qvortrup J 'A voice for children in statistical and social accounting: A plea for children's right to be heard' in James A & Prout A (eds) (1997) *Constructing and reconstructing childhood: Contemporary issues in the sociological studies of childhood* London: Falmer Press

Qvortrup J 'Childhood matters: An introduction' in Qvortrup J *et al* (eds) (1994) *Childhood matters: Social theory, practice and politics* Aldershot: Avebury

Qvortrup J 'Editorial: A reminder' (2007) *14 Childhood* 395

Rajabi-Ardeshiri M 'The rights of the child in the Islamic context: The challenges of the local and the global' (2009) 17 *International Journal of Children's Rights 475*

Rattry R 'The African child in proverb, folklore and facts' (1933) 6 *Journal of the International African Institute* 456

Rawls J (1971) *A Theory of Justice* Harvard: Harvard University Press

Raz J 'Legal rights' (1984) 4 *Oxford Journal of Legal Studies* 1

Reimers C	'Cultural differences in labor force participation among married women' (1985) 75 *American Economic Review Papers and Proceedings* 251
Rensmann T	'Munich alumni and the evolution of international human rights law' (2011) 22 *The European Journal of International Law* 973
Ress G	'The effect of decisions and judgements of the European Court of Human Rights in domestic legal order' (2004-2005) 40 *Texas International Law Journal* 359
Reynaert D *et al*	'A review of children's rights literature since the adoption of the United Nations Convention on the Rights of the Child' (2009) 16 *Childhood* 518
Richardson A	'The politics of childhood: Wordsworth, Blake, and catechistic methods' (1989) 56 ELH 853
Ritchie O & Kollar M	(1964) *The sociology of childhood*
Rochat T & Hough A	(2007) *Enhancing resilience in children affected by HIV and AIDS: children's views and experiences of resilience enhancing family and community practices report* Pretoria, South Africa: Child, Youth, Family and Social Development Book Programme, Human Sciences Book Council
Roose R & Bouverne-De Bie M	'Do children have rights or do their rights have to be realised? The United Nations Convention on the Rights of the Child as a frame of reference for pedagogical action' (2007) 41 *Journal of Philosophy of Education* 43
Rorty R	(2007) *Philosophy as cultural politics* Cambridge: Cambridge University Press
Rosenthal M	'Home to early childhood service: An ecological perspective' (2000) 4 *Childrenz Issues* 7
Rosenthal M	'Out-of-home child care book: A cultural perspective' (1999) *23 International Journal of Behavioural Development* 477
Ruddick S	'At horizons of the subject: Neoliberalism, neo-conservatism and the rights of the child part two: Parents, caregivers, the state' (2007) *14 Gender, Place & Culture: A Journal of Feminist Geography* 627

Ruddick S	'At the Horizons of the Subject: Neo-liberalism, neo-conservatism and the rights of the child Part One: From 'knowing' fetus to 'confused' child' (2007) 14 *Gender, Place & Culture: A Journal of Feminist Geography* 513
Runco M	'Creativity as an extracognitive phenomenon' in Shavinina L & Ferrari M (eds) (2004) *Beyond knowledge: Extracognitive aspects of developing high ability* Mahwah: Lawrence Erlbaum & Associates
Rwenzaura B	'Law, culture and children's rights in Eastern and Southern Africa: Contemporary challenges and present day dilemmas' in Ncube W (eds) (1998) *Law, Culture, Tradition and Children's Rights* Aldershot: Ashgate Dartmouth
Rweraura B	'Competing "images" of childhood in the social and legal systems of contemporary sub-Saharan Africa' (1998) 12 *International Journal of Law, Polity and the Family* 253
Rwezaura B	'The best interests of the child in changing social and economic contexts of sub-Saharan Africa' in Alston P (1994) *The best interests of the child: Reconciling culture and human rights* Oxford: Oxford University Press
Sacramento L & Pessoa A	'Implementation of the rights of the child in the Mozambican context' in Freeman M (eds*)* (1996) *Children's rights: Comparative perspective* Aldershot: Dartmouth
Sanchez-Eppler K	(2005) *Dependant states: The child's part in the nineteenth century American culture* Chicago: University of Chicago Press
Sanchez-Eppler K	'Playing at class' (2000) 67 ELH 819
Sandel M	(1982) *Liberalism and the limits of justice* New York: Cambridge University Press
Sanneh L	(1983) *West African Christianity: The religious impact* Maryknoll: Orbis Books
Sanneh L	(1996) *Piety and Power: Muslims and Christians in the West Maryknoll: Orbis Books*
Sartre J	(1956) *Being and nothingness: An essay on phenomenological ontology* ew York: Philosophical Library

Scanlon T	'Fear of relativism' in Moser P & Carson L (eds) (2001) *Moral relativism* Oxford: Oxford University Press
Scarre G	(ed) (1989) *Children, parents, and politics* Cambridge: Cambridge University Press
Schabas W	(1997) *The abolition of the death penalty in international law* Boston: Northeastern University Press
Schaffner L	'An age of reason: Paradoxes in the US legal construction of adulthood' (2002) 10 *The International Journal of Children's Rights* 201
Schapiro T	'What is a child?' (1999) 109 *Ethics* 715
Scheper-Hughes N *et al*	(1998) *Small wars: The cultural politics of childhood* Berkeley: University of California Press
Schoeman F	'Rights of families: Rights of parents, and the moral basis of the family' (1980) 91 *Ethics* 6
Schrag F	'Children: Their rights and needs' in Aiken W & LaFollette H (eds) (1980) *Whose child? Parental rights, parental authority and state power* Totowa: Rowman and Littlefield
Schwartz S	'A Theory of cultural values and some implications for work' (1999) 48 *Applied Psychology: An International Review* 23
Scott E & Steinberg L	(2008) *Rethinking juvenile justice* Cambridge: Harvard University Press
Scott E	Legal construction of childhood' in Rosenheim M *et al* (eds) (2002) *A century of juvenile justice* Chicago: University of Chicago Press
Scott R	'The English fetus and the right to life' (2004) 11 *European Journal of Health Law* 352
Senghor L	(1966) *Negritude* New York: John Wiley & Sons
Serpell R	'Cultural models of childhood in indigenous socialization and formal schooling in Zambia' in Hwang C & Sigel I(eds) (1996) *Images of childhood* Mahwah: Lawrence Erlbaum Associates
Sgritta G & Wintersberger H	(Eds) (1994) *Childhood matters: Social theory, practice and politics* Vienna: Avebury

Shahar S (1990) *Childhood in the middle ages* London: Routledge

Shahar S (1992) *Childhood in the middle ages* London: Routledge

Sherwood M (2010) *The history of the fairchild family* Whitefish: Kessinger Publishing

Shestack J 'The philosophic foundations of human rights' (1998) 20 *Human Rights Quarterly* 228

Shivji I (1989) *The concept of human rights in Africa* Dakar: CODESRIA

Shutte A (1993) *Philosophy for Africa* Rondebosch: University of Cape Town Press

Siegel H (1987) *Relativism refuted: A critique of contemporary epistemological relativism* Dordrecht: D. Reidel Publishing Company

Sillah R & Chibanda T 'Assessing the African Charter on the Rights and Welfare of the Child (African Children's Charter) as a blueprint towards the attainment of children's rights in Africa' (2013) 11 *IOSR Journal of Humanities and Social Science* 50

Simmons B (2009) *Mobilizing for human rights: International law in domestic politics* Cambridge: Cambridge University Press

Singer P (1994) *Ethics* Oxford, Oxford University Press

Sitaraman S (2009) *State participation in international treaty regimes* Burlington: Ashgate Publishing

Skolnick A 'The limits of childhood: Concept of child development and social context' (1975) 39 *Law and Contemporary Problems* 38

Skovdal M & Daniel M 'Resilience through participation and coping-enabling social environments: The case of HIV-affected children in sub-Saharan Africa' (2012) 11 *African Journal of AIDS Book* 153

Skovdal M & Ogutu V 'Coping with hardship through friendship: The importance of peer social capital among children affected by HIV in Kenya' (2012) 11 *African Journal of AIDS Book* 241

Slaughter M 'Contested identities: The adoption of American Indian children and the liberal state' (2000) 9 *Social and Legal Studies* 227

Sloth-Nielsen J & Mezmur B	'Like running on a treadmill? The 14th and 15th sessions of the African Committee of Experts on the Rights and Welfare of the Child' (2010) 10 *African Human Rights Law Journal* 534
Sloth-Nielsen J & Mezmur B	'Out of the starting blocks: The 12th and 13th sessions of the African Committee of Experts on the Rights and Welfare of the Child' (2009) 9 *African Human Rights Law Journal* 336
Sloth-Nielsen J & Mezmur B	'Surveying the book landscape to promote children's legal rights in an African context' (2007) 7 *African Human Rights Law Journal* 330
Sloth-Nielsen J & Mezmur B	'The dutiful child: The implications of article 31 of the African's Children's Charter' (2008) 52 *Journal of African Law* 159
Sloth-Nielsen J & Mezmur B	'Win some, lose some: The 10th ordinary session of the African Committee of Experts on the Rights and Welfare of the Child' (2008) 8 *African Human Rights Law Journal* 207
Smitherman G	(1977) *Talking and testifying: The language of black American* Boston: Houghton Miffling
Somerville C	(1982) *The rise and fall of childhood* Beverly Hills and London: Sage Publications
Sommerville J	(1991) *The rise and fall of childhood* London: Sage
Steiner H & Alston P	(eds) (2008) *International law in Context: Law, politics and morals* Oxford: Clarendon Press
Steiner H	(1994) *An essay on rights* Oxford: Blackwell
Steiner H	'Individual claims in a world of massive violation: What role for Human Rights Committee?' in Alston P & Crawford J (eds) (2000) *The future of human rights treaty monitoring* Cambridge: Cambridge University Press
Steiner H	'Working rights' in Kramer M *et al* (1998) *A debate over rights, philosophical inquiries* New York: Oxford University Press
Steiner H & Alston P	(2005) *International human rights in context: Law, politics and morals* New York: Oxford University Press
Stephen J *et al*	'Children's rights' (2005) *Encyclopaedia of Education and human development* New York: Myron E. Sharpe

Straus M *et al* 'Spanking by parents and subsequent antisocial behavior of children' (1997) 151 *Archives of Paediatrics and Adolescent Medicine* 761

Sugiyama C 'Inter vivos and transplantation and the human tissue gift act, S.O. 1971 C.83' (1976) 34 *University of Toronto Faculty of Law Review* 124

Summer L (1987) *The moral foundations of rights* New York: Oxford University Press

Sunley R 'Early nineteenth century American literature on childrearing' in Mead M & Wolfenstein M (eds) (1955) *Childhood in contemporary culture* Chicago: University of Chicago Press

Tamanaha B 'Socio-legal positivism and a general jurisprudence' (2001) 21 *Oxford Journal of Legal Studies* 1

Tasioulas J 'Human rights, universality and the values of personhood: Retracing Griffin's steps' (2002) 10 *European Journal of Philosophy* 83

Thairu K (1975) *The African civilization* Nairobi: East African Literature Bureau

Therborn G 'African families in a global context' in Therborn G (ed) (2006) *African Families in A Global* Book Report No.131 Nordiska African Institute

Therborn G 'Child politics: Dimensions and perspectives' (1996) 3 *Childhood* 29

Thomas N 'Towards a theory of children's participation' (2007) 15 *International Journal of Children's Rights* 199

Thompson B 'Africa's Charter on Children's Rights: A normative break with cultural traditionalism' (1992) 41 *The International and Comparative Law Quarterly* 432

Tobin J 'Courts and the construction of childhood: A new way of thinking' in Freeman M (ed) (2012) *Law and childhood studies: Current legal issues 2011* Oxford: Oxford University Press

Todres J *et al* (eds) (2006) *The U.N. Convention on the Rights of the Child: An analysis of treaty provisions and implications of U.S. ratification* Amsterdam: Hotei Publishing

Tomanović S 'Negotiating children's participation and autonomy within families' (2003) 11 *International Journal of Children's Rights* 51

Tomanović S	'Young people's participation within the family: Parent's accounts' (2000) 8 *International Journal of Children's Rights* 151
Tomuschat C	(2003) *Human rights: Between idealism and realism* Oxford: Oxford University Press
Trandis H *et al*	'Individualism and collectivism: Crosscultural perspectives on self-in group relationships' (1988) 54 *Journal of Personality and Social Psychology* 323
Trimier J	'The myth of authenticity: Personhood, traditional culture, and African philosophy' in Solomon R & Higgins K (eds) (2003) *From Africa to Zen: An invitation to world philosophy* Lanham: Rowman and Littlefield
Uka N	(1966) *Growing up in Nigerian culture* Ibadan: Occasional Publication University of Ibadan
Van Bueren G	(1998) *The International law on the rights of the child* The Hague: Kluwer Law International
Van Blerk L	'Progressing street children's rights and participation in policy: Evidence from South Africa' in Imoh A & Ansell N (eds) (2014) *Children's lives in an era of children's rights: The progress of the Convention on the Rights of the Child in Africa* Routledge: Oxon
Van de Vijver F	(1997) *Methods and data analysis of comparative book: Handbook of cross-cultural psychology: Theory and method* Boston: Allyn & Bacon
Van der Brug M	'Strategies to bring about change: A longitudinal book on challenges and coping strategies of orphans and vulnerable children and adolescents in Namibia African' (2012) 11 *African Journal of AIDS Book* 273
Van Nijnatten C	'Authority relations in families and child welfare in the Netherlands and England: New styles of governance (2000) 14 *International Journal of Law, Policy and the Family* 107
Vandenbroeck M & Bouverne-De Bie M	'Children's agency and educational norms – a tensed negotiation' (2006) 13 *Childhood* 127
Vasanthi R	'The politics of childhood: Perspective from the south' (2000) *Economic and Political Weekly* 4055

Veerman P	(1992) *The rights of the child and the changing image of childhood* Norwell: Martinus Nijhoff Publishers
Vengeyi O	(2013) *Aluta continua biblical hermeneutics for liberation: Interpreting biblical texts on slavery for liberation of Zimbabwean underclasses* Bamberg: University of Bamberg Press
Viljoen F	(2012) *International human rights in Africa* Oxford: Oxford University Press
Viljoen F	'Review of the African Commission on Human and peoples' Rights: 21 October 1986 to 1 January 1997' in Heyns C (ed) (1999) *Human rights law in Africa* Leiden: Martinus Nijhoff Publishers
Viljoen F	'Supra-national human rights instruments for the protection of children in Africa: The Convention on the Rights of the Child and the African Charter on the Rights and Welfare of the Child' (1998) 31 *The Comparative and International Law Journal of Southern Africa* 199
Viljoen F	'The African Charter on the Rights and Welfare of the Child' in Davel C (ed) (2000) *Introduction to child law in South Africa* Cape Town: Juta
Viljoen F	(ed) (2012) *Beyond the law: Multi-disciplinary perspectives on human rights* Pretoria: PULP
Walker S & Poe S	'Does cultural diversity affect countries' respect for human rights?' (2002) 24 *Human Rights Quarterly* 237
Walter R	(1972) *How Europe underdeveloped Africa* Dar es Salaam: Tanzania Publishing House
Waltz S	'Universal human rights: The contribution of Muslim states' (2004) 26 *Human Rights Quarterly* 799
Wardle L	'The jurisprudence of parenting and the influence of religion on effective parenting' (2011) 2 *International Journal of the Jurisprudence of the family* 437
Weinberg J *et al*	'Normativity and epistemic intuitions' (2001) 29 *Philosophical Topics* 249
Weisbrod C	(2002) *Emblems of pluralism: Cultural differences and the state* Princeton: Princeton University Press

Weisner T 'Support for children and the African family crisis' in Weisner T *et al* (eds) (1997) *African families and the crisis of social change* Westport: Greenwood Publishing Group

Welch C & Meltzer R (eds) (1984) *Human rights and development in Africa* Albany: University of New York Press

Welch C 'Human rights as a problem in contemporary Africa' in Welch C & Meltzer R (eds) (1984) *Human rights and development in Africa* Albany: State University of New York Press

Werker P 'Universal human rights and the problem of unbounded cultural meanings' (1997) 99 *American Anthropologist* 4

Westman J (1999) *Children's rights, parents' prerogatives, and society's obligations* Child Psychiatry and Human Development

Wiredu K & Gyekye K (1992) *Person and community: Ghanaian philosophical studies* I Washington: Council for Book in Values and Philosophy

Wong D (1986) *Moral relativity* Berkeley: University of California Press

Wong D (2006) *Natural moralities: A defence of pluralistic relativism* New York: Oxford University Press

Wong D 'Pluralistic universalism' (1996) 20 *Midwest Studies in Philosophy* 378

Wong D 'Relativism' in Singer P (ed) (1995) *A companion to ethics* Cambridge: Blackwell

Wood L *et al* 'Read me to resilience': Exploring the use of cultural stories to boost the positive adjustment of children orphaned by AIDS (2012) 11 *African Journal of AIDS Book* 225

Woodhead M 'In search for the rainbow: Pathways to quality in large scale programmes for young disadvantaged children' (1996) 10 *Early Childhood Development: Practice and Reflections*

Ya'ir R 'Redefining the child's right to identity' (2004) 18 *International Journal of Law, Policy and Family* 147

Yeshanew S 'Utilising the promotional mandate of the African Commission on Human and Peoples' Rights to promote human rights education in Africa' (2007) *African Human Rights Law Journal* 191

Yoshihara S	'Human rights and the unborn child by Rita Joseph: Book review' (2011) *The National Catholic Bioethics Quarterly* 599
Young C	(1976) *The politics of cultural pluralism* Madison: University of Wisconsin Press
Young C	(ed) (1993) *The rising tide of cultural pluralism: The nation state at bay?* (Madison: University of Wisconsin Press
Zainaldin J	'The emergence of modern American family law: Child custody, adoption and the courts, 1796-1851' (1978-79) 73 *Northwest University Law Review* 1039
Zeiher H	'Institutionalization as a secular trend' in Qvortrup J *et al the Palgrave handbook of childhood studies* (2009) 127
Zelizer V	(1985) *Pricing the priceless child: The changing social value of children* New York: Basic Books
Zimba R	'Indigenous conceptions of childhood development and social realities in southern Africa' in Zimba R (2002) *Between culture and biology: Perspectives on ontogentic development* Cambridge: Cambridge University Press
Zwart T	'Using local culture to further the implementation of international human rights: The receptor approach' (2012) 34 *Human Rights Quarterly* 546

Case law

the Institute for Human Rights and Development in Africa and the Open Society Justice Initiative (On behalf of Children of Nubian Descent in Kenya) against the Government of Kenya Communication: No. Com/002/2009 22 March 2011.

Gillick v West Norfolk and Wisbech Area Health Authority (1986) AC 112

Lewis v. Bankole (1908) 1 N.L.R.81. pp. 100-101.

Odievre v France [2003] 1 FCR 621 EctHR.

Open Door and Dublin Well Women v Ireland (14234/88) [1992] ECHR 68 (29 October 1992)

Panham v J.R (1979) 442 U.S 584, 602.

Re Gault (1967) US 387 at 12

Re S (A minor) (Independent representation) (1993) 3 All ER 36 at 46-47

Roe v Wade (1973) 410 US 113, 93 S Ct 705, reh den (1973) 410 US 959, 93 S Ct 1409

Roper v Simmons (2005) 125 S. Ct 1183

Santa Clara County v. Southern Pacific Railroad Co (1886) 113 U.S. 394

Secretary, Dept of Health and Community Services, v JWB and SMB FLC 92-3 at 79,191 (1992).

Smith v.Organisation of foster families for equality and reform 431 US, 845 (1977).

Winnipeg Child and Family Services (Northwest Area) v. G. (D.F.), [1997] 3 S.C.R. 925

Concluding observation

Concluding Observations of the CRC Committee, Saudi Arabia, U.N. Doc. CRC/C/15/Add 148 (2001)

Concluding observations of the CRC Committee, Algeria, U.N.Doc CRC/C/15/Add 269 (2005)

The African Committee of Experts on the Rights and Welfare of the Child Concluding Observation to the Republic of Uganda

Concluding Recommendations by the African Committee of Experts on the Rights and Welfare of The Child (African Children's Committee) on the Republic of Tanzania Report on The Status of implementation of the African Charter on the Rights and Welfare of the Child

Constitution

Constitution of Djibouti Approved on 4 September 1992

Constitution of The Gabonese Republic adopted on 26 March 1991, amended on 22 April 1997

Political Constitution of São Tomé and Príncipe adopted on 5 November 1975, Amended on 10 September 1990 through Law 7/90

The Constitution De La Republique Islamique De Mauritanie (avec les projets d'amendements soumis au référendum du 25 juin 2006)

The Constitution of Botswana adopted in September 1966, last amended in 1999

The Constitution of Burkina Faso adopted on 2 June 1991, promulgated on 11 June 1991, amended on 27 January 1997 and on 11 April 2000

The Constitution of Eritrea Ratified by the Constituent Assembly, On 23 May 1997

The Constitution of Kenya 2010; Constitution of Lesotho adopted in 1993, Amended 1996, 1997, 1998, 2001

The Constitution of Mauritius 1968

The Constitution of Morocco adopted on 13 September 1996

The Constitution of Mozambique Approved and enacted on 2 November 1990

The Constitution of Sierra Leone adopted on 1 October 1991

The Constitution of the Arab Republic of Egypt after the amendments ratified on May 22, 1980 Referendum

The Constitution of the Central African Republic adopted on 28 December 1994, promulgated on 14 January 1995

The Constitution of the Federal Republic of Ethiopia, 1995

The Constitution of the Federal Republic of Nigeria 1999

The Constitution of the Fifth Republic of Niger adopted on 18 July 1999, promulgated on 9 August 1999

The Constitution of the Kingdom of Swaziland Act, 2005 (Act No: of 2005)
The Constitution of the United Republic of Tanzania, 1997

The Constitution of the People's Democratic Republic of Algeria adopted on 19 November 1976, amended on 28 November 1996 and on 10 April 2002

The Constitution of the Republic of Benin adopted at the referendum of 2 December 1990

The Constitution of the Republic of Cameroon adopted on 18 January 1996, amendment to the Constitution of 2 June 1972

The Constitution of the Republic of Equatorial Guinea, 1996

The Constitution of the Republic of Guinea-Bissau adopted in 1984, amended in 1991, 1993, and 1996

The Constitution of the Republic of Liberia approved on 3 July 3 1984, entered into force on 6 January 1986

The Constitution of the Republic of Madagascar adopted on 19 August 1992, amended in 1995 and 1998

The Constitution of the Republic of Rwanda Adopted on 26 May 2003

The Constitution of the Republic of Senegal adopted on 7 January 2001

The Constitution of the Republic of Seychelles approved on 18 June 1993, amended by Act No 14 of 1996

The Constitution of Zambia 1996

The Constitutional Law of the Republic of Cape Verde adopted on 25 September 1992, amended on 23 November 1995 and in 1999

The Constitutional Proclamation of Libya adopted on 11 December 1969; The Constitution of Mali Adopted by referendum on 12 January 1992 and promulgated on the 25 February 1992; amended 1999

The first draft of the Tanzanian Constitution made public in June 2013; The Constitution of Tunisia Adopted on 1 June 1959, Amended on 12 July 1988 and by Amendment Act No 93-105 of 8 November 1993

The Fundamental Law of the Second Republic of Guinea Approved on 23 December 1990

The Fundamental Law of the Union Comoros adopted on 23 December 2001
The Constitution of the Republic of Cote D'Ivoire adopted on 24 July 2000

The Interim Constitution of Sudan 2005

The Transitional Federal Charter of the Somali Republic 2004

Dictionary

Black's Law Dictionary 9th edition

The Oxford Dictionary of English 2013

General Comments

CRC Committee General Comment 5 (2003) General measures of implementation of the Convention on the Rights of the Child (arts. 4, 42 and 44, para. 6) CRC/GC/2003/5 27 November 2003

CRC Committee General Comment 8 (2006) The right of the child to protection from corporal punishment and other cruel or degrading forms of punishment (arts. 19; 28, para. 2; and 37, inter alia) CRC/C/GC/8 2 March 2007

CRC Committee, General Comment 7, Children's Rights in Juvenile Justice 2005, CRC/C/GC/7/Rev.1, para. 13)

General Comment 12 (2009) on the rights of the child to be heard, of the CRC Committee. CRC/C/GC/12 20 July 2009

General comment No. 14 (2013) on the right of the child to have his or her best interests taken as a primary consideration (art. 3, para. 1)

General Comment Number 1 of the Committee on Economic, Social and Cultural Rights Report on the 3rd session E/1989/22 E/C.12/1989/5.

Human Rights Committee, General Comment 10, Article 19 (Nineteenth session, 1983), Compilation of General Comments and General Recommendations Adopted by Human Rights Treaty Bodies, U.N. Doc. HRI/GEN/1/Rev.1 at 11 (1994

Human Rights Committee, General Comment 22, Article 18 (Forty-eighth session, 1993). Compilation of General Comments and General Recommendations Adopted by Human Rights Treaty Bodies, U.N. Doc. HRI/GEN/1/Rev.1 at 35 (1994)

National legislation

The Code of Person and Family 1993 (Republic of Burundi)

The French Civil Code 1958 (in force in the Republic of Chad)

The Family Code 1972 of the Republic of Senegal

The Civil Code of the Republic of Gabon 1972

Reports

African Child Policy Forum Report: Realising rights for children: Harmonisation of laws on children Eastern and Southern Africa 2007

African Child Policy Forum: In the best interests of the child: Harmonisation with national laws with the Convention on the Rights of the Child 2007

African Child Policy Forum: In the best interests of the child: Harmonization of laws on children in east and Southern African and in West and Central Africa 2011

Concerned Women for America, The end of innocence: How the UN stole childhood 1999

Curran & E Bonthuys 'Customary law and domestic violence in rural South African communities (2004) Centre for the Book of Violence and Reconciliation

M Hecker Be born and you shall be attended 1992 The Nyae Nyae Foundation.

The CIVICUS State of the World Civil Society Report 2013

The Report of the evaluation of the activities of the African Committee on Experts on the Rights and welfare of the Child 2010

UNICEF 'Children in an urban world' The state of the world's children 2012

UNICEF 'Circles of participation' The state of the world's children 2003

UNICEF Childhood under threat: Why are millions of children losing out on their childhood? 2005

UNICEF's World status of children's Report 2010

State party Reports

Initial Report of the Congo submitted to the CRC Committee

Initial Reports of The Republic of Guinea submitted to the CRC Committee

Initial Reports of States Parties Due in 1995 submitted to the CRC Committee

Initial report of Yemen 1998 Yemen submitted to the CRC Committee

Initial Reports of States Parties Due in 1992 submitted to the CRC Committee

Initial Reports of States Parties Due in 1992 submitted to the CRC Committee

Initial State party report of the Republic of Mali submitted to the African Committee of Experts on the Rights and Welfare of the Child

Initial Report of Arab Republic of Egypt to the African Committee on Experts on the Rights and Welfare of the Child, 2003

Initial and first State Report of the Federal Republic of Nigeria to the African Committee of Experts on the Rights and Welfare of the Child submitted in 2006

Initial State Report of Tanzania submitted to the African Committee of Experts on the Rights and Welfare of the Child in 2006

Initial Report of the Republic of Kenya submitted to the African Committee of Experts on the Rights and Welfare of the Child in 2007

Initial Report of the Republic of Uganda submitted to the African Committee of experts on the rights and Welfare of the Child in 2007

Initial, first and second State Report of the Republic of Senegal 1998-2009 submitted to the African Committee of experts on the Rights and Welfare of the child in 2009

Initial Report of the Republic of Mali 1999-2006 submitted to the African Committee of Experts on the Rights and Welfare of the Child in 2007

Initial Report of the Republic of Sudan submitted to the African Committee of Experts on the Rights and Welfare of the Child in 2010

Initial Report of the Republic of Togo submitted to the African Committee of Experts on the Rights and Welfare of the Child in 2009

Treaties

Additional Protocol I to the Geneva Convention 1949

Additional Protocol II to the Geneva Convention 1949

African Charter on Human and Peoples' Rights 1981

Convention on the Rights of the Child 1989

Declaration on the rights of the child 1924

Declaration on the Rights of the Child 1959

International Convention on Civil and Political 1966

Optional Protocol to the Convention on the Rights of the Child on the Involvement of Children in Armed Conflict 2002

Optional Protocol to the Convention on the Rights of the Child on the Sale of Children, Child Prostitution and Child Pornography 2002

Optional Protocol to the Convention on the Rights of the Child on the involvement of children in armed conflict 2002

Optional Protocol to the Convention on the Rights of the Child on Communication Procedure 2014

Rome Status of the International Criminal Court 2002

The African Charter on the Rights and Welfare of the Child 1990

The African Youth Charter 2007

The Declaration on the Rights and Welfare of the Child 1979

The ILO's Worse Forms of Child Labour Convention 182 of 2000

The Protocol to the African Charter on Human and Peoples' Rights on the Rights of Women in Africa 2003

Universal Declaration of Human Right 1948

Unpublished book

Kruger M 'The development of a protocol to ensure the recognition of the rights of children during a legal process' unpublished PhD book, University of Pretoria, 2006

Made in the USA
Monee, IL
05 November 2026

67811374R00197